THE HISTORY OF CONTINENTAL PHILOSOPHY

THE HISTORY OF CONTINENTAL PHILOSOPHY

General Editor: Alan D. Schrift

1. Kant, Kantianism, and Idealism: The Origins of Continental Philosophy
   Edited by Thomas Nenon

2. Nineteenth-Century Philosophy:
   Revolutionary Responses to the Existing Order
   Edited by Alan D. Schrift and Daniel Conway

3. The New Century: Bergsonism, Phenomenology, and
   Responses to Modern Science
   Edited by Keith Ansell-Pearson and Alan D. Schrift

4. Phenomenology: Responses and Developments
   Edited by Leonard Lawlor

5. Critical Theory to Structuralism: Philosophy, Politics,
   and the Human Sciences
   Edited by David Ingram

6. Poststructuralism and Critical Theory's Second Generation
   Edited by Alan D. Schrift

7. After Poststructuralism: Transitions and Transformations
   Edited by Rosi Braidotti

8. Emerging Trends in Continental Philosophy
   Edited by Todd May

THE HISTORY OF CONTINENTAL PHILOSOPHY

General Editor: Alan D. Schrift

VOLUME 2

NINETEENTH-CENTURY PHILOSOPHY: REVOLUTIONARY RESPONSES TO THE EXISTING ORDER

Edited by Alan D. Schrift and Daniel Conway

The University of Chicago Press
Chicago

The University of Chicago Press, Chicago 60637
© Editorial matter and selection, 2010 Alan D. Schrift and Daniel Conway
Individual contributions, the contributors
All rights reserved. Published 2010
Published simultaneously outside North America by Acumen Publishing Limited
Printed and bound in the UK by MPG Books Group

This book is copyright under the Berne Convention. No reproduction without permission.

19 18 17 16 15 14 13 12 11 10   1 2 3 4 5 6

ISBN-13: 978-0-226-74046-1 (cloth)
ISBN-13: 978-0-226-74049-2 (electronic)
ISBN-10: 0-226-74046-3 (cloth)
ISBN-10: 0-226-74049-8 (electronic)

Library of Congress Cataloging-in-Publication Data

The history of continental philosophy / general editor, Alan D. Schrift.
    p. cm.
  Includes bibliographical references and index.
  ISBN-13: 978-0-226-74046-1 (cloth : alk. paper)
  ISBN-10: 0-226-74046-3 (cloth : alk. paper)
  ISBN-13: 978-0-226-74049-2 (electronic)
  ISBN-10: 0-226-74049-8 (electronic)
  1. Philosophy, Modern. 2. Phenomenology. 3. Structuralism. 4. Science—Philosophy.
I. Schrift, Alan D., 1955–
  B791.H57 2010
  190—dc22
                                                                        2010014182

∞ The paper used in this publication meets the minimum requirements of the
American National Standard for Information Sciences—Permanence of Paper
for Printed Library Materials, ANSI Z39.48-1992.

CONTENTS

Series Preface		vii
Contributors		xiii
	Introduction DANIEL CONWAY	1
1.	Feuerbach and the Left and Right Hegelians WILLIAM CLARE ROBERTS	17
2.	Marx and Marxism TERRELL CARVER	35
3.	Søren Kierkegaard ALASTAIR HANNAY	65
4.	Dostoevsky and Russian philosophy EVGENIA CHERKASOVA	85
5.	Life after the death of God: thus spoke Nietzsche DANIEL CONWAY	103
6.	Hermeneutics: Schleiermacher and Dilthey ERIC SEAN NELSON	139
7.	French spiritualist philosophy F. C. T. MOORE	161
8.	The emergence of sociology and its theories: from Comte to Weber ALAN SICA	177

9.	Developments in philosophy of science and mathematics DALE JACQUETTE	193
10.	Peirce: pragmatism and nature after Hegel DOUGLAS R. ANDERSON	217
11.	Aesthetics and the philosophy of art, 1840–1900 GARY SHAPIRO	239
	Chronology	261
	Bibliography	285
	Index	301

SERIES PREFACE

"Continental philosophy" is itself a contested concept. For some, it is understood to be any philosophy after 1780 originating on the European continent (Germany, France, Italy, etc.). Such an understanding would make Georg von Wright or Rudolf Carnap – respectively, a Finnish-born philosopher of language and a German-born logician who taught for many years in the US – a "continental philosopher," an interpretation neither they nor their followers would easily accept. For others, "continental philosophy" refers to a style of philosophizing, one more attentive to the world of experience and less focused on a rigorous analysis of concepts or linguistic usage. In this and the accompanying seven volumes in this series, "continental philosophy" will be understood *historically* as a tradition that has its roots in several different ways of approaching and responding to Immanuel Kant's critical philosophy, a tradition that takes its definitive form at the beginning of the twentieth century as the phenomenological tradition, with its modern roots in the work of Edmund Husserl. As such, continental philosophy emerges as a tradition distinct from the tradition that has identified itself as "analytic" or "Anglo-American," and that locates its own origins in the logical analyses and philosophy of language of Gottlob Frege. Whether or not there is in fact a sharp divergence between the work of Husserl and Frege is itself a contested question, but what cannot be contested is that two distinct historical traditions emerged early in the twentieth century from these traditions' respective interpretations of Husserl (and Heidegger) and Frege (and Russell). The aim of this history of continental philosophy is to trace the developments in one of these traditions from its roots in Kant and his contemporaries through to its most recent manifestations. Together, these volumes present a coherent and comprehensive account of the continental philosophical tradition that offers readers a unique resource for understanding this tradition's complex and interconnected history.

Because history does not unfold in a perfectly linear fashion, telling the history of continental philosophy cannot simply take the form of a chronologically organized series of "great thinker" essays. And because continental philosophy has not developed in a vacuum, telling its history must attend to the impact of figures and developments outside philosophy (in the sciences, social sciences, mathematics, art, politics, and culture more generally) as well as to the work of some philosophers not usually associated with continental philosophy. Such a series also must attend to significant philosophical movements and schools of thought and to the extended influence of certain philosophers within this history, either because their careers spanned a period during which they engaged with a range of different theorists and theoretical positions or because their work has been appropriated and reinterpreted by subsequent thinkers. For these reasons, the volumes have been organized with an eye toward chronological development but, in so far as the years covered in each volume overlap those covered in the subsequent volume, they have been organized as well with the aim of coordinating certain philosophical developments that intersect in a fashion that is not always strictly chronological.

Volume 1 begins with the origins of continental philosophy in Kant and the earliest responses to his critical philosophy, and presents an overview of German idealism, the major movement in philosophy from the late eighteenth to the middle of the nineteenth century. In addition to Kant, the period covered in the first volume was dominated by Fichte, Schelling, and Hegel, and together their work influenced not just philosophy, but also art, theology, and politics. This volume thus covers Kant's younger contemporary Herder, and his readers Schiller and Schlegel – who shaped much of the subsequent reception of Kant in art, literature, and aesthetics; the "Young Hegelians" – including Bruno Bauer, Ludwig Feuerbach, and David Friedrich Strauss – whose writings would influence Engels and Marx; and the tradition of French utopian thinking in such figures as Saint-Simon, Fourier, and Proudhon. In addition to Kant's early critics – Jacobi, Reinhold, and Maimon – significant attention is also paid to the later critic of German idealism Arthur Schopenhauer, whose appropriation and criticism of theories of cognition later had a decisive influence on Friedrich Nietzsche.

Volume 2 addresses the second half of the nineteenth century, in part as a response to the dominance of Hegelian philosophy. These years saw revolutionary developments in both European politics and philosophy, and five great critics dominated the European intellectual scene: Feuerbach, Marx, Søren Kierkegaard, Fyodor Dostoevsky, and Nietzsche. Responding in various ways to Hegelian philosophy and to the shifting political landscape of Europe and the United States, these thinkers brought to philosophy two guiding orientations – materialism and existentialism – that introduced themes that would continue to play out throughout the twentieth century. The second half of the nineteenth century also saw the emergence of new schools of thought and new disciplinary thinking, including the birth of sociology and the social sciences, the development of French spiritualism, the beginning of American pragmatism, radical developments in science and mathematics, and the development of hermeneutics beyond the domains of theology and philology into an approach to understanding all varieties of human endeavor.

Volume 3 covers the period between the 1890s and 1930s, a period that witnessed revolutions in the arts, science, and society that set the agenda for the twentieth century. In philosophy, these years saw the beginnings of what would grow into two distinct approaches to doing philosophy: analytic and continental. It also saw the emergence of phenomenology as a new rigorous science, the birth of Freudian psychoanalysis, and the maturing of the discipline of sociology. Volume 3 thus examines the most influential work of a remarkable series of thinkers who reviewed, evaluated, and transformed nineteenth-century thought, among them Henri Bergson, Émile Durkheim, Sigmund Freud, Martin Heidegger, Edmund Husserl, Karl Jaspers, Max Scheler, and Ludwig Wittgenstein. It also initiated an approach to philosophizing that saw philosophy move from the lecture hall or the private study into an active engagement with the world, an approach that would continue to mark continental philosophy's subsequent history.

The developments and responses to phenomenology after Husserl are the focus of the essays in Volume 4. An ambiguity inherent in phenomenology – between conscious experience and structural conditions – lent itself to a range of interpretations. While some existentialists focused on applying phenomenology to the concrete data of human experience, others developed phenomenology as conscious experience in order to analyze ethics and religion. Still other phenomenologists developed notions of structural conditions to explore questions of science, mathematics, and conceptualization. Volume 4 covers all the major innovators in phenomenology – notably Sartre, Merleau-Ponty, and the later Heidegger – as well as its extension into religion, ethics, aesthetics, hermeneutics, and science.

Volume 5 concentrates on philosophical developments in political theory and the social sciences between 1920 and 1968, as European thinkers responded to the difficult and world-transforming events of the time. While some of the significant figures and movements of this period drew on phenomenology, many went back further into the continental tradition, looking to Kant or Hegel, Marx or Nietzsche, for philosophical inspiration. Key figures and movements discussed in this volume include Adorno, Horkheimer, and the Frankfurt School,

Schmitt, Marcuse, Benjamin, Arendt, Bataille, black existentialism, French Marxism, Saussure, and structuralism. These individuals and schools of thought responded to the "crisis of modernity" in different ways, but largely focused on what they perceived to be liberal democracy's betrayal of its own rationalist ideals of freedom, equality, and fraternity. One other point about the period covered in this volume is worthy of note: it is during these years that we see the initial spread of continental philosophy beyond the European continent. This happens largely because of the emigration of European Jewish intellectuals to the US and UK in the 1930s and 1940s, be it the temporary emigration of figures such as Adorno, Horkheimer, Lévi-Strauss, and Jakobson or the permanent emigration of Marcuse, Arendt, and Gurwitsch. As the succeeding volumes will attest, this becomes a central feature of continental philosophy's subsequent history.

Volume 6 examines the major figures associated with poststructuralism and the second generation of critical theory, the two dominant movements that emerged in the 1960s, which together brought continental philosophy to the forefront of scholarship in a variety of humanities and social science disciplines and set the agenda for philosophical thought on the continent and elsewhere from the 1960s to the present. In addition to essays that discuss the work of such influential thinkers as Althusser, Foucault, Deleuze, Derrida, Lyotard, Irigaray, Habermas, Serres, Bourdieu, and Rorty, Volume 6 also includes thematic essays on issues including the Nietzschean legacy, the linguistic turn in continental thinking, the phenomenological inheritance of Gadamer and Ricoeur, the influence of psychoanalysis, the emergence of feminist thought and a philosophy of sexual difference, and the importation of continental philosophy into literary theory.

Before turning to Volume 7, a few words on the *institutional* history of continental philosophy in the United States are in order, in part because the developments addressed in Volumes 6–8 cannot be fully appreciated without recognizing some of the events that conditioned their North American and anglophone reception. As has been mentioned, phenomenologists such as Alfred Schutz and Aron Gurwitsch, and other European continental philosophers such as Herbert Marcuse and Hannah Arendt, began relocating to the United States in the 1930s and 1940s. Many of these philosophers began their work in the United States at the University in Exile, established in 1933 as a graduate division of the New School for Social Research for displaced European intellectuals. While some continental philosophy was taught elsewhere around the United States (at Harvard University, Yale University, the University at Buffalo, and elsewhere), and while the journal *Philosophy and Phenomenological Research* began publishing in 1939, continental philosophy first truly began to become an institutional presence in the United States in the 1960s. In 1961, John Wild (1902–72) left Harvard to become Chair of the Department of Philosophy at Northwestern University. With a commitment from the provost of the university and the Northwestern University Press to enable him to launch the Northwestern Series in Phenomenology and Existential Philosophy, Wild joined William Earle and James Edie, thus making Northwestern a center for the study of continental philosophy. Wild set up an organizational committee including himself, Earle, Edie, George Schrader of Yale, and Calvin Schrag (a former student of Wild's at Harvard, who was teaching at Northwestern and had recently accepted an appointment at Purdue University), to establish a professional society devoted to the examination of recent continental philosophy. That organization, the Society for Phenomenology and Existential Philosophy (SPEP), held its first meeting at Northwestern in 1962, with Wild and Gurwitsch as the dominant figures arguing for an existential phenomenology or a more strictly Husserlian phenomenology, respectively. Others attending the small meeting included Erwin Straus, as well as Northwestern graduate students Edward Casey and Robert Scharff, and today SPEP has grown into the second largest society of philosophers in the United States. Since those early days, many smaller societies (Heidegger Circle, Husserl Circle, Nietzsche Society, etc.) have formed and many journals and graduate programs devoted to continental philosophy have appeared. In addition, many of the important continental philosophers who first became known in the 1960s – including Gadamer, Ricoeur, Foucault, Derrida, Lyotard, and Habermas – came to hold continuing appointments at major American universities (although, it must be mentioned, not always housed in departments of philosophy) and, since the 1960s, much of the transmission of continental philosophy has come directly through teaching as well as through publications.

The transatlantic migration of continental philosophy plays a central role in Volume 7, which looks at developments in continental philosophy between 1980 and 1995, a time of great upheaval and profound social change that saw the fruits of the continental works of the 1960s beginning to shift the center of gravity of continental philosophizing from the European continent to the anglophone philosophical world and, in particular, to North America. During these years, the pace of translation into English of French and German philosophical works from the early twentieth century as well as the very recent past increased tremendously, and it was not uncommon to find essays or lectures from significant European philosophers appearing first in English and then subsequently being published in French or German. In addition, the period covered in this volume also saw the spread of continental philosophy beyond the confines of philosophy departments, as students and faculty in centers of humanities and departments of comparative literature, communication studies, rhetoric, and other interdisciplinary fields increasingly drew on the work of recent continental philosophers. Volume 7 ranges across several developments during these years – the birth of postmodernism, the differing philosophical traditions of France, Germany, and Italy, the third generation of critical theory, and the so-called "ethical turn" – while also examining the extension of philosophy into questions of radical democracy, postcolonial theory, feminism, religion, and the rise of performativity and post-analytic philosophy. Fueled by an intense ethical and political desire to reflect changing social and political conditions, the philosophical work of this period reveals how continental thinkers responded to the changing world and to the key issues of the time, notably globalization, technology, and ethnicity.

The eighth and final volume in this series attempts to chart the most recent trends in continental philosophy, which has now developed into an approach to thinking that is present throughout the world and engaged with classical philosophical problems as well as current concerns. The essays in this volume focus more on thematic developments than individual figures as they explore how contemporary philosophers are drawing on the resources of the traditions surveyed in the preceding seven volumes to address issues relating to gender, race, politics, art, the environment, science, citizenship, and globalization. While by no means claiming to have the last word, this volume makes clear the dynamic and engaged quality of continental philosophy as it confronts some of the most pressing issues of the contemporary world.

As a designation, "continental philosophy" can be traced back at least as far as John Stuart Mill's *On Bentham and Coleridge* (1840), where he uses it to distinguish the British empiricism of Bentham from a tradition on the continent in which he sees the influence of Kant. Since that time, and especially since the early twentieth century, the term has been used to designate philosophies from a particular geographical region, or with a particular style (poetic or dialectical, rather than logical or scientistic). For some, it has been appropriated as an honorific, while for others it has been used more pejoratively or dismissively. Rather than enter into these polemics, what the volumes in this series have sought to do is make clear that one way to understand "continental philosophy" is as an approach to philosophy that is deeply engaged in reflecting on its own history, and that, as a consequence, it is important to understand the *history* of continental philosophy.

While each of the volumes in this series was organized by its respective editor as a volume that could stand alone, the eight volumes have been coordinated in order to highlight various points of contact, influence, or debate across the historical period that they collectively survey. To facilitate these connections across the eight volumes, cross-referencing footnotes have been added to many of the essays by the General Editor. To distinguish these footnotes from those of the authors, they are indicated by an asterisk (*).

Alan D. Schrift, General Editor

CONTRIBUTORS

Douglas R. Anderson is Professor of Philosophy at Southern Illinois University Carbondale. He teaches American philosophy, history of philosophy, and philosophy and popular culture. He is editor of the *Transactions* of the Charles S. Peirce Society and coeditor of a series in American philosophy for Fordham University. He is author of three books on American philosophy – *Creativity and the Philosophy of C. S. Peirce* (1987); *Strands of System: The Philosophy of Charles Peirce* (1995); and *Philosophy Americana* (2006) – and editor of several others.

Terrell Carver is Professor of Political Theory at the University of Bristol, UK. He has published extensively on Marx, Engels, Marxism, and the philosophy of the social sciences. He is the editor of the *Cambridge Companion to Marx* (1991) and translator of *Karl Marx: Later Political Writings* (1996). His book *The Postmodern Marx* (1998) has recently been translated into Chinese.

Evgenia Cherkasova is Associate Professor of Philosophy at Suffolk University in Boston, Massachusetts. Her scholarly and pedagogical interests include ethics, moral psychology, philosophy of art, and existentialism. She is the author of numerous essays on Dostoevsky, Kant, Russian philosophy, and philosophy of literature. Her most recent publication is a book entitled *Dostoevsky and Kant: Dialogues on Ethics* (2009).

Daniel Conway is Professor and Head of Philosophy at Texas A&M University. He is the author of three books on Nietzsche – *Nietzsche's Dangerous Game* (1997), *Nietzsche and the Political* (1997), and *Reader's Guide to Nietzsche's* On the Genealogy of Morals (2008) – and a former editor of the *Journal of Nietzsche*

Studies, and the editor of the *Routledge Critical Assessments* volumes on Kierkegaard (2002) and Nietzsche (1998). His current research comprises an investigation of the confrontations with modernity articulated, respectively, by Marx, Kierkegaard, and Nietzsche.

Alastair Hannay is Emeritus Professor of Philosophy at the University of Oslo. He was for many years editor of *Inquiry* and is author of *Mental Images: A Defence* (1971, 2002), *Kierkegaard* (1982, 1999), *Human Consciousness* (1990), *Kierkegaard: A Biography* (2001), *Kierkegaard and Philosophy* (2003), and *On the Public* (2006). He has translated several of Kierkegaard's works and is a Fellow of the Royal Society of Edinburgh as well as a Member of both the Royal Norwegian Scientific Society of Science and Letters and the Norwegian Academy of Science and Letters.

Dale Jacquette is Lehrstuhl ordentlicher Professor für Philosophie, Schwerpunkt theoretische Philosophie (Senior Professorial Chair in Theoretical Philosophy) at the University of Bern, Switzerland. He is the author of numerous articles on logic, metaphysics, philosophy of mind, and aesthetics, and recently *Wittgenstein's Thought in Transition* (1998), *David Hume's Critique of Infinity* (2001), *Ontology* (2002), *The Philosophy of Schopenhauer* (2005), and *Philosophy of Mind: The Metaphysics of Consciousness* (2010). He is the editor of the *Blackwell Companion to Philosophical Logic* (2002), *Cambridge Companion to Brentano* (2004), *Schopenhauer, Philosophy, and the Arts* (1996), and *Philosophy of Logic* (2007).

F. C. T. (Tim) Moore held the first Chair of Philosophy at the University of Hong Kong from 1979 to 2000, and is now Emeritus Professor. Working in the areas of the philosophy of the social sciences, the history of philosophy (especially French philosophy), the philosophy of mind, and computer-assisted logic learning, he is the author of numerous journal articles and contributed chapters, as well as several books, including *The Psychology of Maine de Biran* (1970), *The Psychological Basis of Morality: An Essay on Value and Desire* (1978), and *Bergson: Thinking Backwards* (1996). He was also responsible for two volumes, working from the original manuscripts, of the collected works of Maine de Biran: *Sur les rapports du physique et du moral de l'homme* (1984) and *Essai sur les fondements de la psychologie* (2001).

Eric Sean Nelson is Assistant Professor of Philosophy at the University of Massachusetts-Lowell and has taught at the Universities of Memphis and Toledo. He has published various articles on ethics, epistemology, hermeneutics, and phenomenology in nineteenth- and twentieth-century European philosophy, and is the coeditor of two anthologies: *Addressing Levinas* (2005) and *Rethinking Facticity* (2008).

William Clare Roberts teaches philosophy and political theory at McGill University. He has written essays on Marx, the history of Marxism, Aristotle, and the political thought of Arendt and Strauss. He is currently working on a book on postmodern appropriations of Aristotle in the Marxist and Heideggerian traditions.

Alan D. Schrift is the F. Wendell Miller Professor of Philosophy at Grinnell College. In addition to his many published articles or book chapters on Nietzsche and French and German twentieth-century philosophy, he is the author of *Nietzsche and the Question of Interpretation: Between Hermeneutics and Deconstruction* (1990), *Nietzsche's French Legacy: A Genealogy of Poststructuralism* (1995), and *Twentieth-Century French Philosophy: Key Themes and Thinkers* (2005). He has edited five collections on a variety of topics, including *The Logic of the Gift: Toward an Ethic of Generosity* (1997) and *Modernity and the Problem of Evil* (2005). In addition to serving as general editor of the eight-volume *The History of Continental Philosophy*, he serves as general editor of *The Complete Works of Friedrich Nietzsche*, the Stanford University Press translation of Nietzsche's *Kritische Studienausgabe*.

Gary Shapiro is Tucker-Boatwright Professor in the Humanities-Philosophy at the University of Richmond. Two of his current writing projects focus on Nietzsche's political thought and on the philosophical meaning of the last four hundred years of land art. He has published *Nietzschean Narratives* (1989), *Alcyone: Nietzsche on Gifts, Noise, and Women* (1991), *Earthwards: Robert Smithson and Art After Babel* (1995), and *Archaeologies of Vision: Foucault and Nietzsche on Seeing and Saying* (2003), in addition to many articles on Hegel, aesthetics, American philosophy, and other subjects. Shapiro has also coedited the collections *Hermeneutics: Questions and Prospects* (with Alan Sica; 1984) and *After the Future: Postmodern Times and Places* (1990).

Alan Sica is Professor of Sociology and founder of the Social Thought Program at Pennsylvania State University. He was editor of the American Sociological Association journal, *Sociological Theory*, for five years, and is currently editor of the ASA book review journal, *Contemporary Sociology*. He has published a number of books concerning social thought, Max Weber, hermeneutics, and the 1960s, and has been writing about social theory for thirty-five years.

INTRODUCTION

Daniel Conway

This volume charts the most influential trends and developments in European philosophy in the tumultuous period 1840–1900. Particular emphasis is placed on the theoretical responses to, and anticipations of, the revolutionary fervor of the period. The main figures of the period are situated with respect to the following indices: their relationships to the dominant paradigm of Hegelian philosophy; their debts and contributions to the theme of revolution; their participation in the dawning self-awareness of modernity as a unique historical epoch; their contributions to the emerging project of conducting a critique of modernity; and, finally, their contributions to the current elaboration of the dominant themes and discourses of continental philosophy.

This historical period is essential, we believe, to the development and articulation of those projects – including deconstruction, psychoanalysis, postmodernism, poststructuralism, phenomenology, hermeneutics, negative theology, postcolonial studies, postdemocratic political theory, and transhuman philosophy – that are now widely regarded as integral to the identity and self-understanding of continental philosophy. The period 1840–1900 merits careful study not only for the insights and innovations it birthed, but also for its incubation of so many of the ideas and questions that are central to the currently dominant expressions of continental philosophy.

It has become customary in recent years to frame the development of European philosophy in the nineteenth century as an extended, serial response to the magisterial achievements and expansive influence of Hegel. While this response admits of significant variation across a number of spheres of human endeavor – including religion, art, politics, law, and economics – a single theme tends to prevail: Hegel is understood to have articulated a definitive position or stance that is believed to verge on, or aspire to, comprehensive totality.[1] He is understood to have done so, moreover, on the strength of his dauntingly potent historical–phenomenological method – popularly, if inaccurately, known as the *dialectic* – which many critics regard with elevated suspicion. To capitulate to Hegel, his critics occasionally insist, is to surrender to the totalizing impulse his system supposedly manifests. The consequences of doing so, his critics further insist, include an increasingly normalized and homogeneous existence, which, some might claim, we have a moral duty to resist.

According to proponents of this general line of interpretation, Hegel's philosophy is not simply the powerful expression of a creative intellect attuned to the dynamic rhythms of historical development. It also represents – and, more ominously, celebrates – the victory of those darker impulses to which the modern epoch was (and remains) uniquely vulnerable. These impulses travel and coalesce under a variety of names, but they are generally agreed to have funded the most disturbing political monstrosities of European modernity. That any such identification is patently unfair to Hegel is worth noting, but it is also beside the point of this introduction. For better or worse, Hegel's philosophy has come to stand for an unacceptable degree of accommodation on the part of Europeans to form, structure, order, security, homogeneity, authority, or totality.

This general approach to the development of nineteenth-century European philosophy has proved to be both familiar and productive. Recent years have witnessed a proliferation of successful academic courses and seminars devoted to the theme of "Hegel and his critics," and the nineteenth century is well known to scholars and students for its spirited debates, big ideas, and grand ambitions. The richness and diversity of these curricular innovations, and of the sweeping historical narratives they embroider, faithfully attest to the reach of Hegel's influence, even if the drama they stage is occasionally contrived. This general approach is endorsed, moreover, by many of those thinkers who are integral to the development of philosophy in the nineteenth century. Feuerbach, Marx, Kierkegaard, Nietzsche, and Peirce, to name just a few figures of significance, all understood themselves to be responding, either directly or indirectly, to Hegel. In all of these cases, moreover, Hegel's standing as *the* philosopher of the modern period – and, so, as the perceived guardian of assorted orthodoxies – instilled in his critics an unusual level of energy, audacity, and combativeness. German philosophy in particular was dominated by Hegel, although his shadow extended well across the continent as a whole.

---

1. A representative statement of this concern is expressed by Isaiah Berlin, who includes Hegel among those "rationalist metaphysicians" whose anticipation of "a final harmony in which all riddles are solved, all contradictions reconciled" leads them to favor "monism" over the "pluralism" that Berlin advocates. Isaiah Berlin, *Four Essays on Liberty* (New York: Oxford University Press, 1970), 168–72.

INTRODUCTION

A further attraction of this approach is that it fits the stormy tenor of the times. As Hegel himself was fond of pointing out – most notably, perhaps, with respect to his brush with "world-spirit on horseback" (aka Napoleon) – the political and cultural developments of the century appeared to confirm the larger outlines of his philosophical system. Several of these developments bear noting here: the emergence of the modern nation-state; the acceleration of research in science and technology; the unprecedented mobility of Europeans and the subsequent mixing of social classes; the exportation of European culture (and aggression) via imperial expansion; and the flattering reflection of European culture to be glimpsed in the ongoing struggle to civilize the native peoples and landscapes of the Americas.

The career of philosophy in the nineteenth century reflects in many respects the excitement and turbulence of the times. Freed for the most part from the constraints of academic manners and political patronage, the major figures of the period forwarded daring, irreverent hypotheses, very much in the spirit of Hegel's own philosophy. Grand, sweeping theories were in vogue, and philosophers endeavored to comment instructively on such general themes of vital interest as the nature of the human condition, the meaning of life (and death), the future of humankind, the limits of reason, the aims and bounds of science, and the proper scope of freedom. In many cases, as we will see, the leading philosophers of the period channeled and lent voice to the utopian muse that has inspired so much of Western philosophy. Indeed, despite the emergence in the nineteenth century of several enduring schools of suspicion, the leading figures of the period had not yet abandoned the perennial philosophical quest for the ideal society to which human beings might aspire. In short, that is, the dream of pan-European Enlightenment was not yet extinguished.

The leading philosophers of the period furthermore regarded themselves as both qualified and entitled to weigh in on the scientific debates of the day. Indeed, there was not yet a general sense among European philosophers that science was somehow beyond their ken. In some cases, in fact, the leading philosophers of the period considered themselves to be toiling at the very forefront of scientific research. This was especially true with respect to the nascent "human" sciences, including sociology, history, political economy, and psychology. Thinkers as diverse as Marx, Nietzsche, Comte, Dilthey, and Peirce understood themselves to be contributing productively (if diversely) to the determination of the method that would place the emerging "human" sciences on a firm foundation. Here it bears noting, in fact, that the very concept of *science* (*Wissenschaft*) was contested, and successively refined, throughout the nineteenth century. At the beginning of the century, scholars were inclined to apply the term *science* quite generally, and to virtually any identifiable body of received knowledge. By the end of the century, however, the scope of science had been narrowed considerably, and the distinction between the "natural" sciences and the "human" sciences had become widely accepted.

To be sure, this general approach to the development of nineteenth-century European philosophy also has its limitations. As we have seen, for example, this approach can have the effect of distorting Hegel's philosophical aspirations and accomplishments. As these distortions verge on caricature, moreover, Hegel comes to represent a veritable army of straw men.[2] This state of affairs admits of considerable irony. The name of the philosophical champion of *spirit* (*Geist*) has become a shorthand designation for any comprehensive interpretation, apparatus, or regime that either threatens or promises to crush the human spirit. Similarly, the philosopher who dared to track the maturation of human *freedom*, who located the demonstrable superiority of Western civilization in its elaboration of (and support for) political institutions that reflect the creativity and will of the citizens they serve, has become synonymous with any comprehensive campaign to circumscribe individual expressions of freedom. Accordingly, the political philosopher who sought to defend the ethical relevance of the family and the indispensable contributions of the "corporations" is now seen as the apologist *par excellence* for the hyper-organized, ultra-efficient, pan-surveillant, *über*-policed modern nation-state. Finally, the former Tübingen seminarian who demonstrated how and why God might have entered time is now regarded as the arch-nemesis of appeals to faith, miracles, petitionary prayer, divine intervention, and all other irrational elements of religious practice and experience.

Another limitation of this approach is that it can tend toward unhelpfully reductive strategies of interpretation. A sprawling philosophical enterprise is all too easily compressed into a single big idea, and a voluminous corpus of writings is all too easily condensed into a few pithy slogans. In some cases, this reductive approach is applied to the century as a whole, especially if Hegel is taken to represent the prevailing (Apollonian) impulse toward integration and systematization while his critics are variously taken to represent the (Dionysian) impulse toward disintegration and dissolution. In fact, as we will see, this impossibly neat depiction of nineteenth-century European philosophy fails to capture the divided allegiances, shifting boundaries, complex genealogies, and crosscurrents of influence that produced the rich, unruly diversity of thought that characterizes the period 1840–1900.

For all the clarity afforded us by its most enduring caricatures, the career of nineteenth-century philosophy was marked by ambiguity, uncertainty, and, occasionally, outright confusion. With respect to so many important points of

---

2. Several of these straw men are exposed by Jon Stewart in *Idealism and Existentialism: Hegel and Nineteenth- and Twentieth-Century European Philosophy* (London: Continuum, 2010).

contention, the leading philosophers of the period simply did not know what to think. Part of the problem was that they struggled to digest an overwhelming influx of knowledge about their world. The period was rife with scientific advances, anthropological and ethnological discoveries, empire-driven contact with alien peoples and civilizations, and technological innovations – all of which influenced the development of European philosophy. Even the "big ideas" that are so often attributed to the central figures of the period remained a source of significant mystery to their authors. Feuerbach and Marx, so clear in their opposition to Hegel, are anything but clear about the sensuous character of existence to which philosophers, ideally, should attend. Dostoevsky and Kierkegaard, so perspicacious in reckoning the failings of contemporary Christendom, were notoriously elusive on the question of how to constitute – much less to sustain – a life of genuinely Christian faith and practice. Nietzsche, so insightful in his spot-on critique of the bloated idols of late modernity, is uncharacteristically ineloquent with respect to the nebulous "future" of philosophy. In this light, perhaps, the true, collective genius of nineteenth-century European philosophy may be seen to be largely *diagnostic* – as opposed to *prognostic* or *prescriptive* – in nature.

In recognition of these limitations, we have employed a modified, hybrid approach to the development of European philosophy in the period 1840–1900. Following the familiar strategy outlined above, we have tracked the lively commerce in big ideas for which the nineteenth century is well known. At the same time, however, we have attempted to detail the complex background against which this commerce transpired. Toward this end, we have devoted entire chapters to the major figures of the period, including Feuerbach, Marx, Kierkegaard, Dostoevsky, Nietzsche, and Peirce, while also placing these figures in the broader context of the philosophical movements branded in their names. In addition, we have devoted entire chapters to several thematic developments of central importance – for example, in hermeneutics, spiritualism, sociology, science, mathematics, and art. In all of these chapters, finally, we have taken care to situate the highlighted theories, insights, innovations, and debates in their historical, social, political, and cultural contexts.

As our unifying theme, we have focused on the revolutionary fervor that alternately informed, structured, interrupted, fragmented, and guided the development of European philosophy in the period 1840–1900. This theme is apposite, we believe, for a number of reasons. First of all, the period under consideration was shaped by revolutions of various kinds, from the political struggles of 1848, through the intensifications of the industrial and scientific revolutions, to the geopolitical revolution that was marked by the rise of a unified Germany at the conclusion of the Franco-Prussian War. This theme thus accommodates the general sense of urgency that infused the philosophical debates of the period.

Rightly or wrongly, the philosophers working in this period believed that something important and worthwhile was at stake in their deliberations. This belief was revolutionary, moreover, inasmuch as they deemed something *essential* to European modernity to be either missing, dormant, damaged, or awry. The apparent victory of the Hegelian system signaled the need for philosophy to acquire a new focus and direction, lest the great promise of European modernity come to naught. Indeed, several of the thinkers surveyed in this volume understood themselves to be issuing devastating, if not fatal, challenges to the *status quo* in politics, religion, science, art, and virtually every other sphere of human endeavor.

Second, the theme of revolution captures the contrarian spirit of the period. Many of the philosophers examined in this volume are joined by a common commitment to the suspension of traditional pieties and to the interrogation of received orthodoxies. For these thinkers, nothing was so hoary or venerable as to escape scrutiny and criticism. The penetrating power of reason, channeled by the emerging scientific method, was employed to unmask all manner of sham and humbug. In fact, many of the philosophers treated in this volume shared the conviction that European modernity was other than it appeared. It was up to them, they further believed, to acquaint their fellow Europeans with the reality that lay hidden beneath the beguiling appearances. In short, it is no accident that this period nurtured the overlapping careers of the three great masters of suspicion – Marx, Nietzsche, Freud – and of several others who merit a similar designation.

Finally, the theme of revolution is recommended by the contributions of the philosophers surveyed in this volume, many of whom were actively engaged in what they or others described as revolutionary innovations, movements, or causes. In some cases, of course, the call to revolutionary activity was explicit, literal, and unmistakable. In other cases, the revolutionary response in question was either nascent or imperceptibly under way. In still other cases, a revolution in thinking and practice had already taken hold, obliging the philosopher(s) involved to interpret this revolution on the fly. As we shall see, the revolution in question was presented by some as real, practical, and of determinate consequence, while from others the revolutionary impulse received a more figurative or allusive formulation.

In general, however, the philosophers treated in this volume presented themselves as responding to the exigencies of a perceived condition of crisis.[3] In some cases, the crisis was perceived as current, while in other cases it was understood

---

3. This common orientation to a crisis is helpfully elucidated by Richard Kearney in his "Introduction," in *Modern Movements in European Philosophy*, 2nd ed. (Manchester: Manchester University Press, 1994).

INTRODUCTION

to be gathering or imminent. Although the nature of the crisis was diversely characterized – for example, as either material or spiritual, secular or religious, practical or theoretical, quotidian or eschatological – in most cases philosophy was expected to play a unique, leading role in addressing the crisis in question. (In some cases, to be sure, philosophy was chastised, called to order, and/or challenged to evolve in response to the perceived crisis.) For the most part, in fact, the task of philosophy was seen to lie in providing an interpretation of the crisis in question and, subsequently, in preparing European modernity to address this crisis, whether by adapting to it, deflecting its advance, avoiding it altogether, or accelerating its constituent contradictions.[4]

Chapter 1 charts the development and divergence of "Right" and "Left" articulations of Hegelianism, with a particular emphasis on the contributions of Ludwig Feuerbach.[5] In this chapter, William Clare Roberts explains how Feuerbach attempted to situate himself within the roiling debates of his day, focusing in the process on Feuerbach's elaboration of a nuanced interpretation-*cum*-reception of Hegel's account of the maturation of *Geist* in world history. Known primarily for his influence on the young Marx, Feuerbach played a major role in the elaboration and defense of *humanism* as the hidden truth of Christianity (and, so, of Hegel's account of the movement of history). Rather than treat individual human beings as finite shapes of divine Spirit, Feuerbach identified the God of Christianity as an externalized objectification (or psychological projection) of as-yet-unclaimed perfections of distinctly human provenance. As Roberts ably demonstrates, the interpretation of Christianity for which Feuerbach himself is best known to twenty-first-century audiences was made possible by what Feuerbach regarded as his more important contribution: a new approach to, and direction for, philosophy itself. As envisioned by Feuerbach, the task of philosophy is to lead human beings – potentially for the first time – to engage the world in the sensuous totality of its existence. In doing so, human beings stand to glimpse – albeit ever so obliquely – the concrete truth of their communal existence (i.e. their species-being).

Chapter 2 continues this developmental narrative, documenting the contributions of Karl Marx and the subsequent rise of Marxism. Focusing on Marx's aversion to the antipolitical, ideological abstractions of philosophy, Terrell Carver portrays Marx as a social critic and political activist – more closely allied with journalism than German philosophy – determined to publicize and promote class-based antagonisms throughout Europe. Carver traces the birth of

---

*4. As can be seen in many of the essays in *The History of Continental Philosophy: Volume 3*, this theme of crisis continues in the work of many of the important philosophers in the early decades of the twentieth century.

*5. These developments are treated in a different context in the essay by Lawrence S. Stepelevich in *The History of Continental Philosophy: Volume 1*.

philosophical Marxism to the founding efforts of Friedrich Engels, Marx's friend and collaborator, noting that the subsequent development and exportation of Marxism was contrary to Marx's own antiphilosophical wishes. The inequities of capitalism were best addressed, Marx believed, not through the elaboration of philosophical theories (e.g. of alienation), but through the effective organization of disaffected workers. As presented by Carver, Marx appears not only as the great critic of speculative, ideological philosophy, but also as the (reluctant) inspiration for a new, eminently *practical* articulation of philosophy in Europe and beyond.

Chapter 3 introduces the reader to another outspoken critic of European modernity, the Danish philosopher Søren Kierkegaard. Expertly guided by Alastair Hannay, the reader is introduced in this chapter to a thinker bent on fomenting what might be called a revolution of the spirit. Convinced that contemporary Christendom had strayed dangerously far from the founding insights of Christianity, Kierkegaard embarked on an ambitious campaign to persuade his fellow Danes – via direct and indirect forms of discourse – to aspire for the first time to a life of genuinely Christian faith and practice. In order to do so, he realized, he would need not only to encourage his readers to cultivate habits of introspection and inwardness, but also to loosen the grip on them of the social and cultural institutions that were emblematic of European civilization in the modern epoch. Toward this latter end, Kierkegaard launched a blistering, unrelenting attack on the Danish state church, which, he alleged, had become a pawn of larger forces responsible for the growing secularization of northern Europe in the nineteenth century. Kierkegaard is perhaps most famous for a series of pseudonymous writings in which he brought the full complement of his literary, philosophical, and psychological gifts to bear on a cluster of problems centered on the difficulties involved in leading a life of Christian devotion in late modern Europe.

Chapter 4 documents the contributions of another influential critic of the established practice of Christianity in the modern epoch. The great Russian novelist Fyodor Dostoevsky – who is not typically included in surveys of nineteenth-century European philosophy – was motivated by a set of concerns not unlike those that prompted Kierkegaard to take up his own pioneering investigations into psychology, religion, and politics. Indeed, Dostoevsky's contributions to the development of European philosophy were significant, if largely indirect. As presented in this chapter by Evgenia Cherkasova, Dostoevsky appears as a gifted novelist, to be sure, but also as a keen observer of the social conventions and cultural mores that uniquely characterize the modern epoch. He proved to be an astute critic of modern political movements and institutions, a fearless explorer of the unconscious springs and irrational currents of "civilized" human behavior, a sympathetic expert on the psychology of religion, and a dedicated chronicler of the paradoxes engendered by the desire for freedom. As Cherkasova persuasively maintains, Dostoevsky deserves to be considered, alongside Marx, Nietzsche, and Freud, as one of the "masters of suspicion" who taught scholars and intellectuals of the twentieth and twenty-first centuries to detect the hidden motives, libidinal investments, unacknowledged expectations, and unconscious conflicts that inform and enliven all spheres of human endeavor.

Chapter 5 is devoted to a philosopher who was deeply (and gratefully) influenced by Dostoevsky: Friedrich Nietzsche. At one time a professor of classical philology (at Basel), Nietzsche resigned his university appointment and fled the stifling confines of European academe. Adjusting to the itinerant life of the independent scholar, Nietzsche went on to write a number of important books that eventually became influential for the development of philosophy on the European continent and beyond. Nietzsche is presented here as a persistent critic of the supposed triumphs and accomplishments of European modernity. Where other observers of the European scene claimed to discern evidence of progress, development, maturation, and growth, Nietzsche claimed to detect symptoms of regress, decay, dissolution, and disintegration. Late modernity, he insisted, was a fundamentally decadent epoch, incapable of projecting its highest values and ideals into a meaningful and sustainable future.

The focus of this chapter falls on Nietzsche's famous teaching of the death of God, by means of which he endeavored to report a crisis of confidence in the basic system of beliefs that supported Christian morality. Owing to the death of God, he maintained, European culture would soon find itself slipping into chaos and confusion, as its highest values – for example, God, Truth, Beauty, and so on – continued to suffer a precipitous devaluation. The goal he identified for philosophy in the twilight of the idols was to determine, soberly and scientifically, what the death of God was likely to *mean* for the future of humankind. Indeed, although he understood the death of God to augur a protracted period of disruption, uncertainty, dislocation, and calamity, Nietzsche cautioned against the presumptive conclusion that humankind simply cannot negotiate the vagaries of a godless cosmos. Those human beings who survive the death of God, he believed, will be advantageously positioned to renew the promise of European civilization.

Chapter 6 charts the development of hermeneutics, which comprises the science or method or art of interpretation. The author of this chapter, Eric Sean Nelson, places particular emphasis on the signal contributions to the development of nineteenth-century hermeneutics by Friedrich Schleiermacher and Wilhelm Dilthey. Already well known to scholars of biblical and classical texts, hermeneutics became influential in this period for its actual and proposed applications to research in philosophy, theology, and the emerging "human" (or social) sciences. As philosophers and social scientists grappled with the problem of how to ground or orient their incipient programs of empirical research, they increasingly turned their attention to the method and practice of hermeneutics. In this respect, a perceived strength of the hermeneutic method lay in its attunement to those subjective, affective inflections of human language and behavior – as well as their historical and cultural contexts – that distinguish human beings from the nonhuman objects studied by natural scientists.

Deeply indebted to the culture and literary tradition of German Romanticism, Schleiermacher sought to develop an "art" of understanding that would prevail in the face of chronic, inertial misunderstanding. For him, the promise of hermeneutics lay in its capacity to accommodate one's prereflective intuition of the "singular" and the "infinite," which he later came to associate with the subjective recognition of one's utter dependence on God. It was imperative to express and communicate these affective and intuitive dimensions, Schleiermacher believed, for these alone could provide human beings with the orientation they would need to deflect an otherwise corrosive rationalism and skepticism. Although similarly concerned to elucidate the process or method through which interpretation leads to understanding, Dilthey endeavored to employ hermeneutics to shore up and expand the as-yet-shaky foundations of the nascent "human" sciences. For him, the value of hermeneutics lay in its capacity for further understanding through a careful interpretation of human experience and behavior in relation to their contexts and structures. Notwithstanding their differences in temperament and approach, both thinkers articulated the famous "hermeneutic circle," which describes the movement of understanding, from general to particular and back again, as it approaches and approximates the truth of the text or lived-experience under consideration. As Nelson instructively observes, the development and influence of hermeneutics continue to inform debates central to the articulation of European philosophy.

Chapter 7 documents the contributions of the "French spiritualists," a group of philosophers who shared a common suspicion of materialism and a common inclination toward idealism, especially with respect to the emerging "human" sciences. The author of this chapter, F. C. T. Moore, helpfully situates the school of French spiritualism against the backdrop of nineteenth-century science. Reacting to what they regarded as misplaced enthusiasm for a mechanistic paradigm in the emerging "human" sciences, the French spiritualists resisted the impulse to establish the science of psychology, for example, on the basis of either materialism or determinism. An important influence on the development of French spiritualism was Marie François Pierre Gonthier de Biran (Maine de Biran), who, in stark contrast to the Cartesian valorization of reason, emphasized the role of the will in the conscious activity of human agents. Bucking the increasingly influential trend toward reductive theories and explanations of human behavior, Maine de Biran insisted on the scientific relevance of the "life of the spirit."

Of the French spiritualists themselves, Félix Ravaisson and Jules Lachelier deserve mention for their criticisms of materialism and their insistence that the "human" sciences must account for feeling, will, enthusiasm, freedom, and other subjective indices of human behavior. Charles Renouvier, who is occasionally associated with the school of French spiritualism, in fact represents a return to a Kantian framework for understanding the relationship between philosophy and science.

Moore closes this chapter by documenting the contributions of the eminent philosopher Henri Bergson, who not only served as a bridge figure to twentieth-century philosophy, but also famously developed what might be called a "spiritualist" response to the increasingly influential theory of evolution. Despite being far more favorably disposed toward science than his brethren among the French spiritualists, Bergson nevertheless shared their suspicions of simplistic and reductive appeals to material principles of explanation. Rejecting both materialism and vitalism in its crudest forms, Bergson aspired to design and conduct biological and psychological investigations that would accommodate both spirit and matter. As Moore suggests, we may thus conclude that Bergson's proposal of "creative" evolution expresses something of the spirit of French spiritualism.

Chapter 8 documents the birth and development of sociology in the latter half of the nineteenth century. The author of this chapter, Alan Sica, explains that sociology emerged in this period as a response to the pressing need to develop a scientific method that would allow scholars to collect and interpret the unruly data of the so-called "human" sciences. Sica deftly charts the genealogy of sociological research, from its origins in the investigations of Herbert Spencer and Henri de Saint-Simon, through the innovations of Auguste Comte, Émile Durkheim, and Max Weber, to its consolidation in the early twentieth century as a scientific (and academic) discipline in its own right. Whereas Spencer is perhaps best known for the teleological inflections of his contributions to "social Darwinism," and Saint-Simon for his utopian faith in the progress and prosperity to be enjoyed by a society guided by science, it was Comte who recoiled most decisively from the crypto-theological failings of speculative philosophy. His influential "Law of the Three Phases" was designed to show, *pace* Hegel (and others), that the full maturity of humankind lay in its graduation from a reliance on metaphysics to an appeal to positive facts and empirically confirmed data. Comte's famous positivism was meant not only to place the nascent "human" sciences on a firm empirical foundation, but also to elevate the sociologists themselves to positions of quasi-religious leadership within society.

Durkheim in turn aimed to identify, and build on, those basic insights of Saint-Simon that he (and others) felt Comte had not properly acknowledged. In doing so, Durkheim hoped to recover for the "human" sciences some measure of the philosophical sophistication that, according to him, Comte had sacrificed. This trend was continued by Weber, who reserved for philosophy an indispensable role in determining the criteria for evidence and truth in the "human" sciences. As Sica demonstrates throughout this chapter, the leading social theorists of the period borrowed liberally from their philosophical brethren. Thus it should come as no surprise that the development of sociology in this period so closely parallels related developments in the history of European philosophy.

The theme of Chapter 9 is the development of science and mathematics in the latter half of the nineteenth century. In this chapter, Dale Jacquette tracks several of the most important innovations in scientific method and its mathematical foundations. Central to this account are his treatments of the proliferation of scientific research projects and of the dramatic – and occasionally contentious – expansion of the domain perceived as appropriate to, and ripe for, scientific investigation. In addition to providing a broad overview of the period, Jacquette helpfully draws our attention to several significant developments in scientific method and practice, including John Stuart Mill's contributions to the empiricist method of inductive reasoning, Bernard Bolzano's contributions to a neorationalist philosophy of science and mathematics, Comte's development of his positivism, and Gottlob Frege's contributions to scientific semantics and philosophy of mathematics.

As previously noted in Chapters 6 and 8, this period also witnessed the emergence of the distinctly "human" (or social) sciences, wherein scientific methods were applied, with varying results, to the data encoded in human behavior. As Jacquette demonstrates, the consolidation of research methods and protocols was accompanied by a growing sense of dissatisfaction with the established "laws" of nature. From this contentious, tumultuous situation would arise the influential twentieth-century challenges to classical Newtonian science.

Chapter 10 is devoted to the emergence and development of pragmatism in the latter half of the nineteenth century, with special emphasis on the seminal contributions of Charles Sanders Peirce. As presented here by Douglas R. Anderson, Peirce is best understood as both an appreciative reader and a respectful opponent of Hegel. While indebted to Hegel's focus on dynamic processes of historical development, Peirce resisted Hegel's decision to discount the enduring significance of the universal categories of "Firstness" (or qualitative immediacy) and "Secondness" (or otherness). According to Peirce, that is, Hegel's preoccupation with the logical sublation of opposing theses, which Peirce understood in terms of his own category of "Thirdness" (or mediation), prompted him to ignore, or deny, the perdurance of the categories of Firstness and Secondness.

Pragmatism thus emerged, and subsequently developed, not as a rejection of Hegel's method, but as a unique reception of this method. It was left to the pragmatists, Peirce believed, to fulfill the promise of German idealism and to steer Hegel's method into closer conformity to the emerging paradigm of evolutionary science. As subsequently modified by William James and John Dewey, pragmatism began to take on the form in which it is still familiar today. Indeed, the contemporary influence of pragmatism on the development of European philosophy thus completes the feedback loop that began with Peirce's engagement with Hegel.

In Chapter 11, Gary Shapiro closes our volume with a detailed survey of aesthetics and art history in the period 1840–1900. Reflecting the revolutionary fervor of the period, practitioners (e.g. Richard Wagner) and theorists (e.g. Karl Marx) of art proposed revolutionary advances of their own, with respect both to the goals and methods of artistic production and to the proper cultural role of aesthetic theory. As in previous chapters, the focus is placed here on the rejection of established norms and conventions and the subsequent introduction of innovative practices and approaches. Establishing the uniquely *modern* provenance of the study of aesthetics, Shapiro documents the contributions and concerns of the post-Hegelian generation of European philosophers, including Karl Rosenkranz, F. T. Vischer, Søren Kierkegaard, Robert Zimmermann, and others. Deftly guided by Shapiro, the reader is introduced to the rapidly shifting scene wherein European artists perfected their craft while theorists and critics replaced shopworn pieties with bold, new, experimental measures of evaluation. From Nietzsche's investigation of the "physiology of aesthetics" to the management of nature by landscape gardeners, the latter half of the nineteenth century witnessed a veritable proliferation of new artistic forms and genres.

As these chapters and their authors variously confirm, the period 1840–1900 saw the fruition of those insights, questions, and challenges that are now deemed central to the core ventures of contemporary continental philosophy. By way of conclusion, it may be worthwhile to review several general lines of influence and inheritance from the nineteenth century. First, we may trace the broadly interrogative approach and generally critical stance of continental philosophy to the unmasking and debunking projects that were launched in the nineteenth century. The groundbreaking criticisms developed by Feuerbach and Marx, for example, were instrumental to the articulation of a critique of modernity and of the seemingly "natural" institutions that sustain its supposed "progress." From the pioneering investigations conducted by Kierkegaard, Dostoevsky, and Nietzsche emerged the fully developed schools of psychoanalysis that we now associate with Freud, Jung, Reich, and Lacan. From the seminal contributions of Schleiermacher and Dilthey grew the philosophical hermeneutics practiced by Heidegger, Gadamer, Ricoeur, and their contemporary followers. The current surge of interest in negative theology, the death of God, post-Holocaust ethics, and the new atheism would be unthinkable apart from the contributions of the great nineteenth-century critics of institutionalized religion, including Feuerbach, Marx, Dostoevsky, Nietzsche, and Comte.

Second, continental philosophy owes its abiding attunement to alterity, in all of its innumerable and incommensurate incarnations, to the expansive investigations conducted by the leading thinkers of the nineteenth century. The period 1840–1900 was marked by an explosion of contact with, and interest in, the various others of European modernity. As scientists gathered new data, explorers encountered new cultures, and previously segregated nations, peoples, and classes began to intermingle, European philosophers were generally keen to acknowledge – although not always to include – the others to whom they were introduced. The ongoing debates about what would and would not "count" as true science, or real philosophy, we might speculate, accustomed philosophers on the continent to contested disciplinary borders and permeable (if not porous) disciplinary boundaries. European philosophers, we might further speculate, grew to expect their efforts at categorization and classification to require regular updates and revisions, especially when presented with those others whose unique existence defied the standard systems of classification.[6]

Third, continental philosophy owes its generally inclusive orientation – which we may characterize as multidisciplinary, historically contextualized, politically engaged, scientifically informed, and hermeneutically sophisticated – to the leading thinkers and trends of the nineteenth century. As we have seen, the major figures of the period were not reluctant to enter scientific debates and controversies, and they contributed throughout the century to the continued refinement of scientific methods and practices. In this respect, contemporary continental philosophy may trace its lineage to the efforts of Marx, Nietzsche, Dilthey, Comte, Weber, and Peirce, to name just a few. To be sure, this orientation is also indebted to the resistance mounted by nineteenth-century philosophers to prematurely reductive applications of scientific principles of explanation. The debates surrounding the founding of the "human" sciences were very much concerned to preserve something that is irreducibly human – whether it be freedom, will, or spirit – in the face of increasingly popular mechanistic and deterministic worldviews. In this respect, contemporary continental philosophy is deeply indebted to the labors of the "Left" Hegelians, the French spiritualists, the early sociologists, and the early pragmatists.

Finally, we might conclude, continental philosophy owes its relentlessly inquisitive and self-reflective temperament to the pioneering thought experiments conducted by the leading philosophers of the nineteenth century. In general, the lines of questioning initiated by the nineteenth-century "masters of

---

*6. The crossing of disciplinary borders is a guiding theme of the essays in *The History of Continental Philosophy: Volume 7*.

suspicion" – Marx, Nietzsche, and Freud, although other figures (e.g. Feuerbach, Kierkegaard, and Dostoevsky) are equally worthy of this designation – were instrumental to the development of the critical strategies and techniques that are associated with the most visible and influential contemporary expressions of continental philosophy, including deconstruction, postmodernism, and poststructuralism.[7]

---

7. I wish to thank Alan Schrift for his general guidance of the *History of Continental Philosophy* series and also for his efforts in support of this particular volume. Without his patience, good will, and editorial acumen, this volume would not have been completed. I also would like to thank Dana Lawrence for her editorial assistance in the final stages of the project. Finally, I would like to dedicate this volume to the memory of my mother, Mary Joan Kavanagh Conway, who died as this project was nearing its completion.

1

FEUERBACH AND THE LEFT AND RIGHT HEGELIANS

William Clare Roberts

To those left cold by the bombast, internecine polemics, and melodrama of post-Hegelian German philosophy, it might seem either that Hegel's students failed to attain the height of their master, and so fell into obscure partisan squabbles, or else that the entire project of German idealism contained the germs of this debacle from the beginning, and that it serves as a *reductio ad absurdum* of the whole tradition. Both of these views were common among the post-Hegelians themselves. The first reaction is characteristic of those who came to be known as Right Hegelians. These set themselves the task of conserving the truth of Hegel's philosophy, and defending it against misapplications, misappropriations, and misinterpretations. The second reaction is the developed response of the more radical among the Left Hegelians, Feuerbach[1] and Marx especially. Thus an air of dissatisfaction and restlessness permeates the entire post-Hegelian scene. To the extent that this dissatisfaction continues to characterize philosophical and political discourses, we remain within that scene.[2]

This essay will investigate this scene of restlessness with special attention on the role of Ludwig Feuerbach. Feuerbach is generally treated as the joint between Hegel and Marx, and this essay will to some extent reinforce that tendency by beginning with Hegel and ending with Marx. Nonetheless, Feuerbach is certainly much more than a mere transitional figure, in that he articulates a response to

---

1. Ludwig Feuerbach (July 28, 1804–September 13, 1872; born in Landshut, Bavaria; died in Nuremberg, Germany) was educated at the University of Heidelberg (1823–24), University of Berlin (1824–26), and University of Erlangen (1826–28). His influences included Bacon, Hegel, Kant, Leibniz, and Spinoza, and he held no university appointments.
2. See also Jürgen Habermas, *The Philosophical Discourse of Modernity: Twelve Lectures*, Frederick G. Lawrence (trans.) (Cambridge, MA: MIT Press, 1987), 53.

the post-Hegelian ferment that endures as a recurrent, live option.[3] Marx is certainly not the necessary consequence of Feuerbach's premises; one can start down the path with Feuerbach and travel as far as one wishes without arriving at Marxism. One of the objects of this essay is to identify the point of rupture that separates Feuerbach's position from that of Marx. Whether Feuerbach's position is satisfactory, as opposed to unique and viable, is a separate question, and one that this essay will not seek to answer. Instead, it will identify the problem to which Feuerbach responds, trace in some detail the critique of theology and philosophy by which he responds to that problem, and highlight the distinctive features of his response, by which Feuerbach can be differentiated from Right Hegelians, other Left Hegelians, and Marx.

I. PERSONALITY, SPIRIT, AND THE PROBLEM OF INCARNATION

In order to appreciate Feuerbach's problem, it is helpful to be cognizant of certain aspects of the historical and cultural context of his writings, aspects that are not explicitly acknowledged within those writings, but that function nonetheless as the backdrop against which Feuerbach wrote.[4] Feuerbach was seduced into philosophy by Hegel himself, and left behind his studies in theology to devote himself to *Wissenschaft* (philosophical science). He was never to secure the academic post he desired, however, for he was blacklisted after failing sufficiently to guard his authorship of the anonymous *Thoughts on Death and Immortality*, which argued against the immortality of the personal soul. The ensuing death of his academic career was not due merely to his book's offensiveness to religious orthodoxy. The personality of the soul – its individual and irreducible selfhood – was one leg of the three-legged stool of German order, together with the personality of God and the personality of the king. Warren Breckman has demonstrated that this discourse of personality colored all of the controversy surrounding Hegel and the Young Hegelians. This is because German personalism sustained an elaborate homology between the uniqueness of a personal God, the indivisible and quasifamilial sovereignty of the king, and the singularity of each subject. As Breckman reminds us, "the works of the Young Hegelians unified theological, political, and social themes in large measure because they were written within a context in which this unity was

---

3. For a sense of Feuerbach's living relevance, see Nina Power, "Which Equality? Badiou and Rancière in Light of Ludwig Feuerbach," *Parallax* 5(3) (2009).
*4. This philosophical context is the subject of many essays in *The History of Continental Philosophy: Volume 1*; see, in particular, the essays by Terry Pinkard and Lawrence S. Stepelevich.

taken for granted."[5] Therefore it is necessary to examine in more detail both the personalism of German politics and theology and the aspects of Hegelian and post-Hegelian thought that elicited such a powerful defensive reaction. It is crucial to understand, in other words, how German idealism came to be seen as a threat to the German order.[6]

During and after the *Pantheismusstreit* (pantheism controversy) – the debate between F. H. Jacobi and Moses Mendelssohn about whether Enlightenment rationalism necessarily entails pantheism and fatalism – the line of demarcation between enlightenment and reaction was Spinoza's definition of God as substance, or the totality of nature. It was Jacobi's exchange with Mendelssohn that cemented the identification of Spinozism with what Jacobi called "nihilism," and counterpoised to it the intuitive and emotional certainty in "a transcendent personal intelligence" (MYH 26).[7] Already in Jacobi, the transcendent personality of God is also keyed to the transcendent personality of the human individual. After Napoleon's defeat, Restoration political thinkers such as Carl Ludwig von Haller decisively asserted the personality of the sovereign to be the third leg of the stool, and Pietist reactionaries and the later Schelling unified all three into the Christian personalism that functioned as the *de facto* state ideology of Prussia right up to 1848.[8]

Without delving too deeply into Hegel, it is a fairly straightforward matter to show that his philosophy of spirit is deeply – although not simply – opposed to each branch of orthodox personalism. In his early essay "The Spirit of Christianity and its Fate," he had argued for the incompatibility of Christianity and personalism. According to Hegel, Christ himself was explicitly "against personality, against the view that his essence possessed an individuality opposed to those who had attained the culmination of friendship with him."[9] This view did not change, and is reiterated in his *Lectures on the Philosophy of Religion*. Although his endorsement of monarchy in *The Philosophy of Right* dramatically separates him from the Left Hegelians, Hegel's monarch was not the personal monarch the conservatives wanted, but a mere functionary of the state, a "decider" whose decisions carried not personal authority but only the impersonal authority of

---

5. Warren Breckman, *Marx, the Young Hegelians, and the Origins of Radical Social Theory: Dethroning the Self* (Cambridge: Cambridge University Press, 1999), 15. Hereafter cited as MYH followed by the page number.
6. Throughout this section I rely heavily on Breckman's scholarship.
*7. For a discussion of Jacobi in relation to his criticism of Kant, see the essay by Richard Fincham in *The History of Continental Philosophy: Volume 1*.
8. See the useful account in MYH 63–89.
9. G. W. F. Hegel, *Early Theological Writings*, T. M. Knox (trans.) (Philadelphia, PA: University of Pennsylvania Press, 1948), 239.

the constitution and its laws. On theological and political grounds, then, the conservatives had good reason to count Hegel as an opponent.

It is in relation to the third aspect of personalism, however – the transcendent personality of the individual – that the complexity and depth of Hegel's opposition to personalism comes to the fore. The personality defended by the conservatives was a willful personality, self-contained and sovereign within its own domain.[10] This personality has a place in Hegel's thought, to be sure. Yet it is not the truth of personality, but only an abstract, legalistic moment to be overcome. Just as God the Father is not the truth of God, so, too, the self-contained, sovereign person is not the true person; only *Geist* (spirit) is fully and actually a self-conscious subject. When Hegel introduces spirit in the *Phenomenology*, he writes:

> A self-consciousness, in being an object, is just as much "I" as "object." With this we already have before us the Notion of Spirit. What still lies ahead for consciousness is the experience of what Spirit is – this absolute substance which is the unity of the different independent self-consciousnesses which, in their opposition, enjoy perfect freedom and independence: "I" that is "We" and "We" that is "I."[11]

As opposed to the abstract, legal person, spirit is the concrete person, the person constituted as a subject by a consciousness of its intersubjective reality. This person is not sovereign or willful, for it comes to know itself only through the ethical and rational life it shares with others. Spirit does not transcend and rule over its own private domain, but is always outside itself. In Jean-Luc Nancy's apt phrase, spirit "trembles in desire."[12] Or, as Judith Butler puts it, "if we are to follow *The Phenomenology of Spirit*, I am invariably transformed by the encounters I undergo; recognition becomes the process by which I become other than what I was and so cease to be able to return to what I was."[13]

Hegel's identification of spirit as the truth of personality could not have pleased any of the parties in the theological–political disputes roiling Germany,

---

10. As Breckman puts it, "At the core of both the theological and political discourses of personality was an intense concern with the nature and conditions of indivisible unitary will – in short, with the nature of sovereignty" (MYH 63).
11. G. W. F. Hegel, *Phenomenology of Spirit*, A. V. Miller (trans.) (Oxford: Oxford University Press, 1977), 110 [§177].
12. Jean-Luc Nancy, *Hegel: The Restlessness of the Negative*, Jason Smith and Steven Miller (trans.) (Minneapolis, MN: University of Minnesota Press, 2002), 64.
13. Judith Butler, *Giving an Account of Oneself* (New York: Fordham University Press, 2005), 27. John McCumber's work has also stressed this aspect of Hegel.

for all camps relied, at one point or another, on abstract personality. The political reactionaries stressed the sovereign personality of the king, and the religious reactionaries stressed the same in God. But political liberals were equally invested in the personality of the individual political subject. Attachment to and rejection of the spiritualization of God, of the state, and of the subject, therefore, became the shibboleths of Hegelianism and anti-Hegelianism, respectively. Left and Right Hegelians were as one in their adherence to spirit. What divided them was the question of how to interpret spirit, a question that came unmistakably on the scene with the 1835 publication of David Friedrich Strauss's *The Life of Jesus Critically Examined*.[14]

In the denouement of his argument, Strauss presents the standard Hegelian Christology – every element of the "evangelical history" is "deduced" dialectically from "the concept of God and man in their reciprocal relation"[15] – only to diagnose it with a fatal contradiction:

> If reality is ascribed to the idea of the unity of the divine and human natures, is this equivalent to the admission that this unity must actually have been once manifested, as it never has been, and never more will be, in one individual? This is indeed not the mode in which Idea realizes itself; it is not wont to lavish all its fullness on one exemplar, and be niggardly towards all others: it rather loves to distribute its riches among a multiplicity of exemplars which reciprocally complete each other – in the alternate positing and sublating of individuals. (LJ 48)

With this text, the division between Left and Right Hegelians sprang into existence fully formed, like Athena from the head of Zeus. Whereas Right Hegelians (such as Philip Conrad Marheineke and Karl Rosenkranz) emphasized the differentiation within spirit, and valorized certain historical instantiations of spirit as the actual manifestations of the idea, Left Hegelians followed Strauss in denying equally to all particular historical shapes of spirit the privilege of

---

14. David Friedrich Strauss (January 27, 1808–February 8, 1874; born and died in Ludwigsburg, Württemberg [Germany]) was educated at the University of Tübingen (1825–30) and University of Berlin (1831–32). His influences included Hegel, Kant, Schleiermacher, and Spinoza, and he held appointments at the University of Tübingen (1832–33) and University of Zurich (1839). His major works included *Das Leben Jesu, Kritisch bearbeitet* (*The Life of Jesus Critically Examined*; 1835).
15. Strauss, *The Life of Jesus*, in *The Young Hegelians: An Anthology*, Lawrence S. Stepelevich (ed.) (Amherst, NY: Humanity Books, 1999), 46. I have silently expurgated Massey's editorial insertions, such as brackets and interpolated German words. Hereafter cited as LJ followed by the page number.

actualizing the idea. It is the play of history as an infinite totality that alone incarnates the "infinite spirit" of God, and no incident or moment of that play can, to the exclusion of other moments, condense and hold the infinite within itself.

That this Left Hegelian interpretation amounts to an absolute humanism was made obvious by Strauss from the beginning:

> Humanity is the union of the two natures – the incarnate God, the infinite Spirit alienated in the finite and the finite Spirit recollecting its infinitude; … it is the worker of miracles, insofar as in the course of human history the spirit more and more completely subjugates nature, both within and around man, until it lies before him as the inert matter on which he exercises his active power. Humanity is the sinless one because the course of its development is blameless. … It is Humanity that dies, rises, and ascends to heaven, for from the negation of its natural state there ever proceeds a higher spiritual life; from the sublation of its finitude as a personal, national, and terrestrial spirit, arises its union with the infinite spirit of the heavens.
>
> (LJ 48–9)

There are two dilemmas constitutive of Strauss's spiritual humanism, dilemmas that will in turn frame Feuerbach's own construction and development of a spiritual or transcendental anthropology. The first is the dilemma between Strauss's dispersal of spirit into the infinite play of the species and his obvious commitment to a progressive historical development. If no "particular point in time" can incarnate infinite spirit, how can human history tell the tale of a "more and more" complete spiritualization? It would be easy enough to resolve this first dilemma were it not for a second; on the one hand, Strauss wants to deny any particular incarnation of the infinite within history, but, on the other, he does not want to relapse into a Kantianism that would posit the idea as merely ideal, as approximated but never realized. Infinite spirit cannot be contained within history as a local phenomenon, but nor can it stand outside history as an eternal *ought*.

In his works on teleological judgment and history, Kant had formulated a concept of the species that clearly foreshadowed the post-Hegelian scene.[16] He had claimed that the "natural capacities" of humanity, insofar as they are destined for rational employment, "are to be completely developed only in the species, not in the individual," and that:

---

*16. Kant's philosophy is discussed in detail in the essay by Thomas Nenon, as well as several of the other essays on reactions to Kant's philosophy in *The History of Continental Philosophy: Volume 1*.

[Nature] requires a perhaps incalculable sequence of generations, each passing its enlightenment on to the next, to bring its seeds in our species to the stage of development that completely fulfills nature's objective. And the goal of [man's] efforts must be that point in time, at least among the ideas of men, since the natural capacities must otherwise be regarded as in large part purposeless and vain.[17]

For all Hegelians, this fails to satisfy, as Hegel's Preface to *The Philosophy of Right* attests. The promise and satisfaction of Hegelian philosophy was the "warmer peace" with historical actuality that it brought.[18] For Strauss, that peace took the form of history conceived as a progressive totality that, its progress notwithstanding, had always already constituted the identity of God and the human species. God is not incarnated within that history because it is only the totality in its play that makes the divine materially present. The progressive spiritualization of nature is not progress toward an eschatological completion, either within or outside history, but the ever-triumphant expansion of the totality itself.

Strauss's formulation of spirit was the final nail in the coffin of Hegelianism so far as its conservative critics were concerned, and it made the position of the Right Hegelians a very difficult one, for they had to defend their more conservative Hegel against both the conservative anti-Hegelians and the Hegelian Left. It seemed as if they had no ground on which to stand, their adversaries having already divided the whole terrain – Christianity to the right, Hegelianism to the left – between themselves. There will later be a resurgence of a quasi-conservative position from within the ranks of the Left Hegelians themselves – that of Bruno Bauer[19] – but Bauer's conservatism was a secular, elitist neo-

---

17. Kant, "Idea for a Universal History with a Cosmopolitan Intent," in *Perpetual Peace and Other Essays on Politics, History, and Morals*, Ted Humphrey (trans.) (Indianapolis, IN: Hackett, 1983), 30.
18. G. W. F. Hegel, *The Philosophy of Right*, Alan White (trans.) (Newburyport, MA: Focus Publishing/R. Pullins Company, 2002), 10.
19. Bruno Bauer (September 6, 1809–April 13, 1882; born in Eisenberg, Saxe-Altenberg; died in Rixdorf, Germany) was educated at the University of Berlin (1828–34). His influences included Hegel, and he held appointments at the University of Berlin (1834–39) and University of Bonn (1839–42). His major works include: *Kritik der evangelischen Geschichte der Synoptiker und des Johannes, Dritter und letzter Band* (1840–42); (anonymously) *Die Posaune des jüngsten Gerichts über Hegel, den Atheisten und Antichristen* (*The Trumpet of the Last Judgment against Hegel the Atheist and Antichrist: An Ultimatum*; 1841); *Das Entdeckte Christentum: Eine Erinnerung an das 18. Jahrhundert und ein Beitrag zur Krisis des 19* (*Christianity Exposed: A Recollection of the 18th Century and a Contribution to the Crisis of the 19th*; 1843); *Die Judenfrage* (*The Jewish Problem*; 1843); *Christus und die Cäsaren: Der Ursprung des Christenthums aus dem römischen Griechenthum* (*Christ and the Caesars: The Origin of Christianity from Romanized Greek Culture*; 1879).

conservatism.[20] Christian Hegelianism was, after Strauss, treated generally as an oxymoron. Therefore we can turn to Feuerbach, who turned Strauss's argument into a critical technique by which he sought to revolutionize humanity's self-conception.

II. FEUERBACH'S ANTHROPOLOGY OF SPIRIT

If Feuerbach is known for one thing, it is for coining "species-being" (*Gattungswesen*), the term so important for the young Marx. Species-being is the sort of being, human being, that is – and is conscious of what it is – only in and through its relations with the other beings of the same species. Hence it would not be an exaggeration to say that Feuerbach's concept of the species-being is nothing more than Hegel's spirit – "I" that is "We" and "We" that is "I" – under a different name. That Feuerbach's central philosophical concept differs from Hegel's only verbally is not nothing, however. Indeed, Feuerbach would say this *verbal* difference amounts to an *essential* difference, for it brings out the relation between thought and language, a relation over which Feuerbach seeks to break absolutely with Hegel. Feuerbach takes Hegel to identify thought and language, reason and demonstration, and his first open criticism of Hegel attacks precisely this purported identity.

Feuerbach's essay *Zur Kritik der Hegelschen Philosophie*,[21] appearing in 1839, articulates two basic criticisms of Hegel. First, Feuerbach argues that Hegelian philosophy "is defined and proclaimed as *absolute* philosophy; i.e., as nothing less than *philosophy itself*, if not by the master himself, then certainly by his disciples – at least by his orthodox disciples – and certainly quite consistently and in keeping with the teaching of the master" (TCH 97). This claim, Feuerbach replies, is refuted by the same reasoning Strauss used to refute the claim that God was incarnated in Christ. No infinite species realizes itself in a single individual. Such an incarnation would, indeed, amount to "the end of the world," emptying all future time of any meaning or history (TCH 98).[22] Second, Feuerbach argues that all modern philosophies, including Hegel's, "presuppose philosophy; that is, what they understand by philosophy to be the immediate truth"

---

20. Ironically, Bauer had, at twenty-six, been chosen by Marheineke to deliver the Right Hegelian critique of Strauss's *Life of Jesus*. The ink was barely dry when Bauer went over to the Left. In a further irony, Strauss very quickly abandoned much of his Hegelianism. The fourth edition of his book – the 1842 edition translated into English by George Eliot – contains very little Hegelian terminology.
21. Ludwig Feuerbach, "Towards a Critique of Hegel's Philosophy," in *The Young Hegelians*, Stepelevich (ed.). Hereafter cited as TCH followed by the page number.
22. I will return to the relation between incarnation and history in Feuerbach's writings below.

(TCH 110). The *Logic* and *Phenomenology of Spirit* do not begin, according to Feuerbach, by addressing "sensuous consciousness" – the other of philosophy – but by addressing philosophy itself (TCH 114). In other words, Hegel offers no inducement to sensuous consciousness to get on board with his philosophical project in the first place. His philosophy remains solipsistic.

Both of these criticisms depend on Feuerbach's denial that thought and language are identical. Feuerbach's argument for this denial takes the form of three appeals to experience. His first appeal is to the communication between teacher and student. A "quick-witted person," he reminds us, "can be ahead of his demonstrating teacher" (TCH 105). This shows us that "forms of communication, modes of expression, representations, conceptions" are only "forms in which thought manifests itself," not "active forms of thought, not causal relations of reason" (TCH 104 n.1). The teacher does not "instill his thoughts in me like drops of medicine," and the philosopher cannot "really produce philosophers" (TCH 105). Rather, the teacher presupposes the self-activity of the pupil's understanding: "he only embodies and represents what I should reproduce in myself in imitation of him" (TCH 105–6). Thus linguistic, demonstrative thought, including the dialectical presentation of Hegel, "is only the translation into an idiom comprehensible to us of a highly gifted but more or less unknown author who is difficult to understand," the "genius for thinking" in all of us (TCH 105 n.1).

Second, Feuerbach appeals to the process of writing. To write is to present thought, but "[t]hought is prior to the presentation of thought" (TCH 107). Hegel knew before beginning the *Logic*, for example, that it would culminate in the absolute idea, and yet the *Logic* in its presentation does not begin with this knowledge. Feuerbach concludes:

> This contradiction between the thinker who is without needs, who can anticipate that which is yet to be presented because everything is already settled for him, and the needy writer who has to go through a chain of succession and who posits and objectifies as formally uncertain what is certain to the thinker – this contradiction is the process of the Absolute Idea which presupposes being and essence, but in such a way that these on their part already presuppose the Idea. ... That is why the Idea's lack of self-knowledge at the beginning is, in the sense of the Idea, only an ironical lack of knowledge.
> (TCH 112)

In other words, Hegel is an unwitting ironist, an ironist who cannot admit his own irony in the face of his self-seriousness. He is a self-denying "actor" and "artist" (TCH 105–6). Such is the case with all philosophers who communicate their thought. Every linguistic presentation, including Hegel's dialectic, is communication; hence language – and not merely the propositional language of the understanding – is distinct from thought.

Finally, Feuerbach appeals directly to sensuous consciousness, which, he claims, treats language as a mere means, a tool that sensuous consciousness picks up and discards as it is a help or a hindrance. This is why the opening of Hegel's *Phenomenology* – which claims to begin with sensuous certainty of the "this" and the "now"[23] – fails to address sensuous consciousness at all. Feuerbach has sensuous consciousness respond to Hegel:

> Enough of words, come down to real things! *Show* me what you are talking about! To sensuous consciousness it is precisely language that is unreal, nothing. How can it regard itself, therefore, as refuted if it is pointed out that a particular entity [the presence of consciousness] cannot be expressed in language? (TCH 114)

Whether these criticisms have any real impact on Hegel is unimportant for present purposes. What they reveal about Feuerbach, on the other hand, is critical. Feuerbach's skepticism about systematic presentation and his conviction that language stands outside thought as a mere instrument ought to prepare one to read *The Essence of Christianity* with an eye to what it does not say. If Hegel is unwitting in his irony and unable to acknowledge it, Feuerbach is well aware that he cannot help but be ironic himself. The silent currents of thought that circulate behind his presentation, even as they are communicated by his presentation, are what must concern the reader. As Feuerbach himself wrote to his friend Christian Kapp in November 1840, just as he was finishing *The Essence of Christianity*, he is a "cryptophilosopher."[24]

Thus, when Feuerbach writes, in the preface to the second edition, that *The Essence of Christianity* "contains a faithful, correct translation of the Christian religion out of the Oriental language of imagery into plain speech,"[25] the reader must remember that this is a translation from one set of representations into another set of representations, from concrete, sensuous images into "abstract images" (EC 77). That this translation is possible, and that Feuerbach has set it forth, is itself supposed by him to provide a demonstration in deed of "the real, complete nature of man" (EC xiv–xv). The act of translation indicates without elucidating the reality of the spirit – the species – behind the letter. The "principle"

---

23. Hegel, *Phenomenology of Spirit*, 58–66 [§§90–110].
24. Quoted in Marx Wartofsky, *Feuerbach* (Cambridge: Cambridge University Press, 1977), 404 n.6.
25. Ludwig Feuerbach, *The Essence of Christianity*, George Eliot (trans.) (Amherst, NY: Prometheus Books, 1989), xiii. Hereafter cited as EC followed by the page number.

of Feuerbach's "new philosophy" is "verified practically, i.e., *in concreto*" by the translation of religion into speech (EC xiv). The essence of Christianity speaks in Feuerbach's book, and confesses by this spoken self-representation that its imagistic representation in the hearts and minds of its adherents is no more its essence than is its new, verbal representation. The essence is what speaks, not what is spoken, and what speaks is "Man" (EC xv–xvi).

Since the essence of Christianity is the essence of all religion, and also the essence or principle of Feuerbach's new philosophy, it follows that Feuerbach is not the enemy of religion. Feuerbach's philosophy agrees completely with religion: "it has in itself the true essence of religion – is, in its very quality as a philosophy, a religion also" (EC xxiv).[26] Rather, the enemy of religion is theology, or – what amounts to the same thing – the old, pre-Feuerbachian philosophy, especially Hegel's. By a profound reversal, Feuerbach agrees with the orthodox Right that Hegelianism is the mortal enemy of religion, of spirit, and of "man." What Hegel's orthodox critics did not notice, however, is that they, too, are arrayed against religion and on the side of Hegel. The opposition of the theologians to Hegel is the opposition of one sort of anti-religion to another sort of anti-religion.

Theology and philosophy are anti-religious and anti-human because, whereas religion "is the *immediate object*, the *immediate nature* of man" (EC xxii), theology and philosophy are "the reflection of religion upon itself" (EC xvii), a reflection that makes "real beings and things into arbitrary signs, vehicles, symbols, or predicates of a distinct, transcendent, absolute, i.e., abstract being" (EC xx). Theology and philosophy take the representation of religion to be the essence of religion, and thereby make out the real essence to be a mere representation of the representation. If religion is "the dream of the human spirit" (EC xix, translation modified), it is a spontaneous dream, and so is innocent.[27] Theology, however, takes the dream to be the reality, and tries to derive the dreaming spirit from its dream. Philosophy compounds the sin by translating the sensuous dream-images into the abstract word-images of metaphysics, while continuing theology's attempt to derive the dreamer from the (now abstract) dream. Against this image fetishism of theology and philosophy, Feuerbach proposes to defend religion in its complex reality. Against his age, "which prefers

---

26. See also Ludwig Feuerbach, *Principles of the Philosophy of the Future*, Manfred H. Vogel (trans.) (Indianapolis, IN: Hackett, 1986), §64. Hereafter cited as PPF followed by the section number.
27. Wartofsky is excellent on this point: "Feuerbach is neither a positivist nor an atheist, in the ordinary (and narrower) senses, but rather an emergentist, for whom religion is a serious (and dialectically necessary) expression of a certain stage of human self-understanding" (*Feuerbach*, 6).

the sign to the thing signified," he wants to reduce "the appearance of religion" to its essence, and to explain the dream from out of the dreamer (*ibid.*).

The dreamer is human spirit, the human individual in its constitution by and consciousness of its species-being. In religion, this spirit dreams only of itself. Thus Feuerbach defines religion itself as "identical with self-consciousness – with the consciousness which man has of his nature" (EC 2).[28] But if religion is self-conscious spirit, what need is there for Feuerbach's new antiphilosophy? If religion already confesses all of its secrets without thereby ceasing to be religion (EC 57–8), what does Feuerbach's translation of that confession into speech accomplish? It is easier to say what it does *not* accomplish. It certainly does not do away with religion. For this reason, the standard account, according to which Feuerbach is a critic of religion, is simply wrong if *critique* is taken to be an external, negating stance. Feuerbach *affirms* religion, defends it against theology and philosophy, and asks of it only that it openly avow what it already is: absolute humanism. Feuerbach has long been taken to be an empirically minded materialist, as well as a critic of religion. The Vienna Circle positivists lumped him in with Hume, Bentham, and Comte as a predecessor of their own "hedonism and positivist sociology."[29] Even those who stress his Hegelian heritage tend to portray him as moving toward sensationalism, nominalism, and positivism as he matured. While it should be clear from the above that he is far from being a textbook secularist, the question of how to understand Feuerbach's epistemological statements – his insistence on the priority of sensation, for example – remains unanswered. I think it is better to see Feuerbach as a proto-phenomenologist than as a proto-positivist, anticipating the thought of Husserl and Merleau-Ponty rather than Mach and Ayer. His phenomenological humanism distinguishes him from his Left Hegelian peers, and outlining its distinctive positive features will be the focus of the final section.

---

28. Compare Louis Althusser, "On Feuerbach," in *The Humanist Controversy and Other Writings (1966–67)*, François Matheron (ed.), G. M. Goshgarian (trans.) (London: Verso, 2003). Althusser argues that Feuerbach differs from all "enlightenment" critics of religion (beginning with Epicurus) in that these all attribute religion to "partial and, usually, *aberrant* effects of human nature," while, for Feuerbach, "religion is not only an index of the distinction between man and the animals, but that which constitutes man's humanity, the human essence in its adequation" (*ibid.*, 91–2).

29. Otto Neurath *et al.*, *Wissenschaftliche Weltauffassung. Der Wiener Kreis* (Vienna, 1929), published in English as "The Scientific Conception of the World. The Vienna Circle," in *The Emergence of Logical Empiricism: From 1900 to the Vienna Circle*, Sahotra Sarkar (ed.) (New York: Garland Publishing, 1996), 326.

III. OBJECT RELATIONS AND CONFESSIONAL PRACTICE

The central tenet of *The Essence of Christianity* is Feuerbach's formula, "God is the mirror of man" (EC 63). In this, Feuerbach seeks to encompass two realizations. First, God is the peculiar object of the human being, the inescapable object of human apprehension. Second, this object is nothing other than human being objectified; everything that is in God is in human species-being, if not in each and every particular human being. According to Althusser, "the term 'object' ... sustains the entire edifice of Feuerbach's theory,"[30] and it is the objective character of human being that opens it to the sort of anthropological study Feuerbach undertakes, perhaps the first philosophical anthropology in the modern sense. Therefore, in order to understand the import of Feuerbach's central tenet, it seems necessary to analyze his notion of the object.

Working backwards, Feuerbach denies the possibility of a Cartesian or Fichtean ego, an immediately self-relating subject, explicable via introspection.[31] Consciousness has access to itself – is self-consciousness – only by way of its consciousness of objects. This is the origin of his claim that "for my thought, I require the senses, especially sight" (EC xiv).[32] The true nature of a human being is not inside, but outside. Not only the truth of statements about nature in general, but the truth of statements about human nature, is in objects, not in the subject. The subject has an inside only because it has an outside that it has introjected. Feuerbach is most explicit about this in his *Principles of the Philosophy of the Future*, where he writes, for example, that "a real object is given to me only where a being that affects me is given to me and where my self-activity ... finds its boundary or resistance in the activity of another being" (PPF §32). This discovery of the boundary of one's own subjectivity is precisely the experience of being passive. Thus, Feuerbach continues, "only where I am transformed from an 'I' into a 'thou,' where I am passive, does the conception of an activity existing apart from me, that is objectivity, arise" (*ibid.*). In other words, only by *being* an object can I *experience* objects, only by being an object can I be a subject. Being active – and here Feuerbach means thinking – implies being passive, that is, sensitive, and being sensitive further implies being sensible. This is the anchor of Feuerbach's philosophical anthropology, since anything and everything objective and sensible about human life can serve as a way into the active subjectivity of human species-being.

But there is yet this further wrinkle to Feuerbach's rather elliptical argument. *Being an object* is not co-extensive with *sensation* or *passivity* in the everyday

---
30. Althusser, "On Feuerbach," 94.
31. See Wartofsky, *Feuerbach*, 206–10, for a good discussion.
32. See also PPF §32.

senses of those terms, at least not in the original significance of *being an object*. I am truly or originally an object only when I am the object of another subject, when I am a "thou" to another "I." Intersubjectivity is, in other words, a condition for the possibility of subjectivity. Thus he claims that the object is "originally" only another "I" (PPF §32). This excavation of the conditions for the possibility of the thinking subject Feuerbach takes to mark the fundamental divide between his new philosophy and all other philosophies of the modern age. The "I" is constituted only as a "thou," the subject only as an object, thinking activity only as sensuous passivity.

As a consequence, Feuerbach argues that thought, the activity of the subject as such, must take its place within these conditions of its possibility. In one sense, this "must" is simply descriptive. Human beings cannot but think in an intersubjective context, and in light of an experiential history; there is nothing we can do about it. But Feuerbach also formulates this "must" as a series of "categorical imperatives":

> Desire not to be a philosopher, as distinct from a man; be nothing else than a thinking man. Do not think as a thinker, that is, with a faculty torn from the totality of the real human being and isolated for itself; think as a living and real being, as one exposed to the vivifying and refreshing waves of the world's oceans. Think in existence, in the world as a member of it, not in the vacuum of abstraction as a solitary monad, as an absolute monarch, as an indifferent, superworldly God; then you can be sure that your ideas are unities of being and thought. (PPF §51)

How might these imperatives be fulfilled? How does one think in the world as a member of it? The world is nothing other than the totality of possible objects, of which each human being is one. But the original object is itself a subject. Therefore the totality of possible objects is, in this original sense, the totality of subjects. In other words, the world is identical with the species. Realizing that I am, in Wartofsky's phrase, "species-identical" with my object is the definition of thinking as a member of the world.[33] Human beings look around the world and find nothing but their humanity looking back at them.

Feuerbach seems to mean this in several senses. In one sense, he writes, "The certainty of the existence of other things apart from me is mediated for me through the certainty of the existence of another human being apart from me" (PPF §41). In this sense, certainty is always an intersubjective phenomenon; what is real is what is socially vouched as real. In another way, every object, by

---

33. Wartofsky, *Feuerbach*, 207.

being an object for human consciousness, is a humanized object. Thus, "Even the moon, the sun, the stars, call to man *gnôthi seauton* [know thyself]. That he sees them, and so sees them, is evidence of his own nature" (EC 5). Finally, in a closely related manner, human senses are, according to Feuerbach, "elevated above the limits of particularity and its bondage to needs," in that they know no limits. All human senses are, therefore, "intellectual and scientific acts" (PPF §53). Thus the nature that every possible object shows to us is an infinite nature, a nature that knows no bounds. Human being cannot escape itself into some other; wherever it goes, there it finds itself. Human being is its own "absolute horizon."[34]

But none of this reveals the process whereby human beings are to go from finding their species-being always already mirrored back to them from every object to *realizing* that is what they are finding, and thereby fulfilling Feuerbach's imperatives. Feuerbach's new philosophy is needed because we do not recognize ourselves in our original object. We look in the mirror and see God – the infinite spirit – but we fail to see that we are looking in a mirror. We do not recognize ourselves in God because we do not see the mirror as a mirror. The problem is that "[m]en first see objects only as they appear to them and not as they are; they do not see themselves in the objects, but only their imaginations of the objects" (PPF §43). Imagination and fantasy, like discursive thought, are abstract. Sensuous intuition and feeling are concrete. But we don't find ourselves immediately at home in the concrete. Rather, we have to work to actually see what is in front of our faces. Feuerbach writes:

> Immediate, sensuous perception comes much later than the imagination and the fantasy. ... The task of philosophy and of science in general consists, therefore, not in leading away from sensuous, that is, real, objects, but rather in leading toward them, not in transforming objects into ideas and conceptions, but rather in making visible, that is in objectifying, objects that are invisible to ordinary eyes. (PPF §43)

Truly religious eyes are actually better at seeing than are "the eyes of the anatomists or the chemists," and yet Feuerbach wants to replace even these with "the eyes of philosophers," understood in his new sense, of course (PPF §41). "Historical epochs arise," he writes, "where that which before was only ideated and mediated becomes an object of immediate and sensuous certainty" (PPF §38). The becoming visible of the mirror-function of the object would, it seems, mark the epoch to end all epochs, for in becoming visible as a mirror, the object

---

34. Althusser, "On Feuerbach," 101.

would show us to ourselves as we really are. Our objects, being so many mirrors, would reflect to us our essential nature.

No process has been outlined, however, whereby we could come to see the mirror as a mirror. Because the human subject is constituted only intersubjectively, we must expect that such consciousness can come only socially; the intersubjective context must matter. Feuerbach also tell us explicitly that "[o]nly in feeling and in love ... is the infinite in the finite" (PPF §33). Thus we can expect further that the realization cannot be a merely rational one; it must be felt. Thus Feuerbach becomes himself a preacher and exhorts us:

> The single man for himself possesses the essence of man neither in himself as a moral being nor in himself as a thinking being. The essence of man is contained only in the community and unity of man with man; it is a unity, however, which rests only on the reality of the distinction between I and thou. (PPF §59)

The conditions that authenticity must be communal and must be felt only reinforce what Feuerbach's critique of Hegel already said: even *new* philosophers cannot really produce other philosophers. Feuerbach cannot simply tell the truth and expect that the telling will make the truth manifest to his readers. The telling is only an abstract image of the concrete fact. But the fact itself is attested only by the act of translating it into new images. This, finally, is what Feuerbach means by *praxis*: the act, renewed again and again, of taking the confession of the species, and then publishing the transcription of the confession. This transcription never incarnates the species, nor does it trap the species in amber. Rather, it only witnesses the excessiveness of the species *vis-à-vis* any of its manifestations. It thereby is meant to provoke our wonder at and love of our own species-being.

This confessional practice is Feuerbach's distinctive contribution to post-Hegelian philosophy. The post-Hegelian scene is constituted by the various attempts to discover a happy relation of individual consciousness to the totality, conceived initially as infinite spirit, then as species. In the beginning, Strauss tried to dissolve the problem by denying the possibility of such a happy relation. No exemplar realizes the species; the individual consciousness is the unhappy consciousness. In the end, Max Stirner[35] tries again to dissolve the problem, but in the opposite direction, by completely subjectivizing spirit. Stirner was a quiet figure on the margins of the Left Hegelians gathered around Bruno Bauer until

---

35. Max Stirner (Johann Kaspar Schmidt) (October 25, 1806–June 26, 1856; born in Bayreuth, Bavaria; died in Berlin, Germany) was educated at the University of Berlin, University of Erlangen, and University of Königsberg. His influences included Hegel, and he held no academic appointments. His major works included *Der Einzige und sein Eigentum* (*The Ego and Its Own*; 1844).

he published his polemical and sensationalistic book *The Ego and Its Own* in 1844. Taking Feuerbach's opposition between word and thought to the extremes of nominalism, Stirner argued that Feuerbach's "man" is just as abstract and ideal as the Christian God, and hence just as opposed to the concrete existence of the unique individual, which alone is real. Because these abstract ideas – God, state, humanity, proletariat – are rooted in the artistic externalizations of unique individuals, they are, in fact, merely so many disguises under which individuals affirm themselves egoistically. Stirner therefore urges his readers to abandon their hypocrisy and self-denial, to recognize and embrace the egoism that really drives even their acts of self-abnegation, and to assert the identity of individual and species. The close of his book is Stirner's apotheosis:

> They say of God, "Names name me not." That holds good of me: no *concept* expresses me, nothing that is designated as my essence exhausts me; they are only names. Likewise they say of God that he is perfect and has no calling to strive after perfection. That too holds good of me alone.[36]

Self-consciousness comes to equal the unique consciousness that can appear only in an infinitely self-satisfied individual.

Caught between these two extremes, both temporally and argumentatively, Feuerbach tries to hold them together. Like Strauss, he insists on the reality of the infinite, but, like Stirner, he insists on the possibility of satisfaction. In the experience of love evoked by the true religious–philosophical practice of confession, the veil between individual and species separates and a nonalienated expression of species-being shines through. The veil of history can always serve as a ground for these pinpricks of nonalienated love. The mirror can, at any moment, appear as mirror, thereby bringing us back to the ineluctable truth of our species life.

The post-Hegelian scene, then, is dominated by a problem Hegel thought he had overcome: the problem of how the universal and rational idea is or comes to be present in the particular and confused persons, events, and movements of sensuous experience. Marx breaks with this scene only when – or, more precisely, to the extent that – he abandons spirit, identifying it with an ideological reflection of capital, whose incarnation must be resisted through revolutionary action, not sought. This is the perhaps only half-conscious point of his scribbled promissory note in the margins of the notebooks posthumously published as *The German Ideology*, that "Communism is for us not a state of

---

36. Max Stirner, *The Ego and Its Own*, David Leopold (ed.) (Cambridge: Cambridge University Press, 1995), 24.

affairs which is to be established, an ideal to which reality [will] have to adjust itself. We call communism the real movement which abolishes the present state of things."[37] The extent to which Marx actually succeeds in elaborating this denial in a coherent revolutionary practice is not for this essay to judge. What is clear is that such a coherent revolutionary practice could not be a continuation of Feuerbach's confessional project by other means, a translation of one manifestation of the species into another, both of which manifestations equally fall short of the spiritual activity that effects the translation itself.

MAJOR WORKS

Geschichte der neueren Philosophie. 2 vols. Ansbach: Verlag Carl Brügel, 1833–37.
Pierre Bayle nach seinen für die Geschichte der Philosophie und der Menschheit interessantesten Momenten. Ansbach: Verlag Carl Brügel, 1838.
Das Wesen des Christenthums. Leipzig: Otto Wigand, 1841. 2nd ed. 1843. 3rd ed. 1849. Published in English as *The Essence of Christianity*, translated by George Eliot. Amherst, NY: Prometheus Books, [1854; 2nd ed. 1881] 1989.
Grundsätze der Philosophie der Zukunft. Zürich/Winterthur: Verlag des literarischen Comptoirs, 1843. Published in English as *Principles of the Philosophy of the Future*, translated by Manfred H. Vogel. Indianapolis, IN: Hackett, [1966] 1986.
Vorlesungen über das Wesen der Religion. Leipzig: Verlag Otto Wigand, 1851. Published in English as *Lectures on the Essence of Religion*, translated by Ralph Mannheim. New York: Harper & Row, 1967.
Theogonie, nach den Quellen des klassischen hebräischen und christlichen Altertums. Leipzig: Verlag Otto Wigand, 1857.

---

37. Karl Marx and Friedrich Engels, *The German Ideology: Part 1 and Selections from Parts 2 and 3*, Christopher J. Arthur (ed.) (New York: International Publishers, 1970), 56–7.

2

MARX AND MARXISM

Terrell Carver

I. MARX AND PHILOSOPHY

Karl Marx[1] did not write philosophy as a philosopher, nor would he have been pleased to be read in this way. From his earliest published works, which were topical and provocative newspaper reports and opinion pieces, he dedicated himself to political activism, holding the view that academic philosophers were too little engaged with social questions, and that philosophy as a profession and a genre would never engage properly with the politics of thoroughgoing social change. The interpretation of *some* of his works as philosophical, or as stating philosophical doctrines or using concepts of philosophical interest, developed in his later lifetime, and was the work of others. In the first instance this was done by Friedrich Engels (1820–95), his lifelong friend and occasional collaborator, who provided a biographical and philosophical context for Marx, so that he could be read in this way. In works of his own, and republished texts by Marx, Engels summarized Marx's life and thought for the reading public in this manner, while also maintaining that Marx was a political activist of worldwide and epoch-making significance.

After Engels's death Marxism emerged as a comprehensive philosophy and political practice through which many of the twentieth century's most important social and economic transformations were envisioned and pursued. By the 1930s, however, *some* of Marx's works and ideas were taken up by professional

---

1. Karl Marx (May 5, 1818–March 14, 1883; born in Trier, Rhenish Prussia; died in London, UK) was educated at the University of Bonn (1835–36), University of Berlin (1836–41), and University of Jena (PhD, 1841). Hegel is the primary philosophical influence on his work.

philosophers, at times and to some degree independently of the Marxist philosophical tradition, and often with rather less political fanfare. It must thus be understood that reading Marx as a philosopher, and interpreting his works and ideas as philosophy, is an exercise at odds with their original context as interventions into the politics of the time, as he construed it. Nonetheless, Marx has become a familiar figure in various philosophical traditions, including continental philosophy, and it is the purpose of this essay to explain how and why this happened, and what substantive claims and doctrines have been constructed on this basis.

II. EARLY LIFE AND SUBSEQUENT CAREER

Marx was born into the professional classes of converted Jews who had been afforded civil rights under the Napoleonic occupation of the Rhineland during the French Revolutionary Wars (1792–1802). These reforms survived to an extent during the era of restored monarchical and princely regimes that followed the Congress of Vienna (1814–15). During this period the impetus for antimonarchical campaigns for representative and responsible government grew steadily, culminating in the European revolutions, albeit short-lived, of 1848.

Marx had a classical "*gymnasium*" education in the days when philosophy covered the known and important forms of knowledge. The principal controversies of the time did not presuppose an opposition between it and science; rather, science was comprehended within it as natural philosophy. The intellectual and political diremption running through contemporary works and debates in philosophy was between "free-thinking" philosophical inquiry and the orthodoxies of confessional Christianity. The latter were themselves the principal way through which authoritarian sovereignty and minimal public accountability were promoted by the mutually supportive political establishments of church and state. The struggles between faith and reason were both personal and political. Marx's early life has almost always been read as more aligned with reason than with faith, although his parents were in no way radicals. Karl was encouraged by his father to study at university, first at Bonn, and then at Berlin, in order to become a lawyer.

Given the near absence of public political life in the patchwork of German kingdoms, principalities, and city-states, and the phobias concerning republican ideas and revolutionary violence promoted by the post-Napoleonic regimes, academic philosophy represented a somewhat insulated realm where free-thinking could take place. However, open confrontations with the truths that were the bedrock of Christian faith, and therefore of the moral and political order as such, had to be avoided. Atheism, or even the kind of skepticism that would question the tenets and position of Christianity, was an obvious ground for exclusion and dismissal in the universities and the professions. As a Jew, Marx's father had to become a confessing Lutheran in order to continue practicing law, and some of the "free-thinking" historians and philosophers of the time, including associates of Marx, never obtained the academic positions they sought, or in some cases were dismissed from positions they already held.[2] While the procedures involved were not full-blown inquisition and persecution, the atmosphere and results were clearly restrictive and punitive, rooted in fundamentalism and bigotry. In his university days Marx became associated with free-thinkers in history and philosophy, in particular with appropriations of philosophy for radical political purposes.

The common methodological thread in "free-thinking" was historicization. This was derived from the late eighteenth century onward through the pioneering historical and archaeological researches of German scholars into ancient civilizations and languages. Its effects are profoundly political. One way of claiming and maintaining power is to declare some states of affairs to be natural or necessary, and thus protected by fact, logic, and morality from change. When a history is provided for these phenomena – typically in law, politics, or the economy, and particularly when this history provides comparisons across times and cultures – then the claims of logical or moral necessity and of conformity to an unchanging nature no longer seem credible. Historicization shows that in human institutions at different times there have been different legal, political, and economic systems, justified by different philosophies, religions, and "time-honored" traditions. By eschewing clear statements endorsing the political and economic arrangements of the present, and failing to re-affirm the revealed truths of Christian confession, new histories could promote destabilization in contemporary power structures and open up perspectives on social change. Perhaps current certainties would pass away, as previous ones had done. Perhaps the rejection of past certainties could not be explained away with smug assurances about the secure certainties of the present. Owing to the enforcement of political and religious orthodoxies at the time, there were few published works as bald as this. Instead, a considerable amount of careful ambiguity in language, content, and requisite assurances was the order of the day, since freedoms of expression were not protected. The whole idea of a right to such protection was itself subversive.

Given the appropriation of classical Roman and Greek philosophies into European culture and legal systems, begun in the early Middle Ages and thus the bedrock for the schools and universities that Marx attended, nonradical historicization was little questioned. This was because it was familiarly combined

---

2. David McLellan, *Karl Marx: His Life and Thought* (London: Macmillan, 1973).

with Christian principles and practice, and not seriously challenged by alternative orthodox histories and philosophies derived exclusively from the Bible and other fundamentalisms of the Christian churches. However, a landmark work during the time of Marx's intellectual development addressed itself directly to the historical basis of Christian faith, in particular the life and teachings of Jesus. Then, even more radically, another book propounded a theory of the anthropological processes through which religions of any kind had been produced within societies up to the present. These two books were David Friedrich Strauss's *The Life of Jesus Critically Examined* (1835), and Ludwig Feuerbach's *The Essence of Christianity* (1841).[3] These works went through an impressive number of controversy-provoking editions in Marx's youth, with a fourth edition of Strauss's book published in 1840, and a second of Feuerbach's in 1843.

Strauss's work applied a rigorous historical method to the Gospel accounts of Jesus's life. This was precisely the kind of skepticism that the defenders of orthodoxy were uncomfortable with, and the results were much as they had feared: there were no facts to be had from the Gospels themselves, or indeed from any other reliable sources. While sounding like history and eyewitness reports, much Gospel discourse was merely repetition of earlier texts of prophecy, claiming fulfillment. Feuerbach's work was more radical and more philosophical, proposing a mechanism of projection throughout history (and indeed speculatively, in prehistory) through which humans assuaged their anxieties by constructing fictive supernatural beings. These beings were themselves only the repositories of projected human qualities and activities (courage, love, anger, war, etc.) around which religious practice and institutional power were produced. Humans were thus in thrall to an alien realm supposedly over and above their mundane existence.

Both Strauss and Feuerbach, however, proposed versions of philosophy that would effectively transcend confessional Christianity, at least for the educated classes where free-thinking had the wherewithal to flourish, and thus they would avoid an overt rejection of familiar moral values and the ultimate horror of valueless nihilism. Strauss's solution was a kind of pantheism, where goodness pervades the universe, of which rationalized Christianity was an instance. Feuerbach's was a religion of humanity, where human values were recognized and respected as exactly that. The Christian establishment regarded both new systems as many steps too far, and both philosophers entered a pariah realm where their readers were radicals, and the two were clearly on the wrong side of respectable philosophizing.

---

*[3]. Strauss's and Feuerbach's works are discussed in detail in the essay by Lawrence S. Stepelevich in *The History of Continental Philosophy: Volume 1*.

By historicizing philosophy itself, and expanding the content of philosophy to include history and culture in all aspects, G. W. F. Hegel (1770–1831) had set all these problems up.[4] Writing in language of deliberate ambiguity, though, he was able to achieve the eventual production of his work as a system, comprising published volumes and other materials that were still in editorial production following his death. While his early works excited suspicion that the realization of the rational and the real, as he understood these developmental phenomena in the world, was driven forward by the French Revolution (1789–99), the mature works were generally read as much more sympathetic to the conservative ideals of the restored Prussian monarchy. In the later Hegelian and post-Hegelian world, it was clear, then, that politics and social questions generally were now central to the philosopher's work and vision, rather than excluded or marginalized as ancillary. Hegel had equated knowledge with the philosophization of human historical experience in its entirety, rather than with philosophy as an abstract account of truth and judgment. From the Hegelian perspective, there was no reason to exempt confessional Christianity from occupying a position in the development of *Geist* or – in the usual clumsy English translation, "spirit" – which in Hegel's discourse stood for the driving force within human development. Thus the protected zone for matters of faith was no longer obviously intact and so exempt from philosophical scrutiny.

Keeping the authoritarianism of both church and state in place was a major political project pursued by the rulers of the time, and evinced in numerous antiradical scares and exemplary punishments. It was evident in politicized academic appointments, notably that of the philosopher Friedrich von Schelling (1775–1854) to the Berlin Academy in 1841.[5] His mission was to deradicalize the Hegelian legacy and to discourage the radicalism brewing among "Young Hegelians"[6] (an echo of "Young Germany,"[7] a liberal literary nationalism flourishing a few years previously). Marx's interest in Hegel was thus compulsory, in the sense that any student of the time would need to engage with the great German master. This engagement was necessarily political, because the content and current position of the landmark philosophical system was itself a political issue in almost the only public space – the universities – where debates about politics, however rarefied, could take place, albeit within the coded terms of philosophical engagement.

---

*4. For a discussion of Hegel's philosophy, see the essay by Terry Pinkard in *The History of Continental Philosophy: Volume 1*.

*5. Schelling is discussed in an essay by Joseph P. Lawrence in *The History of Continental Philosophy: Volume 1*.

*6. The Young Hegelians are discussed in this volume in the essay by William Clare Roberts, and in the essay by Lawrence S. Stepelevich in *The History of Continental Philosophy: Volume 1*.

*7. "Young Germany" is discussed in Alastair Hannay's essay in this volume.

During his student days Marx undoubtedly contemplated an academic career on the model of some of his younger teachers and associates, such as Bruno Bauer (1809–82). However, by the time he submitted his doctoral dissertation "Difference Between the Democritean and Epicurean Philosophy of Nature"[8] by post to the University of Jena, he can have had few hopes of obtaining a university position at all. His topic was far from purely academic, however, since he argued against philosophical determinisms that excluded change, and for philosophies where indeterminacy made change possible, thus using philosophy as a convenient metaphor for politics. Moreover his political liberalism – which in context was a subversive radicalism – had pointed him in the direction of the "social" questions of reform and economic transformation. Transformation of the social and political order, as had occurred to an unprecedented degree under the French revolutionary regimes, was of course out of the question, and obviously punishable as sedition.

Unsurprisingly, Marx's alternative career move was into liberal journalism in 1842–43, during a brief window of supervised toleration allowed by the Prussian monarchy. Following the politically motivated closure of his Rhineland newspaper, Marx moved rapidly into expatriate politics, starting in Paris in 1844 and transferring to Brussels the following year. The young radical was by then a self-declared socialist and communist, deriving his views primarily from French utopian works of the 1830s, updated in the early 1840s to include the hardships of the emerging class of industrial workers.[9] He was also an activist for constitutions based on popular sovereignty, representative and responsible government, and elements of male suffrage within the political system. He thus worked in alliance with middle-class liberal groups, advocating representative and responsible government and socioeconomic policies to benefit poor workers. While his communism looked forward to a classless, cooperative society – ideas having their origins in Plato's works and Thomas More's *Utopia* (1516) – his political project was essentially one of pushing liberals leftward, toward a transformative engagement with the economic structures that produce modern class inequalities. He participated as a radical journalist in the vicissitudes of the '48 revolutions in central Europe, and after the swift collapse of the liberal republican regimes, he emigrated to England in 1849, one of many central European '48-ers in exile. He remained there as a German-speaking émigré for the rest of his life, making only brief trips to the continent, and working as a journalist and publicist for working-class political struggles worldwide. Only later on in the 1870s

---

8. In Karl Marx and Frederick Engels, *Collected Works*, 50 vols (London: Lawrence & Wishart, 1975–2004), vol. 1, 25–108. Hereafter cited as CW followed by volume and page numbers.
9. For a detailed account of the political context of this period, and of Marx's perspective within it, see David Leopold, *The Young Marx: German Philosophy, Modern Politics, and Human Flourishing* (Cambridge: Cambridge University Press, 2007).

did he acquire – from his writings alone – a public reputation as a revolutionary, although his activities as a journalist in 1848–49 had been a long way from even partisan activism, let alone violence and street-fighting.

III. AUTOBIOGRAPHY AND POLITICAL ENGAGEMENT

Written in 1859 when he was nearly forty-one, Marx's own account of his life and works up to that point is contained in the "Preface" to his preliminary study, *A Contribution to the Critique of Political Economy*. These few paragraphs pick out a somewhat different selection of texts to explain his career trajectory than are found in, say, the narrative accounts constructed by Engels in Marx's later lifetime, and then again by many others after his death. The list also differs from any standard or specifically philosophical account constructed today. This is precisely because so much more material has become available and current over the years, as opposed to the very limited number of published and accessible works to which Marx could refer his readers at the time, hardly any of whom would have heard of him. Most importantly, in this account Marx clearly presents himself as a social critic and political activist, rather than a philosopher in any sense. He puts little emphasis on the works through which he has been posthumously understood as a philosopher, making no mention of certain now-famous ones at all.

Marx begins, not with his academic dissertation in philosophy, but with an allusion to some of the very few articles[10] that he wrote and published in his time as a liberal journalist on, and then editor of, the *Rheinische Zeitung* (Rhenish Gazette), a legal and therefore moderate paper in Cologne. These were campaigning accounts informing readers about the hardships of workers in the peasant and wine-growing communities of the area, and also opinion pieces on free trade and protective tariffs, which were being discussed in the Rhine Province Assembly, a purely advisory and nonelected body. Alluding to his published criticism of other writers, who were guilty of "an echo of French socialism and communism, slightly tinged with philosophy" (CW 29: 262), Marx then recounts how he had to withdraw into his study following forcible closure of the paper. He then embarked on "a critical re-examination of the Hegelian philosophy of law," self-publishing an introduction in 1844: "Contribution to the Critique of Hegel's Philosophy of Law:[11] Introduction" (*ibid.*). His lengthy *Contribution to the*

---

10. For a detailed discussion of Marx's early journalism, see Heinz Lubasz, "Marx's Initial Problematic: The Problem of Poverty," *Political Studies* 24(1) (1976).
11. Hegel's *Philosophie des Rechts* (1821) has an alternative and more familiar English translation as *Philosophy of Right*.

Critique of Hegel's Philosophy of Law itself survived only in manuscript form and was left wholly unremarked and unpublished until the twentieth century.

This is the point in oft-repeated biographical narratives at which posthumous accounts that frame and justify Marx as in some sense a philosopher, or at least a major contributor to philosophy, generally take hold. It is also the point at which his engagement with Hegel is framed as a detailed critique of the latter's political philosophy as such, allied to a critique of his overall dialectic as a general method. Marx's method of critique is thus generally counterposed to Hegel's as a landmark in post-Hegelian continental thought.[12] And – given Hegel's overt idealism – some kind of Marxian materialism is consequently initiated as a necessary philosophical contrast. However, Marx's critical use of Hegel was no simple reversal or inversion, and certainly never a reversion to the ontological materialisms and epistemological empiricisms that Immanuel Kant (1724–1804) had so notably critiqued a generation or so earlier.

Marx's own view of this conjuncture in 1859 was rather different from the posthumous accounts that paint him as a philosopher engaged in revising Hegel's ideas at length. Marx himself tells his readers that his focus in 1843–46 was on "legal relations" and "political forms" (CW 29: 262), and that these – which were evidently the important *political* problems for him – could not be effectively comprehended as Hegel had attempted, that is, "on the basis of a so-called general development of the human mind" (*ibid.*). Rather, Marx explained that from Hegel he had appropriated the concept of "civil society" (*bürgerliche Gesellschaft*), itself taken from "English and French thinkers of the eighteenth century," and he had concluded that the "anatomy" of this "has to be sought in political economy" (*ibid.*). This was a science, or in Marx's terms *Wissenschaft* or rigorous study, of the production, exchange, distribution, and consumption of the goods and services of ordinary life on an individual, national, and international basis. It notably divided "civilized" society into classes by wealth and income, rather than by hierarchies based on rank or status.[13]

In his "Preface," Marx then historicizes these processes in a way that was more or less common both to some notable political economists, such as Adam Ferguson (1723–1816), and to Hegel himself. However, in opposition to conventional thinking, Marx emphasized that distributive differences in terms of wealth and income were derived from the sphere of production – its technological forces and property relations – and so were not simply reflections of different abilities

---

12. For an alternative framing that emphasizes Marx's intellectual debts to Aristotle, see Scott Meikle, *Essentialism in the Thought of Karl Marx* (London: Duckworth, 1983).
13. Political economy was the precursor to the economics of today, which is generally regarded as having its origin in the "marginalist" revolution in the 1870s. Economics established a clear, mathematical focus on prices, whereas the earlier study had centered on philosophical investigations into the nature of value, money, and profit.

to consume goods and services on the market. Thus his political perspective on change and reform was more radical and thoroughgoing than any adopted by the political economists, precisely because for him mere redistribution of goods and services would never suffice to resolve the social question of inequality. Instead a thoroughgoing transformation of the social relations of production would be required in order to derive the greatest benefits for all from the extraordinary productivity of modern industry, which he could clearly see on the horizon.[14] His perspective was decisively marked off from Hegel's by a practical concern with the nitty-gritty of "material interests" (CW 29: 262) as outlined in his journalism, rather than with any supposed philosophical reversion from idealism to an oppositional materialism. Indeed Marx's engagement with any philosophy as such was secondary to, or explicitly in aid of, his chosen political project, a politically motivated critique of political economy.

Amplifying this point, Marx goes on to mention published works that are specifically "material" in this way, and not generally rated by philosophers for philosophical content: a "brilliant essay on the critique of the economic categories"[15] (CW 29: 264), and a book, *The Condition of the Working-Class in England*[16] (1845), both by his friend Friedrich Engels. He pointedly noted that Engels had come to the same conclusion as himself, but "by another road," that is, *not* through any detailed engagement with Hegel's works on the "social" question, but rather through critical investigation and empirical research of his own (CW 29: 264). Marx next includes his polemical engagement with the then famous French socialist Pierre-Joseph Proudhon (1809–65),[17] *The Poverty of Philosophy* (1847),[18] published in French, and his own French-language "Speech on the Question of Free Trade" (1848).[19] This latter work is now little read, marking the fact that philosophical interest in Marx has generally won out over interest in his "economic" writings.

In equally brief fashion Marx also mentions the *Manifesto of the Communist Party* (1848), jointly written by Engels and himself, but in 1859 quite unavailable to his readers. Significantly in the context, the *Manifesto* was a work whose

---

14. The apparently bucolic and nonindustrial vision of communist society expressed in *The German Ideology* is more plausibly read as a "send-up" by Marx of Engels's lapse into a Fourierist fantasy; see my "Communism for Critical Critics? A New Look at *The German Ideology*," *History of Political Thought* 9(1) (1988).
15. Here Marx refers to Engels's "Outlines of a Critique of Political Economy," first published in 1844; in CW 3: 418–43.
16. Friedrich Engels, *The Condition of the Working-Class in England: From Personal Observation and Authentic Sources*, in CW 4: 295–596.
*17. For a discussion of Proudhon, see the essay by Diane Morgan in *The History of Continental Philosophy: Volume 1*.
18. In CW 6: 105–212.
19. In CW 6: 450–65.

political message would attract difficulties with censors and readers alike. For this reason the politically substantial portions of the 1859 "Preface" are effectively an extremely boiled-down and considerably restrained version of the ideas and arguments put forth ten years earlier in the anonymous pamphlet. In 1848 Marx had made explicit his communist commitments, echoing his short published work of 1844 "Contribution to the Critique of Hegel's Philosophy of Law: Introduction." Nineteenth-century socialism and communism were not then consistently distinguished from each other, and in any case these diverse movements comprised a wide variety of views on human nature, ideal societies, and political tactics. Communists, such as Marx, were generally more radical in focusing on working-class politics and calling for large-scale, revolutionary change, using violence if need be.

Marx's political program can be succinctly summarized as one based on the promotion of class struggle in modern industrial society, where bourgeoisie and proletariat represent opposing class structures at a particular moment in history. He contrasted this with a timeless opposition of wealth and poverty, or a supposedly justified inequality reflecting incentives and rewards, and sacrosanct rights to property. Influenced by Engels's early critical work on political economy, Marx took the view that modern mechanized industry was so productive that very soon human needs could be satisfied with little labor input. However, the current ownership of these enterprises by "private" persons was in radical contradiction with their "public" origin and potential as industrial resources. This contradiction was not merely conceptual, but real in the sense that the knowledge and systems giving rise to this productivity were not the creation of particular individuals who could own them in some sense that others must necessarily respect. Rather, those individuals were all themselves products of society in various ways, and so the products collectively produced by knowledge and systems developed in society should rightly belong to all. Moreover Marx conceived this as a dynamic scheme in which rising productivity would be built on greater use of machines in producing goods and services, and there would therefore be less employment available in the economy as a whole as economic development proceeded. The class structure would assuredly become simpler, as intermediate classes below the bourgeoisie would fall into the proletariat, and actual numbers within the bourgeoisie itself would decline to a small fraction of society as a whole. Social revolution made by the vast majority would necessarily democratize not just governmental structures, but economic ones at the workplace and at points of distribution for goods and services.

Summarizing Marx's own summary of the guiding principle for this analysis, as he put it in the 1859 "Preface," is rather more difficult. On the one hand, he generalizes that humans in society enter into relationships – property and work relations, for instance – that are independent of their individual wills, yet are human constructions, of course, subject to change in history, sometimes profoundly and dramatically so. On the other hand, he argues that in the modern world he can foresee that humans could take charge of these changes in a different and highly self-conscious way, managing a society where abundance can be produced and distributed to the benefit of producers, rather than for the benefit of leisured classes who own or otherwise control productive resources. Overall he links economic and political structures in varying modes to the kinds of technologies and practices through which production occurs in the first place, referring to this as a real foundation. From this real basis there arises a legal and political superstructure, to which there are in correspondence definite modes of social consciousness, that is, political views and commonplaces, broadly understood as ideological, in Marx's sense of the term (CW 29: 262–3).

Ideology in Marx's view referred to ideas and doctrines that in practice help one class to oppress and exploit another. They appear – often in the work of philosophers and other prominent writers and essayists – as generalizations supposedly applicable to all mankind, or at least to all individuals that make up a given society. These "truths" were typically specious claims that ruling or dominant classes were necessary for there to be society at all, or that some classes or ruling orders had necessarily to care for others and to make decisions on their behalf. Ideological generalizations of this kind are – from Marx's perspective – misleading, rather than false, selectively tendentious rather than thoughtfully political, mystifying rather than enlightening. Marx thus did not have an ideology himself, but rather – in his own terms – an outlook or conception that made ideology visible. Perhaps the single phrase that best sums up Marx's outlook on history, society, and politics is the one where he asserts that "the mode of production of material life conditions the general process of social, political and intellectual life" (CW 29: 263).

This synchronic schema then gives way to a diachronic one, in which Marx suggests that there have been four epochs in history that exemplify this: ancient, Asiatic, feudal, and modern bourgeois society. Changes from one social formation to another (and not necessarily inevitably or in this particular order) have arisen from conflicts between productive forces and productive relations. This happens particularly when the property system restricts technological and other workplace developments that enhance productivity and innovation. This was already in evidence as patchwork and antimarket feudal property relations in Marx's own time were already being abolished in favor of "private" ownership of productive resources, in particular land, water, and mineral rights of unrestricted use. Bourgeois society, Marx says, will be under pressure from similar contradictions as increasing productivity reduces employment and therefore consumption, and the dysfunctionality of a market system based on "private" ownership will become evident. This will be the last form of society in which such class antagonism will be a necessary feature, and its successor social formation will provide for collective control of production and distribution for the benefit of all, rather than for the benefit of the propertied few. In this text, subject to censorship at the time, proletarian revolution could not be mentioned, but the implication is clear (*ibid.*).

The manuscript works of 1845–46 that Marx also mentions in his 1859 "Preface," but skips over – tantalizingly – as "self-clarification" (CW 29: 264), are the ones that have excited the attentions of philosophers to an increasing and now dominant degree. These were first published in part in the 1920s and subsequently transmitted in variously edited book-length versions, beginning in a German-language edition of 1932. The materials were posthumously – and now controversially[20] – entitled *The German Ideology*. Marx describes them as a "critique of post-Hegelian philosophy" (*ibid.*), but seems little engaged with either the details or with explaining exactly why and how he had engaged in such a critique. The 1859 "Preface" does not actually mention dialectic or even method at all, and indeed Marx's other comments on these matters are very few and far between. When Engels was writing his own philosophical work on Feuerbach and latter-day Feuerbachians many years later in the 1880s, he dismissed the old manuscripts of 1845–46 as "useless,"[21] save for a very short one, which he published, in edited form, as "Theses on Feuerbach" (1886).[22] The *Economic and Philosophic Manuscripts of 1844*, standardly recommended since the 1960s in order to understand Marx as a philosopher, are not mentioned at all.

---

20. Karl Marx, Friedrich Engels, and Joseph Weydemeyer, *Die Deutsche Ideologie: Artikel, Druckvorlagen, Entwürfe, Reinschriftenfragmente und Notizen zu I. Feuerbach und II. Sankt Bruno*, 2 vols, *Marx-Engels-Jahrbuch 2003* (issued by the Internationale Marx-Engels-Stiftung, Amsterdam), Inge Taubert and Hans Pelger (eds) (Berlin: Akademie, 2004), 5*–28*. The scholarship cited and summarized in this edition reveals – notwithstanding the efforts of the editors – that the so-called *German Ideology* manuscripts do not represent the copy-text of a book-length work by Marx and Engels alone, but rather the remains of various uncompleted publishing projects involving other people, nor was a book with that title ever planned by them; see my "*The German Ideology* Never Took Place," *History of Political Thought* 31(1) (2010).
21. Friedrich Engels, *Ludwig Feuerbach and the End of Classical German Philosophy*, in CW 26: 353–98; "Preface," in CW 26: 519–20.
22. CW 5: 6–8; for Marx's original version, see CW 5: 3–5.

IV. MARX AS PHILOSOPHER, AND MARXISM AS PHILOSOPHY

Engels was Marx's publicist, and he worked hard to make Marx visible. One way of doing this, and – so it seems – gaining political capital of a certain kind, was to make Marx a philosopher. Marx was decisively linked with Hegel, and therefore in a positive sense with philosophy and with philosophers, when Engels wrote his own biographical notes on Marx's career and ideas. This was also in 1859, as both were then engaged in introducing Marx's first substantial published work in his projected multivolume critique of political economy, *A Contribution to the Critique of Political Economy*. Engels's project in his 1859 review[23] of Marx's slim volume was to publicize the expertise of the then unknown author, and to précis his ideas in order to excite a readership. Rather understandably, Engels very prominently attached Marx's name to Hegel's, since the latter was obviously the greatest philosopher – and *German* philosopher – of recent times.

Engels explained how Marx had rectified Hegel's political shortcomings by radicalizing his thought, and how he had built on the notable achievements of his system. In Engels's account, Marx was thus similar to Hegel as a systematizer of all knowledge by means of a universal method. However, Marx was said to have inverted the master's distinctive and reputedly powerful dialectic. In particular, Marx could account for the historical development of human society through a linked scheme of economic and political stages, but root this argument in a material world of human productive activity – as opposed to a "spirit" world of mere philosophical speculation. For Marx, class politics thus replaces the apparently autonomous development of "spirit" (CW 16: 472–5).

Engels also distinguished a logical from a historical method in Marx, while declaring them ultimately compatible and of unquestionable validity (CW 16: 475–6). While Engels could précis Marx's distinctive outlook on historical and political development, introducing the phrase "*materialist conception of history*" (CW 16: 469), his three-part review was never completed. The promised section on the critique of economic theory, commercial practice, and political support structure – which was the point of Marx's new book – was never produced. Engels thus initiated a commonplace disjuncture between what is of philosophical interest, and what is rather separably "economic." This review was the point from which Marxist philosophy was secured, with Marx in pride of place as Hegel's successor intellect. The whole idea that Marx was a philosopher, and that his work makes sense when reconstructed as a philosophy, dates from this period, rather than from Marx's driving political intentions and the politicized context of philosophy itself under the illiberal regimes of the 1830s and 1840s.

---

23. Engels, "Karl Marx, A Contribution to the Critique of Political Economy," in CW 16: 465–77.

Engels was thus effectively the founder of Marxism as a comprehensive system derived from a universal method. He developed this outlook, particularly in influential works of the late 1870s and early 1880s, and then definitively during the twelve years in which he outlived Marx. The most important of these was *Anti-Dühring: Herr Eugen Dühring's Revolution in Science* (1878),[24] and its reprise in the editorially constructed *Dialectics of Nature* (1925).[25] This latter was derived from unpublished notebooks and manuscripts, and was produced with suitable flourishes by a Russo-German team of Marxist scholars anxious to link Marxism with scientific certainty. Engels was thus made central to Marxist philosophy – in his own lifetime and then posthumously – through his reading, presumed authoritative, of Marx as a matter-in-motion materialist from whom only a correspondence theory of truth could proceed. This philosophy was thus widely publicized as Marx's materialist inversion of Hegel's idealism, and the basis of the so-called materialist dialectic. This latter was resolved into three universal laws applicable to nature, history, and "thought" or logic. These three laws of "dialectics" were: law of unity and struggle of opposites – a foundational assumption that all entities and processes contain within themselves opposite properties or terms; law of transformation of quantity into quality – purportedly explaining how purely quantitative and continuous changes to an entity or process can cause discontinuous changes that we understand as qualitative transformations in substance; law of negation of the negation – purportedly explaining how change and development proceed by successive negations, each one taking the resulting positive to a higher level.[26]

From the beginning, Marxist philosophy was marginalized by professional philosophers and regarded with suspicion. This was precisely because of the way it purported to embody and validate a political commitment to a revolutionary transformation of society. The extent to which class struggle and transformative politics required this particular philosophy, or indeed any philosophy at all, was rejected even as a question by academic philosophers. This was because they claimed objectivity and universality, rather than political partiality and practical action, which were suspect orientations on the face of it. In that way the philosophical classics of Marxism are not themselves usually seen as classics of philosophy in academic circles. These Marxist classics included G. V. Plekhanov's (1856–1918) *Fundamental Problems of Marxism* (1908), V. I. Lenin's (1870–1924) *Materialism and Empirio-Criticism: Critical Comments on a Reactionary Philosophy* (1909), J. V. Stalin's (1878–1953) *Dialectical and Historical Materialism* (1938), and Mao Zedong's (1893–1976) *On Contradiction*

---

24. In CW 25: 5–309.
25. In CW 25: 313–588.
26. CW 25: 11, 110–32.

(1937). The last was a major revision emphasizing the fluidity of contradictions over the other organizing concepts of what came to be known by the 1920s as "dialectical materialism," or "diamat." Those philosophers outside the schools of Marxism who did not immediately dismiss Marxist philosophy on grounds that it was political typically dismissed the systematizing generalities of dialectical materialism and its variants as vacuous redescriptions of any entity or process in crypto-Hegelian jargon.

V. CHALLENGES TO MARXIST ORTHODOXIES

It is also the case that, from the beginning, Engels's dialectics was challenged from within the Marxist camp by revisionist writers such as Eduard Bernstein (1850–1932) in his *Evolutionary Socialism* (1899), and Hegelianizers such as Antonio Labriola (1843–1904) in his *Essays on the Materialistic Conception of History* (1896) and *Socialism and Philosophy* (1897), Ernst Bloch (1885–1977) in his *Principle of Hope* (1918) and György Lukács (1885–1971)[27] in his *History and Class Consciousness* (1923). These challenges were on grounds that the scientific determinism promoted by Engelsian orthodoxies was depoliticizing, and, moreover, either false to the fluidities and contingencies of reality, or at least to those of social – as opposed to material – phenomena.

The Institute for Social Research, known as the Frankfurt School,[28] was a notable and systematic attempt to replace Engels's outdated materialism with newer forms of science and philosophy, eclectically conceived. The school dates from the 1930s when its constituents made very early use of Marx's newly published *Economic and Philosophic Manuscripts of 1844* and *The German Ideology*, neither of which had been incorporated by Engels into his Marxist dialectics and materialism, nor used by Hegelianizers of the previous generation. This is particularly reflected in Herbert Marcuse's (1898–1979) *Reason and Revolution* (1941), which re-analyzes the relation of Marx to Hegel, and in other antifascist projects that were critical of capitalist society. Working in the post-Kantian tradition of aesthetic and cultural criticism, Max Horkheimer (1895–1973) and Theodor W. Adorno (1903–69) generalized from Marx's critique of capitalist society to a critique of Western civilization and rationalism in their *Dialectic of Enlightenment* (1947), and again in Adorno's *Negative Dialectics* (1966). Incorporating aspects of psychoanalysis into a Marxian perspective

---

*27. For a discussion of Lukács, see the essay by Chris Thornhill in *The History of Continental Philosophy: Volume 5*.

*28. Essays on the Frankfurt School, with special attention to Adorno, Horkheimer, and Marcuse, can be found in *The History of Continental Philosophy: Volume 5*.

on capitalist society, Marcuse produced the hugely influential works *Eros and Civilization* (1955) and *One Dimensional Man* (1964).

Working in similar ways, and with numerous interconnections, Marxist philosophers writing in French appropriated Marx in a selective and critical fashion, very closely allied with their political adherence to the Communist Party in France and their suspicions of the Marxist orthodoxies propounded by the Communist Party of the Soviet Union. They followed the early Hegelianizers in reading Marx in ways that undermined the materialism and determinism fostered by the later Engels. The Russian Marxist philosopher Alexandre Kojève[29] lectured in Paris on Hegel's *Phenomenology of Spirit* (1807) during the 1930s and conjoined his focus on the so-called "master–slave" dialectic[30] with allusions to Marx's *Economic and Philosophic Manuscripts of 1844*, only recently published. These lectures and the general outlook on Marxism were hugely influential in French philosophy, in particular with relation to a further critique, that of German phenomenology, where ideas from Marx – rather than from deterministic Marxism – were used to amend its "existential" focus on consciousness and individual experience. Interpretations of Marx's views on laboring activities in social settings, and on the constraints imposed by class structures in capitalist societies, featured in philosophical works such as Jean-Paul Sartre's (1905–80) *Critique of Dialectical Reason* (1960),[31] drawing on the earlier essay "Search for a Method" (1957), and in the writings of other philosophers, such as Maurice Merleau-Ponty (1908–61),[32] and sociologists such as Henri Lefebvre (1901–91). The common thread was the application of Marxian notions of social production, class structure, and ideological critique to cultural criticism, social science, and historical research. As a result these areas of intellectual endeavor were substantially revised and redefined.

However, the most important thinker and activist succeeding to these unorthodox efforts was Antonio Gramsci (1891–1937),[33] a Communist Party worker in Italy during his short lifetime. His lengthy *Prison Notebooks* were circulated in parts after the Second World War and published in a collected edition in 1975. Rejecting Hegelian teleologies, but retaining a historicization of knowledge,

---

*29. For a discussion of Kojève, see the essay by John Russon in *The History of Continental Philosophy: Volume 4*.

30. Numerous attributions notwithstanding, Marx did not make use of these passages from Hegel at all.

*31. For a discussion of Sartre's Marxism, see the essay by William L. McBride in *The History of Continental Philosophy: Volume 5*.

*32. Merleau-Ponty is discussed in the essay by Mauro Carbone in *The History of Continental Philosophy: Volume 4*.

*33. Gramsci is also discussed in Thornhill's essay in *The History of Continental Philosophy: Volume 5*.

Gramsci argued against a materialism of matter-in-motion, or analogies thereto. Marxism should not claim access to an ideal realm reflected in philosophy as a matter of objective truth, but should opt instead for a "praxis" account, where the intersubjective categories of practical life and cultural understanding themselves constitute the human realm where political judgments must take place.

Gramsci's critique was therefore essentially one of Engels's reading of Marx both as a philosopher and as a materialist, but was necessarily and interestingly constructed from much the same textual materials as Engels had used, rather than from hitherto uncirculated manuscripts. Moreover, like Marx's work, Gramsci's was written to resolve the political issues of the time, specifically the difficulties of negotiating a communist consciousness within the worker and peasant classes in a newly industrializing country. This was of course the same problem that Marx had set for himself. As a philosophy, rather than as the meditations of a political activist, Gramsci's thought is a postwar reconstruction. But it is one that set the terms, ironically, not so much for a reading of Marx's well-known works largely independent of Engels, as Gramsci himself had done, but rather for a philosophical "new Marx," who was derived from manuscript materials that were widely circulated in translation in the postwar period.

VI. THE "HUMANIST" MARX

The postwar international political and economic settlements set the stage for the practice and promotion of philosophy that was profoundly different from prewar circumstances. The intense politicization and polarization of class politics was subsiding, and the professional tendency to dismiss politicized philosophies out of hand, or to dismiss philosophies that concerned themselves with political, historical, and economic issues, gradually waned. The political commitment characteristic of Marxist philosophers, and their use of Marx's texts and interest in what came to be known as his "theory of history," became respectable, if not necessarily universally accepted. The Lysenko affair, wherein Stalinist dialectics came to direct science in the USSR with disastrous results, together with a declining faith in the Soviet system among "progressive" intellectuals, marked the end of even hostile concern in Western philosophical circles with "diamat." The continental tradition in philosophy, itself largely a postwar construction, admitted Marx and his historicizing and Hegelianizing successors, but not the dialectics and materialism promoted by Engels in his most deterministic and positivistic writings and correspondence.

Isaiah Berlin's prewar book *Karl Marx: His Life and Environment* (1939) prefigured these developments in a remarkable way. While acknowledging the "diamat" of the time, Berlin (1909–97) simply sidelined it and read the available texts of Marx within the historical context of liberalizing revolutionary movements fighting for social and economic transformation in mid-nineteenth-century Europe. Eventually Berlin's work, and his contextualizing successors, made Marx, and a philosophical interest in Marx, increasingly visible in philosophical circles and, in principle, separable from Marxist doctrines derived from Engels. Given Berlin's own visibility in academic circles at the highest level (All Souls College, Oxford) and his gifts in writing and broadcasting for an educated and middle-class audience, it is unsurprising that the politics in portrayals of Marx in this tradition was safely in the past. It was also, with suitable caveats, well insulated from Cold War "red scares" and other contemporary issues.

In the postwar period, Marx was also re-read independently of Engels's systematizing materialism and determinism, but in a much more Hegelian manner than in Berlin's rendition of his thought. Bertell Ollman's (1936–) and Norman Levine's (1931–) studies elaborated the way that Marx, self-consciously or otherwise, drew on Hegel's understanding of language as composed of interrelational rather than precisely demarcated terms. The philosophical point is both anti-empiricist and sociologically holistic, arguing that Marx's views on language and society match, because language and society match. The Hegelian heritage can thus be stripped of the very mystifications about which Marx had complained, namely the apparently suprahuman or quasireligious source of movement and change implied by Hegel's entity – or metaphor – of *Geist*.[34]

Concurrently with these developments in reading Marx came new texts to read, in particular the *Economic and Philosophic Manuscripts of 1844* and *The German Ideology* manuscripts of 1845–46. Both were suited to the construction of Marx's work as a philosophy. This was because the discourse of the manuscripts themselves appeared philosophical in comparison with the detailed historical works, polemics, and economic critiques that – according to standard typologies – had succeeded this "early" phase. Marxology then took up questions of continuity, development, and innovation within this burgeoning field that was preoccupied with making sense of Marx rather than Marxism.

Philosophers, whether identified with Marxism in any sense or not, were generally content to receive these works as of obvious philosophical interest, and to leave contextualizing questions to the side, including the ones surrounding the production of these rather disparate manuscripts themselves as edited and readable entities. However, it is also true that contextualizers produced accounts of these works as philosophy, but equally as a stage on a journey to more empirical concerns that left philosophy behind. Both ways of receiving these texts failed to

---

34. Norman Levine, *Dialogue within the Dialectic* (London: George Allen & Unwin, 1984); Bertell Ollman, *Dialectical Investigations* (London: Routledge, 1993); *Dance of the Dialectic: Steps in Marx's Method* (Urbana, IL: University of Illinois Press, 2003).

set out clearly the context of the 1840s in which philosophy itself was a contentious practice, and to grasp clearly Marx's radical ambitions for transforming what would count in liberal and radical circles as practical and progressive views and tactics concerning the social question. The philosophical "new Marx" was thus somewhat depoliticized. Philosophers were excited in the postwar period by the young Marx's terminology of alienation, estrangement, species-being, and other so-called humanist ways of setting out his concerns.

These elements of the "humanist" Marx were largely expounded, rather than rigorously debated, in works that constructed the "new Marx" philosophically. These included numerous studies of alienation as a critical category figuring importantly in the *Economic and Philosophic Manuscripts of 1844*.[35] The common threads in the "theory of alienation" that was constructed for Marx from these early manuscript materials is that the modern industrial worker is alienated or separated from the product of labor, productive activity itself, fellow workers, and "species-being." Alienation as a concept derives from an array of preexisting German philosophical terms describing an essential fissure with "oneness," which is regrettable and requires resolution or transcendence through transformation. Marx's apparent contrast is with craftwork, where a worker knows his work in the object, understands and controls the productive process, has cooperative relationships with fellow producers and known consumers, and is at one with the universal human experience of producing goods and services. This is not to say that Marx in any way endorsed craftwork as a solution to any social questions whatsoever in the world of modernizing industrial production and consumption, but rather that this kind of (largely unpublished) philosophical analysis could help him to understand the socialist and communist critique through which *political* issues of proletarian poverty were then being addressed.

However, there were dissenting voices. In *Marx and Human Nature: Refutation of a Legend* (1986), Norman Geras (1943–) offered a more critical perspective on this way of philosophizing the "early Marx," arguing that it was a mistake to attribute a philosophy of human nature to him at all. Leszek Kołakowski's (1927–2009) three-volume study, *Main Currents of Marxism: Its Rise, Growth and Dissolution* (1978), argued from a wholly contrary perspective that there was no "humanist" Marx. Kołakowski's view was that Marx's thought was in essence seamless not only with Engels's and with Soviet "diamat" but also with

---

35. See, among others, C. J. Arthur (1940–), *Dialectics of Labour: Marx and his Relation to Hegel* (Oxford and New York: Blackwell, 1986); David McLellan (1940–), *Marx Before Marxism* (London: Macmillan, 1970); István Mészáros (1930–), *Marx's Theory of Alienation* (London: Merlin, 1970; 4th ed. 1975); Bertell Ollman, *Alienation: Marx's Conception of Man* (Cambridge: Cambridge University Press, 1971; 2nd ed. 1976); and John Plamenatz (1912–75), *Man and Society: A Critical Examination of Some Important Social and Political Theories from Machiavelli to Marx*, 2 vols (Oxford: Oxford University Press, 1963).

the policies and practices of authoritarian and oppressive self-styled Marxist parties and regimes.

VII. "OTHER" MARXES

There are, of course, further ways of engaging philosophically with Marx, and therefore with Marx as a supposed philosopher. In *For Marx* (1965), Louis Althusser (1918–90) published a notable critique of both the orthodox Engelsian "diamat" reading of Marx, and the new "humanist" one.[36] He sought instead to find the philosophical and chronological point at which Marx "broke" with a philosophy centered on the human subject and then launched into a science that could be specified in philosophical terms. In Althusser's view this was a science of structures, explaining how human subjects are hailed or "interpellated" into existence, one way or another, and also an explanation of how such structures occur in historical succession. While ultimately unsuccessful in finding such a point where this self-styled anti-Hegelian science succeeded philosophy in Marx's work, or specifying its existence philosophically in a way that was independent of Marx's supposed attempts to realize this achievement, Althusser's assimilation of Marx into the French structuralist tradition was formidably influential. Structures, of course, could be identified as continental in some sense derived from Kantian critiques of British empiricisms. These were rooted by contrast in accounts of perception taking individuals to have essential and defining presocial capacities in their essence or nature. For a time in the 1970s, Althusserianism was said by many radical philosophers to be a more productive way of examining social life than either liberal individualisms emphasizing choice, or Engelsian teleologies of historical and ontological certainty.

The analytical or rational-choice school of Marxist thought, inaugurated in the mid-1970s by G. A. Cohen (1941–2009), Jon Elster (1940–), John Roemer (1945–), Robert Brenner (1943–), Erik Olin Wright (1947–) and others, took a quite different approach. While internally various, the common thread was a rejection of what its adherents termed Hegelianism, and thus of the continental tradition as such, on grounds that it was methodologically unrigorous, as indeed was French structuralism, in their view. By contrast, rigor was identified with a variety of presuppositions and methodologies, among them an individualism of a rational and economic character (rather than any kind of humanism), a method of propositional hypothesis and evidential testing (derived from the logical positivism and philosophy of science of the Vienna Circle of the 1930s),

---

*36. For a detailed discussion of Althusser, see the essay by Warren Montag in *The History of Continental Philosophy: Volume 6*.

and a claim to clarity and precision in language (derived from the "linguistic turn" in Oxford philosophy of the later 1950s). Marx's role from this perspective was to have contributed two notable puzzles to be resolved in a decidedly noncontinental way.

One puzzle was the validity (or not) of his "guiding principle" as articulated in the 1859 "Preface" (CW 29: 262). These few paragraphs famously but ambiguously derive epochal change in human society from linked transformations in the forces and relations of production, contradictions that are in turn reflected in political struggles for class dominance. H. B. Acton (1908–74) had produced an influential critique in *The Illusion of the Epoch: Marxism-Leninism as a Philosophical Creed* (1955), arguing that Marx was logically muddled and empirically incorrect. Analytical Marxists essentially elaborated and reworked this. The other puzzle was the validity (or not) of Marx's theory of exploitation, rooted in the value-theory of commodity production and exchange as outlined in the opening sections of his late work, *Capital: A Critique of Political Economy, Volume 1, Book 1: The Process of Production of Capital*. Mainstream economics had no truck with this, but then analytical Marxists wagered that perhaps Marx could be shown to be right after all.

The first puzzle was addressed by Cohen in a major work where a "rigorous" version of Marx's prose was produced and defended. But Cohen's later verdict was that Marx's theory, stated that way, was ultimately false.[37] The second puzzle was addressed in a "rigorous" way by Roemer and others, adopting strict assumptions from economic modeling and game theory. This produced exploitation as a logical result, but the initial assumptions were precisely the ones that Marx himself had always argued were constitutive of capitalist exploitation in the first place, so in the absence of alternative ones, there was thus no critical purchase.[38]

One notable debate in which academic philosophers engaged with Marx's texts and with Marxist philosophers – albeit those imbued with the "new Marx" of the postwar period – was the "Marx and justice" controversy of the later 1970s and early 1980s. This was the first time that Marx's texts were selectively deployed and then debated in a nonsectarian, although not completely depoliticized, way. Justice and morality are of course topics in philosophy with an ancient tradition of debate, through which any number of ontological, epistemological, and ultimately political positions have been articulated. Marx's texts, selectively quoted, were said to pose a puzzle within this tradition in two ways.

---

37. G. A. Cohen, *Karl Marx's Theory of History: A Defence* (Oxford: Clarendon Press, 1978); *Self-Ownership, Freedom and Equality* (Cambridge: Cambridge University Press, 1996).
38. John E. Roemer, *A General Theory of Exploitation and Class* (Cambridge, MA: Harvard University Press, 1982).

One puzzle was the apparent contradiction in his views. On the one hand, he had apparently argued that morality was epiphenomenal to the material processes through which human society constructs itself, and he had certainly dismissed contemporary philosophizing about politics as mere moralizing that could never be effectual. This seemed to follow from the dismissive (unpublished) comments that Marx had made in *The German Ideology* that all morality was ideological, because it was mere moralizing that covertly served the interests of the possessing classes. But on the other hand, he clearly had a political project to assist with the destruction of capitalism, on grounds that the exploitation inherent in it was to be condemned, and a successor communistic system to be instituted – violently, if necessary – for the benefit of all. How could such a political, and indeed personal, program not be rooted in a theory of morality, and an ethical vision? This seemed to follow because of Marx's overt espousal of the proletarian cause, precisely as an effect of class interest, albeit the one that he had announced to be a human universal, and indeed species-defining characteristic.

The other puzzle was that Marx had apparently dismissed justice as an effect of the capitalist system, precisely because its rules of equal treatment were applied through supposedly consensual contracts between laborers and capitalists, exchanging a day's work for a day's pay. But his commitment to communism evidently entailed a commitment to a distributive scheme. In the *Manifesto of the Communist Party* he had said, "we shall have an association, in which the free development of each is the condition for the free development of all" (CW 6: 506), and in the "Critique of the Gotha Programme," he offered a maxim: "From each according to his abilities, to each according to his needs!" (CW 24: 87). How could this not entail a theory of justice? Or was Marx merely inconsistent, by accident or design?

The debate drew on a wide variety of Marx's texts, reflecting the increased availability and respectability of standard and collected texts of Marx and Engels, particularly in English translation, that occurred from the 1960s onwards. In general, contributors were aligned with Marx, not as Marxists or as anti-Marxists, but as scholars respecting his gestating status as a major philosopher who could be examined in a reasonably neutral way, unaccompanied by political dogmatizing. The resolution of the "Marx and justice" debate was not a clear or consensus position, but rather a typology of defensible answers linked to the different kinds of theories that would count, on the one hand, as morality or justice, and on the other hand, the different kinds of philosophical positions that could plausibly support them.[39] Notably in the debate Marx had re-arrived on the philosophical scene in textual readings construed independently of previous

---

39. Philip J. Kain, *Marx and Ethics* (Oxford: Clarendon Press, 1988). R. G. Peffer, *Marxism, Morality and Social Justice* (Princeton, NJ: Princeton University Press, 1990).

Marxisms. But it is also the case that this mainstream anglophone position was constructed in a way that did little to link him directly to any post-Kantian position in the continental tradition.

However, philosophers who took a broader view in contextualizing the "new" Marx as a philosopher drew on the full range of texts available from the 1960s. They produced a series of notable studies, all of which took the Hegel–Marx relationship as central, and therefore they necessarily engaged continental philosophy.[40] Reading Marx as primarily interesting as a critic of Hegel, commentators have extracted a substantive account and critique along the following lines. On the plus side, in his works Marx praised Hegel for presenting basic human social institutions – ethical relationships, family structures, economic organizations, and governmental forms – as historically varied, malleable, and developmental. But on the minus side, Marx took Hegel to task for a teleology of progress that was merely asserted and couched in rather mystical terms, and for his evident view that human life and change was all ultimately a matter of ideas. These were presented as a movement of abstractions, rather than in an empirically plausible historical account of socioeconomic and political practices, particularly those through which most people have actually lived their lives. At the time, right-wing Hegelians asserted the truth of the master's philosophical presumptions and conservative politics, whereas left-wing "Young Hegelians" adopted the vision of historical change and progressive development through conceptual negation. Unlike both, Marx's new political philosophy historicizes human development in specifically economic and everyday practical terms rather than in merely ideational terms such as morality, ethics, religion, philosophies, and the like, and it puts itself into overt engagement with processes of social change through struggle, specifically class struggle. Class struggle takes place, overtly or covertly, between different classes within a structure, where class itself is rooted by definition in intergenerational patterns of wealth and poverty. These structures were often defended at the time as natural and necessary, or conversely as open enough for exceptional individuals to rise up from poor circumstances. Marx's thinking was that both these claims are implausible. In line with socialist and communist social criticism of the time, Marx finds that Hegel's work apologizes for middle-class wealth and power, and constructs a state that secures this

---

40. See, in particular, Alex Callinicos (1950–), *Marxism and Philosophy* (Oxford: Oxford University Press, 1983); William L. McBride (1938–), *The Philosophy of Marx* (London: Hutchinson, 1977); Richard W. Miller (1945–), *Analyzing Marx: Morality, Power and History* (Princeton, NJ: Princeton University Press, 1987); David-Hillel Ruben, *Marxism and Materialism: A Study in the Marxist Theory of Knowledge* (Hassocks: Harvester/Atlantic Highlands, NJ: Humanities Press, 1977); and Allen W. Wood, *Karl Marx* (London and Boston, MA: Routledge & Kegan Paul, 1981; 2nd ed. New York: Routledge, 2004).

privilege over "the people" whom Marx construes as workers, not as the unruly rabble that Hegel obviously feared.

While Marx rejected right-wing Hegelian views as merely reactionary, he ruthlessly criticized left-wing Hegelians in print for failing to get beyond a movement of concepts to a history and politics of genuine revolutionary confrontation. Both Hegelian schools were dismissed by Marx as "German ideologists," thinkers who unwittingly promoted a class perspective – that of the bourgeoisie or property-owning class – while apparently philosophizing in universal, abstract terms about humanity. The universal human subject, Marx countered, was the proletarian or *homo faber*, "man the worker." The proletariat collectively would produce the most decisive change in human history, through which human productive instruments and processes would be put to the service of all on the basis of need, rather than serving the interests of property owners and their heirs alone.

For contextualizing commentators the methodological puzzle that arises, then, is how exactly Marx had appropriated Hegel's dialectic, and, given his decisively different political and orientation, why exactly he wanted to. Hegel's dialectic is difficult to summarize, and the commonplace triad thesis–antithesis–synthesis is a particularly bad attempt. Rather, dialectic for Hegel indicates that conceptual relations are fluid and – somehow – in motion, and the overall effect is to produce a philosophy that emphasizes change. Hegel's philosophy addresses itself systematically to the constitutive ideas through which social life is lived in different ways at different times. Marx objected to what he termed a mystification in Hegel's discourse, namely that ideas somehow "move" and that human lives are some kind of consequence or effect of this motion-through-contraries. Hegel's reconciliation of all negation as ultimately progressive struck Marx as quasi-religious, and politically smug. Nonetheless as a mode of critical thinking founded on assumptions of change and development, rather than timeless truths or descriptive certainties, Marx found Hegel's dialectic very stimulating and highly useful.

In this way, then, the twentieth-century reception of Marx as a philosopher follows the general outlines set by Engels in 1859: Marx is said to be a world-class philosopher, worthy critic of the great Hegel, and very much Feuerbach's superior in that regard. The crucial terms for articulating this view set out by Engels in 1859 also remain much the same by name at least, if not necessarily by content: materialism, idealism, and dialectic. They go along with a supposedly helpful set of metaphors through which Marx is said to invert Hegel and in that way to have extracted a rational kernel from a mystical shell. However, the selection of texts, philosophical issues, and political projects are necessarily very different from Engels's, and differ somewhat among the academic commentators themselves, as one would expect.

VIII. POSTMODERN "TURNS"

As a modernist thinker Marx has largely been rejected by self-styled postmodernists within the continental tradition of philosophizing. This philosophical "turn" is centered on historicizing the categories of consciousness through which the phenomena of human experience are intersubjectively constructed, and on producing language-centered accounts of meaning and communication. These emphasize the discourses through which certainties are claimed and enforced out of what is necessarily contingent and indeterminate. If taken in an Engelsian sense, Marx's work is clearly a modernist discourse of power/knowledge through which an authoritarian politics has unsurprisingly been practiced, in fact promoting the interests of communist elites in Marxist countries rather than those of the supposedly favored working class. If taken in an alternative humanist sense, Marx's work is clearly rooted in prelinguistic universalizing presumptions about human life and consciousness that reproduce Eurocentric modernist structures of capitalist dominance, political claims to liberation notwithstanding.

The classic critique of both positions is that of Ernesto Laclau (1935–) and Chantal Mouffe (1943–),[41] which counterposes Gramsci's flexible and contingent constructions of cultural power to alternative readings of Marx, including Gramsci's own.[42] What is new in their work is the assimilation of Gramsci's view that political consciousness is a cultural project, not an inevitable economic result, to the view that the discourses through which consciousness is articulated and changed are themselves the media of persuasion and power, rather than propositions to be tested for truth and thus (supposedly) efficacy. This of course is an application of a wider redefinition within the continental tradition as to what philosophy is, what its proper concerns are, what is mainstream, and what is "dangerous," an attribute generally attached to alleged relativisms that postmodernists incur yet celebrate.

If Marx were to be re-read as himself a postmodern thinker, however, this would itself be an exercise that many would dismiss out of hand as an anachronism or, if not, certainly at odds with the certainties that, so it is presumed, his texts expound, and through which his political project proceeded (even if he himself were never an authoritative political actor). Marx would have to be re-understood as a thinker allowing contingency and indeterminacy in human

---

*41. Laclau and Mouffe's work is discussed in detail in the essay by Lasse Thomassen in *The History of Continental Philosophy: Volume 7*, and in the essay by Emily Zakin in *The History of Continental Philosophy: Volume 8*.

42. Ernesto Laclau and Chantal Mouffe, *Hegemony and Socialist Strategy: Towards a Radical Democratic Politics* (London: Verso, 1985).

historical development, admitting necessary and inevitable uncertainties in his own generalizing theories, and focusing peculiarly on language itself as the means through which social relations are constructed as power relations, not simply as the medium through which knowledge of the human social world appears if the correct methodology is employed.

Reading Marx against the grain of his previous reception as a modernist is not quite as difficult or improbable as it sounds. As presented above, his intellectual and political trajectory from as early as 1842 was toward the social question of class power and oppression rather than to philosophizing as an activity abstracted from such practical concerns. For him this was swiftly resolved into an investigation of the discourses through which contemporary knowledge of these matters was generated. Specifically this meant accounts in natural philosophy (*both* Hegelian philosophizing *and* contemporary political economy). His lifelong project from an early stage was thus a "critique of the economic categories,"[43] in his own turn of phrase. Natural philosophy and political economy represented *both* specialist discourses (whether of Hegelian accounts of civil society or of economic accounts of production, consumption, and class division) *and* everyday discourses, through which newly emerging commercial and industrial societies articulated their legal systems, histories, and political systems – indeed the common currency of daily life. On this view, Marx's economic work represents not an analytical discourse of certainty but a complex and parodic re-presentation of economic science as a discourse that constructs and sustains a class structure. On this postmodern reading, Marx's historical works then appear as investigative and exploratory, drawing out contradictions between events as he understood them and his own generalizing theories, always aiming for progressive political effect. Understood in this way, his theories and predictions do not exclude negative, regressive, or catastrophic outcomes, which he sometimes mentions. Marx is thus grounded in a view not only of language as constructive but of human activities as performative: they name what they act out, and they act out what they name.[44]

IX. NOTHING OUTSIDE THE TEXT

Reading Marx in this way, as indeed reading him in any way, involves a selection of texts that have themselves increased dramatically in number over time and have also been through diverse and controversial contextualizations and

---

43. Marx to Lassalle, February 22, 1858, in CW 40: 270.
44. Terrell Carver, *The Postmodern Marx* (Manchester: Manchester University Press/New York: St. Martin's Press, 1998).

editorial treatments. Even the production of large-scale uniform editions of published and manuscript works, letters, and notebooks involves overt or covert categorizations and necessarily controversial introductions and disciplinary framings (e.g. those of Engels or succeeding editors). This has a distinct effect on the way that Marx can be constructed as a philosopher (or not), and in the continental tradition (or not), given that uniform texts are a medium that "evens out" texts, making everything look like grist to the mill. A facsimile edition, say of pamphlets or letters, would by contrast emphasize the quotidian and often ephemeral character of political interventions that were only later philosophized into doctrines, propositions, or other discourses that speak directly to overtly philosophical concerns. Philosophical treatments of Marx tend to emphasize the 1859 "Preface" as a supposed methodological work at the expense of *Capital, Volume 1* as a so-called "economic" one; or the *Economic and Philosophic Manuscripts of 1844* as a supposed "humanist" work as opposed to so-called political works, such as the *Manifesto of the Communist Party*; or *The German Ideology* as a supposed "philosophical" work, in preference to so-called historical works, such as *The Eighteenth Brumaire of Louis Bonaparte* (1852).[45] Works that are newly published and circulated, as many of Marx's were after the turn of the twentieth century, often excite interest and commentary, suggesting that what is to be found in these unfamiliar works cannot be located elsewhere. Given Marx's capacity for developmental repetition, and the vast quantity of his output, this is really rather unlikely.

X. AN ANTIPHILOSOPHY

Overall, Marx's relationship to philosophy, and thus to any continental tradition, is highly problematic at the outset, although there are affinities with other antiphilosophical philosophies, as it were. These can be found, for example, in certain parallels between the later Ludwig Wittgenstein (1889–1951),[46] who made remarks that are critical of philosophical puzzle-setting as the kind of activity devoted (ineffectually) to resolving what need never have been doubted or made problematic in the first place.[47] Marx, of course, was disinclined to find certainties in the commonplace antiskeptical small change of ordinary life, as Wittgenstein did; rather the reverse, as his project was to argue that these are areas of mystification where political power accumulates in the hands

---

45. CW 11: 99–197.
*46. For a detailed discussion of Wittgenstein, see the essay by John Fennell and Bob Plant in *The History of Continental Philosophy: Volume 3*.
47. Ludwig Wittgenstein, *Philosophical Investigations*, G. E. M. Anscombe (trans.) (Oxford: Blackwell, 1958).

of exploiting classes. However, in terms of scorn for philosophers who were addressing political issues abstractly and ahistorically yet claiming truth and certainty, there is a certain family resemblance.[48]

Taken as a philosopher, at least in most of the ways described above, Marx falls within a continental tradition critical of empiricisms. Yet his thoroughgoing indictment of Hegelian (or indeed any) subjective idealism thus raises an issue for constructions of a continental tradition that require a central focus on mind, consciousness, and the self, as does phenomenology.[49] His focus not just on society but on the specifically economic processes therein, sometimes identified – provocatively – as "material," begins to raise questions about empirical aspects of social life and empirical knowledge thereof, such that a philosophy could possibly emerge. The issue here is that Marx's writings that are taken to be of most philosophical interest were themselves produced as an antiphilosophy, yet were written in the terms through which certain philosophies were articulated at the time. Thus they may easily be read anachronistically today as speaking to us in locutions that we familiarly characterize as philosophical. Marx's own political project, however, represents a challenge not just to philosophy itself but to our traditional conceptions of disciplinary boundaries, and indeed to what is or is not acceptably academic or political. This is because it is rooted in concerns that are central to some philosophies but not argued through by him as a philosophical project with an audience of philosophers or students of philosophy in mind. While Marx relied on philosophers and philosophical methods in interpreting the world in political and economic terms for himself and his intended public, it seems unlikely that he regarded philosophizing as itself the kind of activity through which transformative social change could be effected. Indeed, the thrust of his scathing critiques of the philosophers of his time was that they either ignored the need for social change, or mistook the nature and scale of the problems. Marx himself was not particularly successful in unifying his critique of contemporary, class-based society with the kind of communist transformation that he and his (rather few) colleagues envisioned. While his self-styled Marxist successors in the political arena were rather more effective in practical terms, it is questionable whether the ideas involved really bore much resemblance to his in any sense. Paradoxically Marx has been highly but posthumously successful as a philosopher, appropriated by – and reconstructed as such within – a surprising range of traditions, including the continental one.

---

48. Gavin Kitching and Nigel Pleasants (eds), *Marx and Wittgenstein: Knowledge, Morality and Politics* (London: Routledge, 2002).
49. See Trân Duc Thao, *Phenomenology and Dialectical Materialism*, Robert S. Cohen (ed.), Daniel J. Herman and Donald V. Morano (trans.) (Dordrecht: Kluwer, 1986) for an early attempt to use Marxist philosophy to make the phenomenological tradition more overtly social, economic, and political; the work was published first in French in 1951.

MAJOR WORKS

German titles are taken from Maximilien Rubel, *Bibliographie des œuvres de Karl Marx avec en appendice un Répertoire des œuvres de Friedrich Engels*. Paris: Marcel Rivière, 1956.

References are given to, and translations are taken from, this standard edition: Karl Marx and Frederick Engels, *Collected Works*. 50 vols. London: Lawrence & Wishart, 1975–2004.

The works below are arranged in chronological order of writing, where they are manuscript works that were posthumously published in the twentieth century; works published in Marx's lifetime are included in the list in chronological order of first publication.

Kritik des hegelschen Staatsrechts. Unpublished ms. 1843. Published in English as *Contribution to the Critique of Hegel's Philosophy of Law*, in CW 3: 3–129.

Zur Kritik der Hegelschen Rechtsphilosophie/Einleitung. Paris: Deutsch-Französische Jahrbücher, 1844. Published in English as "Contribution to the Critique of Hegel's Philosophy of Law: Introduction," in CW 3: 175–87.

Zur Kritik der Nationalökonomie/mit einem Schluszkapitel über Hegelsche Philosophie. Unpublished ms. 1844. Also known as *Ökonomische-philosophische Manuskripte aus dem Jahre 1844*. Published in English as *Economic and Philosophic Manuscripts of 1844*, in CW 3: 229–346.

Thesen über Feuerbach. Unpublished ms. 1844. Published in English as "Theses on Feuerbach" in CW 5: 3–5.

With Friedrich Engels. *Die deutsche Ideologie/Kritik der neuesten deutschen Philosophie in ihren Repräsentanten Feuerbach, B. Bauer und Stirner und des deutschen Sozialismus in seinen verschiedenen Propheten*. Unpublished ms. 1845–46. Published in English as *The German Ideology: Critique of Modern German Philosophy According to Its Representatives Feuerbach, B. Bauer and Stirner, and of German Socialism According to Its Various Prophets*, in CW 5: 19–539.

Anonymously, with Friedrich Engels. *Manifest der kommunistischen Partei*. London: J. E. Burghard, 1848. Also known as *Das Kommunistische Manifest*. Published in English as *Manifesto of the Communist Party*, in CW 6: 477–519.

Vorwort: Zu Kritik der Politischen Ökonomie. Erstes Heft. Berlin: Franz Duncker, 1859. Published in English as "Preface," in *A Contribution to the Critique of Political Economy*, in CW 29: 261–5.

Das Kapital/Kritik der politischen Ökonomie. Erster Band. Buch I: Der Produktionsprozess des Kapitals. Hamburg: Otto Meissner /New York: L.W. Schmidt, 1867. 3rd ed. 1883. Published in English as *Capital: A Critique of Political Economy, Volume 1, Book 1: The Process of Production of Capital*, in CW 35: 1–761.

Randglossen zum Programm der deutschen Arbeiterartei. Unpublished ms. 1875. Published in English as "Critique of the Gotha Programme," in CW 24: 75–99.

3

SØREN KIERKEGAARD

Alastair Hannay

I. THE WORKS AND THEIR CONTEXT

Søren Aabye Kierkegaard,[1] now considered one of the most important writers of the nineteenth century, was born in Copenhagen, the youngest of a family of seven, five of whom died before he was twenty-one, as did his mother. Kierkegaard was brought up strictly both at school and at home, where his father, who was once in feudal bondage but retired as a highly successful tradesman at the age of forty-one, attended personally to his family's upbringing. After his father's death in 1838 at the age of eighty-one, Kierkegaard and his surviving elder brother inherited a considerable fortune. His long-delayed theological studies completed, he became engaged to Regine Olsen, and one year later received his doctorate with a dissertation *On the Concept of Irony with Continual Reference to Socrates* (1841). Scandalously, and to his own unending personal disquiet, he broke off his engagement immediately afterward and, renouncing an academic career, left for Berlin, where, on the first of four visits to that city, he began the pseudonymous authorship on which his international fame chiefly rests.

Apart from a first publication, *From the Papers of One Still Living* (1838), in which he had criticized a novel by Hans Christian Andersen (1805–75), and the doctoral dissertation three years later, Kierkegaard's main authorship is divided into two series: the pseudonymous works and the signed "edifying" (or

---

1. Søren Kierkegaard (May 5, 1813–November 11, 1855; born and died in Copenhagen, Denmark) was educated at the University of Copenhagen (1830–40; degree in theology), pastoral seminary (1840) and became a Magister (later Doctor) in 1841. He was a freelance writer (1841–55), whose influences included Aristotle, Hamann, Hegel, Luther, and Socrates.

"up-building") and later "Christian" discourses. The two series were written in parallel, publication from both sometimes occurring simultaneously. The first pseudonymous work was *Either/Or: A Fragment of Life* (1843), which became an immediate success. It was quickly followed in the same year by *Repetition* and *Fear and Trembling*. Then in 1844 there followed *Philosophical Crumbs* (originally translated as "Fragments") and *The Concept of Anxiety*, and in 1845 *Stages on Life's Way*. Kierkegaard intended to bring the pseudonymous series to a close with the lengthy *Concluding Unscientific Postscript to the Philosophical Crumbs* (1846), but following a famous feud with a satirical weekly and abandoning plans for retirement to a country pastorate, he chose to take up his pen once more.

Notable among the several publications that ensued were the signed *Works of Love* (1847) and two further pseudonymous works. The former expounds an ideal of unselfish, Christian love, while the first of the latter two, *The Sickness unto Death* (1849), offers a systematic analysis of progressively deliberate renunciations of a Christian conception of human fulfillment, all of them characterized as forms of despair and, in the second part of the work, as sin. In *Practice in Christianity* (1850) the same pseudonym resumes the theme of the paradox of the God-Man (that the eternal should have become historical), central in the earlier *Philosophical Crumbs*. Through its emphasis on the degradation suffered by Christ, and against the background of what Kierkegaard saw as an absence of any corresponding self-denial in the Danish clergy, this reworking of the paradox theme paved the way for an open attack on the Danish state church, provoking a conflict that reached its peak at the time of Kierkegaard's untimely death, in 1855, at the age of forty-two.

On the map of cultural history, Kierkegaard appears, along with Karl Marx, as an archcritic of Hegel. He is also cited as the father of existentialism and more.[2] On closer inspection these identifications speak more of the reception at a later time than of his impact in his own. Kierkegaard's immediate targets are now recognized as having been the Danish Hegelians, first among them Johan Ludvig Heiberg and Hans Lassen Martensen, rather than Hegel himself. However, since Kierkegaard was well read in Hegel and the Hegelian "right wing," it would be rash to conclude that Kierkegaard's concern with philosophy and his times was confined to his settlement with local contemporaries. In order to arrive at a more accurate picture of Kierkegaard's place in the world of nineteenth-century thought, and a more focused portrait of Kierkegaard himself as thinker, it pays to take into account the context both of his writings as a whole and of their wider cultural and polemical origins.

---

*2. For a discussion of existentialism, see the essay by S. K. Keltner and Samuel J. Julian in *The History of Continental Philosophy: Volume 4*.

Alongside its place as a prosperous trading center, Copenhagen in Kierkegaard's time was a lively marketplace of ideas.[3] These two sectors are not disconnected, with concentrated wealth both motivating and supporting scientific and cultural progress and generating new political pressures. The previous century's transition from an agrarian economy to one based on trade (and centered in Copenhagen) generated an increasingly concerted liberal opposition that put an outdated monarchical system of government on the defensive. Freedom of expression and suffrage had become topical issues, and so, too, the problem of creating stability in a society whose current support system belonged to the past. Not least, there was now the question of where to look for authority and guidance: to the church or to philosophy and reason?

II. KIERKEGAARD AND HEGEL

In his student years Kierkegaard, like most of his contemporaries, succumbed to the strong appeal of Hegelian thinking. The five-years-older Martensen later recorded that Schleiermacher's and Hegel's names "were [the] two ... that glittered in the scientific world and denoted the zenith of the era's knowledge."[4] Schleiermacher (1768–1834),[5] the great Romantic interpreter of religion, had visited Copenhagen the year before he died, but in Kierkegaard's early formative period Hegel had become the dominant influence. Hegel himself had died in 1831, the year Kierkegaard took his two-part first-year university examination (the first part with distinction in Latin, Greek, Hebrew, and history and exceptional distinction in lower mathematics, and the second with exceptional distinction in theoretical and practical philosophy, physics, and higher mathematics). A few years earlier his closest mentor Poul Martin Møller (1794–1838) had held introductory courses on Hegelian philosophy at the newly instituted King Frederick University in Oslo (Christiania). And just following Hegel's death, Heiberg (1791–1860), the most powerful, and in many ways most gifted, cultural personality in Copenhagen in Kierkegaard's lifetime, provided Copenhagen's intellectuals, in lectures and in writing, with extraordinarily clear summary versions of Hegel's thought. Heiberg, a theater director and stage writer, had

---

3. For details see Joakin Garff, *Søren Kierkegaard: A Biography*, Bruce H. Kirmmse (trans.) (Princeton, NJ: Princeton University Press, 2004); Bruce H. Kirmmse, *Kierkegaard in Golden Age Denmark* (Bloomington, IN: Indiana University Press, 2001).
4. Hans Lassen Martensen, *Af Min Levnet: Meddeleser* [From my life: communications] (Copenhagen: Gyldendal, 1882–83), vol. 1, 65–8. See Curtis I. Thompson and David J. Kangas, *Between Hegel and Kierkegaard: Hans L. Martensen's Philosophy of Religion* (Atlanta, GA: Scholars Press, 1997), 41.
*5. Schleiermacher's work is discussed in detail in the essay by Eric Sean Nelson in this volume.

even managed (in the unpublished "Grundlinien zum System der Ästhetik als speculativer Wissenschaft") to extrapolate, from his attendance in the summer of 1824 of Hegel's lectures in Berlin, a version of the latter's aesthetic theory that anticipated the actual publication more than a decade later of the lectures themselves. As for Martensen (1808–84), he was an astute and up-and-coming academic who was temperamentally Kierkegaard's opposite. By the time of the latter's untimely death, Martensen had become primate of Denmark. Early on, prior to a three-year spell in Germany on a research grant, he had on his own suggestion tutored Kierkegaard on Schleiermacher. He returned in 1836 as a convert to Hegel, giving a highly successful series of lectures, some of which Kierkegaard himself attended and on which his notes (and those of others) are preserved.

At this time Kierkegaard showed no sign of antipathy toward Hegelian philosophy. In fact his teacher and friend Frederick Christian Sibbern (1785–1872) spoke later of Kierkegaard himself as having been "Hegelianized."[6] We also have Kierkegaard's own word for it. In a journal entry from 1850, he confesses to having been "influenced ... by Hegel and everything modern," so enduringly that as late as his dissertation of 1841 he had been "Hegelian fool" enough to criticize Socrates for having regard only for individuals and not seeing the significance of the collective for ethics.[7]

Too sharp a focus on Kierkegaard's later obvious opposition to Hegelian thought tends to bring much out of focus, not least the subtle and largely hidden interaction between Kierkegaard as a writer who disdained the academic style and Martensen, who self-consciously represented it. The work most often cited as the *locus classicus* of Kierkegaard's anti-Hegelianism is *Concluding Unscientific Postscript* (subtitled "A Mimic, Pathetic, Dialectic Compilation: An Existential Contribution"). However, the fact that *Postscript* was written at a time when Hegel's own influence in Germany had sharply declined speaks for some caution in regarding it simply in this light. It is true that in a retrospective "report to history" published posthumously, Kierkegaard appears to confirm the standard view when he says that *Postscript* was designed to guide people "back" from the Hegelian "System,"[8] but circumstances indicate that it is plausible to read this

---

6. See Bruce H. Kirmmse (ed.), *Encounters with Kierkegaard: A Life as Seen by His Contemporaries*, Bruce H. Kirmmse and Virginia R. Laursen (trans.) (Princeton, NJ: Princeton University Press, 1996), 217.
7. Søren Kierkegaard, *Søren Kierkegaards Papirer*, P. A. Heiberg and V. Kuhr (ed.), 2nd ed. Niels Thulstrup (ed.) (Copenhagen: Gyldendal, 1909–69), vol. X3, A477; Søren Kierkegaard, *Papers and Journals: A Selection*, Alastair Hannay (trans.) (Harmondsworth: Penguin, 1996), 506.
8. Søren Kierkegaard, *Synspunktet for min Forfatter-Virksomhed: En ligefrem Meddelelse, Rapport til Historien* [The point of view of my work as an author: a direct communication,

as an inclusive reference embracing the continuing debate in Denmark among those who were still pursuing Hegelian ideas on their own account.

What appear to be strong arguments for making Hegel directly the focus of *Postscript* often prove on inspection not to be so. One such argument points to the fact that the work calls itself "unscientific." Taken in context, this can indicate a demonstrative rejection of the Hegel of *Enzyklopädie der philosophischen Wissenschaften.* Yet "Wissenschaft" and the Danish "Videnskab" refer far more widely than to what Hegel labels his "science." They refer to scholarship in general and to what might be called the philosophy of mind (which incorporated many concepts drawn from theology) of the time. It is therefore just as natural to take the contrast here to be with the scholarly approaches to *Postscript*'s topic detailed and dismissed in the work's relatively brief first part. These are rejected because they treat what is a subjective problem as if it were objective. Disturbingly for the aforementioned arguments, the working title that Kierkegaard adopted until at least half-way through his preparation of this work was "Concluding Simple-Minded Postscript,"[9] suggesting that the book was promoting a democratic point of view, undermining the assumption that the work's advertised task, how to become a Christian, was reserved for those with sufficient intellectual talent. Why he changed the title is not clear, but perhaps, as the text unfolded under his pen, he realized that it was indeed for this intellectual audience that the book was being written. By amply demonstrating an ability to speak to the elite in its own terms (to mimic them), but doing so in a deliberately "unscholarly" vein, the author might hope to catch that elite's ear and convey to it, from above rather than below, so to speak, that its expertise was not required.

The association of the label "unscientific" with mimicry suggests another such argument. It has been proposed by several commentators that what appears to be the substantial content of *Postscript* is intended as a parody of Hegel, an interpretation that brings Hegel directly in focus. What these commentators in effect claim is that *Postscript* adopts a Hegelian conceptual apparatus simply in order to demonstrate its inappropriateness for the task at hand. One version of the argument finds a piece of deliberately false reasoning in the pseudonymous Johannes Climacus's account of becoming a Christian. It says that although the work makes every appearance of providing a criterion of Christian faith, the one offered by Climacus fails so conspicuously (to those able to see this) to guarantee Christian faith as its object that the whole thing must be seen as an

---

report to history] (1859), in *Søren Kierkegaard Samlede Værker*, A. B. Drachmann et al. (eds) (Copenhagen: Gyldendal, 1962), 106.

9. In Søren Kierkegaard, *Søren Kierkegaards Skrifter*, Søren Kierkegaard Research Centre (ed.) (Copenhagen: Gads Forlag, 1997–), vol. K7, 35.

elaborate joke.[10] Another version, drawing on a fashionable interpretation of the ladder metaphor in Wittgenstein's *Tractatus Logico-Philosophicus* (1921), construes what appears to be a philosophical project of clarifying what it is to be a Christian as a deliberate *reductio ad absurdum* of the project itself, it being stated at the start that there is no doctrine or method available, simply a practical task.[11] According to both versions, the reader is supposed to detect nonsense beneath the appearance of sense. Supporters of such arguments point to three things: first, the fact that Climacus is a self-ascribed humorist; second, his insistence that the task that concerns him is a practical and not a theoretical one; and third, Climacus's sudden "revocation" of *Postscript* in its conclusion. It is then inferred that the point of the latter is to say that once you understand *Postscript*, you can simply put the book away and forget it, for there is nothing there that can help you with the practical task of becoming a Christian.

That Kierkegaard had at this time no reason to fasten his polemic on Hegel suggests there may be alternative explanations for all three facts, as indeed there are. The role of humorist, as Climacus himself defines it, in no way disqualifies him from speaking meaningfully and in general terms of what becoming a Christian is and is not. The humor that he himself fictively represents (at, as he says, the boundary between ethics and religiousness) is such as to distance him from the actual task, analogously to the way in which he saw philosophers who seek to solve the matter in thought and understanding also distancing themselves from it, although in their case with a misplaced seriousness. Climacus's humor contrasts with the earnestness of the real task itself. In his remarks toward the close of *Postscript*, Climacus admits that for all his talk, here and in the previous *Crumbs*, of seeking a point of departure beyond that of Socrates, he himself has come no further. In the earlier work, the Socratic and more-than-Socratic positions are simply "A" and "B," the former assuming, as in traditional metaphysics, that the eternal preexists human being and can be retrieved in thought, while in the latter human cognitive capacity is confined to time and history. In *Postscript*, the two positions reappear as religiousness A (the religiousness of "immanence") and religiousness B ("paradoxical" religiousness). For Climacus, the humorist able to talk in general terms of the paradox and without bearing witness himself to what appropriating it personally implies, the eternal is still something "behind" rather than ahead of him, as in the religiousness of immanence. From an existential point of view, however, the eternal can exist only in a frame of mind (in "inwardness") in which the individual faces the future with

---

10. Henry E. Allison, "Christianity and Nonsense," *Review of Metaphysics* 20(3) (1967); reprinted in *Kierkegaard: Critical Assessments of Leading Philosophers*, Daniel W. Conway (ed.), vol. 3 (London: Routledge, 2002).
11. James Conant, "Kierkegaard, Wittgenstein and Nonsense," in *Pursuits of Reason*, Ted Cohen et al. (eds) (Lubbock, TX: Texas Technical University Press, 1993).

finite purposes subordinated to an eternal *telos*. As for the mimicry admitted in *Postscript*'s subtitle, although that is something that may well be used in the service of parody, it differs from the latter. Mime is closer to burlesque, itself a good characterization of much of what we find in a polemical work by a self-styled humorist.

III. REVOCATION

But why then the revocation? Those who see the whole work as a jest might consider reading this too as a joke. But commentators may also bear in mind that this apparent lack of nerve on the part of the author is not something specific to *Postscript*. There is a step in the same direction in Kierkegaard's first (and signed) publication, *From the Papers of One Still Living*. Its very preface has a postscript, "for readers who might possibly be worse off for reading the preface." Kierkegaard goes on: "they could of course skip it, and skip so far that they skipped over the dissertation too, which wouldn't matter."[12] This seemingly flippant remark is open to many interpretations. It might conceal anything, from an author's natural fear of being misunderstood to the hope that he will be read only by those capable of the kind of concern he wishes to implant (in this early work the importance of having a life-view, something he criticizes his contemporary, Hans Christian Andersen, for lacking). That the pseudonymous Climacus appends a similar postscript, in this case *to* a postscript, is likewise open to several interpretations. There is the motto of the work (*Philosophical Crumbs*) to which it is the postscript: "Better well hanged than ill wed," a wish to be spared the imperial attentions of those concerned with the world-historical advance of thought. Or the revocation might be seen as not so much the author's withdrawal *of* the work as the author's withdrawal *from* the work, a matter usually explained by pseudonymity. Here, however, that seems not to be what the still pseudonymous author would have us bear in mind. Rather, assuming that the positive content of the work is not nonsense, but makes sense to those who "have a sense" of the eternal in the way indicated above, Climacus may be saying that, to those with this sense, the book will not be saying anything new that they need to be told, while if they do not possess that sense, there is no use in their going back over it again in order to try to acquire it.

---

12. Søren Kierkegaard, *Af en endnu Levendes Papirer*, in *Søren Kierkegaards Skrifter*, vol. 1, 14, my translation.

IV. KIERKEGAARD'S DIALECTIC

One unfortunate effect of the parody and jest argument is to draw attention away from what now seems undeniable, namely that Kierkegaard himself inherits and draws heavily on the Hegelian apparatus. As is natural for someone early influenced by Hegel, Kierkegaard's first criticisms take the form of a careful dissection of dissertations and journal articles by contemporary German and Danish academics. His comments, almost always concerned with the need to separate religion from philosophy, are serious, probing, and indeed generally philosophical except when commenting on Heiberg and Martensen, where animus is present. On the dissertation of a theology student, Adolph Peter Adler (1812–69), who had also converted to Hegelianism on a visit to Germany, he speaks (in 1840) of Hegel as "a conclusion," but then "only of the development that began with Kant." Through Hegel "we have arrived in a deeper form at the result which previous philosophers took as their immediate point of departure, i.e., that there is any substance to thinking at all." This even sounds as though Kierkegaard accepts Hegel's criticism of Kant's critical philosophy for leaving the objects of knowledge "in-themselves" out in the cognitive cold. But he adds that "a properly anthropological contemplation is still to come."[13] Five years later, in *Postscript*, this reservation had developed into the thought of a new "in-itself" intractable to thought, namely "existing,"[14] an *an sich* at the subject end, as it were, replacing the Kantian one that Hegel closed off at the object end.

The argument in *Postscript* might be roughly summarized as follows: if we take thought to be the instrument with which philosophers establish essential truth, and accept that Hegel has overcome the regrettable "skepticism" in which Kant's critical philosophy is forced to leave the world-in-itself beyond the reach of thought, we now find our very existence separating being from thought once more, the elusive *an sich* now the very medium in which we have our own being. The terms philosophy employs to define its own task are the Aristotelian oppositions of the finite and the infinite, the temporal and the eternal, the contingent (historical) and the necessary. Where Hegelians purport to be able to reconcile these, through the operation of mediating between the opposites in a higher understanding, Climacus insists that the oppositions confront us in our lives as a tension defining an ethical space in which reconciliation is possible only within the individual's "God-relationship." Mediation, he constantly and humorously repeats, is an operation possible only for those too distracted to see that, besides being thinking beings, they also exist.

---

13. Kierkegaard, *Søren Kierkegaards Papirer*, vol. III, A510; *Papers and Journals*, 127–8.
14. Søren Kierkegaard, *Concluding Unscientific Postscript*, Alastair Hannay (ed. and trans.) (Cambridge: Cambridge University Press, 2009), 275.

This is the basis on which becoming a Christian is to be understood. Christianity offers the existing individual a reconciliation of the finite and the infinite in acceptance of the absurd notion of the God-Man, or the eternal in time. For the understanding, such a concept is an offense. The term Climacus uses, "repulsion," is drawn from Hegel's *Science of Logic* but borrowed by Hegel in turn from Kant. It becomes evident, therefore, that the thought expressed in Kierkegaard's most nearly philosophical pseudonyms follows a pattern meriting the description "dialectical." It is concerned with the need to make oppositions clear in order, in this case, to reconcile them not in any advance in thinking, as in the case of that other dialectical thinker, Hegel, but in appropriating the both appealing and repellent Christian idea in one's own existence.

Johannes Climacus owes his name to a seventh-century abbot who acquired it as author of *Scala paradisi* (Divine ascent). Kierkegaard also used the name in the title of a manuscript of an unpublished cautionary tale written while *Either/Or* was in press (Johannes Climacus or *De Omnibus Dubitandum Est* [Everything is to be doubted]). There its possessor is a young student who unsuccessfully seeks eternal consciousness by way of philosophy. In the two works later assigned to him as a pseudonym (*Philosophical Crumbs* and *Postscript*), readers are urged in the language of philosophy to see that philosophy is not the way. Appropriating the Christian idea is a personal project for which the only encouragement or authority is an active interest in an "eternal consciousness" (for Climacus, Christianity's promise of an "eternal happiness"). The claimed merits of a proffered position can be judged only on the basis of a present ability to grasp in one's person the force of arguments, examples, and ironic observations in its favor. The "stages" (aesthetic, ethical, and religious), developed in the pseudonymous series culminating in *Postscript*, can indeed be said to form a kind of "divine ascent." These works present characters in a dialogue of sorts in which the inadequacies of a "lower" position are brought to light, together with the hint of a need for one that is "higher." However, to follow that need requires a radical change of vision. Someone who maintains a preference for the cultivated melancholy and hedonistic opportunism of the aesthete reveals an undeveloped sense of the nature of the rewards (self-identity, an inner history, public recognition) brought to light by the ethicist. Similarly, failure on the part of the ethicist to see the moral claims of the "exceptional" individual, not covered by the norms of a visible virtue, is due to a failure to appreciate the position of the single individual. It is from this latter position of the single individual, making room for a sense of a need for redemption, that the Christian promise can first be appreciated. The method employed in the pseudonymous series from *Either/Or* to *Stages on Life's Way* is what Climacus in *Postscript* calls "indirect communication." Since Christianity is not a doctrine that one follows, its content or "truth" can be grasped only subjectively in the form of an "existential communication." The teacher does not teach but prompts the novice, not, however, as with Socrates in Plato's *Meno* for the novice to discover what he already knows, but to enable the single individual to face the eternal in the future in the creative form of his or her own actions. Reaching that point is the topic of the "dialectic" pursued by Climacus in his elaboration of the thesis (taken from the eighteenth-century German philosopher and dramatist G. E. Lessing) that you cannot determine an eternal happiness on the basis of contingent historical fact. Increasing awareness of the opposition between time and eternity introduces urgency or "pathos," which reaches its extreme in the transition from religiousness A to religiousness B in the realization that the absolute can be found only in the unintelligible idea – which Kierkegaard calls in *Postscript* "the absurd" – that the eternal itself has entered time, so that the focus must now be on something historical.

V. KIERKEGAARD AND MODERNISM

The characterization of Kierkegaard as a dialectical thinker invites a reading of him as a modernist, like Kant and the paradigmatic Hegel before him. In this he can be compared to his near-contemporary and fellow critic of Hegel, Karl Marx (1818–83), who also had a Hegelian past.[15] For both writers, reality continued to reveal itself most cogently and truthfully in the form of oppositions whose ultimate resolution forms the goal of human life proper. For Marx the tensions are found in the working arrangements of society, and the corresponding resolutions require political action on the part of those collectives best placed to grasp the situation and to bring them about. The tensions that Kierkegaard brings to mind concern dilemmas faced by individuals in their personal confrontation with life and independently of such historical variables as the political and economic situation. Some recent commentators prefer to read Kierkegaard as a prophet of postmodernism, but it is impossible to ignore the indications or analogies that suggest quite strongly that his authorship is at core modernist though aimed at introducing a not hitherto envisaged radical form of faith.

Up to and even including the infamous attack on the church and "Christendom," that "theatrical" version of Christian observance prevailing in Denmark into which he spoke of introducing true Christianity, Kierkegaard's aim looks much like an alternative to Hegel's, replacing the Hegelian absolute with another (although also, as in Marx too, another kind of) single truth on which, now in faith, every individual's understanding can converge. However, with Kierkegaard one may raise the same question as can be asked of Marx:

---

*15. Marx's relation to Hegel is discussed in the essay by Terrell Carver in this volume, as well as in the essay by Lawrence S. Stepelevich in *The History of Continental Philosophy: Volume 1*.

what happens to the Hegelian metaphysics? In Marx it can be seen to reduce, in the end, to theories of social and political development, theories that can be confirmed or proved false by comparison with the facts. Does something analogous happen in the case of Kierkegaard's use of the familiar oppositions? The fact that the finite/infinite, temporal/eternal, possible/necessary contrasts form the basis of Kierkegaard's analysis of despair in the late *The Sickness unto Death*, together with the fact that despair itself is subsumed under the concept of sin, speaks against such a view.

That commentators and interpreters may not want to leave it there is understandable when they come upon certain comments by Kierkegaard himself, such as that made on completing his late works: that he must now "dare to believe that [he] can be saved through Christ from the thrall of melancholy in which he has lived" (adding "and I must try to be more sparing with my money").[16] The thought that Christian belief is a response to a profound existential need parries, as it were, the official Kierkegaardian line that you have to see Christianity from the point of view of that need if you are to recognize its true nature. This complementary thought leads in the direction of a Feuerbach who would translate the metaphysical vocabulary into that of a human pathology that transcribes religious ideals into expressions of corresponding deficits in the human condition, leaving the latter with no "eternal possibility."

At the very least, comments such as the above by Kierkegaard can hint at some sense of the way in which a Hegelian and a Kierkegaardian way of asking questions about human fulfillment differ in what might be called their teleological mood. It is a not uninteresting fact that Hegel himself in his earlier years expressed views very close to those with which Kierkegaard came to oppose the Hegelians. The suggestion has been made that Hegel's early comments on God, religion, and the individual (in the *Theological Writings*) earn him and not Kierkegaard the title of father of existentialism. The French philosopher Jean Wahl (1888–1974)[17] was prompted to remark on the "curious phenomenon" that Hegel was a "'precursor of his own criticism and of the most violent anti-Hegelianism ever formulated";[18] or, still more curious, a precursor of the anti-Hegelianism of the one-time Hegelian Kierkegaard.

To an anti-Hegelian, this circumstance can indicate that the mature Hegel's thought is a failure to follow up an important intuition about human life. The entire Hegelian philosophy, and metaphysics itself, or reason, might then take on the appearance of a diversion, a convenient but illusory substitute for the

---

16. Kierkegaard, *Søren Kierkegaards Papirer*, vol. X1, A510; *Papers and Journals*, 363.
*17. For a discussion of Jean Wahl's interpretation of Hegel, see the essay by John Russon in *The History of Continental Philosophy: Volume 4*.
18. Jean Wahl, *Études Kierkegaardiennes* (Paris: Fernand Aubier, 1938), 166, my translation.

kind of satisfaction Christianity offers to those able to dispel the clouds and see their situation clearly. In one of his notebooks Kierkegaard contrasts the "greater honesty in even the bitterest attacks on Christianity in the past," which still left it "reasonably clear what Christianity is," with "the danger with Hegel," that he "changed Christianity – and by doing so got it to conform with his philosophy." Pointing to his own time, he adds that it is "characteristic of an age of reason in general not to let the task remain intact," and that "[t]he hypocrisy of reason is infinitely insidious," which is why it "is so difficult to catch sight of."[19]

In its attempt to reinstate the task, *Postscript* presents the human condition as in a kind of constant state of emergency. The exclusively finite nature of the world, as we know it, confronts an innate longing for fulfillment (an eternal closure perhaps). The work's "dialectic" attempts to bring this to the fore and adverts to the fact that the distinction between finite and infinite has continually been obscured or "mediated" by Kierkegaard's Danish contemporaries. In order to reintroduce an element of revelation that Hegel's bias in favor of philosophy disallowed, Martensen had gone so far as to introduce a speculative theology that mediates between philosophy and religion, thereby muddying the distinction between religion and philosophy that it had been Kierkegaard's constant preoccupation to keep in view. Martensen is not mentioned by name, but readers, and especially Martensen himself, would have had little difficulty in making the reference, just as, even if they had not been told, they would have immediately recognized the educationist, historian, and reformist pastor N. F. S. Grundtvig (1783–1872) as the butt of the arguments in a section in the *Postscript*'s first part entitled "On the Church." Kierkegaard describes Martensen in his journals as "asseverative" and as "not at all a dialectician."[20] The latter might be read as implying that, in this respect, Kierkegaard himself was the better Hegelian.

VI. A NEED FOR DISTANCE

That Kierkegaard did not involve himself openly in the exchanges that interested him in the intellectual debates of the time, but only from the sidelines and in an evasively unscholarly style underlined by the literary device of pseudonymity, could be explained by his taking the differences with his would-be colleagues to be too comprehensive, or their positions too entrenched, to offer common ground. That would allow us to bracket Kierkegaard along with Dadaists and the

---

19. Kierkegaard, *Søren Kierkegaards Papirer*, vol. X4, A429, Notebook 26; *Papers and Journals*, 533.
20. Kierkegaard, *Søren Kierkegaards Papirer*, vol. X1, A558; *Papers and Journals*, 401.

Theater of the Absurd, or even Aristophanes – not such a far-fetched idea in view of his one foray into this field,[21] as a critic of an entire and still well-established intellectual tradition. It would also speak for the parody interpretation. But if, as indicated, there was much that Kierkegaard had philosophically in common with his contemporaries, the explanation could just as well be his own appreciation of where his creative, and not just his destructive, talents lay.

It is easy from the vantage point of Kierkegaard's acknowledged importance to forget that while most of his illustrious contemporaries in Golden Age Denmark had strong intellectual ties with Germany and sought a response in German culture, he himself wrote exclusively in his native tongue, one that he claimed was particularly well suited to his creative powers. The fact that after defending his dissertation Kierkegaard rejected his teacher's suggestion that he apply for a position at the university indicates that he was already aware of the uses to which literary writing could be put. His examiners had already noted expressions of a kind inappropriate to the academic setting.

This, however, invites the thought that Kierkegaard himself may nevertheless have had some feelers out in the direction of Germany. His life as a student and writer falls almost exactly within the period (*c.*1830–50) in which the Young Germany movement (*Junges Deutschland*) flourished. This group of young writers sought to pursue their goal of political and social justice through a belletrist or "poetic" approach, something that would in itself appeal to the Kierkegaard of the "aesthetic" production. But his aims differed from theirs. In a comment in that posthumously published "report to history," and parallel to the corresponding comment on *Postscript* and the System, Kierkegaard describes this production as designed to draw readers "back from the aesthetic and toward becoming a Christian."[22] The Young Germans looked on Christianity as just another aspect of petrified convention to be demolished. This would make the dialectical Kierkegaard want to distance himself from the movement and from any inclination for its Danish offshoots to enroll him in their cause. Yet, for the aesthetic Kierkegaard, the example was there to be followed and his library records indicate that he kept himself well abreast of the Young Germans. He would also be alert to their criticism of the later Romanticism. Here again Kierkegaard would have to be on the defensive; the dialectical Kierkegaard's stress on the passion of faith can easily trap the unwary reader into thinking that Kierkegaard has much in common with the Romantics, and in his younger days he had indeed expressed his appreciation of J. G. Hamann (1730–88), and of the

---

21. Søren Kierkegaard, "The Conflict Between the Old and the New Soap Cellar," in *Kierkegaard's Journals and Notebooks*, vol. 1, Journals AA–DD (Princeton, NJ: Princeton University Press, 2007), 272–89.
22. Kierkegaard, *Synspunktet for min Forfatter-Virksomhed*, 106.

humor that allowed that figure of the counter-Enlightenment to rise above his time. But it is clear from what his dialectical alter ego writes that the passion in question is not one that brings you, as Schleiermacher would claim, to the object of faith itself; it merely puts you in the proper position to begin the task of faith. Focused as it is on Christianity, *Postscript* demolishes any belief in the possibility of *arriving* at a saving truth, whether achieved (as discussed in Part One) through objective means (history, idealist philosophy, or the mere test of time) or (as in the major part of the work) in the form of some truth-guaranteeing quality of experience. For Climacus, subjectivity is a passionate state of what might be called truthfulness in which the meaning of Christianity becomes apparent although without the force of revelation. The democratic aspect of Kierkegaard's positive remarks on Christianity, that it is available to all equally and requires no special intellectual talent, would have gained an appreciative ear with the Young Germans, but the *Postscript* project of making explicit what it takes to become a Christian would not have found its place on an agenda drawn up by a movement many of whose most prominent members were in any case Jewish. It is nevertheless thinkable that, sensing the surface similarities between his and their approaches, Kierkegaard would feel the need to stress the differences. He might do this simply in order to escape identification with the Young German cause, or with any cause for that matter, preferring to chisel out alone his polemical notion of "the individual," the "category through which," as he says, "in a religious respect, this age, history, the human race, must pass."[23]

VII. PSEUDONYMITY AND THE INDIVIDUAL

But what kind of radical was Kierkegaard himself? In his time and locally he appeared to be the opposite. In the ongoing transition to constitutional monarchy, Kierkegaard consistently opposed the rapid introduction of liberal reform, not, however, because he had monarchical sympathies but because he claimed that the ideals that politicians opposed to the established order were unreal because untried. This did not necessarily even mean that he opposed the ideals themselves, but Kierkegaard seems consistently to have believed that ideas and ideals have to be generated in the hearts and lives of individuals. An idea has to acquire form, and form for Kierkegaard is a matter of enthusiasm. In *A Literary Review*, written while *Postscript* was in press, he says that the age of the French Revolution possessed form because in its ideals it had passion: "In the world of individuals, remove the essential passion, the one purpose, then everything becomes an insignificant featureless outwardness; the flowing

---

23. Kierkegaard, *Kierkegaard's Journals and Notebooks*, vol. 4, NB3:77.

current of ideality stops and the life that people share becomes a stagnant lake – and that is rawness [i.e. lack of form]."[24] In that signed work Kierkegaard nevertheless gives revolutionary zeal only qualified approval; it is better than the cool prudence of modern life where everything is settled by something else, be it reason, a committee, the ballot box, a way of life in which passion has to find its outlets in shapeless and short-lived eruptions not informed by a constant ideal. But as with the qualified approval given to the monastic movement by Johannes Climacus (in *Postscript*), that it shows passion but concentrates it in a conspicuous kind of solitude that belies its alleged focus on the eternal, so too Kierkegaard in the *Review* regards revolutionary activity as a misplaced passion for the eternal concentrated here in time. The true revolution will be undertaken by unrecognizable revolutionaries working in indirect ways to bring the passion of the infinite back to individuals. As for the actual turmoil about to beset Europe in 1848, Kierkegaard remained aloof.

Kierkegaard's own focus on the individual struck many, and not just Martensen, as exaggerated. But in the time to come it was this radical aspect of Kierkegaard's thought that captured the imagination. In the early 1920s, Kierkegaard was translated into several languages, including Russian, and was widely read in both academic and literary circles in Germany, where as a student the Hungarian and later communist apologist Georg Lukács (1885–1971) was an admirer (and later critic).[25] But it was not until the late 1920s and the 1930s, through the intermediaries of Karl Jaspers (1883–1969), Martin Heidegger (1889–1976), and Jean-Paul Sartre (1905–1980),[26] the second of whom is heavily indebted to the Danish thinker, that Kierkegaard became a familiar point of reference among intellectuals and was heralded as the father of existentialism. In a theological context Kierkegaard was perceived as the creator of a radical faith with a new, spare theology. This latter exerted a powerful influence on the Swiss theologian Karl Barth (1886–1968).[27] In the United States, Kierkegaard acquired a solid Lutheran following, while in more recent times a focus on the variety and complexity of his writings, his recourse to pseudonyms and the refusal of his writings to fit into the traditional academic and literary categories, has attracted

---

24. Søren Kierkegaard, *A Literary Review*, Alastair Hannay (trans.) (London: Penguin, 2001), 53, 54.
*25. For a discussion of Lukács, see the essay by Chris Thornhill in *The History of Continental Philosophy: Volume 5*.
*26. For a discussion of Jaspers and Heidegger, see the essays by Leonard H. Ehrlich and Miguel de Beistegui, respectively, in *The History of Continental Philosophy: Volume 3*. Sartre is discussed in an essay by William L. McBride in *The History of Continental Philosophy: Volume 4*.
*27. Karl Barth's theology is discussed in detail in the essay by Felix Ó Murchadha in *The History of Continental Philosophy: Volume 4*.

the attention of those who see Kierkegaard as a precursor of postmodernism and perhaps even a prophet of styles of thought and literary expression still to come.

However, this emphasis, too, like that on the Hegel critique, easily distorts the fuller picture. It is easy, for instance, to overemphasize the importance of the pseudonyms and to lose sight of what pseudonymity makes possible. As for the first, several pseudonyms were adopted by Kierkegaard only at the last moment. This is true of such central pseudonyms as Johannes Climacus, Vigilius Haufniensis, and Anti-Climacus, for whose appropriation of the authorship Kierkegaard offers explanations in his journals. Some pseudonyms come within the category of private jokes. "Victor Eremita" (Triumphant Recluse), he explains later, signified that the author of *Either/Or*, having given up all plans for marriage, was "already in a monastery" while writing a work that included over three hundred pages in its defense.[28] "Hilarius Bogbinder" (Hilary Bookbinder) serves to combine the initially two separate parts of what became the one-volume *Stages on Life's Way*. A pseudonym that has provoked much speculation is "Johannes *de silentio*" author of *Fear and Trembling*. That is hardly surprising since, as Kierkegaard predicted, this would be his most widely read book and by itself "enough to immortalize my name."[29] Kierkegaard's own comments confirm what might be one's first guess: that Johannes *de silentio* tries hard to talk about that of which one cannot speak. He was initially considered for authorship of some comments on the art of divine oratory in connection with conveying what one means by saying as little as possible in the way of "results," or, as one may perhaps put it, in respect of what is or may be the case.[30] *Fear and Trembling* (a "dialectical lyric" in which the poet prepares the ground for the polemicist) sets up Abraham as a counterinstance to Hegel's ethics. From Johannes's point of view, which may be Martensen's or for that matter most people's, but could also be called Hegelian, anything that might justify Abraham's intended sacrifice of Isaac is beyond the sayable, which is to say that no generally acceptable justification can be given. In his notes Kierkegaard distinguishes Johannes *de silentio* from Johannes Climacus as concerned with the "formal definition" of the absurd, while the latter handles the absurd itself as an object of belief.

Regarding the role of pseudonymity, some recent commentators have pointed out that far from being an author's way of withdrawing his or her factual personality from the written text, it can be a diversionary tactic allowing much more self-revelation than would otherwise be acceptable or, in Kierkegaard's case,

---

28. Kierkegaard, *Søren Kierkegaards Papirer*, vol. IV, A97.
29. *Ibid.*, vol. X2, A15; *Papers and Journals*, 425.
30. Kierkegaard, *Søren Kierkegaards Papirer*, vol. VI, A146–50.

strategically desirable.[31] It seems clear that Kierkegaard found in his own life material for a kind of philosophizing that ran directly counter to the objectifying spirit of his times. Climacus is, as he says, a relation of his, one aspect of his more than usually complex personality, part of an individual life developing also in the form of an authorship that resulted from a kind of inner dia- or even multi-logue. Climacus addresses a task that the real author might accept was also his own but that, under pseudonymity, he need not admit to be undertaking. The (aesthetic, ethical, and religiousness A and B) stages or "spheres" of existence whose development from *Either/Or* to *Stages* is recounted and commented on in a section of *Postscript* ("A Glance at a Contemporary Effort in Danish Literature") have an admitted autobiographical base but are literary products in the service of religion, at least as Kierkegaard retrospectively assures us in the posthumously published "report to history" and elsewhere. In this light the pseudonymous authorship may be seen to complement as well as to stand in clear contrast to the writings of Young Germany. The contrast is underscored even further by the edifying and Christian discourses that appeared alongside under Kierkegaard's own name and were addressed, under the guise of "that single individual," to his once fiancée Regine Olsen and dedicated to his father Michael Pedersen Kierkegaard, a man of a simpler faith than that of the luminaries of Golden Age Denmark. These discourses, in a strongly oratorical and compelling form, present stark, cut-to-the-bone readings of a wide range of scriptural texts.

Those who see the separation of texts from their authors as an extension of other forms of desirable freedom, and, perhaps in view of what Climacus has to say about indirect communication, have interpreted the pseudonymity as signaling Kierkegaard's total personal withdrawal from the texts, as if his aim was to let readers make of his writings what they may. Or even, if the expression of that aim too is an infringement, as if what the texts say is whatever the reader by right and opportunity can make of them. But then they face the problem of what it means to talk of indirect communication. For indirectness is still a relation and assumes that the author is still somehow there, if only indirectly. Another interpretation of the pseudonymity would allow the author to be there in the background hoping for a reader disposed to see things in the way that motivates the authorship. The point of the pseudonymity would then be twofold: to disown any *rapport* with a reader lacking that disposition, and to prevent the reader who possesses it from appealing to the real author as an authority for accepting what is written, since any acceptance has to be the reader's alone, as part of his or her own *Bildung* or development.

---

31. See my *Kierkegaard: A Biography* (Cambridge: Cambridge University Press, 2001); Garff, *Søren Kierkegaard: A Biography*.

VIII. THE RELIGIOUS PREMISE AND ITS PROSPECTS

The issue of Kierkegaard's modernity or otherwise is also contested. Some will see the answer depending on whether or not, or to what extent and in what form, the "religious premise" is placed in abeyance. Others may see it rather as a matter of whether Kierkegaard's version of Christianity so departs from anything that could count as modernism as to be either a reversion to something premodern or a pointer to some new and even postmodern version of Christian religiousness. The issue might also be seen in the light of indirect communication. What if the indirect communicator's hope in this case was that the reader see things in the light of the kind of experience in which notions of repentance and grace assume meaning for the individual? This would bring the Climacus of 1846 into line with the early Kierkegaard of 1835.[32] If that were granted, then the further question would be whether, within that frame, it was possible to read Kierkegaard as having abandoned what has been called the "reassuring framework of a classical, Aristotelico-Hegelian metaphysics of infinity"[33] or, alternatively, as having exploited it in a radically new fashion, even one that makes its reassurances less reassuring and less easy to come by.

The extraordinary richness of Kierkegaard's writings, both the published texts and the *Nachlass* now made available, permits the reader to pursue his thoughts and insights in many directions, some perhaps still unsuspected. The religious "premise," which has led some sympathetic commentators to focus on Kierkegaard the literary innovator, rather than the religious thinker, may harbor still untold possibilities, as indicated by recent interest in Kierkegaard shown by a dedicated defender of reason – Jürgen Habermas – who now dares to herald a "post-secular" age.[34] Although just these innovations may cause some to hesitate (also on Kierkegaard's own behalf) to call Kierkegaard a "philosopher," philosophy itself – existential, postmetaphysical, or postsecular – will surely continue to find in his writings a valuable resource for renewal, this in spite of Kierkegaard's own railing against the profession as he found it in his time. Philosophy may even find reason there, one way or the other, to revise its own professional parameters.

---

32. See Kierkegaard, *Kierkegaard's Journals and Notebooks*, vol. 1, AA:13.
33. John D. Caputo, *More Radical Hermeneutics: On Knowing Who We Are* (Bloomington, IN: Indiana University Press, 2000), 47.
34. Jürgen Habermas, "Religion in the Public Sphere," *European Journal of Philosophy* 14(1) (2006), 17.

SØREN KIERKEGAARD

MAJOR WORKS

Kierkegaard's works are collected in *Søren Kierkegaards Skrifter*, edited by the Søren Kierkegaard Research Centre. Copenhagen: Gads Forlag, 1997– . Hereafter SKS.

Om Begrebet Ironi (1841). In SKS 1 (1997). Published in English as *The Concept of Irony*, translated by Howard V. Hong and Edna H. Hong. Princeton, NJ: Princeton University Press, 1989.

Enten/Eller. Et Livs Fragment (1843). In SKS 2 and 3 (1997). Published in English as *Either/Or*. (i) Translated by Howard V. Hong and Edna H. Hong. Princeton, NJ: Princeton University Press, 1988. (ii) Abridged and translated by Alastair Hannay. Harmondsworth: Penguin, 1992.

Gjentagelsen (1843). In SKS 4 (1997). Published in English as (i) *Repetition*, translated by Howard V. Hong and Edna H. Hong. Princeton, NJ: Princeton University Press, 1983; (ii) *Repetition and Philosophical Crumbs*, translated by M. G. Piety. Oxford: Oxford University Press, 2009.

Frygt og Bæven (1843). In SKS 4 (1997). Published in English as *Fear and Trembling*. (i) Translated by Howard V. and Edna H. Hong. Princeton, NJ: Princeton University Press, 1983. (ii) Translated by Alastair Hannay. Harmondsworth: Penguin, 1985. (iii) Translated by Sylvia Walsh. Cambridge: Cambridge University Press, 2006.

Philosophiske Smuler (1844). In SKS 4 (1997). Published in English as (i) *Philosophical Fragments, or a Fragment of Philosophy*, translated by Howard V. Hong and Edna H. Hong. Princeton, NJ: Princeton University Press, 1985; (ii) *Repetition and Philosophical Crumbs*, translated by M. G. Piety. Oxford: Oxford University Press, 2009.

Begrebet Angest (1844). In SKS 4 (1997). Published in English as *The Concept of Anxiety*, translated by Reidar Thomte. Princeton, NJ: Princeton University Press, 1980.

Opbyggelige Taler (1843, 1844, 1845). In SKS 5 (1998). Published in English as (i) *Eighteen Upbuilding Discourses*, translated by Howard V. Hong and Edna H. Hong. Princeton, NJ: Princeton University Press, 1992; (ii) in George Pattison, *Kierkegaard's Devotional Writings: Gift, Creation, Love*. New York: HarperCollins, 2010.

Stadier paa Livets Vei (1845). In SKS 6 (1999). Published in English as *Stages on Life's Way*, translated by Howard V. Hong and Edna H. Hong. Princeton, NJ: Princeton University Press, 1988.

Afsluttende uvidenskabelig Efterskrift (1846). In SKS 7 (2002). Published in English as *Concluding Unscientific Postscript*. (i) Translated by Howard V. Hong and Edna H. Hong. Princeton, NJ: Princeton University Press, 1992. (ii) Translated by Alastair Hannay. Cambridge: Cambridge University Press, 2009.

En literair Anmeldelse (1846). In SKS 8 (2004). Published in English as (i) *Two Ages: The Age of Revolution and the Present Age: A Literary Review*, translated by Howard V. Hong and Edna H. Hong. Princeton, NJ: Princeton University Press, 1978; (ii) *A Literary Review*, translated by Alastair Hannay. London: Penguin, 2001.

Kjerlighedens Gjerninger (1847). In SKS 9 (2004). Published in English as *Works of Love*, translated by Howard V. Hong and Edna H. Hong. Princeton, NJ: Princeton University Press, 1995.

Christelige Taler (1848). In SKS 10 (2004). Published in English as *Christian Discourses*, translated by Howard V. Hong and Edna H. Hong. Princeton, NJ: Princeton University Press, 1997.

Sygdommen til Døden (1849). In SKS 11 (2006). Published in English as *The Sickness unto Death*. (i) Translated by Howard V. Hong and Edna H. Hong. Princeton, NJ: Princeton University Press, 1983. (ii) Translated by Alastair Hannay. Harmondsworth: Penguin, 1989.

Indøvelse i Christendom (1850). In SKS 12 (2008). Published in English as *Practice in Christianity*, translated by Howard V. Hong and Edna H. Hong. Princeton, NJ: Princeton University Press, 1991.

Synspunktet for min Forfatter-Virksomhed (1859). In SKS 16 (forthcoming).

Kierkegaard's Journals and Notebooks. Edited by Niels Jørgen Cappelørn, Alastair Hannay, David

Kangas, Bruce H. Kirmmse, George Pattison, Vanessa Rumble, and K. Brian Söderquist. Princeton, NJ: Princeton University Press, 2007–. Vols 1–11.
Søren Kierkegaards Papirer. Edited by P. A. Heiberg and V. Kuhr, 2nd ed. Niels Thulstrup. Copenhagen: Gyldendal, 1909–69.
Søren Kierkegaard. *Samlede Værker*. Edited by A. B. Drachmann, J. L. Heiberg, and H. O. Lange. Copenhagen: Gyldendal, 1962–64. Vols 1–20.

4

DOSTOEVSKY AND RUSSIAN PHILOSOPHY

Evgenia Cherkasova

The nineteenth-century Russian writer Fyodor Dostoevsky[1] hardly needs an introduction. His stories, which masterfully weave together philosophical reflections, unique personalities, and gripping plots, have earned the author praise as a literary genius, a prophetic political thinker, a keen psychologist, and an expert on human nature and the human condition. His work inspired generations of intellectuals, among them prominent figures of the continental tradition including, among others, Friedrich Nietzsche, Sigmund Freud, Martin Heidegger, Jean-Paul Sartre, Albert Camus.

Even the most cursory look at Dostoevsky's legacy reveals an immense body of work in many disciplines and languages; consequently, any brief account of the novelist's contribution to the development of ideas in Russia and Europe is bound to be incomplete. My presentation of the topic of Dostoevsky and Russian philosophy will be thematic rather than genealogical. I will begin with a brief overview of the novelist's historical–intellectual milieu and then proceed to explore Dostoevsky's artistic treatment of two philosophical questions: the limits of rationality and the problem of freedom. Renowned features of Dostoevsky's *oeuvre*, these themes are also central to many of the diverse sources composing continental philosophy. For the purposes of this essay, I limit textual references to two seminal pieces – *Notes from Underground*, which was published shortly after the novelist's return from exile in Siberia, and the "poem" about the Grand

---

1. Fyodor Dostoevsky (November 11, 1821–February 9, 1881; born in Moscow, Russia; died in St. Petersburg) was educated at the St. Petersburg Academy of Military Engineering (1837–41). His influences included Balzac, Fourier, Gogol, Petrashevsky, Pushkin, Sand, and Schiller.

Inquisitor from the monumental novel *The Brothers Karamazov*, the crown of his literary career.

I. PHILOSOPHICAL REVELATION AS POLITICAL ACTION: PHILOSOPHIZING À LA RUSSE

The nineteenth century in Russia was an epoch of instigation and rapid growth of extremely diverse ideas and movements. They ranged from mystical–religious visions to socialist utopias; from idealism to "scientific" materialism; from moderate reformist programs to extreme nihilist and anarchist manifestoes. Many of these movements were characterized by active engagement with contemporary European philosophy – predominantly German idealism and French social–political thought[2] – and its creative, often quite radical, interpretations.[3] Ubiquitous censorship and constant governmental persecution of free-thinking did not stifle private philosophical discussions. To the contrary, they intensified the intellectuals' profound dissatisfaction with their country's socioeconomic conditions and their eagerness to put new ideas into practice. Long before Russian thinkers had heard of Feuerbach or Marx, they were determined to forgo theoretical speculations about the world in favor of changing it.

For young Dostoevsky and his contemporaries, philosophical education, study of European thinkers, and exchange of ideas commonly took place in informal settings: private conversations, literary salons, and *kruzhki* (circles or discussion groups). Having emerged from heated debates, ideas and theories found expressions in popular essays, novels, sociopolitical commentaries, literary criticism, and philosophical correspondence. William Barrett in his study of existentialism observes:

> precisely because Russia … had no developed tradition of professional or professorial philosophy there was no insulating screen between the questions and the personal passion such questions ought to arouse. The absence of a philosophical tradition, however, does not mean necessarily the absence of philosophical revelation: the

---

*2. Several of the essays in *The History of Continental Philosophy: Volume 1* address these German and French philosophical developments.

3. It is interesting to note that in the preceding years (late 1700s–early 1800s) the Russian language itself was considered *dialectus vulgaris*, not suitable for literary or philosophical purposes. In her book *Fiction's Overcoat* (Ithaca, NY: Cornell University Press, 2004), Edith Clowes traces the development of Russian philosophical discourse in an atmosphere of opposition created by many intellectuals who did not believe in the possibility of expressing philosophical ideas in their native language and would rather communicate in German or French.

Russians did not have philosophers, but they did have Dostoevsky and Tolstoy.[4]

From the very beginning of his intellectual career Dostoevsky was deeply immersed in the contemporary discussion. As a young writer he was sympathetic to Romantic and utopian socialist ideas, and in the late 1840s he belonged to the infamous Petrashevsky circle, an ill-fated secret society of young intellectuals. His involvement resulted in his arrest, imprisonment, and a subsequent death sentence, which, however, was commuted at the very last moment to hard labor and exile in Siberia. By his own account, the terrifying experience of being subjected to a mock execution instilled in him an insatiable feeling of the fullness of life that never failed him, even at the most unbearable moments of loss and despair. Conspicuous in his post-Siberian writings are profound meditations on human existence in the face of death coupled with a sense of passionate life affirmation.

In 1861, on his return to St. Petersburg, Dostoevsky published *Notes from the House of the Dead* – a thrilling fictional account of his Siberian impressions, offering unique insight into the criminal psyche, its violent, self-destructive impulses, and its all-too-human longing for appreciation. This book marks the birth of Dostoevsky the psychologist, or the "realist in the highest sense," as he later came to characterize himself. The tragic, dark, and irrational traits of humanity he observed in Siberian prison continued to inform his later works. *Notes from the House of the Dead* was soon followed by Dostoevsky's celebrated *Notes from Underground* (1864), which, one hundred and fifty years later, is still praised as one of the most poignant portrayals of modernity and its discontents.

II. DOSTOEVSKY'S UNDERGROUND

A peculiar blend of confession, psychological struggle, buffoonery, and philosophical dispute, the *Notes* is written from the perspective of a spiteful "anti-hero" who rages against the contemporary rationalist, determinist, and socialist-utopian projects. Because of its uncompromising exploration of the irrational in human nature and its precise, if bizarre, formulation of the paradoxes of freedom, *Notes from Underground* is considered a classic of existentialist literature. It is this book that deeply impressed Nietzsche, who ranked Dostoevsky as the only psychologist from whom he had something to learn. Nietzsche considered his accidental discovery of the French translation of the

---

4. William Barrett, *Irrational Man: A Study in Existential Philosophy* (New York: Doubleday Anchor, 1962), 135.

Notes in a bookstore one of the "most beautiful strokes of fortune in [his] life," not least because the novelist's lacerated prose apparently challenged the philosopher by "offending [his] most basic instincts."[5] Let us take a closer look at the story and its narrator.

The nameless protagonist, the "underground man," is an intellectually agitated loner who is up in arms against some of the most influential philosophical ideas of his time. Characteristically, his attacks on "the statisticians, sages, and lovers of mankind" take the form of a personal polemic with both individual thinkers (among whom one easily discern Rousseau, Kant, and Hegel) and whole intellectual movements. In striking contrast with both Rousseau's *l'homme de la nature et de la vérité* and Kant's autonomous rational agent, the anti-hero describes himself as "the man of heightened consciousness": someone who is painfully aware of the existential angst that accompanies self-reflection but who thrives on contradiction and doubt. The problem of human nature is at the very center of his diatribe and he approaches it by first taking issue with rationality as a proposed final end of humanity and reason as foundational for human existence.

"Reason, gentlemen, is a fine thing," the underground man argues:

> but reason is only reason and satisfies only man's reasoning capacity, while wanting is a manifestation of the whole of life – that is, the whole of human life, including reason and various little itches. And though our life in this manifestation often turns out to be a bit of trash, still it is life and not just the extraction of a square root.[6]

Here one of the underground man's interlocutors is the ideologue of the nihilist–socialist movement in Russia – Nicolai Chernyshevsky[7] – whose theories were largely based on truncated versions of Feuerbach's historical anthropologism, Comte's positivism, and John Stuart Mill's utilitarianism. Chernyshevsky's "realism" efficiently reduced human nature to a sum of psychological and physiological factors: people were considered good or evil depending on their circumstances and the key to moral development lay in the improvement of social

---

5. For these and other references to Dostoevsky in Nietzsche's writings and correspondence, see C. A. Miller, "Nietzsche's 'Discovery' of Dostoevsky," *Nietzsche-Studien* 2 (1973).
6. Fyodor Dostoevsky, *Notes from Underground*, Richard Pevear and Larissa Volokhonsky (trans.) (New York: Vintage, 1993), 28. Hereafter cited as NU followed by the page number.
7. Nicolai Chernyshevsky (July 12, 1828–October 17, 1889; born and died in Saratov, Russia) was educated at St. Petersburg University (1846–50). His influences included Comte, Feuerbach, Fourier, John Stuart Mill, Proudhon, Ricardo, and Adam Smith. His works include *Aesthetic Relations to Art of Reality* (1855), *What is to be Done?* (1863), and *The Nature of Human Knowledge* (1885).

and material conditions. Along the same lines, his doctrine of "rational egoism" grew from the alleged psychological fact that people invariably act in accordance with their idea of what is beneficial for them. In his novel *What is to be Done?* (1863), Chernyshevsky portrayed a pleiad of "new people" – rational egoists with a socialist vision – determined to build a harmonious society of rational agents who, while seeking their own benefit, would benefit society as a whole. It is against this worldview – which stirred up a whole generation of revolutionaries and whose future admirers included Marx, Plekhanov, and Lenin – that Dostoevsky's underground man fires his most acid remarks.

How does it happen, he asks, that all these philosophers, in calculating human profits, constantly omit one profit? Yet this omitted "profit" happens to be the most essential, "the most profitable profit," for which some are ready to go against reason, honor, peace, and prosperity. According to the underground man, this most essential component of human existence is nothing else but *volia* – the Russian word that means at the same time "freedom," "liberty," "spontaneity," "unfettered will," and "arbitrariness." Thus, the underground man argues:

> One's own free and voluntary wanting, one's own caprice, however wild, one's own fancy, though chafed sometimes to the point of madness – all this is that most profitable profit, the omitted one, which does not fit into any classification, and because of which all systems and theories are constantly blown to the devil. And where did all these sages get the idea that man needs some normal, some virtuous wanting? What made them necessarily imagine that what man needs is necessarily a reasonably profitable wanting? Man needs only *independent* wanting, whatever this independence may cost and wherever it may lead. ... I believe in this, I will answer for this, because the whole human enterprise seems indeed to consist in man's proving to himself every moment that he is a man and not a [piano key]! With his own skin if need be, but proving it.
> (NU 25–6, 31)

For the underground man, a human being is not merely an arbitrary creature; he is a creature that possesses *the power* of arbitrariness, which allows him, being "predominantly a creating animal," at the same time to "swerve aside" and do something completely unfitting, unreasonable, and destructive. But the originality of the underground man's message consists not in his asserting the existence of such power (although this is still something that some determinists and rationalists would dispute) but in his prescriptive claim: not only does man act out of his *volia*; he sometimes "positively must" (NU 25) live solely by *volia*, be it against reason, security, or even happiness. For the underground man, it is precisely this primordial freedom for good or evil that makes a person who he is: a human being and not a "piano key" played on by the laws of nature.

The view of a human being as a creature endowed with freedom is not new in the history of philosophy. The question is what one understands by "freedom." The underground man insists on a radical understanding of free will – *volia*, sometimes translated as "self-will" – as arbitrary, indiscriminate will, a congenital wild force that finds its expression in anything from the most sublime human deeds to the most base and cruel. *Volia* could be the attribute of a genius or that of a criminal, for its very nature is transgression, and it does not discriminate between creation and destruction. This view poses a serious challenge to the liberal rationalist tradition, which focuses on identifying freedom with moral autonomy on the one hand and reason on the other. This powerful existential critique is carried over to the issue of human progress in general – historical, technological, moral.

The underground man cannot help but laugh at Rousseau's nostalgic view of the "natural" state of man and his belief that people can be brought up to rediscover their original goodness in a carefully planned civil community. He is equally dismissive of the views of modern materialists, who associate economic and technological progress with moral development and cessation of violence:

> What is it that civilization softens in us? Civilization cultivates only a versatility of sensations in man, and … decidedly nothing else. And through the development of this versatility, man may even reach the point of finding pleasure in blood. Indeed, this has already happened to him. Have you noticed that the most refined blood-shedders have almost all been the most civilized gentlemen …? (NU 23)

Even a cursory glance at world history would show that no unified theory can explain all the conflicting differences, senseless suffering and sacrifice, unjustified violence and destructiveness that accompany both human achievement and failure. Yet philosophers continue to offer such theories, or metanarratives, because, as the underground man notes, "man is so partial to systems and abstract conclusions that he is ready intentionally to distort truth, to turn a blind eye and a deaf ear, only so as to justify his logic" (*ibid.*). This accusation, voiced earlier by the Romantics,[8] may be equally applied to the nineteenth-century idealists and materialists.

Thus, it is suggestive that Hegel's description of "human history as an altar on which individuals and entire nations are immolated" appears as a quick

---

8. To be sure, the underground man takes issue with Romanticism as well. The analysis of his critique of the Romantic tradition lies beyond the scope of the present essay.

remark in an afterword to his grand philosophical vision of the world-historical process in which conflicts get resolved as particular ends get "submerged" in the universal end.[9] The Absolute Spirit develops in and through individuals and nations toward self-knowledge, rationality, and freedom;[10] and while empirical history may appear tragic and disjointed, it is in effect an embodiment of the necessary dialectical movement of the Absolute.

Dostoevsky's fictional character belongs to the generation of Russian intellectuals familiar with Hegel's dialectics and his philosophy of history. In the 1840s it captured the minds of the educated Russians to the extent that some of them would stop speaking to each other if they disagreed over some key passage in Hegel's work. At the time of the underground man's writing, many versions of historical progressivism, directly or indirectly influenced by Hegel, were being developed and discussed. The underground man's response to such attempts is quite blunt: "In short, anything can be said about world history, anything that might just enter the head of the most disturbed imagination. Only one thing cannot be said – that it is sensible" (NU 30). Moreover, even if it turned out to be the case that there is some final, reasonable, noble purpose to the existence of the human race, could this glorious end possibly justify individual sacrifices at the altar of history here and now?

What is at stake here is more than just a theoretical polemic with Hegel, the Left Hegelians or other progressivists. For Dostoevsky and for some of his philosophically inclined characters, the issue is first of all ethically and politically charged. He insists that a universal theory that dismisses the destiny of a particular person has a tendency to degenerate into an ideological dictatorship in the name of justice and future happiness of mankind. In the novels following *Notes from Underground*, Dostoevsky develops this theme in painstaking detail. Its psychological, ideological, and political implications unfold in the analysis of nihilism and revolutionary terror in *Demons* (1871–72); the same issue, among others, is presented in its metaphysical and existential complexity in the "Grand Inquisitor," an extraordinary chapter in *The Brothers Karamazov*.

---

9. G. W. F. Hegel, *Lectures on the Philosophy of World History*, H. B. Nisbet (trans.) (Cambridge: Cambridge University Press, 1975), 212.
10. Interestingly, Hegel's philosophy of history labels whole geographical regions as not capable of attaining "a distinct form in the world-historical process." Thus, according to Hegel, Siberia is a quintessential *Geist* – forsaken place. It is ironic that Dostoevsky's study of Hegel, however fragmentary, took place during his exile in Siberia, "outside history and culture." László Földényi offers a fascinating discussion of this ironic juxtaposition in his essay "Dostoevsky Reads Hegel in Siberia and Bursts into Tears," *Common Knowledge* 10(1) (2004).

III. THE GRAND INQUISITOR

The prophetic "poem" about the Grand Inquisitor is a culmination of Dostoevsky's lifelong preoccupation with a cluster of problems surrounding the human quest for freedom. The ninety-year-old Inquisitor is a literary creation of one of Dostoevsky's beloved characters, a passionate young philosopher–dilettante, Ivan Karamazov. Ivan tells the story to his brother Alyosha, an aspiring monk.

The poem imagines the second coming of Christ and is set in the dark and gloomy days of the Spanish Inquisition. In the hot streets of Seville, where hundreds of heretics are burned every day, the Grand Inquisitor recognizes Christ and orders his guards to take him to prison. Their conversation – or rather the Inquisitor's monologue, for Christ is silent throughout the poem – takes place in the dungeon of the Sacred Court. The story of the three temptations of Christ in the desert becomes the pivot of their encounter. The Grand Inquisitor dramatically asserts that in the three temptations, or questions posed by the wise spirit in the desert, "all of subsequent human history [was] as if brought together into a single whole and foretold; three images [were] revealed that will take in all the insoluble historical contradictions of human nature over all the earth."[11]

The Grand Inquisitor's words reveal Dostoevsky's own perception of the "scale of the event."[12] For him the three questions represent, in the most forceful and concentrated form, the three ultimate challenges of the human condition: the need for material comfort and security; a longing for spiritual guidance that would alleviate the existential anxiety associated with freedom of choice; and, finally, a quest for universal harmony and the unity of all people on earth. All three are also the supreme expressions of a human being's search for happiness.

The Grand Inquisitor powerfully questions the motivation of his prisoner, who apparently was given the opportunity to address these needs on behalf of humanity but rejected the offer. How could Christ, who loves people and knows their aspirations and weaknesses, refuse to alleviate their physical suffering and their spiritual angst? The cardinal accuses Christ:

---

11. Fyodor Dostoevsky, *The Brothers Karamazov*, Richard Pevear and Larissa Volokhonsky (trans. and annot.) (New York: Farrar, Straus & Giroux, 1990), 252. Hereafter cited as BK followed by the page number.
12. Thus, addressing one of the readers of his *Diary of a Writer*, Dostoevsky stresses that "in the temptations of the devil are blended three colossal universal ideas and after eighteen centuries the more difficult of these ideas have not and still cannot be settled" ("Letter to V. Alekseev of June 7, 1876," in *Polnoe sobranie sochinenii v tridtsati tomakh* [Complete collection of Dostoevsky's writings in 30 volumes], G. M. Fridlender [ed.] [Leningrad: Nauka, 1986], vol. 29(II), 84–5, my translation).

> Instead of taking over men's freedom, you increased it and forever burdened the kingdom of the human soul with its torments. You desired the free love of man, that he should follow You freely, enchanted and captivated by You. Instead of the firm ancient law, man had henceforth to decide for himself, with a free heart, what is good and what is evil, having only Your image before him as a guide – but did it not occur to you that he would eventually reject and dispute even Your image and Your truth if he was oppressed by so terrible a burden as freedom of choice? …. Is it the fault of the weak soul that it is unable to contain such terrible gifts? Can it be that you indeed came only to the chosen ones and for the chosen ones?
> (BK 255–6)

Initially as a follower of Christ, the Grand Inquisitor himself spent years in the wilderness preparing for the spiritual ordeal. Yet. unlike Christ, he "awoke" and refused to "serve madness" (BK 260). His decision was based on his penetrating knowledge of human nature, which, according to him, Christ deliberately ignored in the name of a higher ideal. He bitterly questions his prisoner as to how he could treat people as equals and expect them to transcend their limited nature. By contrast, the Inquisitor claims to be committed to people's happiness and security and he does not ask for anything that is beyond his subjects' abilities.

The cardinal's monologue deepens into an almost biblical rhetoric when he accuses his prisoner of not loving humanity at all. He goes so far as to suggest that Christ himself must be a messenger from Hell because of the unbearable suffering and unhappiness his Promethean gifts have brought to the poor rebels. What people need, according to the Grand Inquisitor, is not freedom but an illusion of freedom; radical freedom for good or evil not only demands too much; it breeds anxiety, uncertainty, and misery. Furthermore, even for God's elect a quest for spiritual freedom proves to be a double-edged sword: the stronger one becomes, the more susceptible one is to the ideas of spiritual superiority and domination.

The perennial conflicts between freedom and happiness, freedom and security, freedom and human nature, are not resolved within Ivan's poem. According to Dostoevsky's design, *The Brothers Karamazov* as a whole functions as a response to the Grand Inquisitor. "The burden of freedom" becomes the central theme for later existentialists, most notably for Sartre, who famously proclaimed that we are "condemned to be free."[13] Sartre insists that one is never in the position to

---

*13. For a discussion of Sartre and his account of freedom, see the essay by William L. McBride in *The History of Continental Philosophy: Volume 4*.

forfeit one's freedom. Indecisiveness, indifference, cowardice, and weakness are not just human traits; they are chosen attitudes. At the same time, no attitude ever defines a human being completely. Even under the direst of circumstances, a human being remains freedom incarnate and no one can deprive him of that. Yet, the Grand Inquisitor's question still stands: why does one have to live under the curse of freedom? What is wrong with one's freely choosing a comfortable bondage? In other words, by urging individuals to take full responsibility for their character and destiny, Sartre seems to be putting an unrealistically positive spin on what the Grand Inquisitor brilliantly identifies as the central existential–spiritual challenge of humanity: our burning desire for independence and our inability to bear the burden of ultimate existential responsibility.

It may seem as if at the beginning of the twenty-first century, after the collapse of several sinister totalitarian systems, we have achieved a much better understanding of the consequences of forfeiting freedom in favor of material security and peace of mind. Some protest banners used in the demonstrations in East Germany in 1989 before the fall of the Berlin Wall directly invoked *der Gross Inquisitor* as a symbol of ideological enslavement, deception, and brazen contempt for humanity disguised as love and care.[14] However, despite crucial shifts on the contemporary political stage, it is far from obvious that we have learned enough from Dostoevsky's psychological and political insights. Dostoevsky clairvoyantly predicted the rise and fall of totalitarian regimes; yet most importantly, he spoke of the totalitarianism of the mind, which, in its many forms, ranges from banal domestic despotism and degrading paternalism to sophisticated operations of self-tempting consciousness that act on behalf of all suffering humanity. This internal enslavement still looms large in the aftermath of the massive twentieth-century struggles for political liberties and economic independence. For example, one is prompted to ask why Russia, the country that produced so many "fanatics of freedom," the birthplace of modern anarchism and nihilism, the testing ground of all possible revolutionary lunacies, keeps losing its battle with the shadow of the Grand Inquisitor.

At the beginning of the twentieth century, Nikolai Berdiaev[15] offers one of the most perceptive commentaries on the phenomenon of totalitarianism. Taking Dostoevsky's "Grand Inquisitor" as a point of departure, Berdiaev eloquently describes dangerous metamorphoses of libertine mentality into a tyrannical

---

14. Travis P. Kroeker and Bruce K. Ward, *Remembering the End: Dostoevsky as Prophet to Modernity* (Boulder, CO: Westview Press, 2001), 76.
15. Nikolai Berdiaev (March 6, 1874–March 24, 1948; born in Kiev, Ukraine; died in Paris, France) was educated at the University of Kiev (1894–98). His influences included Dostoevsky, Hegel, Kant, Marx, Nietzsche, and his works included *The Meaning of the Creative Act* (1916), *The Meaning of History* (1923), *Dostoevsky's Worldview* (1923), *The Origin of Russian Communism* (1937), and *Slavery and Freedom* (1939).

one. Thus, in the *Origin of Russian Communism* and the *Russian Idea*, Berdiaev exposes the pseudoreligious, messianic rhetoric of Russian revolutionaries and predicts the devastating consequences of the state-sponsored ideological infiltration of people's conscience. According to Berdiaev, all radical movements in Russia, including nihilism and Marxism, were man-created religions, illegitimate children of Orthodox mysticism. As such, they may all claim the Grand Inquisitor as their forefather.[16] Berdiaev's brilliant work in Christian existentialism, personalism,[17] and philosophy of creativity during his exile years in Europe (1922–48) exhibit a clear mark of Dostoevsky's influence. And his heroic attempts at keeping philosophy alive in Bolshevik Russia before he was forced to leave the country reflect his devotion to the individual freedom of conscience which both he and Dostoevsky so passionately defended.

IV. DOSTOEVSKY'S LEGACY: UNDERGROUND AND BEYOND

Dostoevsky's well-known critique of scientism, positivism, and utilitarian ethics aligns him with the continental tradition, as does his wariness of the alleged power and coherence of rational discourse. He masterfully depicted the precarious metaphysical situation of a modern man who finds himself confronted with a world that defies rational explanations. Reason demands consistency, intelligibility, order; it craves justice and purpose. But life is ambiguous and messy; it does not cater to rational demands. Yet it would be a mistake to view Dostoevsky as an antirationalist, for he does not oppose reason as such. Instead, he rejects the hegemony of abstract reasoning that tends to subsume the paradoxes and controversies of human existence under the laws of necessity and universality. Albert Camus,[18] whose encounter with Dostoevsky has been aptly described as "intellectual intoxication, a life-time attraction, due to a genuine

---

16. As early as 1901, Vladimir Lenin identified Berdiaev as someone he and his comrades "need to smash and not just his philosophy." Shortly after coming to power, Lenin ordered the arrest and deportation of many writers and scholars, whom he considered "the lackeys of capital." In the summer of 1922, 160 intellectuals and their families, Berdiaev among them, were involuntarily sent abroad on two German cruise ships that later became known as "philosophy steamers." See Lesley Chamberlain, *Lenin's Private War: The Voyage of the Philosophy Steamer and the Exile of the Intelligentsia* (New York: St. Martin's Press, 2007).
*17. Other representatives of Christian existentialism and personalism are discussed in essays by Felix Ó Murchadha and Andreas Grossman in *The History of Continental Philosophy: Volume 4*.
*18. Albert Camus is discussed in the essay by S. K. Keltner and Samuel J. Julian in *The History of Continental Philosophy: Volume 4*.

and deep affinity,"[19] made much of this tragic confrontation between the mind and the world. In the exploration of his two major themes – philosophy of the absurd and rebellion – Camus continually chooses Dostoevsky's characters as his interlocutors because of their unprecedented openness to the absurd and the paradoxical.[20]

Likewise, many of Jean-Paul Sartre's novellas and plays invoke both Dostoevsky's protagonists and his major themes. Sartre's heroes engage in Dostoevsky-inspired self-experiments when they rebel against conventional values and principles, drive themselves to the limit in political action, and reflect on their own thinking to the point of nausea. The novelist and the philosopher also converge in their penetrating depictions of self-deceiving consciousness and their belief in the dynamic volatility of human personality and intention.

As a champion of paradoxes and contradictions, Dostoevsky is often linked to Kierkegaard, Nietzsche, and Kafka. Kierkegaard once said that "the thinker without the paradox is like the lover without passion – a mediocre fellow."[21] Neither Dostoevsky nor his protagonists could ever hope to be seen as mediocre on this count. Paradox is a driving force behind many transformations of characters and ideas in his novels: hyperconsciousness paralyzes thinking in the underground; *Demons* and *The Brothers Karamazov* flesh out horrific mutations of freedom into tyranny and humanism into unabashed misanthropy; libertarian ideas solidify as suffocating dogmas; social reformers prove to be degenerates; and revolutionaries become ruthless dictators.[22]

These mutations are closely connected with another "continental" theme of Dostoevsky's art, namely, his preoccupation with the gap between abstract principles and their practical consequences, between conjuring up theories and living them through. Take the underground man's revolt against "bookishness" and his glorification of "living life."[23] It is, of course, deeply ironic that the denizen of the underground, an avid reader, compulsive writer, and himself a literary creation, would rage against the written word; it is also bizarre to hear the life-affirming speech from someone who spends most of his energy assiduously avoiding life. Yet quite true to his intent to depict a "paradoxalist,"

---

19. George Strem, "The Theme of Rebellion in the Works of Camus and Dostoevsky," *Revue de littérature comparée* 1 (1966), 246.
20. For detailed study of the connection between Dostoevsky and Camus, see, for example, Ray Davison, *Camus: The Challenge of Dostoevsky* (Exeter: University of Exeter Press, 1997).
21. Søren Kierkegaard, *Philosophical Fragments, or a Fragment of Philosophy*, Howard V. Hong and Edna H. Hong (trans.) (Princeton, NJ: Princeton University Press, 1985), 37.
22. For a deep, yet entertaining discussion of the many intentional absurdities and paradoxes populating Dostoevsky's artistic world, see Gary Saul Morson's essay "Paradoxical Dostoevsky," *Slavic and East European Journal* 43 (1999).
23. The "living life" is a theme that runs through all Dostoevsky's post-Siberian novels. *Notes from Underground* contains one of its early expressions.

Dostoevsky again entrusts his anti-hero with the task of delivering a speech on a modern intellectual's terror in the face of life:

> [W]e've reached a point where we regard real "living life" as almost a labor, almost a service, and we all agree in ourselves that it's better from a book .... Leave us to ourselves, without a book, and we'll immediately get confused, lost – we won't know what to join, what to hold to, what to love and what to hate, what to respect and what to despise. It's a burden for us even to be men – men with real, *our own* bodies and blood; we're ashamed of it, we consider it a disgrace, and keep trying to be some unprecedented omni-men. We're stillborn, and have long ceased to be born of living fathers, and we like this more and more. We're acquiring a taste for it. Soon we'll contrive to be born somehow from an idea.   (NU 129, 130)

In this passage one hears Dostoevsky's own voice with an adamant diagnosis of his society and his century. The novelist's portrayal of tragic estrangement from life and the hypertrophy of self-defeating consciousness, two maladies of modernity, fits quite well with the philosophical sensibilities most clearly pronounced in Kierkegaard and Nietzsche.

As we have already seen, the other leading underground motifs are obvious forerunners of existentialism. The narrator is an impersonation of raging individuality. He insists that some differences cannot and should not be reconciled; that freedom and rationality often clash in a grave conflict; that the human condition is not a sum total of observable social and psychological influences; and that life is irreducible to the laws of nature. The avid rejection of reason as a source of meaning, on both the individual and the global level, would become a common theme in twentieth-century philosophy and literature, as would the underground man's uncompromising focus on radical freedom, with all the misery and anxiety accompanying it.[24]

---

24. Joseph Frank thus characterizes the appeal of the anti-hero: "The term 'underground man' has become part of the vocabulary of contemporary culture, and this character has now achieved – like Hamlet, Don Quixote, Don Juan, and Faust – the stature of one of the greatest archetypal literary creations. No book or essay dealing with the precarious situation of modern man would be complete without some allusion to Dostoevsky's explosive figure. Most important cultural developments of the present century – Nietzscheanism, Freudianism, Expressionism, Surrealism, Crisis Theology, Existentialism – have claimed the underground man as their own or have been linked with him by zealous interpreters; and when the underground man has not been hailed as a prophetic anticipation, he has been held up to exhibition as a luridly repulsive warning" (*Dostoevsky: The Stir of Liberation, 1860–1865* [Princeton, NJ: Princeton University Press, 1986], 310).

The underground is also the place where Dostoevsky's famous narrative style first takes shape. The very manner in which the anti-hero addresses his reader – whether in the form of self-mocking confession, sarcastic questioning, provocation, or insult – was eagerly adopted by twentieth-century authors as a form of literary philosophizing. Indeed, why would someone suspicious of reason's ability to address vital, painful questions of human existence resort to systematic rational argumentation? As Lev Shestov pointed out, Dostoevsky's *Notes from Underground* can be considered the most effective and consistent critique of pure reason because it manages to capture the convulsive movements of the irrational and the absurd.

Following Shestov's lead, Camus in *The Myth of Sisyphus* scorns the "thesis-writers" whose speculations serve to support a preconceived idea but could never reach the depth of insight characteristic of "philosophical novelists." In his writings and interviews, Camus never fails to credit Dostoevsky as one of the greatest masters of philosophical narration. But what exactly is the style of Dostoevsky's literary philosophizing? While some commentators emphasize Dostoevsky's fascination with irrationality and contradiction, others defend the analytical and argumentative aspects of his work.[25] Volumes have been written, in the spirit of Mikhail Bakhtin's classic, *Problems of Dostoevsky's Poetics*, on the dialogic–polyphonic nature of Dostoevsky's writing, the style that corresponds to the challenge of depicting the ambiguity of the themes he was set to explore. These features of Dostoevsky's narrative style have been much studied and there is no need to revisit them here. It is a less popularized connection between Dostoevsky and the acclaimed "masters of suspicion" that I would like to discuss.

In their recent book on Dostoevsky and modernity, Travis Kroeker and Bruce Ward suggest that the novelist should be recognized as a preeminent teacher within the "school of suspicion." They write:

> Was it not Dostoevsky, before Nietzsche and before Freud, who began to teach readers to observe what a character reveals only in order then to ask: "What is it supposed to hide? From what is it supposed to distract our attention?" The underground man, himself the most striking early instance of the artistic embodiment of *hinterfragen*, prods, even bullies the reader into an attitude of suspicion .... To seek meaning in Dostoevsky's work is not simply a matter of explicating the consciousness of meaning but of "attempting to *decipher its expressions*."[26]

---

25. James Scanlan, *Dostoevsky the Thinker* (Ithaca, NY: Cornell University Press, 2002).
26. Kroeker and Ward, *Remembering the End*, 137.

Indeed, Dostoevsky not only practiced the "hermeneutics of suspicion," but he kept perfecting this technique throughout his career. In the Grand Inquisitor's monologue and surrounding chapters, it reaches its pinnacle. The story of Christ's ordeal, the Inquisitor's own story, and their setting within Ivan's conversation with Alyosha invite the reader to decipher a whole cluster of hidden motives: the Grand Inquisitor seduces people and he was himself seduced by the wise spirit; the cardinal's speech, the aim of which is to tempt Christ, is itself a reflection of Ivan's tempted consciousness. Ivan's poem becomes an epicenter of his larger argument, whose seductive power is eventually turned on Alyosha; finally, behind all these layers there is Dostoevsky – the tempted and the tempter. In confronting his heroes with the "cursed questions" with which he struggled all his life, the novelist invites his readers to share the struggle and question their own deepest commitments.

With this multilayered narrative methodology, Dostoevsky not only establishes a personal dialogue with the reader but also effectively calls into question the traditional philosophical approach to the problem of truth. While the rationalists put an emphasis on *what* is being said, their critics would shift the focus on *how* and by *whom* it is said. Kierkegaard's famous rendering of truth as subjectivity drives the point home: the only truth that matters is sustained in the existing individual's committed, passionate relation to it. It is precisely what Kierkegaard calls "the inward 'how'" that Dostoevsky is depicting through an extraordinary array of diverse characters. He also speaks directly about one's relation to one's truth, if only in the underground man's merciless internal dialogue with himself:

> You thirst for life, yet you yourself resolve life's questions with a logical tangle. And how importunate, how impudent your escapades, yet at the same time how frightened you are! ... You may indeed have happened to suffer, but you do not have the least respect for your suffering. There is truth in you, too, but no integrity; out of the pettiest vanity you take your truth and display it, disgrace it, in the market place .... You do indeed want to say something, but you conceal your final word out of fear, because you lack the resolve to speak it out, you have only cowardly insolence. (NU 38)

As both Kierkegaard and Dostoevsky knew very well, it is not enough to know or tell the truth; one must live it and be truthful to it. Yet Dostoevsky would not be himself if he did not allow this very truth to be subverted as well. The anti-hero remarks snidely: "To be sure, I just made it all up. This, too, is from underground" (*ibid.*). The seemingly genuine, living words about truth and integrity are dropped like lifeless fossils. By making this happen, Dostoevsky shows that it would take much more than bloodless moralizing to bring back to life a deprived, unloved, spiteful anti-hero disabled by endless self-reflection.

The distinction between the abstract truth of speculative philosophy and the personal, passionate truth of a living individual separates two incommensurable ways of philosophizing. As I mentioned at the beginning, Russian philosophy, for all the diversity of its subject matter, has always been characterized by engagement and existential commitment. For better or worse, the risk-taking nature of Russian philosophy, its favoring of ideas for which one could live or die, was a powerful symptom of the intellectual climate in which Dostoevsky wrote. This intellectual energy of the epoch was creatively transformed in Dostoevsky's novels, whose tremendous success in turn inspired many European and Russian thinkers and legitimized the connection between philosophy and literature.

Indeed, it is one of Dostoevsky's greatest artistic achievements that in his novels he created a unique forum for personal, engaged discussions of the most pressing philosophical questions, the questions that the readers of the twenty-first century still find vitally relevant. In an impassioned speech at the recent International Dostoevsky Symposium, the prominent Dostoevsky scholar Robert Louis Jackson said:

> *Dostoevsky is ours. We were educated on him, he is native to us, he is reflected everywhere in European development.* His moral vision, his spiritual outlook, his profound understanding of the human psyche, his grasp of the deep crises of our times – the crisis of faith, of reason, of the moral principle itself, and of the ideal, and above all his deep humanity and sensitivity to suffering – all this, embodied in the imagery of sublime art – is our heritage.[27]

Undoubtedly, Dostoevsky's legacy is present everywhere; for this reason any study that focuses on thematic connections between his art and a whole intellectual tradition (in this case continental philosophy) is bound to be incomplete. In this essay, structured around Dostoevsky's philosophy of freedom and his critique of rationality, many Russian and European thinkers, as well as many topics, remain unexplored. However, I hope that my brief study nonetheless succeeds, at least in part, in conveying the philosophical depth and complexity of the novelist's contribution to the development of some distinctly "continental" themes.

---

27. Robert Louis Jackson, "Dostoevsky Today and for All Times," *Dostoevsky Studies*, n.s. 6 (2002), 12.

MAJOR WORKS

Polnoe sobranie sochinenii v tridtsati tomakh [Complete collection of Dostoevsky's writings in 30 volumes]. Edited by G. M. Fridlender. Leningrad: Nauka, 1972–90.
Zapiski iz mertvogo doma. St. Petersburg: Vremya, 1861. Published in English as *The House of the Dead*, translated by David McDuff. New York: Penguin, 1985.
Zapiski iz podpol'ia. St. Petersburg: Epokha, 1864. Published in English as *Notes from Underground*, translated by Richard Pevear and Larissa Volokhonsky. New York: Vintage, 1993.
Prestuplenie i nakazanie. St. Petersburg: Russkii vestnik, 1866. Published in English as *Crime and Punishment*, translated by Richard Pevear and Larissa Volokhonsky. New York: Alfred A. Knopf, 1992.
Idiot. St. Petersburg: Russkii vestnik, 1868–9. Published in English as *The Idiot*. Translated by Richard Pevear and Larissa Volokhonsky. New York: Vintage, 2003.
Besy. St. Petersburg: Russkii vestnik, 1871–2. Published in English as *Demons*, translated by Richard Pevear and Larissa Volokhonsky. New York: Vintage, 1995.
Dnevnik pisatelia (periodical, monthly publication). St. Petersburg, 1873–81. Published in English as *A Writer's Diary*, translated by K. A. Lantz, 2 vols. Evanston, IL: Northwestern University Press, 1994.
Brat'ia Karamazovy. St. Petersburg: Russkii vestnik, 1879–80. Published in English as *The Brothers Karamazov*, translated by Richard Pevear and Larissa Volokhonsky. New York: Farrar, Straus & Giroux, 1990.

5

LIFE AFTER THE DEATH OF GOD: THUS SPOKE NIETZSCHE

Daniel Conway

The madman jumped into their midst and pierced them with his eyes. "Whither is God?" he cried; "I will tell you. *We have killed him – you and I*. All of us are his murderers. But how did we do this? How could we drink up the sea? Who gave us the sponge to wipe away the entire horizon? What were we doing when we unchained the earth from its sun? Whither is it moving now? Whither are we moving? Away from all suns? Are we not plunging continually? … Are we not straying as through an infinite nothing?"

(Friedrich Nietzsche, *The Gay Science*, §125)

As we approach the close of the first decade of the twenty-first century, no European philosopher of the nineteenth century is more influential, notorious, and controversial than Friedrich Nietzsche.[1] Even Marx, who not so long ago was reviled as the gray eminence behind the red menace – and, so, as the scourge of free-market democratic societies throughout the West – is now regarded as far less relevant, and considerably less threatening, than Nietzsche. Whereas Marx is now widely regarded as passé, which may explain why scholars are free to introduce his "revolutionary" ideas to impressionable college students, Nietzsche presents an enduring, dangerous temptation to young people, malcontents, outcasts, loners, free-thinkers, subversives, sociopaths, iconoclasts, and

---

1. Friedrich Wilhelm Nietzsche (October 15, 1844–August 25, 1900; born in Röcken, Germany; died in Weimar) was educated at the University of Bonn (1864–65) and the University of Leipzig (1865–69). His influences included Burckhardt, Dostoevsky, Emerson, Schopenhauer, Voltaire, and Wagner, and he held an appointment in classical philology at the University of Basel (1869–79).

free spirits. The persistence of his influence and notoriety is attributable to a diverse array of insights, allegations, pronouncements, and provocations – he was, after all, a master aphorist and sloganeer – but one teaching in particular stands out as quintessentially Nietzschean: *the death of God*. Even those who know nothing else about Nietzsche know that he dared to announce the death of God *and* that he has been memorialized for having done so by poets, playwrights, anarchists, and graffiti artists.[2]

As it is popularly understood, in fact, this signature teaching neatly divides Nietzsche's disciples and defenders from his enemies and critics. For those who have suffered and stumbled under the burdens of divine law, original sin, Church dogma, and ecclesiastical authority, Nietzsche's announcement of the death of God heralds the possibility of a life of unimagined independence and unprecedented freedom of thought and action. Such readers would happily live without the constraints, order, and guilt that are popularly associated with God, organized religion, and morality. For those who have drawn sustenance and support from the traditions and routines associated with the practices native to Christianity, Nietzsche's announcement of the death of God augurs a potentially terrifying slide into relativism, uncertainty, disorientation, and chaos. With respect to Nietzsche's teaching of the death of God, both camps agree, one is not free to remain indifferent. The presumed authority of God has simply meant too much for too long to too many Europeans for Nietzsche's readers to fail to form an opinion one way or the other.

Both camps also agree that Nietzsche fully intended for this teaching to *provoke* his readers and to contribute thereby to the realization of its stipulated truth. This teaching is typically received, that is, *not* as a simple statement of fact, along the lines of a conventional obituary, but as a rallying cry and galvanizing call to action. The intended perlocutionary effects of Nietzsche's teaching are generally recognized as twofold: (i) it is meant to expose the vulnerability of Christian authority to internal and external challenges; and (ii) it is meant to encourage Nietzsche's readers to probe and exploit this vulnerability, by any means available to them. As we might expect, the value of these perlocutionary effects is assessed very differently by the two camps. Whereas Nietzsche's supporters cheer his efforts to challenge the authority of the Church and the viability of Christian morality, his critics warn that civil society may not survive a reckless, intemperate assault on its sustaining institutions. Nietzsche's teaching is thus received as enflaming the embers of rebellion – and, it must be said, of

---

2. Peter Berkowitz, for example, asserts that "The death of God is the great speculation that drives Nietzsche's contest of extremes" (*Nietzsche: The Ethics of an Immoralist* [Cambridge, MA: Harvard University Press, 1995], 2). He also points out that Nietzsche offers very little by way of evidence in support of this speculation (*ibid.*, 270–71).

resentment – that lie smoldering within so many of his late modern European readers. Those readers who find themselves drawn to both Nietzsche and Marx, for example, may discover that the source of this dual attraction lies in the anarchic implications of their respective (and very different) confrontations with European modernity.

It is generally agreed, moreover, that Nietzsche did not intend to restrict the challenge encoded in this teaching to the relatively narrow precincts of religion and theology. His declaration of the death of God is understood to report an escalating crisis of confidence that permeates (and weakens) *all* spheres of endeavor that fall under the general umbrella of late modern European culture. His teaching of the death of God thus issues a challenge to all forms of traditional or conventional authority, regardless of whether they are social, political, aesthetic, cultural, or ecclesiastical in nature. As such, this teaching is understood to underwrite a generic declaration of independence from the established order in all of its familiar manifestations.

That this teaching was intended to provoke is perhaps beyond dispute. But how well known is the *content* of this teaching? How many of Nietzsche's readers venture beyond their initial impressions of this teaching, whether *pro* or *contra*, to explore its intended meaning? Most readers, confident in their immediate, prereflective grasp of the truth or blasphemy this teaching conveys, never pause to ask after the full meaning of the death of God. On the one hand, self-assured atheists, staunch humanists, and confirmed secularists are all certain that Nietzsche, much like Feuerbach before him, meant to expose the God of Christianity as a persistent infantile fantasy, as a psychological projection of those virtues that humankind has been unwilling, until now, to acknowledge as its own. For such readers, the announcement of the death of God is supposed to put an immediate end to a pernicious fiction that has retarded the spiritual and emotional maturation of humankind. On the other hand, devout and sympathetic Christians are just as certain that Nietzsche wishes to subvert the authority of the Church, precisely so that he might deprive civil society of its single most reliable stabilizing institution. They point, plausibly, to the ongoing authority of the Church and to the continued relevance of the altruistic virtues that are integral to the practice of Christian morality.

In both cases, or so it would seem, the rhetorical success of Nietzsche's teaching has been achieved at the expense of a more general appreciation of the philosophical complexity of its motivating insight. As we will see, in fact, Nietzsche's philosophical insight is far less scandalous in its totality than its most provocative rhetorical presentations would tend to suggest. It is not meant, for example, either as an affront to Christian theology or as a challenge, narrowly construed, to the ecclesiastical authority of the Church. Rather than ridicule Christians for their persistent belief in a deceased deity, Nietzsche's teaching actually explains both why and how the belief in God has become inextricably entangled with those other beliefs that collectively have sustained the development and expansion of European civilization. As slogans go, in fact, we could do much better. *God is dead* is not nearly as close a fit to Nietzsche's signal insight as, for example, *The end is near*.

I. NIETZSCHE'S LIFE

Friedrich Wilhelm Nietzsche was born on October 15, 1844, in the village of Röcken, in Prussian Saxony. The son and grandson of Lutheran ministers, young Fritz spent his early years in and around the local parsonage. Bereaved early on by the premature deaths of his younger brother and father, he was raised in a matriarchal household that included his mother, grandmother, maiden aunts, and sister. Finding solace in his books, his music, and in the Pietism of his family, he acquired early on the serious, reflective cast of mind that would suit him for a life of quiet study and contemplation.[3]

After the death of his father in 1849, his mother moved the family to the town of Naumburg, where young Fritz attended the local *Gymnasium*. He was later selected for matriculation at the prestigious boarding school in Pforta, where he received a traditional education in classical studies. At the University of Bonn, he initially studied theology before studying classical philology under the direction of Friedrich Ritschl (1806–76), whom he subsequently followed to the University of Leipzig. Largely on the strength of Ritschl's effusive recommendation, Nietzsche was appointed in 1869 to the Chair in Classical Philology at the University of Basel in Switzerland, even though he had not yet completed the requirements for his doctorate.

Nietzsche's tenure at Basel was interrupted by military service (as a medical orderly in the Franco-Prussian War), punctuated by recurring bouts of illness, and clouded by a growing sense of disenchantment with the field of academic philology. While posted at Basel, he published a number of books and essays, which failed to attract the (positive) attention he thought they deserved. Citing poor health, he resigned his university appointment in 1879 and was granted a modest pension from the Swiss government.

Nietzsche spent the remainder of his sane life writing books and leading a nomadic existence. In restless pursuit of a more suitable climate for his various

---

3. See Ronald Hayman, *Nietzsche: A Critical Life* (New York: Penguin, 1982), 14–20; and Julian Young, *A Philosophical Biography of Friedrich Nietzsche* (Cambridge: Cambridge University Press, 2010), 3–11. On the enduring influence of the Pietism of Nietzsche's youth, see Bruce Ellis Benson, *Pious Nietzsche: Decadence and Dionysian Faith* (Bloomington, IN: Indiana University Press, 2008), 15–26.

maladies – he was unusually sensitive to even slight variations in temperature, atmosphere, and climate – he shuttled regularly between the Upper Engadine region in Switzerland and various destinations in Italy, including Venice, Nice, and Turin.[4] In this prolific postacademic period of his career, Nietzsche slowly began to acquire an international reputation as a thinker and critic.

In January 1889, Nietzsche's sanity and philosophical career came to an abrupt end. As legend has it, he collapsed into madness while protecting a carriage horse from the cruel blows of its driver.[5] After a brief period of hospitalization in Basel, followed by a year-long period of institutionalization in Jena, he returned with his mother to her Naumburg home. In 1893, Nietzsche and his mother were joined in Naumburg by his sister, Elisabeth, the opportunistic widow of Bernhard Förster, a prominent Aryan supremacist whom Nietzsche had despised. Elisabeth had married Förster against the wishes of her brother, who refused to attend their wedding ceremony and subsequently broke off all contact with them. Shortly after their wedding, Elisabeth and her new husband sailed for Paraguay, where they contributed to the founding of a colony devoted to the protection of the purity of the Aryan race.[6]

Following the suicide of her husband and the failure of their colonial adventure in Paraguay, Elisabeth returned to Germany and promptly set out to capitalize on her estranged brother's growing fame and reputation. She fostered a cult-like enthusiasm for Nietzsche's books and teachings, oversaw the founding of the Nietzsche Archive, and eventually convinced their mother to cede to her (and a cousin) the trusteeship of Nietzsche's writings. At the time of their mother's death in 1897, Elisabeth had already moved her brother and the archive to Weimar, where she redoubled her efforts to exploit his fame and notoriety.

Nietzsche finally died on August 25, 1900. Against his wishes, he received a traditional Protestant funeral service and burial, authorized by his friend and amanuensis, Heinrich Köselitz (aka Peter Gast). Following his death, Elisabeth oversaw the renovations of the Nietzsche Archive, from which she launched her aggressive campaign to promote international interest in what she understood to be the political expression of her brother's philosophy. In the process of steering her brother's teachings into progressively closer conformity with her own (strongly nationalistic) convictions, she offered her brother's reputation and legacy to admirers such as Mussolini and Hitler, each of whom claimed to

---

4. The connections between Nietzsche's travels and his preoccupation with health are helpfully illuminated by Gregory Moore, "Nietzsche, Medicine, and Meteorology," in *Nietzsche and Science*, edited by Gregory Moore and Thomas H. Brobjer (Aldershot: Ashgate, 2004), 71–3.
5. Rüdiger Safranski, *Nietzsche: A Philosophical Biography*, Shelley Frisch (trans.) (New York: Norton, 2002), 316. See also Young, *A Philosophical Biography of Friedrich Nietzsche*, 531–3.
6. Ben MacIntyre, *Forgotten Fatherland: The Search for Elisabeth Nietzsche* (New York: Farrar, Straus & Giroux, 1992), 119–48.

find inspiration in Nietzsche's writings.[7] Elisabeth Förster-Nietzsche died in Weimar in 1935. Her lavish, state-sponsored funeral was attended by none other than *der Führer* himself.[8]

II. NIETZSCHE'S WRITINGS

Nietzsche's first book, *The Birth of Tragedy from the Spirit of Music* (1872), is now widely esteemed as a classic text of nineteenth-century European philosophy. His seminal insight into the Dionysian roots of Greek tragedy has been confirmed beyond reasonable dispute. In the nineteenth century, however, the received opinion of Professor Nietzsche's first book was strongly negative, owing in large part to the author's apparent disdain for the scholarly customs and manners of academic philology. Still, no critic was as unrelenting as Nietzsche himself. In 1886, he issued a new edition of *The Birth of Tragedy*, as it was to be known henceforth, to which he appended a preface entitled "An Attempt at a Self-Criticism." In this brief preface, Nietzsche lampooned the romantic sentimentalism of his youth, exposed and lamented the influences of Arthur Schopenhauer and Richard Wagner, and generally chastised himself for continually misplacing his central insights. Later, in *Ecce Homo* (1888), he took another swipe at his first book, ridiculing its Hegelian pretensions while celebrating the "tremendous hope [that] speaks out of [it]" (EH:bt 4).[9]

Nietzsche followed *The Birth of Tragedy from the Spirit of Music* with his four *Untimely Meditations*, wherein he articulated his unorthodox (= "untimely") reception-cum-judgment of four influential intellectual trends of his day: the deflationary, miracle-debunking Christology of David Friedrich Strauss (1808–74), which he exposed as symptomatic of the creeping philistinism of the newly unified *Reich* (*David Strauss, The Confessor and Writer*); the Hegelian and neo-Hegelian fascination with history, which he identified as potentially disadvantageous for life itself (*The Uses and Disadvantages of History for Life*); the pessimism of Schopenhauer, whose salutary influence on his own development he presented as emblematic of genuine education (*Schopenhauer as Educator*); and the larger cultural significance of Richard Wagner's move from Tribschen

---

7. *Ibid.*, ch. VIII.
8. *Ibid.*, 196–9; see also Young, *A Philosophical Biography of Friedrich Nietzsche*, 558.
9. Citations identify Nietzsche's works using abbreviations as follows: *The Antichrist* (A); *Beyond Good and Evil* (BGE); *The Birth of Tragedy* (BT); *Ecce Homo* (EH); *On the Genealogy of Morality* (GM); *The Gay Science* (GS); *Twilight of the Idols* (TI); *Thus Spoke Zarathustra* (Z). Lower case instances of these abbreviations refer to Nietzsche's reviews of his "good books" in *Ecce Homo*. Roman numerals refer to parts of a work, Arabic numerals refer to sections rather than to pages, and P refers to prefaces.

to Bayreuth, which was to become synonymous with the annual music festival staged there (*Richard Wagner in Bayreuth*).

In preparation for his next book, *Human, All Too Human* (1878–80),[10] Nietzsche abandoned the essay form and began to perfect the aphoristic style for which he is now well known. *Human, All Too Human* constitutes his first attempt to illuminate the rudiments of moral psychology and moral epistemology. He continued these efforts in his next two books, *Daybreak* (1881) and *The Gay Science* (1882), wherein he endeavored to expose the basic "prejudices" (or unexamined presuppositions) of contemporary morality.

Nietzsche's most influential book was *Thus Spoke Zarathustra*, which was published in four parts over the period 1883–85. Although originally envisioned as a tripartite work, culminating in the central character's lyric expression of love for eternity, *Zarathustra* also comprises a parodic fourth part that places into question the larger aims (and accomplishments) of the book. The central character, modeled loosely on the Persian prophet Zoroaster, is best known for his peripatetic teaching of the *Übermensch*, which has been widely received as conveying Nietzsche's postmoral, post-theistic ideal of human (or transhuman) flourishing. Throughout the course of his travels, however, Zarathustra is routinely frustrated by his failure to disseminate this novel teaching to his disciples. Convinced that his obtuse auditors are largely responsible for this failure, he experiments with various forms of delivery and address while attempting to tailor his teaching to the diverse audiences he encounters. These experiments are punctuated by his occasional retreats to, and returns from, the solitude of his mountaintop cave, where he reflects on his pedagogical successes and develops his plans for establishing an improved rapport with his auditors.

As Nietzsche explains in *Ecce Homo*, he devoted his post-Zarathustran writings to the task of cultivating a sympathetic readership for his *Zarathustra* (EH:bge 1). Toward this end, he endeavored in his first post-Zarathustran book, *Beyond Good and Evil* (1886), to expose the illusions, fictions, and prejudices that have dominated the practice of philosophy and science thus far and stalled their progress. In support of this endeavor, he advanced a sustained criticism of the metaphysical oppositions on which philosophers have typically relied for their normative evaluations, recommending instead a more nuanced appreciation for the (non-oppositional) differences that obtain between varying perspectives, shades, and gradations. Having exposed the prejudices at work in

---

10. When Nietzsche authorized a new, two-volume edition of *Human, All Too Human* in 1886, he bundled together the original book (now Volume I), the *Assorted Opinions and Maxims* that he had published in 1879 as an "Appendix" to *Human, All Too Human* (now Volume II, Part One), and *The Wanderer and His Shadow*, which he originally had published late in 1879 as a separate work (now Volume II, Part Two). See Young, *A Philosophical Biography of Friedrich Nietzsche*, 564–66.

contemporary philosophy and science, he then interpreted the currency of these prejudices as symptomatic of the decline and disintegration of European culture. The recommended emigration "beyond good and evil" would happily coincide, he believed, with the renewal of a distinctly European culture.

In *On the Genealogy of Morality* (1887), Nietzsche advanced his influential hypothesis that contemporary Christian morality is descended from an ancient *slave morality*, which arose in reaction and response to the oppressive material conditions that both expressed and reinforced the primacy of a historically prior *noble morality*. Although the material conditions of slavery have largely disappeared from late modern Europe, the servile pedigree of contemporary Christian morality is apparent in its beatification of suffering and inwardness, its praise for the virtues of passivity and hostility toward the virtues of activity, its simplistic opposition of "good" to "evil," its allegiance to the ascetic ideal, and its orientation to reward (and revenge) in a promised afterlife. By employing terms that immediately recall Hegel's famous "master–slave dialectic," Nietzsche hoped to correct for what he perceived to be the undue optimism of Hegel's familiar story. Without discounting the importance of the struggle for recognition in the formation and maturation of the self, Nietzsche wished to disclose the full, sordid truth of the triumph of the "slave" over the "master." Rather than lead to the development of self-consciousness and the proliferation of political freedom, the victory of the self-loathing "slave" may eventuate in the eradication of nobility and the extinction of the human species.

The slave revolt in morality is Nietzsche's term for the process that culminated in the founding of a morality in which unwarranted suffering is honored as the primary index of one's "goodness." The noble morality, he explains, was predicated on the virtues of spontaneous self-assertion, uncompromising self-possession, and martial physicality. Noble types naturally and instinctively celebrated themselves (and everything pertaining or belonging to them) as *good* (*gut*), while regarding everything and everyone else as *common* or *bad* (*schlecht*). By way of contrast, slavish types always launch their evaluations by first denouncing the hostile external world against which they must struggle. The slaves pronounce their masters *evil* (*böse*), and only as an afterthought proclaim themselves *good* on the basis of the suffering they endure. The most enduring and potent creation of the slave morality is thus a triumph of reclassification: Those deemed *good* by the noble morality are in fact *evil*. Whereas someone or something deemed *bad* by the noble morality is thereby marked as *common, other, different*, and therefore *insignificant*, someone or something deemed *evil* by the slave morality is thereby marked as *lacking adequate warrant to continue to exist as such*.

The psychological key to the slave revolt in morality is the creative expression of *ressentiment* (or resentment), which Nietzsche identifies as the propensity of the slave type to repudiate everything that it is not, as a means of generating affect and thereby distracting itself from its failure to establish an integrated identity. Because the slave type has no coherent self to affirm, moreover, it is utterly reliant on its enabling fantasy of a hostile external world. In order to ensure the permanence of the hostility it detects in the external world, and thereby preserve the intensity of its animating *ressentiment*, the slave type targets as its mortal enemies all earthly exemplars of beauty, nobility, self-possession, and goodness.

In developing his genealogical approach, Nietzsche made novel use of resources and methods drawn from scholarly disciplines as diverse as etymology, psychology, history, psychology, and anthropology. He did so while attempting to pursue his investigations squarely within the emerging paradigm of scientific naturalism. He consequently refused himself recourse to all principles of explanation that appealed to occult forces, supernatural causes, and spectral agencies. Even the venerable *conscience*, long thought to be "the voice of God in man" (EH:gm), was to be understood as a naturally occurring outgrowth of human psycho-physiology. Toward this end, Nietzsche explained the emergence of human interiority, of which the conscience is emblematic, as resulting from the mandatory inward discharge of instinctual energy. Prohibited from visiting upon others their natural instinct for cruelty, he hypothesized, the earliest civilized human beings were obliged to vent their pent-up aggression against themselves. Under the civilizing influence of this enforced regimen of self-directed aggression, human beings involuntarily acquired with respect to themselves an internal point of reference and a corresponding set of self-regarding relationships and prohibitions, which became popularly associated with the hectoring voice of God.

The typical human experience of interiority thus manifests itself as what Nietzsche calls the *bad conscience*, inasmuch as this experience pertains exclusively to a reckoning of one's failings, shortcomings, debts, disabilities, errors, vices, and sins. The suffering one endures as a consequence of this inward discharge of instinctual aggression is thus interpreted as a nagging reminder of one's unfulfilled promise and unrealized aspirations. From here it is but a short step to the *guilty* conscience. According to Nietzsche, the experience of *guilt* is nothing more than a particular, moralized interpretation of the suffering associated with the "bad conscience." Guilty parties suffer, or so they have come to believe, because they *deserve* to suffer – owing, supposedly, to an irreparable flaw or defect in the very nature of their being. This interpretation of the pain of the "bad conscience" is ingenious, Nietzsche concedes, for it renders our suffering meaningful and charges us with the impossible task of atoning for our guilt.[11]

---

11. *On the Genealogy of Morality* has recently received considerable attention in the secondary literature. Book-length treatments of note include: my *Reader's Guide to Nietzsche's* On the Genealogy of Morals (London: Continuum, 2008); Lawrence J. Hatab, *Nietzsche's* On the

In the following year, 1888, Nietzsche produced several short books that collectively elaborated his critique of modernity and its representative institutions. In these books, he developed his earlier account of European nihilism and advanced his diagnosis of late modernity as a *decadent* epoch. The crisis of will that he earlier associated with the onset of nihilism is presented in these books as symptomatic of a much larger (and inevitable) process of cultural decay. It is the decay of European culture, he conjectured, that explains the rise and currency of those projects in terms of which European modernity tends to define its putative success, including democracy, liberalism, science, progress, cosmopolitanism, feminism, and secularism. While questions remain about his prescriptions, if any, for treating the decadence he claimed to detect, these books present a deeply skeptical appraisal of the generative and regenerative resources available to late modern European culture.

The first of these books, *The Case of Wagner*, lays out the particulars of his case against Richard Wagner, the great German composer who had exerted such a profound influence on the young Nietzsche. His subsequent estrangement from Wagner, he now explains, was a necessary – if excruciatingly painful – element of his own development as an independent thinker. This development, he now reveals, has positioned him to appreciate Wagner's magisterial music-drama as symptomatic of the degeneration of German culture, and *not*, as he had once believed, as indicative of the rebirth in Europe of a genuinely tragic culture. In his next book, *Twilight of the Idols*, Nietzsche took aim at the bloated idols of his epoch, delivering blistering indictments of the contemporary scene in morality, science, politics, religion, literature, and the arts.

Nietzsche followed *Twilight of the Idols* with *The Antichrist(ian)*,[12] which was meant to constitute Book One of his proposed *Hauptwerk*, provisionally entitled *The Revaluation of All Values*. *The Antichrist(ian)* is known both for its angry, no-holds-barred attack on Christian morality, and for its original psychological profile of the historical Jesus. Rather than rush *The Antichrist(ian)* into print, however, Nietzsche decided that he first needed to prepare his German readers for its appearance, which he immodestly believed would be explosive. Toward this end, he quickly penned his *faux* autobiography, *Ecce Homo*, which he apparently believed would cultivate a readership keen (or at least curious) to

---

Genealogy of Morality: *An Introduction* (Cambridge: Cambridge University Press, 2008); Christopher Janaway, *Beyond Selflessness* (Oxford: Oxford University Press, 2006); Brian Leiter, *Nietzsche on Morality* (London: Routledge, 2001); Simon May, *Nietzsche's Ethics and his War on "Morality"* (Oxford: Oxford University Press, 1999); David Owen, *Nietzsche's Genealogy of Morality* (Stocksfield: Acumen, 2007); and Aaron Ridley, *Nietzsche's Conscience: Six Character Studies from the "Genealogy"* (Ithaca, NY: Cornell University Press, 1998).

12. Nietzsche's title, *Der Antichrist*, carries the meaning both of the biblical Antichrist (Satan) as well as the anti-Christian (analogous to the anti-Semite).

receive *The Antichrist(ian)*.[13] *Ecce Homo* delivers an idealized – and occasionally fictitious – account of Nietzsche's life and works, which he endeavored to present as culminating in his accession to his "destiny" as the first *immoralist*. In this capacity, or so he claimed, he became the first critic to discover and expose the real truth of Christian morality – namely, that it is a *decadent* morality, bent on eradicating from the world all remaining traces of truth, beauty, nobility, and the natural order of rank.

Nietzsche closed this remarkably productive year with two relatively minor works: *Nietzsche contra Wagner*, in which he diagnosed the decadence of Richard Wagner while documenting his longstanding aversion to Wagner; and *Dithyrambs of Dionysus*, a collection of poems and songs dedicated to Catulle Mendès, the librettist of *Isoline*. His oft-promised *Hauptwerk*, envisioned first under the title *The Will to Power* and subsequently under the title *Revaluation of All Values*, never materialized. The book that first appeared in 1901 under the title *The Will to Power: Attempt at a Revaluation of All Values* was produced without Nietzsche's knowledge or consent. Working from a plan developed (and discarded) by Nietzsche for a four-volume *Hauptwerk*, Elisabeth Förster-Nietzsche, assisted by others (including Köselitz), arranged and edited 1067 entries drawn from his various notebooks.[14] Although *The Will to Power* affords Nietzsche's readers a wealth of valuable insights into the development of his philosophy over the period 1883–88, it cannot be regarded, as Elisabeth hoped it would, as a reliable statement of Nietzsche's mature philosophizing. Nor should it be understood to confirm, as Elisabeth also hoped it would, the validity of her wishfully opportunistic, broadly nationalistic interpretation of her brother's philosophy.[15]

III. NIETZSCHE'S PHILOSOPHICAL TEACHINGS

The German philosopher Martin Heidegger began his 1940 lecture course on Nietzsche by noting that Nietzsche's philosophical thinking may be collected

---

13. Nietzsche's plan was thwarted by the onset of madness, which delayed the eventual publication of these books. *Ecce Homo* did not appear until 1908, some fourteen years after the appearance of the book for which it was meant to create a sympathetic audience.
14. According to Kaufmann, the first edition of *The Will to Power* included only 483 entries. Subsequent editions – the last in two volumes – expanded *The Will to Power* to its now-familiar 1067 entries. See *The Will to Power*, Walter Kaufmann (ed.), Walter Kaufmann and R. J. Hollingdale (trans.) (New York: Random House/Vintage, 1968), xvii. See also Young, *A Philosophical Biography of Friedrich Nietzsche*, 534–6. For a detailed discussion of the history of the construction of *The Will to Power* and its relationship to Nietzsche's other literary remains, see Alan D. Schrift, "Nietzsche's Nachlass," in *A Companion to Friedrich Nietzsche*, Paul Bishop (ed.) (London: Camden House, forthcoming).
15. See Young, *A Philosophical Biography of Friedrich Nietzsche*, 534–42.

under "five major rubrics," each of which affords us a distinct route of entry into Nietzsche's "metaphysics," which was the focus of Heidegger's investigation.[16] (Heidegger famously identified Nietzsche as "the last metaphysician of the West," suggesting thereby that Nietzsche had succeeded in articulating a critique of metaphysics that relied only minimally on the basic presuppositions of Western metaphysics. Presumably, successor critics, including Heidegger himself, would be poised to complete Nietzsche's attempted overcoming of Western metaphysics, "twisting free" once and for all of its unwanted legacy.[17]) While Heidegger's interpretive aims may not coincide with our own, the "rubrics" he identifies nevertheless suggest a useful heuristic for an initial survey of Nietzsche's contributions to philosophy. These "five major rubrics," which we will review in order, are nihilism, the revaluation of all values hitherto, will to power, the eternal recurrence of the same, and the overman.[18]

Nihilism

Nihilism is Nietzsche's term for the general condition in which human beings find themselves beset by a crisis of will, which renders them unable to invest resolute belief in anything, including (or especially) the authority of God (or any other putatively transcendent value). In the shadow of nihilism, in fact, human beings lose the capacity to muster a will for – that is, a commitment to – the very future of humankind itself. Future-oriented projects, especially those of the sort that have founded enduring cultures and civilizations, give way to goals and tasks of a far more modest scope. As life itself is drained of its former meaning, human beings turn ever more aggressively to ascetic practices of self-destruction. Bereft of a goal whose pursuit might justify the suffering that attends the human condition, human beings inevitably will commit themselves to the goal of self-annihilation. According to Nietzsche, the persistence of nihilism thus signals the advent (or activation) of the "will to nothingness," which he identifies as the last will of human beings, the will never to will again.

Nietzsche often presents his diagnosis of nihilism as pertaining to the history, culture, and destiny of Europe itself. As such, this diagnosis presupposes a particular understanding of the historical development of a unified European culture, the recent disintegration of which Nietzsche links to the current experience of nihilism. Integral to the development of this unified culture, he insists, was the

---

16. Martin Heidegger, *Nietzsche, Volume IV: Nihilism*, David Farrell Krell (ed.), Frank Capuzzi (trans.) (San Francisco: Harper & Row, 1982), 3–12.
*17. Heidegger's work is discussed in essays by Miguel de Beistegui in *The History of Continental Philosophy: Volume 3*, and Dennis J. Schmidt in *The History of Continental Philosophy: Volume 4*.
18. Heidegger, *Nietzsche, Volume IV: Nihilism*, 9–10.

uniquely European reverence for a kind of human being – amoral, creative, and semi-barbarian – whose exploits could inspire both fear and admiration. With the rise of the Church and the spread of its timid virtues, however, this kind of human being – affectionately likened by Nietzsche to a "beast of prey" – has all but disappeared from the cultural landscape of late modern Europe. Although hailed by progressives as indicative of the moral improvement of European culture, the disappearance of these "beasts of prey" strikes Nietzsche as a grave and potentially fatal development: "The sight of humankind now makes us weary – what is nihilism today if it is not *that*?" (GM I: 12).

Nietzsche's own relationship to nihilism is widely debated. On the one hand, he is regularly credited with identifying the harrowing prospect of nihilism and rallying his readers to resist its thrall. On the other hand, he is often accused of promoting the spread of nihilism, perhaps in support of his own designs on a legacy of world-historical significance. What is undeniable in this debate is that Nietzsche was and is widely understood by his readers as urging them to hasten or facilitate the collapse of those social institutions that were and are indicative of the decadence of late modern European culture. Those who applaud Nietzsche's diagnosis and celebrate his candor typically appeal to his image of the wise vintner who prunes an overburdened vine so that it might produce more perfect grapes. Those who refuse Nietzsche's diagnosis and recoil from his amoral calculations typically point to the anarchic impulses that inform his critique of modernity. These critics maintain, for example, that Nietzsche's uplifting rhetoric of restoration and rejuvenation serves, at least in part, as a pretext for his more basic pursuit of the joy that attends acts of gratuitous destruction.

Revaluation of all values

Revaluation of all values is Nietzsche's term for a decisive, pivotal re-orientation of human beings either to their defining values or to the act (or process) of determining and assigning values. The slave revolt in morality, by means of which oppressed human beings convinced themselves (and others) of their genuine preference for the suffering, humiliation, poverty, and destitution they were made to endure, marks one such revaluation of values. For several millennia, Nietzsche maintains, the dominant religious and moral traditions of Western civilization have succeeded in promulgating ascetic, anti-affective values that have placed human beings at odds with themselves and their natural environment. As an expression of these values, Western civilization has promoted ideals of human flourishing that rely heavily on suffering, guilt, self-deprivation, and alienation. While indirectly productive of the art, politics, and culture that define the glory of Western civilization, the reign of these ideals has exacted from humankind a nearly mortal toll. Centuries of self-inflicted aggression have so thoroughly wearied the species that Nietzsche now fears for its future. As we have seen, he understands the historical situation of late European modernity in terms of the ominous re-awakening of the *will to nothingness*.

Nietzsche both anticipates and claims to work toward the possibility of another revaluation of all values, which effectively would reverse or negate the slave revolt in morality. As envisioned by Nietzsche, the coming revaluation of values would accomplish, first of all, a reversal of the ascetic, anti-affective values that have sustained the metaphysical systems of Western religion and philosophy. The highest value will be re-assigned to what is most real: the body and its affects, the earth and its ecosystems, and the cosmos and its constituent quanta of power. The envisioned revaluation of values also will accomplish a change in the source or provenance of values. Humankind will no longer orient its future to values that reflect a condition of lack, deprivation, or defect, but will take its bearings instead from values that express a condition of surfeit, overflow, and wealth. The precise target of Nietzsche's revaluation of values is Christian morality, which has succeeded in denaturing human beings and setting them at odds against themselves.

Nietzsche's understanding of his own relationship to the envisioned revaluation of all values is not entirely clear. On some occasions he presents his writings as preliminary to the envisioned revaluation of values, while on other occasions he presents himself as participating in the envisioned reversal. In the course of explaining why he is a "destiny," for example, he intimates that he in fact *embodies* the revaluation of all values, which, he insists, has "become flesh and genius in [him]" (EH: "destiny" 1). As this passage suggests, and as Nietzsche goes on to confirm, his contribution to the revaluation of all values lies in his discovery and subsequent exposé of the truth of Christian morality – namely, that it both promotes and exacerbates the decay of the highest human types. As he also indicates, his contribution to the revaluation of all values also includes his contradiction (or negation) of Christian morality itself (*ibid.*).

Finally, *Revaluation of All Values* is the title Nietzsche proposed for his ill-fated *Hauptwerk*, of which he completed only the Preface and "First Book," which we know as *The Antichrist(ian)*. He concluded this vituperative book by pronouncing on Christianity a summary "curse," which he apparently believed would play a decisive, catalytic role in the historical destruction of Christian morality. As such, the "curse" he pronounced on Christianity may have been meant either to inaugurate or to accomplish the anticipated revaluation of all values. Even if his rhetorical aims in *The Antichrist(ian)* are difficult to sort out, however, he clearly regarded his challenge to Christian morality as contributing uniquely to the re-appraisal of Christianity that would inform the envisioned revaluation of all values.

Will to power

Will to power (*Wille zur Macht*) is the name Nietzsche gives to his central cosmological hypothesis and to the active principle featured therein. First elaborated in *Thus Spoke Zarathustra*, this hypothesis maintains that every being, whether animate or inanimate, both shares in and articulates a will to express its native power. Nietzsche thus envisions a cosmos in constant flux, as "centers" of power aggregate, grow, and disaggregate in accordance with the blind, impulsive strivings of their constituent beings. The hypothesis of will to power thus suggests an amoral, chaotic cosmos, whose "quanta" continuously re-organize themselves into transient configurations that promise, at any given moment, the greatest possible expression of power. In an influential passage, Nietzsche speculates that "The world viewed from inside ... would be 'will to power' and nothing else" (BGE 36).

Although best known as a proposed contribution to physics and/or cosmology, Nietzsche's hypothesis of will to power appears most frequently – and, some scholars believe, most persuasively[19] – in the context of his attempt to account for the basic processes of life itself. When first elaborated in *Zarathustra*,[20] in fact, the will to power is presented as the very essence of life itself (Z II: 12).[21] In his post-Zarathustran writings, Nietzsche consistently identifies the will to power – and *not* the will to self-preservation – as the "cardinal impulse [*Trieb*]" of all living beings (BGE 13). Every living being, he explains, blindly pursues the optimal conditions under which it might express its native "strength" and thereby achieve the desired "feeling of power" (GM II: 12). Just as surely, he continues, every living being instinctively avoids any impediment or obstacle it might encounter in the path of its pursuit of these optimal conditions (*ibid.*). He is quick to add, however, that the pursuit of these optimal conditions does *not* place a living being on "its path to 'happiness,' but its path to power, to action, to the most powerful activity, and in most cases actually its path to unhappiness" (GM III: 7). As this last remark is meant to convey, living beings pursue

---

19. Maudemarie Clark maintains that this restricted, psychological interpretation of the will to power, as what she calls "a second-order drive that [Nietzsche] recognizes is dependent for its existence on other drives," is all that he may "claim knowledge of" (*Nietzsche on Truth and Philosophy* [Cambridge: Cambridge University Press, 1990], 227). The extensions and applications of this account, especially into the realms of metaphysics and cosmology, may be more famous and influential, but they amount to unwarranted "generalizations" of his basic psychological thesis (*ibid.*).
20. The first reference to will to power in *Zarathustra* appears in Z I: 15. See *Thus Spoke Zarathustra*, Graham Parkes (trans.) (Oxford: Oxford University Press, 2005), xx–xxii. This reference is not explained until Z II: 12.
21. For a persuasive statement of the objection that Nietzsche already goes astray in presenting life as will to power, see Clark, *Nietzsche on Truth and Philosophy*, 218–27.

the desired "feeling of power" even at their own expense. In a healthy organism, that is, the will to power always trumps the will to self-preservation.

Although Nietzsche fancied himself an opponent of Darwin, the actual target of his opposition was the "social Darwinism" espoused by those popular figures – he mentions Herbert Spencer and Thomas H. Huxley by name (GM II: 12) – who asserted the primacy of reactive forces in the microcosm of molecular biology and in the macrocosm of European culture.[22] He thus condemned "the whole of English Darwinism" (GS 349), which, he insisted, mistakenly confused the *exceptional* circumstances of late modernity with the *normal* circumstances in which human beings have pursued the optimal conditions under which they might accumulate, reserve, and expend their native strength. That bourgeois Europeans value self-preservation above all else is indicative, he allowed, of nothing more than the abject *decadence* of late modern European culture, that is, of its decline from the norms and standards established in bygone epochs. While it is true that sick and declining organisms naturally seek to preserve themselves, healthy and ascending forms of life naturally seek to accumulate and expend their strength – even at the expense of their own self-preservation.

Eternal recurrence

The teaching of *eternal recurrence*[23] is presented by Nietzsche as performing a divided office: (i) it advances a model of an amoral, godless cosmos in which all atoms and their transient configurations eternally recur; and (ii) it articulates an emblematic expression of one's affirmation of life within such a cosmos, stripped bare of all supernatural contrivances and metaphysical comforts. In Nietzsche's most influential formulation of the idea of eternal recurrence, as found in Section 341 of *The Gay Science*, his readers are asked how they would respond if they were to learn (from a demon, no less) that their lives have recurred in every detail innumerable times and will continue indefinitely to do so.

Two general lines of response are anticipated: either we will curse the impudent demon, gnashing our teeth in despair (and thereby failing the implicit test

---

22. As scholars have noted, Nietzsche's understanding of Darwin was at best sketchy and at worst uninformed. It is not clear that he ever undertook a careful study of Darwin's theories, and he was in any event far more concerned to combat the pernicious influence of these theories – distorted or not – on science and culture. See, for example, Keith Ansell-Pearson's excellent discussion in *Viroid Life: Perspectives on Nietzsche and the Transhuman Condition* (London: Routledge, 1997), ch. 4, "Nietzsche contra Darwin." See also John Richardson, *Nietzsche's New Darwinism* (Oxford: Oxford University Press, 2004), esp. 11–26.

23. Here I depart somewhat from Heidegger's proposed "rubrics," preferring the more familiar "eternal recurrence" to the less familiar (although friendlier to Heidegger's peculiar interpretation) "eternal recurrence of the same."

of affirmation), or, recognizing the demon as a god, we will rejoice and *will* the eternal recurrence of our lives in every detail (thereby passing the implicit test of affirmation).[24] This section ends by posing the following question, which has led some scholars to conclude that the thought of eternal recurrence is meant to perform a diagnostic function not unlike that of Kant's famous "categorical imperative": "[H]ow well disposed would you have to become to yourself and to life *to crave nothing more fervently* than this eternal confirmation and seal?" (GS 341). If we assume that becoming well disposed to oneself and to life ranks among the highest goods available to human beings, then the thought experiment described in this section would appear to serve the diagnostic function that is popularly assigned to it. To be capable of affirming the eternal recurrence of one's life in every detail is thus presented as the single most reliable index of human flourishing.[25]

The teaching of eternal recurrence is apparently meant to express or represent an epiphany Nietzsche experienced in 1881 while walking, as was his wont, in the mountains near Sils-Maria in the Upper Engadine region of Switzerland. "6000 feet beyond man and time" is how he described his experience at the time. Translating this personal epiphany into a communicable philosophical teaching proved to be extremely challenging, however, and Nietzsche's success in doing so remains difficult to gage. Even today, scholars vigorously dispute what, if anything, this teaching is meant to convey. Part of the problem here is that the teaching of eternal recurrence receives relatively little treatment in Nietzsche's published writings. It figures prominently in only one book (*Thus Spoke Zarathustra*, whose form is closer to a prose-poem than a philosophical treatise), while in other books it is scarcely mentioned. When the teaching *is* presented, moreover, it is often placed in the mouths of characters and personae (e.g. the "demon" in GS 341) whom Nietzsche's readers cannot trust to profess reliably on his behalf. In his autobiography, Nietzsche further confuses his readers by attaching "[his] formula for greatness in a human being" *not* to the teaching of eternal recurrence, but to the (potentially kindred) teaching of *amor fati* (love of fate) (EH: "destiny" 10). Finally, it is not at all clear how we are supposed to reconcile the cosmology suggested by the teaching of eternal recurrence, wherein each of us is but a "speck of dust" within the perpetually overturned "eternal hourglass of existence" (GS 341), with the broadly ethical implications of its diagnostic function.

---

24. As Clark points out, the demon does not offer us a *choice* between these two responses (*Nietzsche on Truth and Philosophy*, 281).
25. This interpretation of the eternal recurrence has been advanced most influentially by Bernd Magnus, *Nietzsche's Existential Imperative* (Bloomington, IN: Indiana University Press, 1978), esp. 111–54. See also Clark, *Nietzsche on Truth and Philosophy*, 245–86.

Nietzsche describes the idea of eternal recurrence as the "fundamental conception" of his greatest work, *Thus Spoke Zarathustra* (1883–85). (The "tragedy" of Zarathustra is introduced to Nietzsche's readers in Section 342 of *The Gay Science*, which immediately follows his introduction of the idea of eternal recurrence in Section 341.) Zarathustra's struggles to embrace this elusive idea, presumably so that he might someday promulgate it to others, furnishes the book with its central dramatic structure.[26] Throughout his various journeys and speeches, Zarathustra strives to grow into the role supposedly reserved for him as the teacher of the eternal recurrence.[27] While his growth is in many respects remarkable, and even quasi-heroic, the open-ended conclusion of the book (in Part IV) leaves some doubt about the success of his endeavor to embrace the teaching of eternal recurrence.[28] In the final scene of the book, he sets out to meet his ideal companions (whom he calls his "children") and, presumably, to commence the postmoral, post-theistic epoch of human history. Indeed, the dramatic trajectory of the book suggests that a successful meeting between Zarathustra and his "children" could take place only if he has in fact become the teacher of the eternal recurrence. But the book closes on an inconclusive note: the narrator neither confirms nor denies the eventuality of this fateful meeting. We therefore cannot know if Zarathustra has in fact grown into the role reserved for him, or if he has simply failed once again to connect with his chosen audience.

The overman

The overman (*der Übermensch*) is the other teaching of Nietzsche's Zarathustra and, by association, of Nietzsche himself. In *Thus Spoke Zarathustra*, the central

---

26. The dramatic structure of *Thus Spoke Zarathustra* has received a great deal of attention in the recent literature on Nietzsche. Edifying interpretations are advanced in the following books: Robert Gooding-Williams, *Zarathustra's Dionysian Modernism* (Stanford, CA: Stanford University Press, 2001); Kathleen Higgins, *Nietzsche's Zarathustra* (Philadelphia, PA: Temple University Press, 1987); Laurence Lampert, *Nietzsche's Teaching: An Interpretation of* Thus Spoke Zarathustra (New Haven, CT: Yale University Press, 1986); Paul Loeb, *The Death of Nietzsche's Zarathustra* (Cambridge: Cambridge University Press, 2010); Stanley Rosen, *The Mask of Enlightenment: Nietzsche's* Zarathustra (Cambridge: Cambridge University Press, 1995); T. K. Seung, *Nietzsche's Epic of the Soul* (Lanham, MD: Lexington Books, 2005); and Greg Whitlock, *Returning to Sils Maria* (New York: Peter Lang, 1990).
27. After Zarathustra completes his seven-day period of convalescence, his companion animals inform him that it is his "fate" to be "*the teacher of eternal recurrence*" (Z III: 13). He does not respond, however, and nothing that follows this exchange indicates that he accepts their determination of his fate.
28. Such doubts are viable, of course, only if Part IV is understood to conclude *Zarathustra*. For an alternative account of the basic structure of *Zarathustra*, see Loeb, *The Death of Nietzsche's Zarathustra*, esp. 86–101.

character is initially concerned to acquaint his auditors with the mysterious figure of the "overman," who supposedly embodies a new ideal of human (or transhuman) flourishing. Upon descending to the marketplace from his mountaintop retreat, Zarathustra devotes his very first public address to his teaching of the "overman," which he presents as both an alternative and antidote to the moral and religious ideals that have presided over the development of the Western tradition. Whereas these ideals have collectively demeaned humankind, teaching us to despise our finitude and frailty, the overman is presented as a celebration of humankind as it is, including what is most powerful and unique about us. Zarathustra's teaching of the overman is thus meant to promote and facilitate a life of self-possession, self-mastery, and self-sufficiency, wherein human beings might lay undivided claim to their passions, creativity, physicality, and sexuality.

The teaching of the overman is inextricably linked to Zarathustra's (and Nietzsche's) pronouncement of the "death of God," by which they mean to convey the erosion of theological authority that is specific to the epoch of late modernity.[29] With God out of the picture, or so Zarathustra initially believes, humankind may finally take its rightful place at the value-positing center of the cosmos. Unencumbered by the crushing weight of religious tradition and theological superstition, humankind may finally accede to full maturity as a species. The "death of God" thus furnishes the historical context for Zarathustra's teaching of "the overman," which heralds the advent of human beings who are prepared to serve as guarantors of their own value and meaning.

With the exception of his *Zarathustra*, Nietzsche's writings scarcely mention the overman. It may be more accurate, in fact, to think of this teaching as belonging more fundamentally to Zarathustra than to Nietzsche. Nevertheless, many readers interpret the teaching of the overman as generally continuous with Nietzsche's more common references to those higher human beings – typically architects of empire (e.g. Caesar and Napoleon) and artists (e.g. Goethe and Stendhal) – who command our admiration on the strength of their amoral imposition of form and order onto an otherwise unruly existence. According to this line of interpretation, an overman would be anyone who stands to us and our epoch as these exemplars of higher humanity stood to their respective peoples and epochs. While it is indisputable that Nietzsche encouraged his best readers to admire even the most terrifying exemplars of higher humanity, it is not entirely clear that this is what Zarathustra meant, at least initially, for his teaching of the overman to convey. If humanity must be "overcome," as

---

29. Upon descending from his mountaintop retreat, Zarathustra concludes his first exchange, with a God-fearing hermit whom he encounters in the forest, by remarking, "Could this be possible! This old holy man in his forest has heard nothing of this yet, that *God is dead!*" (Z: P2). This means, I take it, that the death of God is a presupposition or condition of Zarathustra's pedagogy. See Loeb, *The Death of Nietzsche's Zarathustra*, 228–30.

Zarathustra apparently believes, then the teaching of the overman may very well point to the emergence of beings who are discontinuous with, and perhaps radically so, the collective perfections of higher humanity. Indeed, scholars remain divided on the interpretive question of whether or not the teaching of the overman should be understood to locate the most promising future for the human species in the achievement of a transhuman mode of existence.[30]

While undeniably influential – even notoriously so – in the century following its initial presentation, the teaching of the overman remains somewhat elusive. In evaluating this teaching, we would do well to bear in mind that Zarathustra himself was largely unsuccessful in promulgating it, despite his various attempts to tailor this teaching to the needs and interests of his auditors. Although both Zarathustra and Nietzsche were quick to blame this failing on others (e.g. Zarathustra's obtuse auditors, Nietzsche's inept readers), they may bear some responsibility as well. In any event, the failure of Zarathustra and Nietzsche to disseminate their redemptive teaching(s) of the overman is entirely consistent with Nietzsche's diagnosis of late modernity as an epoch hospitable only to teachings of decadence and despair. If the teaching of the overman is meant to re-acquaint human beings with their estranged passions, bodies, and natural surroundings, then perhaps we should not be surprised that this teaching has fallen thus far on deaf ears.

IV. REVISITING THE DEATH OF GOD

When Nietzsche decided in 1886 to add a Fifth Book to *The Gay Science*, along with a new preface and some other materials, he also decided to begin this Fifth Book, entitled "We Fearless Ones," by revisiting the theme of the death of God. Although not advertised as such, this treatment of the death of God is apparently meant to update, and perhaps supplant, the treatment found in the original 1882 edition of *The Gay Science*. There, as we recall, the death of God was announced by a Madman who proceeded to identify himself and his auditors – and, by extension, all of contemporary humankind – as the *murderers* of God.[31] That his auditors were ignorant of their alleged crime was not indicative of their innocence, the Madman insisted, for a crime of this magnitude takes time to penetrate and inform the awareness of its perpetrators. He thus concluded that

---

30. An exemplary statement of a transhuman articulation of Nietzsche's philosophy is provided by Ansell-Pearson in *Viroid Life*.
31. David Owen provides a helpful diagram and supporting analysis of this scene in *Nietzsche's Genealogy of Morality*, 51–2. I am also indebted here to the analysis provided by Robert Pippin in *Nietzsche, Psychology, and First Philosophy* (Chicago, IL: University of Chicago Press, 2010), 47–51.

he had arrived on the scene "too early" to perform his appointed task – namely, that of apprising the murderers of God of their responsibility for the aftermath of this heinous crime (GS 125).

In revisiting this important teaching, Nietzsche apparently hoped to disabuse his best readers of their confusions surrounding his earlier treatment of the death of God. In particular, he apparently meant to clarify that *no one* is responsible for causing the death of God, even if *everyone* is responsible for addressing the death of God as the defining event of our time. In short, that is, Nietzsche wanted his readers to know that he does not share the Madman's preoccupation with identifying, and belonging among, the murderers of God. *His* preoccupation lies instead with the determination of an adequate practical response to the death of God, a task for which the Madman was, by design, ill suited.

To be sure, much of what the Madman says is recognizably and authentically Nietzschean. That God is dead, that contemporary humankind is largely ignorant of the meaning of the death of God, that the event of the death of God remains "distant" from most human beings, that the future is likely to host upheavals and calamities unknown to human history thus far – all of these insights are corroborated by and throughout Nietzsche's other writings. To this limited extent, then, the Madman may be said to play the role that is typically assigned to him – namely, that of Nietzsche's reliable spokesperson. Indeed, the Madman's teaching overlaps sufficiently with Nietzsche's own teaching that we generally do not object if scholars attribute the Madman's words directly to Nietzsche, as if the two were indistinguishable with respect to the teaching of the death of God.

On at least one important point, however, the Madman most certainly does not speak for Nietzsche. On this point, the Madman speaks for himself, revealing in the process the particular illness that afflicts him.[32] Unlike the Madman, Nietzsche does *not* believe that "we have killed [God] – you and I" (GS 125). He does not believe that God was murdered by anyone, much less by "all of us" together. In fact, Nietzsche regards the death of God not as a *deed* at all – which might imply a *doer* or *agent* – but as an *event*. God died, as it were, of natural causes. That the dead God was murdered, by the likes of *us* no less, is the Madman's own unique contribution to the otherwise Nietzschean story he relates to the crowd assembled in the marketplace. Although the Madman is keen to advertise his self-incrimination as the ultimate expression of responsibility, his admission of guilt is more accurately understood as the ultimate *refusal* of responsibility. By convicting himself of an irremediable offense, he effectively pronounces his nature to be both fixed and fallen. As he patiently awaits the

---

32. See my "Revisiting the Death of God: On the Madness of Nietzsche's Madman," *Acta Kierkegaardiana* 4 (2009). See also Loeb, *The Death of Nietzsche's Zarathustra*, 226–9.

maturation of auditors who are not likely to gain awareness of their complicity in a crime they did not commit, he may feel free to postpone indefinitely any obligation to determine the true meaning of the death of God. Pronouncing himself guilty-but-not-yet-responsible, he refuses to contribute to the formulation of a practical response to the death of God.[33]

As this brief sketch of the Madman indicates, Nietzsche's allegory was actually meant to alert us to the enormous difficulties involved in arriving at a sensible, sober reckoning of what the death of God is likely to mean for us.[34] So long as we remain susceptible to the Madman's peculiar brand of flattery, for example, we are unlikely to conduct an unflinching inventory of the physiological, psychological, and cultural resources at our disposal. The smug, know-it-all atheists among us are woefully unprepared to assess the meaning of the death of God, but so are the (equally smug) self-appointed preachers of atheism. In either case one is waylaid by the unshakable conviction that one already knows what the death of God will and must mean for us: on the one hand, unqualified liberation; and on the other, irremediable guilt. When these two types of atheist meet, moreover, the difficulties involved in confronting the death of God are only amplified and exacerbated.

We are now in a position to see why Nietzsche may have wished in 1886 to distance himself from the Madman's particular interpretation of the death of God.[35] There is simply no good reason to assume, as the Madman does, that humankind is not equal to the task of surviving in a godless cosmos.[36] This is something that we simply do not, and cannot, yet know. Nor is there any good reason to believe, as the Madman does, that contemporary human beings played an active, causal role in the death of God. It might be flattering, and even therapeutic, to think of oneself in such grandiose terms, but this belief is in no way warranted. Indeed, virtually everything that Nietzsche says about his contemporary and late modern readers militates against this possibility. We have witnessed the death of God, and we are uniquely responsible for navigating the aftermath

---

33. I agree with David Owen that "GS 125 presents a parable of (a failure of) enlightenment," and I also agree that Nietzsche "calls for an enlightening of the Enlightenment" (*Nietzsche's Genealogy of Morality* [Stocksfield: Acumen, 2007], 54). The failure here is further attributable, I would add, to the failure of the self-appointed enlightener – namely, the Madman himself.
34. Here I take up the line of interpretation advanced by Pippin, *Nietzsche, Psychology, and First Philosophy*, ch. 3.
35. I am persuaded by Pippin's claim that Nietzsche wishes "to draw critical attention to, rather than express or identify with, the 'melancholic' tone" of the Madman's speech (*ibid.*, 50).
36. As Pippin points out, for example, the Madman's "melancholic" tone is as yet unearned and undermotivated (*ibid.*, 49–51). While the Madman may turn out to be right, taking this as a founding assumption of his pedagogy virtually ensures that he will not muster a creative, viable response to the death of God.

of this event, but we deserve neither the guilt nor the credit that would accrue, supposedly, to the actual murderers of God.

V. AN UNBELIEVABLE BELIEF

Bearing in mind Nietzsche's likely desire to distance himself from the Madman's presentation of the death of God, let us turn now to consider an extended extract from Section 343 of *The Gay Science*:

> *The meaning of our cheerfulness.* – The greatest recent event – that "God is dead," that the belief [*der Glaube*] in the Christian God has become unbelievable [*unglaubwürdig*] – is already beginning to cast its first shadows over Europe. For the few at least, whose eyes – the *suspicion* [*Argwohn*] in whose eyes is strong and subtle enough for this spectacle [*Schauspiel*], some sun seems to have set and some ancient and profound trust has been turned into doubt; to them our old world must appear daily more like evening, more mistrustful, stranger, "older." But in the main one might say: The event itself is too great, too distant, too remote from the multitude's capacity for comprehension even for the tidings of it to be thought of as having *arrived* as yet. Much less may one suppose that many people know as yet *what* this event really means – and how much must collapse now that this faith has been undermined because it was built upon this faith, propped up by it, grown into it; for example, the whole of our European morality. This long plenitude and sequence of breakdown, destruction, ruin, and cataclysm that is now impending – who could guess enough of it today to be compelled to play the teacher and advance proclaimer of this monstrous logic of terror, the prophet of a gloom and an eclipse of the sun whose like has probably never yet occurred on earth?

Here we immediately note the familiarity of address and reliance on the first-person plural that increasingly characterized Nietzsche's post-Zarathustran writings.[37] The dramatic–rhetorical distance that separated him in earlier writings from the Madman and Zarathustra, respectively, is missing from this discussion.

---

37. He addresses them, inclusively, as "philosophers and 'free spirits'" (GS 343). His qualification of this designation – they are not free spirits, but "free spirits" – recalls a similar distinction drawn in GM III: 24, where he apparently reserved the designation of *free spirit* for the Assassins, for whom "everything is permitted." Not everything is permitted for Nietzsche and his "we." In particular, they are not permitted to renounce their bedrock faith in truth.

No figure or character speaks for Nietzsche, and the bustling "marketplace" is nowhere in sight. Treating the event of the death of God as a palpably evident condition of the lives of his intended readers, Nietzsche moves expeditiously to explore the *meaning* of this event. Indeed, the *fact* of God's death is simply noted in passing, as if it were scarcely worth mentioning to this particular audience.

As a result, Nietzsche does not labor in this section under the (self-imposed) constraints that ensured the failure of the pedagogy conducted by the Madman. Unlike him, Nietzsche is not alone in his appreciation for the death of God, which means that he is in a position to share the burden of this insight and its attendant responsibilities. It is for this reason, perhaps, that Nietzsche evinces no desire to convince anyone else – much less the "multitude" – that God is in fact dead. The "multitude" will find out soon enough, and its likely response is of little interest to him. Whereas the Madman chose to speak in the proverbial marketplace, moreover, Nietzsche seeks the relative seclusion afforded him by the nearly deserted shore of a newly open sea. Although he does not say so explicitly, Nietzsche addresses his readers as if he were preparing to "go under," that is, to bequeath his wisdom to those who are worthy to receive it.[38] The seriousness of his enterprise is evidenced, in fact, by his disdain for the idle gossip, incessant commotion, and cheap distractions that are staples of the marketplace.[39] Unwilling to waste his time with the kind of companions collected by the Madman, Nietzsche immediately zeroes in on his target audience, speaking in this passage only to those kindred spirits for whom the death of God *already* matters.

As this passage confirms, moreover, the point of Nietzsche's teaching is far more deeply philosophical than his provocative rhetoric would tend to suggest. Speaking here in his own voice, he calmly reports a crisis of confidence in the basic belief structure that informs and supports the prevailing morality of late modern European culture. Here it may be helpful to note that he does not say that belief in the Christian God has become *impossible* or *inconceivable*. He is perfectly well aware that belief in the Christian God persists, albeit in diminished intensity, and he fully expects that Europeans will continue, perhaps for centuries to come, to rehearse the familiar motions of Christian practice. If only it were the case, he might have mused, that belief in the Christian God were now as unthinkable as, for example, belief in astrology or the geocentric model of the cosmos.

---

38. On the relationship of "going under" to death and the consolidation of one's final audience, see Loeb, *The Death of Nietzsche's Zarathustra*, 98–101.
39. Zarathustra urged his auditors to flee the marketplace (Z I: 12), which is precisely what Nietzsche has done here.

In an important sense, in fact, this is precisely the problem Nietzsche wishes to address: belief in the God of Christianity remains both possible and widespread, even though it is no longer credible as such. This means, among other things, that the belief in God cannot be banished, or its clients disabused, by a simple recitation of the facts or the proposal of an alternative belief. Those who believe in the Christian God are not confused or ignorant in any way that is readily or obviously corrigible. Their confusion, if that is the right word, is fully consistent with the regnant system of core beliefs that has authorized the most recent development and advance of Western civilization. In short, readers hoping to parlay the teaching of the death of God into a declaration of the unconditional victory of atheism are likely to be disappointed.

Although Nietzsche is popularly known as an atheist, this particular designation actually tends to obscure the point of his teaching of the death of God.[40] What he means for this teaching to disclose is that belief in the Christian God can no longer be counted on to play a central role in sustaining the ongoing development of European culture. This is not to suggest that belief in the Christian God is now worthless or absurd, for it is not. Belief in the Christian God has become "unbelievable" inasmuch as it is now one belief among many that we are likely to hold. As such, this belief is important, significant, and *useful* (in the sense preferred by the American pragmatists), but its possession no longer serves as a guarantee of our blessedness, redemption, and salvation. Belief in the Christian God remains possible, but it no longer enjoys a privileged, superlative status, no longer commands our full attention, no longer trumps all other beliefs, and no longer authorizes a quest that might consume and hallow a lifetime. The irony, then, is that Nietzsche actually accounts for the conditions under which belief in the God of Christianity could be, and has been, warranted. Of course, with this account comes his assertion that these conditions no longer obtain.

One now believes in the Christian God as one believes in the stock market, in the value of sensible shoes and a favorable first impression, or in the efficacy of regular brushing to avoid tooth decay. Accordingly, the possession of this belief is now understood to require very little effort or preparation, and there is no longer a general sense that it must be earned and cherished, whether by committing oneself to a life of monkish devotion or by risking oneself in the performance of good works. As noted by Johannes *de silentio*, the pseudonymous narrator of Søren Kierkegaard's *Fear and Trembling*, faith in God is now generally believed to be available throughout European Christendom simply for the asking (or the saying), as if it were offered on deep discount at the clearance sale of ideas.[41]

---

40. See Loeb, *The Death of Nietzsche's Zarathustra*, 226–34; Pippin, *Nietzsche, Psychology, and First Philosophy*, 47–62.

*41. Kierkegaard is discussed in an essay by Alastair Hannay in this volume.

Indeed, the ease with which faith is now obtained is accurately reflected in the (distinctly limited) meaning it provides to those who believe in God.

Still, we might ask, *so what*? Is it not possible that a devalued belief in God will be sufficient to support the advance of an increasingly secular culture? The problem, as Nietzsche sees it, is that our regnant system of core beliefs simply cannot survive the demotion in status and intensity suffered by its centerpiece belief. The very project of European culture is dependent for its viability on the superlative status formerly accorded to the belief in God. The oft-remarked stability of this belief in its current, diminished condition, especially by those who only now find it tolerable, is therefore illusory, and dangerously so. As this system of core beliefs buckles, he warns, the culture it has nourished must wither and perish.

In this respect, Heidegger's interpretation of Nietzsche's teaching has been particularly influential. According to Heidegger, the teaching of the death of God is best understood as a shorthand designation for the end of the tradition of Western metaphysics that began, supposedly, with Plato: "The pronouncement 'God is dead' means: The suprasensory world is without effective power. It bestows no life. Metaphysics, i.e., for Nietzsche Western philosophy understood as Platonism, is at an end."[42] According to Heidegger, that is, this teaching is meant to announce the collapse of the suprasensory canopy of transcendent ideas in which Western philosophy and religion have consistently endeavored to locate the truth. Now that the belief in God is "unbelievable," the world of transcendent ideas, long believed to redeem the imperfect world of immanence, must fall to earth.

Nietzsche's teaching of the death of God thus signals the loss of the security of the future. Today and tomorrow remain secure, which is why so few lives have been changed thus far by the event of the death of God. But "the day after tomorrow" – a figure favored by Nietzsche to capture the unique situation and role in which he and his kindred "free spirits" find themselves (cf. A P) – is no longer secure. What the "death of God" *means*, then, is that the entire system of morality that has guided the advance of European civilization now wobbles on the verge of collapse. Faithful Christians will be disinherited, to be sure, *but so will everyone else*, including the smug, know-it-all atheists who believe themselves to be impervious to the reach of this calamity. In other words, the bleak future foretold by the Madman in his marketplace jeremiad remains a distinct possibility.

---

42. Martin Heidegger, "The Word of Nietzsche: God is Dead," in *The Question Concerning Technology*, William Lovitt (trans.) (New York: Harper & Row, 1977), 61.

VI. THE OPEN SEA

As we have seen, Nietzsche's primary concern in GS 343 is not to announce the death of God, which, he presumes, is already well known to his intended audience, but to explore the *meaning* of this event. Toward this end, he forwards his interpretation of the *cheerfulness* with which he and his unknown companions have received the initial consequences of this event. Thus far, he observes, they have embraced the death of God as if it were a positive event, opening up for them a new menu of possibilities.

Nietzsche endorses the Madman's claim that the death of God is so pivotal, so thoroughly world-historical, that its full meaning is not yet available to most human beings. Only now is this event "beginning to cast its first shadows over Europe." Not belonging to the multitude, Nietzsche and his unnamed companions are not similarly removed from the arrival of this event. Even as they steel themselves for the "long plenitude and sequence of breakdown, destruction, ruin, and cataclysm that is now impending" (*ibid.*), they face the future with a "cheerfulness" that surprises even Nietzsche. This may change, he concedes, especially when the full meaning of the death of God finally arrives. The ultimate consequences of this event, he realizes, may be very different from its initial consequences.

Still, their cheerfulness is a genuinely hopeful sign. Rather than experience the death of God as an occasion for despair, regret, disappointment, resignation, and the gnashing of teeth, Nietzsche and his unnamed companions instead "look forward to the approaching gloom." As he now makes clear, he and his unknown companions are advantageously positioned to "guess at" what the Madman claims to know, but they are not tempted to take on the role of the "prophet" or "advance proclaimer" of gloom (*ibid.*). Unlike the Madman, they have no interest in holding forth in the marketplace or in teaching the intractable multitude. Ingredient to their appreciation of this event, we apparently are meant to understand, is the realization that their own needs for recognition, attention, flattery, and so on must be subordinated to the more general task of preparing humankind to survive the death of God. Unlike the Madman, moreover, they cannot pretend to tremble before the "approaching gloom," for they find themselves "without any worry and fear for [*themselves*]" (*ibid.*). Their cheerfulness may bode well for the future of humankind as a whole, especially if they assume the leading role that Nietzsche envisions for them in the endgame of late modern European culture. If he and his unnamed companions continue to receive the death of God with good cheer – a big *if* – they (or, more likely, their heirs) may survive the impending collapse of Christian morality.

The significance of their cheerfulness thus lies in their decisive victory over the presumptive pessimism of the Madman and all kindred doomsayers. As we have seen, the "initial consequences" of the death of God indicate the *opposite* of what the Madman and his ilk have led us to expect. Rather than descend, as predicted, into chaos, disorientation, self-recrimination, and general disenchantment, Nietzsche and his unknown companions bask in the refulgence of a "new dawn." While the events described in the Madman's jeremiad may yet come to pass,[43] we have no reason at this point to conclude that humankind is ill prepared to negotiate the aftermath of the death of God.

This victory in turn secures a foothold for the scientific project that Nietzsche endorses, wherein he and like-minded truth-seekers will conduct an unflinching inventory of the cultural, physiological, and psychological resources available to late modern human beings. This is the point of Nietzsche's recourse in this passage to the familiar trope of the "voyage of discovery," on which he now bids his unknown companions to join him. Crafting one of the most haunting images to be found in the writings from his post-Zarathustran period, he observes, "At long last the horizon appears free to us again even if it should not be bright… the sea, *our* sea, lies open again; perhaps there has never yet been such an 'open sea'" (GS 343). As the seafaring imagery is meant to confirm, Nietzsche and his unnamed shipmates are focused on the task that lies before them. Although they refuse credit (or blame) for the death of God, they accept full responsibility for the aftermath of this event, wherein, they believe, the future of humankind can and will be determined. United in their desire to *respond* to the death of God – thereby ignoring the petty distractions that waylaid the Madman – they prepare to embark on a perilous voyage of discovery. The horizon may not be bright, as he observes, but an "open sea" now beckons them. Indeed, the simple fact that "the sea, *our sea*, lies open again" is meant to confirm the meaningfulness – indeed, the urgency – of the scientific project endorsed by Nietzsche.[44] They are, as he suggests, "Argonauts of the ideal" (GS 382), intrepid voyagers in search of the undiscovered country that lies somewhere beyond good and evil.

As we have seen, Nietzsche does not hold us responsible for the death of God. He *does* hold us responsible, however, for navigating the aftermath of this event. On this point, in fact, he departs most decisively from the Madman, who convicted himself and his contemporaries of this heinous crime precisely so that they would *not* be held responsible for its aftermath.[45] According to Nietzsche, in fact, we now owe it to ourselves to disown all such irresponsible imputations of responsibility, especially inasmuch as they impede our prepara-

---

43. Walter Kaufmann, in *Nietzsche: Philosopher, Psychologist, Antichrist*, 4th ed. (Princeton, NJ: Princeton University Press, 1974), suggests the link here between Nietzsche and the prophets of the Hebrew Bible, and he mentions Jeremiah by name (*ibid*., 96–9). See also Berkowitz, *Nietzsche: The Ethics of an Immoralist*, 16.
44. See Hatab, *Nietzsche's* On the Genealogy of Morality, 160–63.
45. I am indebted here to Berkowitz, *Nietzsche: The Ethics of an Immoralist*, 16–17.

tions for an honest, truthful appraisal of our capacity for mounting an effective response to the death of God. Nietzsche's emphasis on the *meaning* of the death of God thus reflects his wish to shift the focus of the question of responsibility. What matters now is that we address the death of God in a manner that allows us to pursue a meaningful post-theistic existence.[46] Far from an unhinged champion of irrationality, Nietzsche places his hopes for the future of humankind in the practice of *science*, a practice that he envisions as duly expunged of the "democratic prejudices" and sentimental pieties that continue to lead modern scholars astray.

One science in particular claims Nietzsche's attention: *psychology*.[47] While an inventory of the cultural and political resources available to us is crucial to our survival, Nietzsche attaches a higher priority to the task of conducting an inventory of the resources available *within* us. If we are to mount an effective response to the death of God, we first need to know who (or what) we are. What sorts of creatures have we become over the course of several thousand years of breeding, training, habituation, and acculturation? How closely do we approximate the kind of memorial animal that nature would deem worthy of continued selection for survival? What powers, passions, potentialities, and plasticities do we now possess, including those that remain as yet untested and unpracticed by us? How likely are we to participate in the creation of new values or the creative recycling of old values? In short, Nietzsche's goal is to foster in his best readers an attunement to the death of God that will enable them to respond creatively to the demands and challenges of the new, post-theistic cosmos.

A serious attempt at this inventory will require us, finally, to set aside the pieties and prejudices of folk psychology, even at the risk of sacrificing our fragile sense of self-understanding and our bogus sense of self-esteem. We late moderns can no longer afford the luxury of remaining so thoroughly unknown to, and estranged from, ourselves. While much of what we will discover about ourselves is bound to be unflattering and distasteful, we also may be pleasantly surprised – perhaps even empowered – by what we learn about ourselves.

---

46. I am indebted here to Pippin's observation (*Nietzsche, Psychology, and First Philosophy*, 52–9) that our protracted failure to address "the problem of nihilism" is exacerbated, in Nietzsche's eyes, by our refusal thus far – as exemplified in the Madman's intricate dance of deferral – to pose the problem to ourselves in such a way that would invite, or at any rate make possible, a cogent, affirmation-worthy response to the death of God.
47. Here too I follow Pippin, who persuasively identifies psychology – in particular, an approach to psychology indebted to Montaigne and the French moralists – as central to Nietzsche's philosophical project in general and his critique of modernity in particular. Pippin is especially effective in explaining how and why Nietzsche claims to regard psychology as "the queen of sciences" (*ibid.*, 1–21).

Here, too, the cheerfulness displayed by Nietzsche and his unknown companions is significant, for it emerged unexpectedly from their experience of the initial consequences of the death of God. Nietzsche elsewhere refers to *cheerfulness* as the "reward" that awaits those who, like him, have taken very seriously the vexing problems of morality (GM P7). Far from the *opposite* of seriousness, that is, cheerfulness arises naturally from a serious investigation of those serious matters that other philosophers take too lightly. Who knows what other surprises may await us, what additional "rewards" we unwittingly may have earned?

Nietzsche thus hopes that his best readers will receive the death of God as befits their legacy as "good Europeans" – namely, as *scientists* and *scholars* inspired by the will to truth (GS 357; cf. GM III: 27). He hopes, that is, that they will employ their own will to truth to determine what opportunities and challenges a post-theistic cosmos is likely to present to us. This is why he is so keen in his post-Zarathustran writings to perfect and display what he calls his *gay science*, which blends scholarly seriousness (*Ernst*) with buoyant good cheer (*Heiterkeit*) to ward off fits of premature optimism and unwarranted pessimism. Indeed, he offers his own contribution to the development of a gay science as an example of how he and his unknown companions might avoid the equally nihilistic extremes of pessimism and optimism.

VII. NIETZSCHE'S ENDURING INFLUENCES

Nietzsche believed that it was his fate to be "born posthumously" (A P), and he proved to be prophetic in this belief. Writing in 1899, the Danish critic Georg Brandes observed that Nietzsche's name had "flown round the world" in the decade following his public lectures on Nietzsche in Copenhagen and his publication of the first scholarly treatment of Nietzsche's philosophy.[48] Read widely and claimed by diverse, feuding constituencies scattered across the political spectrum, Nietzsche became a central figure in the stormy culture of *fin de siècle* Europe. His influence today is both extensive and multifarious. Six such influences are especially noteworthy:

(i) Nietzsche's first book, *The Birth of Tragedy*, is now widely read and cited by philosophers, historians, and classicists. It is especially influential for its ingenious pairing of Dionysus and Apollo as the patron deities of Attic tragedy and as the twin impulses responsible for the overflowing health of the tragic culture

---

48. George Brandes, *Friedrich Nietzsche*, A. G. Chater (trans.) (London: William Heinemann, 1914), 59.

of the Greeks. *The Birth of Tragedy* is also influential for its heterodox exposé of Socrates as a hyper-rational enemy of tragedy. In general, Nietzsche is acclaimed not only for his unique appreciation of Attic tragedy, but also for his renewed attention to the relevance of ancient Greek culture for modern scholars, artists, and political leaders.

(ii) The psychological insights that informed *The Birth of Tragedy* were later developed and expanded in support of Nietzsche's groundbreaking research in the field of depth psychology.[49] In sharp contrast to the models of subjectivity delivered, respectively, by the Enlightenment and German idealism, Nietzsche located the core of human agency in the prereflective operation of the unconscious drives and impulses. He thus treated human psychology as a complicated instance of animal psychology, which, as he understood it, is predicated on the instinctive pursuit of optimal conditions under which an organism may amass, expend, and replenish its native stores of strength. Every animal aims above all else to attain a maximal feeling of power, and all of human psychology can be derived from this simple, naturalistic principle of explanation.

Nietzsche's investigation of the unconscious, amoral drives that motivate human behavior exerted a profound influence on the development of both depth psychology and psychoanalysis. Particularly noteworthy in this respect is his influence on the pioneering figures in these fields of research, including Sigmund Freud (1856–1939),[50] Alfred Adler (1870–1937), and Carl Jung (1875–1961). These figures in turn propagated Nietzsche's influence to a host of scholars who were similarly concerned to explore the broader sociological implications of Nietzsche's psychological insights. Nietzsche's influence, and especially his controversial diagnosis of the sickliness of late modern European culture, is discernible in the work of Herbert Marcuse (1898–1979), Eric Fromm (1900–1980),[51] Rollo May (1904–1994), and Norman O. Brown (1913–2002).

(iii) Nietzsche is also influential for his attention to the personal, rhetorical, and performative dimensions of philosophy. Well known for his experiments with multiple styles, tropes, voices, personae, and forms of address, he possessed a keen critical eye for the subjective inflections of philosophical discourse. Believing every great philosophy to essay the "personal confession of its author and a kind of involuntary and unconscious memoir" (BGE 6), he sought to

---

49. The definitive study of this topic is Graham Parkes, *Composing the Soul: Reaches of Nietzsche's Psychology* (Chicago, IL: University of Chicago Press, 1994), esp. chs VII–IX.
*50. For a discussion of Freud, and his relationship to the continental philosophical tradition, see the essay by Adrian Johnston in *The History of Continental Philosophy: Volume 3*.
*51. Marcuse, Fromm, and others associated with the first generation of the Frankfurt School are discussed in an essay by John Abromeit in *The History of Continental Philosophy: Volume 5*.

isolate the personal "prejudices" lurking behind seemingly impersonal and ostensibly objective philosophical pronouncements.

Nietzsche is widely recognized for his seminal contributions to the "hermeneutics of suspicion" that spurred the development of literary, aesthetic, political, and cultural criticism in the twentieth century. Generally acknowledged, along with Marx and Freud, as a "master of suspicion,"[52] Nietzsche has inspired twentieth- and twenty-first-century readers to challenge orthodoxies across a broad range of human endeavors, including philosophy, science, history, literature, religion, art, psychoanalysis, and politics. His influence in this respect is evident in the writings of postmodern philosophers and critics such as Maurice Blanchot (1907–2003), Paul de Man (1919–83), Gilles Deleuze (1925–95), Michel Foucault (1926–84), Jacques Derrida (1930–2004), and Sarah Kofman (1934–94).[53]

Nietzsche's attention to the personal and rhetorical dimensions of philosophy is furthermore consistent with the larger, expressivist sympathies that inform his own philosophizing. Praising as exemplary those rare individuals who assert themselves in defiance of prevailing norms and conventions, he regularly urged his readers toward lives of greater risk, urgency, passion, and authenticity. His influence on the philosophical and literary movements associated with *existentialism* is well known,[54] and this influence largely derives from his general affirmation of unfettered acts of self-assertion – even, it should be added, at the expense of established customs and morality. His influence on the development of existentialism is evident in the writings of Martin Buber (1878–1965), Paul Tillich (1886–1965),[55] Heidegger (1889–1976), André Malraux (1901–1976), John-Paul Sartre (1905–80),[56] and Albert Camus (1913–60).

(iv) Nietzsche remains influential for his sweeping critique of European modernity. Flatly rejecting the familiar modernist narratives of growth, progress,

---

52. Paul Ricoeur, *Freud and Philosophy: An Essay on Interpretation*, Denis Savage (trans.) (New Haven, CT: Yale University Press, 1970), 32–6.
53. Many of these lines of influence are productively explored by Alan D. Schrift in *Nietzsche's French Legacy: A Genealogy of Poststructuralism* (New York: Routledge, 1995); [*] see also his essay on "French Nietzscheanism" in *The History of Continental Philosophy: Volume 6*. Deleuze, Foucault, and Derrida are each the subject of an essay in *The History of Continental Philosophy: Volume 6*.
*54. For a discussion of existentialism, see the essay by S. K. Keltner and Samuel J. Julian in *The History of Continental Philosophy: Volume 5*.
*55. For a discussion of Buber and Tillich, see the essay by Andreas Grossman in *The History of Continental Philosophy: Volume 4*.
*56. Sartre is discussed in an essay by William L. McBride in *The History of Continental Philosophy: Volume 4*, as well as in the essay by S. K. Keltner and Samuel J. Julian in *The History of Continental Philosophy: Volume 5*.

amelioration, and maturation, he diagnosed European modernity as irreversibly decadent. He exposed its defining institutions and projects as unmitigated failures, and he disclosed with considerable prescience its growing thirst for blood. He also lamented the disintegration of what he regarded as a distinctly European culture and the concomitant rise of squabbling nation-states bent on imperial expansion. Even a full century after his death, Nietzsche remains one of the most formidable critics of the signature projects of modernity itself. His criticisms were so penetrating, and his diagnoses so astute, that no serious champion of modern ideals can afford to ignore them. The influence of his diagnosis of European modernity is most evident in the work of critics such as Georg Brandes (1842–1927), Oswald Spengler (1880–1936), Sigmund Freud, Leo Strauss (1899–1973), Allan Bloom (1930–92), and Francis Fukuyama (1952–).

The larger sociological implications of Nietzsche's diagnosis of late modern European culture influenced a number of prominent writers of the twentieth century. Authors as diverse as George Bernard Shaw (1856–1950), D. H. Lawrence (1885–1930), Hermann Hesse (1877–1962), Thomas Mann (1875–1955), André Gide (1869–1951), Franz Kafka (1883–1924), and Nikos Kazantzakis (1883–1957) were inspired by Nietzsche to analyze the discontents of the modern world – including repression, guilt, despair, alienation, and anxiety – and to explore the possibility that certain individuals – dare we call them *Übermenschen*? – might succeed in escaping (or deflecting) the stifling demands of civilization.

(v) Nietzsche's proffered contribution to a "genealogy of morality" has been enormously influential on philosophers, anthropologists, historians, and other scholars who are keen to purge their studies of history – in particular, the history of morality – of unwanted assumptions, unwarranted presuppositions, and undetected sympathies. Scholars as diverse as Deleuze and Alasdair MacIntyre have acknowledged their debts to Nietzsche's "genealogical" approach to the history of morality.

Most notably, Nietzsche's contribution to a "genealogy of morality" was taken up and adapted by the French philosopher, historian, and social critic Michel Foucault.[57] Early in his career, Foucault developed an *archaeological* approach to history that allowed him to identify periods of epistemic convergence across various related sciences and disciplines. Within any such period of epistemic convergence, he discovered, the discursive practices of science not only had a common structure but also expressed significant agreement on the general conditions and criteria of truth, knowledge, and certainty. Later in his career,

---

*57. Foucault is discussed in an essay by Timothy O'Leary in *The History of Continental Philosophy: Volume 6*.

Foucault developed a *genealogical* approach to history that enabled him to investigate the intricate power relations that inform discursive practices. As a genealogist, he tracked the shifting relationships between power and knowledge within particular discursive practices, and he charted the resulting fluctuations in the exclusionary power of these practices. He was especially concerned to conduct genealogical investigations of those discursive practices that were responsible for enforcing the institutionalized definitions of *madness, criminality*, and *sexual deviancy*.

(vi) Finally, as we have seen, Nietzsche remains influential for his insight into, and announcement of, the *death of God*. The enduring influence of this insight is apparent throughout the history of twentieth-century literature, drama, music, philosophy, and religion. The influence of this teaching is perhaps most evident in the emergence of negative theology, religious existentialism, and other sustained efforts to rethink the nature and place of religion in the culture of twentieth- and twenty-first-century Europe. It is on the strength of this insight, moreover, that Nietzsche made his greatest contributions to the development and subsequent ramifications of European philosophy.[58]

MAJOR WORKS

Werke: Kritische Gesamtausgabe. Edited by Giorgio Colli and Mazzino Montinari. Berlin: de Gruyter, 1967– .

Sämtliche Werke: Kritische Studienausgabe in 15 Bänden. Edited by Giorgio Colli and Mazzino Montinari. Berlin: dtv/de Gruyter, 1980. Published in English as *The Complete Works of Friedrich Nietzsche*, edited by Ernst Behler and Bernd Magnus (1995–99), and Alan D. Schrift *et al.* (2005–). Stanford, CA: Stanford University Press, 1995– .

Sämtliche Briefe: Kritische Studienausgabe in 8 Bänden. Edited by Giorgio Colli and Mazzino Montinari. Berlin: dtv/de Gruyter, 1986.

Die Geburt der Tragödie (1872; exp. ed. 1886). Published in English as *The Birth of Tragedy*, (i) in *The Birth of Tragedy and The Case of Wagner*, translated by Walter Kaufmann. New York: Random House/Vintage, 1967; and (ii) translated by Ronald Speirs. Cambridge: Cambridge University Press, 1999.

Unzeitgemäße Betrachtungen I–IV (1873–76). Published in English as: (i) *Untimely Meditations*, translated by R. J. Hollingdale. Cambridge: Cambridge University Press, 1983; and (ii) *Unfashionable Observations*, translated by Richard T. Gray. Stanford, CA: Stanford University Press, 1995.

---

58. My thanks to Alan D. Schrift for his valuable comments on earlier drafts of this chapter. This chapter occasionally draws on material that originally appeared elsewhere, including my *Reader's Guide to Nietzsche's* On the Genealogy of Morals, and several entries I contributed to *The Edinburgh Dictionary of Continental Philosophy*, John Protevi (ed.) (Edinburgh: Edinburgh University Press, 2005).

I. *David Strauss der Bekenner und der Schriftsteller* (1873). Published in English as (i) *David Strauss, the Confessor & the Writer*, in *Untimely Meditations*, translated by Hollingdale; and (ii) *David Strauss the Confessor and the Writer*, in *Unfashionable Observations*, translated by Gray.

II. *Vom Nutzen und Nachtheil der Historie für das Leben* (1874). Published in English as (i) *On the Uses and Disadvantages of History for Life*, in *Untimely Meditations*, translated by Hollingdale; and (ii) *On the Utility and Liability of History for Life*, in *Unfashionable Observations*, translated by Gray.

III. *Schopenhauer als Erzieher* (1874). Published in English as *Schopenhauer as Educator*, in *Untimely Meditations*, translated by Hollingdale, and in *Unfashionable Observations*, translated by Gray.

IV. *Richard Wagner in Bayreuth* (1876). Published in English as *Richard Wagner in Bayreuth*, in *Untimely Meditations*, translated by Hollingdale, and in *Unfashionable Observations*, translated by Gray.

Menschliches, Allzumenschliches I und II (1878–80; new ed. 1886). Published in English as (i) *Human, All Too Human*, translated by R. J. Hollingdale. Cambridge: Cambridge University Press, 1986; and (ii) *Human, All Too Human (I)*, translated by Gary Handwerk. Stanford, CA: Stanford University Press, 1997, and *Human, All Too Human (II)*, translated by Gary Handwerk. Stanford, CA: Stanford University Press, forthcoming.

Morgenröte (1881; new ed. 1887). Published in English: (i) as *Daybreak*, translated by R. J. Hollingdale. Cambridge: Cambridge University Press, 1982; and (ii) as *Dawn*, translated by Brittain Smith. Stanford, CA: Stanford University Press, forthcoming.

Die fröhliche Wissenschaft (1882, exp. ed. 1887). Published in English as *The Gay Science*. (i) Translated by Walter Kaufmann. New York: Random House/Vintage, 1974. (ii) Translated by Josefine Nauckhoff. Cambridge: Cambridge University Press, 2001.

Also sprach Zarathustra (1883–85). Published in English as *Thus Spoke Zarathustra*. (i) Translated by Walter Kaufmann in *The Portable Nietzsche*, edited and translated by Walter Kaufmann. New York: Viking Penguin, 1954. (ii) Translated by Graham Parkes. Oxford: Oxford University Press, 2005. (iii) Translated by Adrian Del Caro. Cambridge: Cambridge University Press, 2006.

Jenseits von Gut und Böse (1886). Published in English as *Beyond Good and Evil*. (i) Translated by Walter Kaufmann. New York: Random House/Vintage, 1966. (ii) Translated by Judith Norman. Cambridge: Cambridge University Press, 2002.

Zur Genealogie der Moral (1887). Published in English as (i) *On the Genealogy of Morals*, translated by Walter Kaufmann and R. J. Hollingdale, in *On the Genealogy of Morals and Ecce Homo*, edited by Walter Kaufmann. New York: Random House/Vintage, 1967. (ii) *On the Genealogy of Morality*, translated by Maudemarie Clark and Alan J. Swensen. Indianapolis, IN: Hackett, 1998. (iii) *On the Genealogy of Morals*, translated by Douglas Smith. Oxford: Oxford University Press, 1996. (iv) *On the Genealogy of Morality*, translated by Carol Diethe. Cambridge: Cambridge University Press, 2006.

Der Fall Wagner (1888). Published in English as *The Case of Wagner*. (i) Translated by Walter Kaufmann, in *The Birth of Tragedy and The Case of Wagner*, translated by Walter Kaufmann. New York: Random House/Vintage, 1967. (ii) Translated by Judith Norman, in *The Anti-Christ, Ecce Homo, Twilight of the Idols, and Other Writings*, edited by Aaron Ridley and Judith Norman. Cambridge: Cambridge University Press, 2005.

Götzen-Dämmerung (1888; pub. 1889). Published in English as *Twilight of the Idols*. (i) Translated by Walter Kaufmann, in *The Portable Nietzsche*, edited and translated by Walter Kaufmann. New York: Viking Penguin, 1954. (ii) Translated by R. J. Hollingdale, in *Twilight of Idols and Anti-Christ*. New York: Penguin, 1968. (iii) Translated by Duncan Large. Oxford: Oxford University Press, 1998. (iv) Translated by Judith Norman, in *The Anti-Christ, Ecce Homo, Twilight of the*

Idols, and Other Writings, edited by Aaron Ridley and Judith Norman. Cambridge: Cambridge University Press, 2005.

Der Antichrist (1888; pub. 1894). Published in English as *The Antichrist*. (i) Translated by Walter Kaufmann, in *The Portable Nietzsche*, edited and translated by Walter Kaufmann. New York: Viking Penguin, 1954. (ii) Translated by R. J. Hollingdale, in *Twilight of Idols and Anti-Christ*. New York: Penguin, 1990. (iii) Translated by Judith Norman, in *The Anti-Christ, Ecce Homo, Twilight of the Idols, and Other Writings*, edited by Aaron Ridley and Judith Norman. Cambridge: Cambridge University Press, 2005.

Ecce Homo (1888; pub. 1908). Published in English as *Ecce Homo*. (i) Translated by Walter Kaufmann, in *On the Genealogy of Morals and Ecce Homo*, edited by Walter Kaufmann. New York: Random House/Vintage, 1967. (ii) Translated by Judith Norman, in *The Anti-Christ, Ecce Homo, Twilight of the Idols, and Other Writings*, edited by Aaron Ridley and Judith Norman. Cambridge: Cambridge University Press, 2005. (iii) Translated by Duncan Large. Oxford: Oxford University Press, 2007.

Nietzsche contra Wagner (1888; pub. 1889). Published in English as *Nietzsche contra Wagner*. (i) Translated by Walter Kaufmann, in *The Portable Nietzsche*, edited and translated by Walter Kaufmann. New York: Viking Penguin, 1954. (ii) Translated by Judith Norman, in *The Anti-Christ, Ecce Homo, Twilight of the Idols, and Other Writings*, edited by Aaron Ridley and Judith Norman. Cambridge: Cambridge University Press, 2005.

Die Wille zur Macht. Edited by Elisabeth Förster-Nietzsche *et al.* (1901; exp. ed. 1904, 1906). Published in English as *The Will to Power*, edited by Walter Kaufmann, translated by Walter Kaufmann and R. J. Hollingdale. New York: Random House/Vintage, 1968.

6

HERMENEUTICS: SCHLEIERMACHER AND DILTHEY

Eric Sean Nelson

I. INTRODUCTION

The thought of the German philosophers Friedrich Schleiermacher[1] and Wilhelm Dilthey[2] is often assessed and criticized according to the interests and standards of twentieth-century philosophical hermeneutics. This common yet increasingly questioned account is misleading insofar as these two authors have divergent research agendas, approaches, and contexts, including the notion of hermeneutics itself, from each other as well as from later hermeneutical philosophy.[3]

---

1. Friedrich Daniel Ernst Schleiermacher (November 21, 1768–February 12, 1834; born in Breslau, Silesia; died in Berlin) was educated at Moravian Brethren institutions in Niesky and Barby (1783–87), and the University of Halle (1787–90). His influences included Fichte, Herder, Kant, Plato, Schelling, Friedrich Schlegel, and Spinoza, and he held academic appointments at the University of Halle (1804–1807) and University of Berlin (1810–34).
2. Wilhelm Dilthey (November 19, 1833–October 1, 1911; born in Biebrich am Rhein, Hesse; died in Siusi allo Sciliar, Italy [Seis am Schlern, South Tyrol]) was educated at the Universities of Heidelberg and Berlin (DPhil., 1864). His influences included A. Boeckh, K. Fischer, Hegel, Kant, John Stuart Mill, L. v. Ranke, Schleiermacher, and F. Trendelenburg, and he held appointments at the Universities of Basel (1866–68), Kiel (1868–71), Breslau (1871–82), and Berlin (1882–1905).
3. On the inadequacy of Gadamer's approach to Schleiermacher, see Andrew Bowie, *Aesthetics and Subjectivity: From Kant to Nietzsche*, 2nd ed. (Manchester: Manchester University Press, 2003), 183–219; "The Philosophical Significance of Schleiermacher's Hermeneutics," in *Cambridge Companion to Friedrich Schleiermacher*, Jacqueline Mariña (ed.) (Cambridge: Cambridge University Press, 2005), 75; and my "Schleiermacher on Language, Religious Feeling, and the Ineffable," *Epoché* 8(2) (Spring 2004). On the problematic character of Gadamer's reading of Dilthey, see my "Disturbing Truth: Art, Finitude, and the Human Sciences in Dilthey," *theory@buffalo* 11 (2006): 121–42. Bowie argues that these distortions

Schleiermacher and Dilthey are frequently mentioned together as representatives of nineteenth-century hermeneutics and hermeneutical philosophy. This portrayal is problematic given the historical breaks and philosophical differences between their positions, and the more limited sense of the term "hermeneutics" in their writings. Despite Schleiermacher's formative influence on Dilthey, and the centrality of Dilthey's interpretation of Schleiermacher to his subsequent reception, there are crucial differences between them. Schleiermacher's thought occurs within the context of the modern appropriation and transformation of traditional metaphysics and Protestant theology. His basic point of departure is the felt intuition of the infinite in his early Romantic works and the feeling of absolute dependence on God in his mature academic works. The latter claim is not only a religious and theological one. The prereflective feeling of God replaces the Cartesian *cogito* in grounding both knowledge and metaphysics in his *Dialectic*, and is the only locus of certainty in the face of skepticism.[4]

In contrast with Schleiermacher, whose thought he helped to revive and reinterpret, philosophy took an epistemic, social-historical, and social-scientific turn in Dilthey. Instead of asserting the unity of the world and the sciences, of being and knowledge, Dilthey developed an epistemic pluralism or nonreductive empiricism in relation to knowledge, and moderate skepticism in response to metaphysics.[5] Without the inherent unity of nature and spirit as an object of knowledge, Dilthey differentiated the natural and human sciences according to their contexts, methodologies, and objects. Even if all sciences involve previous processes of interpretation and meaning-formation, insofar as knowing is never free of presuppositions and a larger human context of significance, the human sciences are concerned with self-experiencing and self-interpreting individuals and groups for whom the first-person perspective of relations of meaning is – at least in part – performatively constitutive of practices or how they act and do not act.[6]

The distance between these two authors can be further seen in their attitude toward metaphysics and ancient Greek philosophy. Schleiermacher belonged

---

begin with Dilthey and become canonical in Gadamer in a note to Friedrich Schleiermacher, *Hermeneutics and Criticism*, Andrew Bowie (ed.) (Cambridge: Cambridge University Press, 1998), xxxiv–xxxv. Hereafter cited as HC followed by the page number.

4. Gunter Scholtz, *Ethik und Hermeneutik* (Frankfurt: Suhrkamp, 1995), 239.
5. On Dilthey's empiricism without doctrinal empiricism, or "*Empirie, nicht Empirismus*," see my "Empiricism, Facticity, and the Immanence of Life in Dilthey," *Pli: Warwick Journal of Philosophy* 18 (Spring 2007): 108–28.
6. Rudolf A. Makkreel notes how interpretation in the human sciences involves reinterpretation of previous interpreted realities in *Dilthey: Philosopher of the Human Studies*, 2nd ed. (Princeton: Princeton University Press, 1992), 152; on the priority of practice in Dilthey, see my "Interpreting Practice: Epistemology, Hermeneutics, and Historical Life in Dilthey," *Idealistic Studies* 38(1–2) (2008).

to the generation of early German Romanticism that was more empirically and realistically oriented than German idealism. He remained committed to a revised form of Platonic metaphysics, influenced by his engagement with early modern and German idealist philosophy, and translated the works of Plato in an influential German edition still in use today.[7] Dilthey, however, interpreted modernity – prefigured in thinkers such as Augustine, who opened up the first-person perspective of already meaningful individual lived-experience (*Erlebnis*) in contrast to impersonal objective structures of classical ontology – as an irrevocable break with premodern forms of thought, which included Schleiermacher's dialectics.[8] While dialectic was the central philosophical discipline for Schleiermacher, to which hermeneutics was subordinate, epistemic logic in the context of the fullness of social-historical life played the primary role for Dilthey.[9] In conjunction with his organic and vitalist yet still causal conception of the universe, Schleiermacher was a post-Kantian thinker of religious transcendence and of the ethical ideal of the highest good that informs and orients ordinary life.[10] Dilthey was a philosopher of experiential immanence, as he reformulated the Kantian project as a "critique of historical reason" in his early work *Introduction to the Human Sciences*. There Dilthey describes a critique of historical reason as "a critique of the capacity of man to know himself and the society and history which he has produced."[11] Schleiermacher's faith and intuition of the divine lose their priority as they become one way of expressing lived-experience, mood, and worldview, and infinity is transformed into an immanent yet self-interrupting characteristic of life itself that does not necessarily entail a transcendent God.[12]

---

7. On Schleiermacher's revised Platonism and his translations of Plato, see Julia A. Lamm, "The Art of Interpreting Plato," in *Cambridge Companion to Friedrich Schleiermacher*, Mariña (ed.), 91–108.
8. Scholtz, *Ethik und Hermeneutik*, 243.
9. Ibid., 236–7.
10. God is transcendent and the world is an immanent organic whole for Schleiermacher, who transformed Spinoza's metaphysics in an individualistic and vitalistic direction oriented by a transcendent God and the highest good as the realization of individual personality. Compare the discussion of these issues in Frederick C. Beiser, "Schleiermacher's Ethics," in *Cambridge Companion to Friedrich Schleiermacher*, Mariña (ed.), esp. 61, 65, 67, 69.
11. Wilhelm Dilthey, *Introduction to the Human Sciences*, Rudolf A. Makkreel and Frithjof Rodi (eds), Michael Neville (trans.) (Princeton, NJ: Princeton University Press, 1989), 165. Hereafter cited as IHS followed by the page number. Michael Ermarth pursues this central thread in Dilthey's works in *Wilhelm Dilthey: The Critique of Historical Reason* (Chicago, IL: University of Chicago Press, 1978).
12. On the argument that Dilthey secularized the feeling of God into the feeling of life, moving from the feeling of faith to a more general "reflexive awareness" (*Innewerden*), see Scholtz, *Ethik und Hermeneutik*, 240, 250–51.

II. SCHLEIERMACHER: LANGUAGE, PSYCHOLOGY, AND INTERPRETATION

Friedrich Schleiermacher led an intellectually and publicly active life as a Romantic literary figure, reformed pastor, theologian, university teacher and administrator, public intellectual, and political reformer.[13] The son of a reformed clergyman, he was educated by the Moravian Brethren, who advocated a strict devotional Pietism, and subsequently at the more liberal University of Halle where he continued his studies of early modern and Enlightenment era philosophy and the classics. He is well known for his youthful associations with German Romantic literary circles[14] and the celebration of religion as an intuition and feeling of the universe and the infinite in early writings such as *On Religion: Speeches to its Cultured Despisers*, and he is also noted for being the primary proponent of liberal Protestant theology in his mature theological works such as *The Christian Faith*.

Schleiermacher's writings concerning hermeneutics are all based on lecture courses and lectures, and consequently have a fragmentary character. They continue and transform the early modern Protestant and Enlightenment trends in hermeneutics from the eighteenth century, which are primarily concerned with the interpretation of biblical and classical texts as well as related to rhetoric and Aristotelian logic.[15]

Hermeneutics is a doctrine of art (*Kunstlehre*) oriented according to the idea of understanding given the universality of misunderstanding, which is caused by hastiness or prejudice (HC 23). For Schleiermacher, non- or misunderstanding is the ordinary condition, and understanding needs to be pursued in order to be achieved.[16] That is, where the laxer practice of hermeneutics assumes that understanding is automatic and misunderstanding to be avoided, "[t]he [stricter] practice assumes that misunderstanding results as a matter of course and that understanding must be desired and sought at every point" (HC 21–2). As in Kant, the practice of art is not the doctrine of science, nor does art deductively or mechanically apply rules and method.[17] Art can never be solely based on

---

13. This section refines my interpretation in "Schleiermacher on Language," 297–312.
*14. For a discussion of German Romanticism, see the essay by Daniel Dahlstrom in *The History of Continental Philosophy: Volume 1*.
15. Matthias Jung, *Hermeneutik zur Einführung* (Hamburg: Junias, 2001), 46.
16. *Ibid.*, 59.
17. See Hans-Georg Gadamer, *Truth and Method*, Joel Weinsheimer and Donald Marshall (trans.), 2nd ed. (New York: Continuum, 1989), xxiii. Compare my discussion of the distinction between art and science in Kant and Schleiermacher in "Moral and Political Prudence in Kant," *International Philosophical Quarterly* 44(3) (September 2004), 307, and "Schleiermacher on Language," 299–300.

rules insofar as this involves the infinite regress of always needing another rule to apply a rule. Art requires judgment or a sense of appropriate application that is cultivated. Kant clarifies this distinction in the *Critique of Judgment*: whereas science demands determinate judgment, which subsumes a particular under a concept, art calls for reflective judgment, which articulates the general from the particular – that is, without a pregiven rule.[18]

Art is not the imposition of science on tradition or system on the life-world for Schleiermacher. Art originates in ordinary experience itself. It is always already at work in ordinary understanding to the degree that even the child is engaged in the art of hermeneutics in language acquisition.[19] Because there is no rule for how to apply a rule, art is a practice of a finite sensuous being. Method alone is inadequate for Schleiermacher and Dilthey, since it is the cultivation of a sense already at work in everyday communication and as such it requires lived-experience.[20] Although the goal of truth or correctness is an important one in Schleiermacher's hermeneutics, as Dilthey noted, art and imagination characterize all knowing (HSH 695). Cognitive representation is indispensable to the work of the sciences. Yet it is not itself primary since it is always based on prior feeling. Schleiermacher is consequently already engaged in a critique of a purely representational model of knowledge. Schleiermacher insisted on the priority of feeling in understanding the human agent and, as we shall see, the receptivity and responsiveness of the imagination in interpreting others through their expressions, which is the medium of understanding and interpretation.[21] To this extent, one strength of "Romantic" hermeneutics – in contrast with its impersonalist opponents – is its recognition of the role of feeling, desire, and affectivity as part of linguistic interaction, interpretation, and

---

18. For an examination of this distinction and its implications see Rudolf A. Makkreel, *Imagination and Interpretation in Kant* (Chicago, IL: University of Chicago Press, 1990).
19. Friedrich Schleiermacher, *Hermeneutics: The Handwritten Manuscripts*, James Duke and Jack Forstman (trans.), 2nd ed. (Atlanta, NJ: Scholars Press, 1997), 49, 52; hereafter cited as HHM followed by the page number. Compare Bowie's discussion of interpretation and language inquisition in *Aesthetics and Subjectivity*, 207–8.
20. Wilhelm Dilthey, "Das hermeneutische System Schleiermachers in der Auseinandersetzung mit der älteren protestantischen Hermeneutik," in *Gesammelte Schriften* (Göttingen: Vandenhoeck & Ruprecht, 1985), vol. 14, 605; published in English as "Schleiermacher's Hermeneutical System in Relation to Early Protestant Hermeneutics," in *Selected Works*, vol. 4, *Hermeneutics and the Study of History*, Rudolf A. Makkreel and Frithjof Rodi (eds), Theodore Nordenhaug (trans.) (Princeton, NJ: Princeton University Press, 1996); hereafter cited as HSH followed by the page number in the German *Gesammelte Schriften*, which appears in the margins of the English translations in Dilthey's *Selected Works*. Dilthey critiques rule-based hermeneutics in HSH 710.
21. Jung, *Hermeneutik zur Einführung*, 64.

individuation.[22] Schleiermacher and Dilthey do not segregate the subjective, psychological, or emotional dimensions of interpretation from their linguistic and social-historical contexts.[23]

Hermeneutics, according to Schleiermacher, is the art of understanding. Understanding is an art to the extent that it is neither fully reducible to nor independent of the application of rules (HC 6). Hermeneutics is an art, concerned with language, through which we interpret texts and indirectly understand others. This art has three levels operating between the minimum degree of reflection in ordinary common discourse and the maximum degree of interpretative and reflective effort in approaching classical or original texts (HC 13): that is, (i) the everyday prereflective use and interpretation of language; (ii) the skilled interpretation of language; and (iii) the reflective interpretation of language. Hermeneutics, which does not constitute the whole of philosophical, theological, and scientific inquiry for Schleiermacher, is concerned with understanding only as it occurs through language: "Language is the only presupposition in hermeneutics, and everything that is to be found, including the other objective and subjective presuppositions, must be discovered in language" (HHM 50).

Dilthey unfolded in his work *Schleiermacher's Hermeneutical System in Relation to Earlier Protestant Hermeneutics* of 1860 how hermeneutics is essentially concerned with language. Further, language and language acquisition have, for Dilthey, an interpretive character from the beginning (HSH 745). Accordingly, hermeneutics shares the structure – both the limits and possibilities – of language. If language is always already related to what cannot be said, then the incommunicable does not occur only as a limit for hermeneutical understanding but as a condition that cannot be sublimated and thus positively defines the tasks of interpretation. The object of understanding demands that it be understood immanently from out of itself and accordingly that the one addressed be receptive to the claim being made.[24]

---

22. In *Hermeneutics and Criticism* (HC 93), Schleiermacher associated divination – as receptivity to others and their individuality – with the feminine, and the comparative approach – emphasizing universality – with the masculine. Philosophers and men tend to one-sidedly stress their own thoughts in approaching others (HC 6, 93, 135). Julie Ellson analyzed the "hermeneutics of desire" and its gendered character in Schleiermacher, who often ethically and aesthetically privileges the feminine, and in Romanticism in *Delicate Subjects: Romanticism, Gender, and the Ethics of Understanding* (Ithaca, NY: Cornell University Press, 1990).
23. Bowie demonstrates how divination in Schleiermacher is not the emotional-psychological felt projection of *Einfühlung*, yet misses the expressive-linguistic and social-historical character of interpretation in Dilthey in *Aesthetics and Subjectivity*, 207.
24. Friedrich Schleiermacher, *Über die Religion* (Stuttgart: Reclam, 1969), 28; published in English as *On Religion: Speeches to Its Cultured Despisers*, Richard Crouter (ed. and trans.) (Cambridge: Cambridge University Press, 1988). This connection between responsiveness and immanence is further developed by Dilthey – for example, in the thesis that life needs to be

The further claim that hermeneutics is the art of understanding "the utterance first just as well and then better than its author" seeks to bring to consciousness what remained unconscious in the author (HC 23). This task is driven by the absence of any immediate knowledge of what is within an author (*ibid.*), and indicates, as Dilthey noted, the need in interpretation to consider the unthought of an author (HSH 707). Articulating the unconscious in consciousness follows the hermeneutical model of receptively determining the indeterminate through interpretation (HC 33, 49), and of bringing to concepts the sensual and preconceptual sources of language (HC 34–8). For Schleiermacher, and to the chagrin of Karl Barth and neo-orthodoxy, even the divine word of the Bible is available only through interpretation (HC 41). Inspiration and enthusiasm cannot eliminate the need for contextualization and mediation in order to articulate God's word (HC 82). Owing to the potential infinity of interpretation, as both past origins and future possibilities and transformations are not directly given, and "because it is an infinity of past and future that we wish to see in the moment of the utterance," hermeneutics is an infinite or "endless task" that no synthesis or fusion can overcome (HC 23, 31).

In addition to the interpretation of language that Schleiermacher called "grammatical," there is also "psychological interpretation" involving receptiveness to the traces of the singularity of the other as they are indicated in communication. As Dilthey argued in his reading of Schleiermacher, the individual and the singular would be lost in a discourse that denies the possibility of psychological interpretation (HSH 717–18). Individuals do not only instantiate a pregiven language, and even as the individual is placed within a general location and context, it is irreducible to it (HC 279). Language is used and created through the language-forming power and style of individuals, such that it is inadequate to consider language purely in propositional or structuralist terms. The emphasis on psychological understanding is subsequently not so much the correct representational reproduction by the interpreter of some "mental content" of the author. The "psychological" concerns the individual side of interpretation just as "grammatical" concerns the structural and more universal side of linguistic mediation as a relational system (HC 8–9, 67). Although psychological interpretation has priority from the perspective of the individual and grammatical from the perspective of language as a systematic impersonal whole, both sides are equal and necessary for interpretation (HC 10). Both varieties of interpretation, which are ends of a continuum rather than contraries, are needed, as propositions can be interpreted in relation to individual life-acts, linguistic systems, and the provisionally and indeterminately given whole of a life that is

---

articulated from out of itself – and by Heidegger (*circa* 1920) in describing the hermeneutics of facticity as the self-articulation of life in its enactment.

the intersection of both moments.[25] They are a spectrum and yet each side has to be grasped in its own terms as one transitions between the grammatical and the psychological without either one being complete or sufficient in itself and without there being determinate rules for how these transitions can be accomplished (HC 10–11).

Schleiermacher's approach is no mere "external reconstruction" aiming at correctness, as Gadamer contended.[26] It is oriented toward the question of truth through receptivity to what addresses and claims us, as hermeneutics is constructive in order to envision an organic whole (HC 65). Schleiermacher also noted the integrating and mediating character of language. Although he emphasized the unifying and conforming power of language and tradition, Schleiermacher showed the importance of linguistic transformation such as in the artist of language who each time individualizes language anew (HHM 49), and in the language-forming power of the new and the individual (HC 12, 86).

Schleiermacher's approach to language emphasized the differences that occur in relation to the identity of language; that is, with that which differentiates languages and, further, with that which resists and withdraws from linguistic mediation. Hermeneutics concerns language, which is the only presupposition and defines the scope of hermeneutics (HHM 50). Yet language is not a system that can close itself to what is other than language in a pure immanence of linguistic integration or mediation. Despite the limits that language and its interpretation impose, such limits cannot eliminate the infinity of sense, such as the infinite significance of a book such as the Bible, or the relation of the finite to the infinite (HHM 53, 55). The incommunicable confronts language on the side of both the whole and the individual.

Jean Grondin has emphasized the quest for the whole understood as completeness in Romantic hermeneutics.[27] Yet the whole is not so much a complete system as it is an infinity of intercrossing relations that are ultimately referred to the nonrelational. In this way, Dilthey characterized three senses of "whole" in Schleiermacher's thought: (i) organizing inner form, (ii) system, and (iii) relational context or *Zusammenhang* (HSH 679). Whereas organizing inner form refers to an organic immanent teleology and the idea of a system points to the completeness of a totality, *Zusammenhang* indicates the nexus or contextuality that allows singularity to be interpreted in relation to the infinite. If there is a common quest in "Romantic hermeneutics," it is characterized more by the question of the singular and the ineffable than it is by the systematic complete-

---

25. This is an implication, for instance, of HC 18–19, 92.
26. Gadamer, *Truth and Method*, 165–9; Scholtz, *Ethik und Hermeneutik*, 124.
27. Jean Grondin, *Introduction to Philosophical Hermeneutics* (New Haven, CT: Yale University Press, 1994), 64.

ness of representational knowledge. Dilthey could therefore suggest that individuality is the form of the whole (HSH 709). If we could know the whole, then we would know the whole in its concrete singularity rather than as a universal or concept.

If Schleiermacher's hermeneutics emphasized the correctness of an understanding to be guided by the theoretical articulation of an art and practice, this is far from meaning that he presupposed correctness as the sole model of truth, since interpretation calls for responsive feeling and imagination. Nor does this imply that the world is inherently and fully comprehensible and intelligible, since as finite beings we relate to the infinite through what Schleiermacher called in various places traces and seeds (*Spuren und Keime*). The notion of trace or seed is helpful for interpreting its use in Schleiermacher and the paradox of speaking about that which cannot be spoken. The trace is that which is given as not being able to be given, the presence of that which cannot be thought as presence, the disclosure of nondisclosedness, the revelation of that which is concealed *as* concealed.[28] This trace does not stand alone as a brute singularity or fact, since it bears a fundamental relationship to the word for Schleiermacher.

III. DILTHEY: INTERPRETATION AND THE HUMAN SCIENCES

Wilhelm Dilthey was a philosopher, intellectual and cultural historian, and social thinker, who is most recognized for his contributions to hermeneutics, the human sciences, aesthetics and literary criticism, interpretive psychology, and what later became known as "life-philosophy" (*Lebensphilosophie*). As with Schleiermacher, the hermeneutical tendencies of Dilthey's thought, which concerned understanding and interpretation as epistemic and social-historical phenomena, should be placed in the larger context of Dilthey's project.

Dilthey's primary early work *Introduction to the Human Sciences* (1883) is an attempt to develop a postmetaphysical epistemology of the human sciences, without positivistically truncating human experience, by systematically and historically investigating "the whole of human nature as it is revealed in experience, in the study of language, and in the study of history, and thus seek the connection of these components" (IHS 51). Dilthey developed his analysis of the human investigation of the human world in the context of his early epistemological project of explicating "the empirical without empiricism" in order to

---

28. One of the few thinkers to explore Schleiermacher's appeal to the "trace" in the context of recent literary theory is Werner Hamacher; see his "Hermeneutic Ellipses: Writing the Hermeneutic Circle in Schleiermacher," Timothy Bahti (trans.), in *Transforming the Hermeneutical Context: From Nietzsche to Nancy*, Gayle L. Ormiston and Alan D. Schrift (eds) (Albany, NY: SUNY Press, 1990).

unfold a "critique of historical reason" that would clarify, validate, and extend the distinctive forms of inquiry of the human sciences in the context of social-historical life (IHS 165).

The human sciences can be grounded only through immanent self-reflection on experience, based in and interpreting the "feeling of life" or precognitive reflexive awareness, which includes epistemological and psychological inquiry (IHS 174, 227–8). Dilthey argued for a nonreductive experientialism in epistemology, which expanded it beyond cognitive or theoretical knowledge and hence transformed it. According to Dilthey:

> All science is experiential; but all experience must be related back to and derives its validity from the conditions and context of consciousness in which it arises, i.e., the totality of our nature. We designate as "epistemological" this standpoint which consistently recognizes the impossibility of going behind these conditions. (IHS 50)

In his critique of reductive forms of empiricism and positivism, Dilthey argued for the irreducible richness and variety of experience understood and articulated from out of itself. Experience is bound to meaning-relating activities and structures that are only understandable in their life-context (*Lebenszusammenhang*). Dilthey utilized this account of lived-experience to reject traditional and speculative metaphysics. Metaphysics conceives the world through a unified point outside the world, assumed to be inherently intelligible, in order to represent the world as a systematic totality. Metaphysics separates knowledge from its historical context and the "totality of human nature," whereas what is called for is "historical reflection together with epistemological self-reflection [*Selbstbesinnung*]" (IHS 52).[29]

In his *Life of Schleiermacher* (1870) and *Introduction to the Human Sciences*, Dilthey interpreted the processes of life immanently and in relation to a dynamic context that is never fully visible. This "inner" perspective of life implies the original givenness from the first-person perspective of co-agents or participants of meaningful social-cultural structures and processes. "Inner" thus refers to the first-person life-context, which is inherently bodily, perceptual, and worldly as well as social-historical, and in which objects are preconceptually "understood." In contrast, "outer" or "external" refers to the abstraction of objects from their life-nexus in the third-person perspective of observation and explanation characteristic of modern natural sciences (IHS 61–2, 67). Without the metaphysical unity of the world, which has collapsed into paradox and aporia, we are faced

---

29. On life-reflection (*Besinnung*), see Makkreel, *Dilthey: Philosopher of the Human Studies*, 376–80.

with incommensurable data derived from myriad sources that cannot be conclusively combined insofar as they are explained and interpreted phenomenally and immanently from out of themselves rather than related to an external standard (IHS 61–4).Although Dilthey is repeatedly misinterpreted as an idealist philosopher of spirit or an epistemological dualist, radically opposing causal explanation of nature from the interpretive understanding of human life, the incommensurability of the natural and human sciences does not exclude their overlapping or pluralistic employment in inquiry: "Knowledge of the natural sciences overlaps with that of the human sciences" (IHS 70). Accordingly, for instance, the human sciences are irreducible to causal explanation even as they continue to use it. Third-person causal and structuralist-functionalist approaches in the human sciences, which analyze persons as the results of previous natural causes or as the tools and mechanisms of greater social forces and structures, are legitimate for Dilthey to the extent that they can be related to the perspective of persons as conscious co-agents involved in the formation of social life (IHS 55). Social forces, structures, and processes are in turn necessary for interpreting and explaining the phenomena associated with "spirit" in German idealism, including the individual person, groups, eras, and nations (IHS 56, 58). Nature as a causal order conditions individual and social life, just as that life in turn impacts and reshapes nature (IHS 69). History cannot be understood except through its natural conditions and as the "domination of nature" that is a primary purpose of human social activity from agriculture to technology (IHS 71).

Pluralism is necessary for the human sciences given their distinctive kinds of objects: "the external [or structural] organization of society, the cultural systems [of the reproduction of meaning] within it, and individual peoples" (IHS 93). The latter is the most complex object, since it does not correspond to an entity insofar as there is no such thing as a soul, organism, or essence to a nation or people (IHS 55, 121). Dilthey rejected what is now called "strong holism" in the philosophy of the social sciences, that is, the assertion of the existence of collective entities, while retaining a role for a "weak holism" that allows statements about collective or group phenomena such as an era, generation, or nation. Dilthey's focus on the context of individual life thus differs from the methodological individualism that reduces individuals to the ahistorical self-interested monadic agents of rational choice.

The primary intention of the human sciences is the empirical description of individuality in its life-context. Consequently, in an argument that would arouse neo-Kantian criticism insofar as they excluded psychology from the cultural sciences in classifying it as a natural science, the human sciences require descriptive and empirical psychology (IHS 109). Psychology is not then purely a natural science, as it involves purposes, norms, and values, as seen, for instance, in ethical, legal, and other practically oriented claims. The individual presents itself as both the goal and limit of understanding, which is explicative through the expressions and practices of the individual rather than directly intuited or introspected, as individuality evades full disclosure and articulation.[30] For Dilthey, we often know expressions that have a kind of objectivity for understanding while being uncertain of the life being expressed.[31]

During his middle period from 1883 to 1896, Dilthey focused on developing his aesthetics and a descriptive and interpretive psychology, including his argument for the "acquired psychic structural nexus" from the tension and differentiation of self and world in the experience of resistance via reflexive awareness to the fullness and specificity of an individual life. In this context, Dilthey articulated the lived – or performatively enacted rather than purely transcendentally constitutive – "categories of life" or life's immanent articulation-character that proved so significant for the early Heidegger.[32] The acquired psychic nexus indicates the complexity of overlapping functions of the individual as it develops in a historical situation. Dilthey's "proof" of the external world through the experience of resistance indicates the thereness and co-givenness of self and world.

Dilthey's writings from the early 1890s should be interpreted in the context of his articulation of an interpretive psychology occurring in the space and intersection of epistemology and life. In his *Beiträge zur Lösung der Frage vom Ursprung unseres Glaubens an die Realität der Außenwelt und seinem Recht* (1890), Dilthey formulated the basis for such a project by arguing for a phenomenality or immanence prior to the intellectualism of phenomenalism and for the independence of reality from the subject through the resistance and tension of the co-givenness of self and world. Under the traditional guise of an argument for the "external" existence of the world, Dilthey would radicalize this canonical epistemological problem by anticanonically showing the bodily-worldly character of human life. This work suggests a hermeneutics of bodily being in the world that provides the basis for interpretive psychology. Epistemological categories have their basis in the bodily-perceptual and social-historical character of life. Categories such as substance and cause are derived from the pre-intentional and prereflective categories of life through which the world is experienced and expressed.[33]

---

30. On the explicative character of understanding, see Jung, *Hermeneutik zur Einführung*, 84.
31. *Ibid.*, 86, 88.
32. Wilhelm Dilthey, *The Formation of the Historical World in the Human Sciences*, Selected Works, vol. 3, Rudolf A. Makkreel and Frithjof Rodi (eds), Rudolf A. Makkreel *et al.* (trans.) (Princeton, NJ: Princeton University Press, 2002), 228–45; hereafter cited as FHW followed by the page number; Makkreel, *Dilthey: Philosopher of the Human Studies*, 381–91.
33. Compare Frithjof Rodi, *Erkenntnis des Erkannten: zur Hermeneutik des 19. und 20. Jahrhunderts* (Frankfurt: Suhrkamp, 1990), 159.

Schleiermacher's "hermeneutical circle" is a model of education or cultivation. As one moves between the particular and general, each movement enriches one's previous understanding (HC 24). For Dilthey, it is the unending and irreducible intersection of and movement of prereflective elementary understanding and reflective interpretation between self and other, individual and context, and singular and whole. This dynamic of the determinate and the indeterminate is productive of understanding, which is practical rather than theoretical, selective rather than universal, and productive rather than merely reconstructive.[34] Understanding attempts to move from the exteriority of the utterance to the internal first-person perspective of the speaker or writer.[35]

In the final phase of his work, from 1896 until his death in 1911, Dilthey focused on the hermeneutical and social character of sense and meaning in the context of Hegel's objective spirit, which signifies the constitution of intersubjectivity in and through human practices and products. Dilthey analyzed historical life in *The Formation of the Historical World in the Human Sciences* (1910) through the relation of lived-experience (*Erlebnis*), expression (*Ausdruck*), and understanding (*verstehen*). He further articulated a "philosophy of worldviews" in order to account for the genesis and conflict of systems of interpretation of meaning in relation to the feeling and nexus of life. Worldviews express the tendency to unify experience even as the conflicts (*Widerstreit*) inherent in life prevent the closure of life in conceptual systems, since they inevitably face their limits in the antinomies and aporias generated by life itself.

It is in this late period that Dilthey explicated the experiential structures of consciousness in his three preliminary "Studies toward the Foundation of the Human Sciences," his exploration of the import of the productive systems of historical life for knowledge in *The Formation of the Historical World in the Human Sciences*, and his final and perhaps best formulation of hermeneutics in "The Understanding of Other Persons and Their Manifestations of Life." While Rudolf Carnap and others utilized the word *Aufbau* in the sense of epistemic "construction," Dilthey stressed the formation-character of both the human sciences and the historical reality that they investigate.[36] That is, the formation

---

34. Jung, *Hermeneutik zur Einführung*, 83.
35. Wilhelm Dilthey, *Die Entstehung der Hermeneutik*, in *Gesammelte Schriften*, vol. 5, 318–19; published in English as *The Rise of Hermeneutics, in Selected Works, Vol. 4: Hermeneutics and the Study of History*, Rudolf A. Makkreel and Frithjof Rodi (eds), Fredric R. Jameson and Rudolf Makkreel (trans.) (Princeton, NJ: Princeton University Press, 1996); hereafter cited as HSH followed by the page number in the German *Gesammelte Schriften*.
36. On Dilthey's significance for the early Carnap, particularly on metaphysics as a feeling of life and worldview, which Carnap employed in his critique of Heidegger, see Gottfried Gabriel, "Introduction: Carnap Brought Home," in *Carnap Brought Home: The View from Jena*, S. Awodey and C. Klein (eds) (Chicago, IL: Open Court, 2004), 3–20.

of the historical world refers to its articulation in the human sciences, which themselves theoretically reflect this historical world (FHW 1). Dilthey's theory of the human sciences is not merely an epistemology (*Erkenntnistheorie*) in the conventional sense, but a theory of knowledge (*Theorie des Wissens*) that relates knowing to its context. Whereas epistemology seeks to establish the foundations of conceptual cognition (*Erkenntnis*), Dilthey places the epistemology of the human sciences within a larger context of the knowledge (*Wissen*) embodied in social practices and historical forms of life.

Thought can and does generalize, intensify, and transform life, even as it remains bound to the factical and empirical context of that life (FHW 27). Knowledge encompasses not only the conceptual cognition of reality, but also the values and purposes established concerning it. It is inevitably selective and bound to a perspective. Dilthey accordingly situated the human sciences, which are determined by their respective object and how the object is given, in relation to a pretheoretical life-nexus and its forms of elementary or ordinary understanding (FHW 38). These are tied up with the temporality, historicity, and structures of social life; with an epochal "objective spirit." Objective spirit indicates the ways in which the past has been objectified and continues to shape contemporary practices, and it is analyzed in the human sciences as cultural systems and the external organization of society.

A significant characteristic of the *Formation of the Historical World* is the development of the notion of "productive system or nexus." *Wirkungszusammenhang* suggests a historical efficacy or productivity prior to any analysis of it as either causal or teleological (FHW 4). The human sciences involve the study of dynamic interconnected systems that articulate the intersection of meaning, value, purpose, and force. Dilthey interpreted these temporally, such that meaning primarily concerns how humans are determined by their past, value is based on their present feeling of life, and purpose is projective striving into the future in the face of productive forces (*Kräfte*) that cannot always be predicted or controlled.[37]

Understanding, which should be construed verbally as "to understand" (*verstehen*), is intrinsically interpretive for Dilthey. Since human agents are conscious and reflective beings who are bound to the facticity of their bodies and world, they can cognize themselves and others only indirectly through expressive and interpretive means (FHW 108). Given that we know ourselves and others primarily through actions, life-expressions, and their effects – rather than through introspection or intuition – and that everyday understanding can

---

37. Heidegger's portrayal of the unity of the temporal ekstases is in part a response to temporality in Dilthey. See Ilse Nina Bulhof, *Wilhelm Dilthey: A Hermeneutic Approach to the Study of History and Culture* (The Hague: Martinus Nijhoff, 1980), 172.

face breakdowns and what seems distant or strange, elementary understanding leads to higher forms of understanding and interpretation; that is, hermeneutics. Dilthey's project of a critique of historical reason proceeds from the context of life in all of its complexity and concreteness to the conceptual cognition of the sciences and, finally, to reflective awareness (*Besinnung*). This reflection is made possible by the prereflective reflexivity (*Innesein* or *Innewerden*) of the human subject and, with its double meaning of "sense" (*Sinn*) as meaning and bodily awareness, constitutes the basic movement of Dilthey's thought. Understanding is not merely subjective but mediated through the expressions and practices of human life. It also provides more than a scientific access to objects; it is fundamentally world-opening (FHW 226).

Understanding aims at truth or validity, and such understanding is described as being the most complete (FHW 227). Yet understanding is also concerned with the contextuality and facticity of human expressions. The objectifications of human life in practices and institutions, in behaviors and expressions, are the medium through which we understand and interpret others and ourselves. Dilthey's phenomenological descriptions of kinds of attitude (*Verhaltungsweise*), taking a stance (*Stellungsnahme*), and life-concern (*Lebensbezug*) show how historical life is both about and matters to the individual in its relational context (FHW 2). The human sciences justifiably strive to this extent for objectivity, universality, and truth.

Objectivity in the human sciences links lived-experiences with the social-historical structures that inform them. Yet this objectivity cannot consist of a mimetic copying of reality "as it is" (FHW 23). The human sciences relate the unique, the accidental, and the momentary to the nexus of norms, values, and meanings operative in social-historical reality. They explicate the intersection of the unique and the general in the "historical presentation of the singular occurrence [*die historische Darstellung des einmal Geschehenen*]."[38] The significance of the singular in relation to its context indicates that Dilthey's concern is not exclusively epistemological or scientific. It is practical, and the human sciences cannot extricate themselves from this non-"value-free" context. Possibilities for historical vision need self-reflection (*Selbstbesinnung*) if we are to be truly responsive to our own hermeneutical situation.

---

38. Wilhelm Dilthey, *Der Aufbau der Geschichtlichen Welt in den Geisteswissenschaften*, B. Groethuysen (ed.), 2nd ed. (Göttingen: Vandenhoeck & Ruprecht, 1956), 3, my translation.

IV. HERMENEUTICS AND PHILOSOPHY IN SCHLEIERMACHER AND DILTHEY

The word "hermeneutics" retained its early modern meaning and function in the writings of Schleiermacher and Dilthey. Although they intermittently gave the word more extensive meanings, hermeneutics is principally the art of understanding another's utterance through interpretation (HC 3–5). Hermeneutics is one discipline among other disciplines, correlated in particular with its fellow philological discipline of criticism as the art of evaluating the authenticity of texts rather than a style of philosophizing as a whole (HC 3).[39] It is further subordinate to ethics, which concerns any form of human activity, and dialectic – or the art of thinking – for Schleiermacher.[40] Hermeneutics refers to the exegesis of texts or, more broadly, communicative utterances in terms of their sense and meaning. Whereas earlier Protestant and idealistic hermeneutics stressed the "spirit" of the text, Schleiermacher and Dilthey focus on the individuality, personality or style, and sensibility of the author in his or her historical context.[41] Despite this more limited use of the word hermeneutics, their thought has been retrospectively designated as "hermeneutical" owing to their interest in associated issues of sense and meaning, context and historicity, understanding and interpretation, and in the communicative and explicative dimensions of human life and inquiry.

Even given this potential continuity through issues of interpretation, their responses to such issues are distinct. Schleiermacher and Dilthey emphasized the central role of language in hermeneutics and inquiry but they did not minimize or neglect the material-empirical, social-historical, and biographical-psychological dimensions of human life and knowledge. The art of interpretation is the art of understanding communication, involving the reflective and philosophical elaboration of understanding, within a larger context of intellectual and empirical inquiry. Twentieth-century hermeneutics – beginning with Heidegger's critical reception of Dilthey in the 1920s – is largely hostile to these merely ontic empirical, historical, and psychological moments in Schleiermacher and Dilthey. Where later hermeneutically defined philosophy stressed the integrating power and truth of language, narrative, and communication to disclose, construct, and mediate the world through basic concepts such as linguisticality (Gadamer), narrativity (Ricoeur), and mutual consensus (Habermas), Schleiermacher and

---

39. Compare Jung, *Hermeneutik zur Einführung*, 72; Scholtz, *Ethik und Hermeneutik*, 235.
40. On the ethical and dialectical context of hermeneutics, note Schleiermacher, HC 8. One flaw of the twentieth-century hermeneutical reception of Schleiermacher's hermeneutics is that it ignores its context in his dialectic, the art of thinking in conversation that is the basis of both ethics (to which hermeneutics belongs as a variety of human activity) and physics. On the dialectical context of hermeneutics, also see Bowie, "The Philosophical Significance," 76.
41. Jung, *Hermeneutik zur Einführung*, 56.

Dilthey emphasized not only the linguistic character of thought and the disclosive power of language but also its reversals, limitations, and breakdowns. Since everything cannot be said in language given the conflict, facticity, and resistance constitutive of life, and language is as much evocative as representational, all the resources of indirect communication are needed in order to articulate the singularity and affective life of the individual, on the one hand, and the complexity of any given context or nexus (*Zusammenhang*) of relations, on the other.

Besides the inability to fully determine or signify the individual and the whole in language, which calls forth and demands the interpretive oscillation and circling between them, communication and interpretation were confounded and inspired by the transcendence and ineffability of God in Schleiermacher and the unfathomable and ungroundable immanence of life in Dilthey.[42] This finitude and facticity in relation to the infinite beyond in Schleiermacher, or infinite empirical plurality in Dilthey, orients their intellectual endeavors.[43] Instead of being directly or immediately disclosed to intuition or reason, phenomena require interpretation, which indirectly addresses, articulates, and indicates the singular and complexly mediated phenomena of human existence. Given this context, the work of interpretation is tied to empirical scientific research.

The need for reflectively informed interpretation emerges when elemental or ordinary everyday understanding is confounded by that which is not communicated or understood – whether it is a text (the domain of traditional hermeneutics), the author, other persons, the historical context, life itself, or God. As there is no absolute difference between the transcendental and the empirical, or the ontological and the ontic, interpretation cannot be purely philosophical. Whether in Schleiermacher's dialectic or Dilthey's epistemic logic, philosophy thinks through scientific inquiry and cannot be separated from it without dogmatism. It accordingly cannot avoid or bracket empirical and ontic inquiry into the anthropological, natural, psychological, and social-historical dimensions of human life. Whereas traditional hermeneutics is primarily concerned with the explication of biblical and classical texts, understanding and interpretation are increasingly associated – already in Schleiermacher to a lesser degree, and for Dilthey more centrally – with the first-person participant perspective of lived-

---

42. On Dilthey's notion of life and its epistemic role, see my "Self-Reflection, Interpretation, and Historical Life in Dilthey," *Dilthey International Yearbook for Philosophy and the Human Sciences*, vol. 1 (2010), and "Impure Phenomenology: Dilthey, Epistemology, and Interpretive Psychology," *Studia Phaenomenologica* 10 (2010).
43. On facticity in nineteenth- and twentieth-century European philosophy, see the introduction to François Raffoul and Eric Sean Nelson (eds), *Rethinking Facticity* (Albany, NY: SUNY Press, 2008), 1–21. On Dilthey as a thinker of finitude, see Jos de Mul, *The Tragedy of Finitude: Dilthey's Hermeneutics of Life* (New Haven, CT: Yale University Press, 2004).

experience (*Erlebnis*), epistemic and social-historical reflection (*Besinnung*), and the empirically oriented inquiry of the human sciences (*Geisteswissenschaften*).

It is striking that Schleiermacher and Dilthey conceive of interpretation as aiming both at the individual and the singular *and* at the context and the whole in their relational interdependence. Understanding and interpretation occur to one degree or another as an oscillation between these two poles, as universality demands returning to particularity and particulars require universalization in order to begin to be recognized and understood. The oscillation between the conceptual and the nonconceptual, the universal and the particular, and the individual and the whole became characterized as the "hermeneutical circle," which Schleiermacher adopted from Friedrich Ast.[44] Rather than being a closed system or hierarchy of meanings, where particulars are subsumed under universals never to be heard from again, interpretation occurs through both contextualization and individuation. It is a potentially infinite iteration of departure and return to its object. Similar to empirical research, interpretation is provisional and can always begin anew as more is learned about the individual and the context.

Interpretation is not only the analysis of language, narrative, or communicative action for Schleiermacher and Dilthey; it concerns "meaning" in all its potential guises and expressions. This includes the disruption and incompleteness of meaning in encountering "non-meaning" and the counter-purposive. This insight is related to the role of the nonconceptual and prereflective in experience, the affectivity and emotional character of lived-experience and understanding, and the priority of music and art as expressions of human life. Instead of highlighting reason or intuition alone, they emphasized the need to address human existence in its fullness and variety, which embraces rationality and affectivity, reflection and the basic "feeling of life" (*Lebensgefühl*).[45]

Meaning is "holistic" in the sense of its being relational and interconnected. Yet, in contrast with visions of an impersonal systematic integration in a conceptual or social totality, or the "occult subordination" of every aspect of the text to an esoteric doctrine (HC 17), this is an open-ended, interpretive, and "first-person" holism that is constantly referred back to the experience and interpre-

---

44. Friedrich Ast (1778–1841), one of the leading philologists of the nineteenth century, initially formulated the circle in Section 78 of his *Grundlinien der Grammatik, Hermeneutik und Kritik*, published in 1808, as Schleiermacher himself noted (HHM, 195). See Ronald Bontekoe, *Dimensions of the Hermeneutic Circle* (Atlantic Highlands, NJ: Humanities Press, 1996), 8, 23.
45. On *Lebensgefühl* from Kant's third critique to Dilthey, see Rudolf A. Makkreel, "The Feeling of Life: Some Kantian Sources of Life-Philosophy," *Dilthey-Jahrbuch für Philosophie und Geschichte der Geisteswissenschaften* III (1985).

tation of individuals.[46] Even as the individual is in a sense fundamental, the interpretation of the individual leads back to the context and the potentially universal through the comparative, the generalizable, and the typical. Both the individual and the whole are more or less indeterminate, as interpretations attempt to increasingly articulate their determinateness.[47] In this process, both sides change, readjust in relation to one another, and are reinterpreted.

The provisional character of interpretation does not only hold for the interpretation of other humans. Self-understanding is more complex and questionable than is usually thought, as the self does not have direct or self-certain access and knowledge of itself. Self-knowledge consequently proceeds through self-interpretation, with all the risks that this involves. The individual does not have direct or unmediated self-knowledge, much less an intuitive self-transparency, as evident in biographical and autobiographical writing. The motto of Dilthey's unfinished multivolume biography of Schleiermacher is "the individual is ineffable."[48] Rather than being statically given as an unalterable boundary, or posited as being outside interpretation, the unsayable occurs in the context of communication.[49] It is owing to finitude and alterity that all words and expressions call for interpretation and assessment – whether they are our own or even those of God. Andrew Bowie notes that Schleiermacher's self "is not an absolute point of beginning"; the self is infinitely reflective and interpretive, as it lacks presence to itself and at the same time needs to respond to this lack.[50]

Meaning is inevitably of "diverse provenance," or pluralistic.[51] It involves a multiplicity of elements and sources that entail, for example, addressing and researching the text, the author, the context, and the truth claims of a work in order to interpret and evaluate it. These myriad elements and resources cannot be eliminated prior to the work of interpretation, even as some are highlighted and others remain in the background, depending on the interpretive task. Hermeneutics is methodologically pluralistic in drawing on both generalizing (linguistic) and individualizing (psychological) tendencies, which exemplify the

---

46. Jung discusses the "holism of the first-person perspective," which also differentiates the human from the impersonal third-person perspective of the natural sciences, in *Hermeneutik zur Einführung*, 76.
47. On the difference between an indeterminate and a determinate whole, and the necessity for contextualization in making an utterance more determinate, see HC 28–30.
48. Wilhelm Dilthey, *Leben Schleiermachers: Auf Grund des Textes der 1. Auflage von 1870 und der Zusätze aus dem Nachlaß*, M. Redeker (ed.), in *Gesammelte Schriften* (Göttingen: Vandenhoeck & Ruprecht, 1970), vol. 13, 1; also note HSH 330.
49. Scholtz, *Ethik und Hermeneutik*, 111, 125.
50. Bowie, *Aesthetics and Subjectivity*, 249.
51. This is a key point of contention for Heidegger in *Einleitung in die Philosophie* (*Gesamtausgabe* 27), 2nd ed. (Frankfurt: Klostermann, 2001), 347–9. On Heidegger's critique and Misch's defense of Dilthey's meaning pluralism, see Frithjof Rodi, *Erkenntnis des Erkannten*, 137–40.

two primary tasks of hermeneutics for Schleiermacher and Dilthey. Likewise, ordinary life is differentiated by a diversity of practical interests, and scientific inquiry by its objects and how they are approached.

V. CRITICISMS AND CONCLUSIONS

Despite the incorporation of many of their insights by philosophers as diverse as Heidegger and Habermas,[52] a number of overlapping critiques of Schleiermacher and Dilthey emerged in reaction to their thought. Owing to their concern with the psychological and aesthetic dimensions of human existence, some critics accused them of "psychologism" and "aestheticism," that is, the reduction of truth or validity claims to psychological dispositions and the overprioritizing of art as a model of human activity.[53]

Likewise, on account of their attention to the historical nexus or context in which individuals and groups live, act, and produce, they were criticized to varying degrees for "historicizing" texts and experiences in a way that threatened their truth or cognitive validity; for example, the truth of the Bible (by Orthodox and neo-Orthodox theological critics of Schleiermacher such as Barth[54]), the sciences (by positivism and logical positivism), philosophy (twentieth-century hermeneutics[55]), or the very idea of validity itself (by Neo-Kantianism and Husserl).

Finally, because of their accentuation of the ineffable, individual, and affective aspects of human life and on the epistemology, methodology, and rationality of philosophical and human scientific inquiry, opponents of Schleiermacher and Dilthey – especially Gadamer – have criticized their works for being incoherently beholden to positivistic scientism and Romantic aestheticism, Enlightenment rationality and the irrational affirmation of God or life.[56] Nonetheless, insofar as philosophy does not one-sidedly abandon reflection or feeling, reason or

---

*52. For a discussion of Heidegger's hermeneutic theory, see the essay by Daniel L. Tate in *The History of Continental Philosophy: Volume 4*. Habermas's relation to hermeneutics is discussed in essays by Christopher F. Zurn and Wayne J. Froman in *The History of Continental Philosophy: Volume 6*.

53. On the role of art and aesthetics, and a response to the aestheticism charge, see Nelson, "Disturbing Truth," 121–42.

*54. For a discussion of Barth's theology, see the essay by Felix Ó Murchadha in *The History of Continental Philosophy: Volume 4*.

*55. Twentieth-century hermeneutics is discussed in detail in the essays by Daniel L. Tate in *The History of Continental Philosophy: Volume 4* and Wayne J. Froman in *The History of Continental Philosophy: Volume 6*.

56. Hans-Georg Gadamer, "Wilhelm Dilthey nach 150 Jahren: Zwischen Romantik und Positivismus," in *Dilthey und Philosophie der Gegenwart*, E. W. Orth (ed.) (Freiburg: Karl Alber, 1985), and *Hermeneutik in Rückblick* (Tübingen: Mohr Siebeck, 1995), 9, 186.

imagination, science or art, or universality or individuality, their work continues to be significant in elucidating a nonreductive interpretive experientialism in both knowledge and practical life.

MAJOR WORKS

Friedrich Schleiermacher

Gesamtausgabe der Werke Schleiermachers in drei Abteilungen. Berlin, 1834– .
Kritische Gesamtausgabe. Berlin: de Gruyter, 1980.
Über die Religion (1799). Stuttgart: Reclam, 1969. Published in English as *On Religion: Speeches to Its Cultured Despisers*, edited and translated by Richard Crouter. Cambridge: Cambridge University Press, 1988.
Monologen (1800; 3rd ed. 1822). Hamburg: Felix Meiner, 1978. Published in English as *Soliloquies*, edited and translated by Horace Leland Friess. Chicago, IL: Open Court, 1957.
Dialektik. Edited by Manfred Frank. 2 vols. Frankfurt: Suhrkamp, 2001.
Dialektik (1811). Edited by Andreas Arndt. Hamburg: Felix Meiner, 1986. Published in English as *Dialectic or the Art of Doing Philosophy (1811)*, edited by Terence N. Tice. Atlanta, NJ: Scholars Press, 1996.
Dialektik (1814/15) & Einleitung zur Dialektik (1833). Edited by Andreas Arndt. Hamburg: Felix Meiner, 1988.
Hermeneutik und Kritik. Frankfurt: Suhrkamp, 1977. Published in English as *Hermeneutics and Criticism*, edited by Andrew Bowie. Cambridge: Cambridge University Press, 1998.
Hermeneutik. Nach den Handschriften. Edited by Heinz Kimmerle. 2nd ed. Heidelberg: Carl Winter, 1974. Published in English as *Hermeneutics: The Handwritten Manuscripts*, translated by James Duke and Jack Forstman, 2nd ed. Atlanta, NJ: Scholars Press, 1997.
Der christliche Glaube (1821–22; 2nd ed. 1830–31). Berlin: de Gruyter, 1999. Published in English as *The Christian Faith*, edited by H. R. Mackintosh and J. S. Stewart. Edinburgh: T&T Clark, 1999.

Wilhelm Dilthey

The primary edition of Dilthey's works is *Gesammelte Schriften*. Stuttgart: B. G. Teubner (former publisher)/Göttingen: Vandenhoeck & Ruprecht (current publisher), 1914– . The primary edition of Dilthey's works in English translation is *Selected Works*. Edited by Rudolf A. Makkreel and Frithjof Rodi. Translated by Rudolf A. Makkreel et al. 6 vols. Princeton, NJ: Princeton University Press, 1989– .
"Das hermeneutische System Schleiermachers in der Auseinandersetzung mit der älteren protestantischen Hermeneutik" (1860). In *Gesammelte Schriften*, vol. 14, 597–787. Published in English as "Schleiermacher's Hermeneutical System in Relation to Earlier Protestant Hermeneutics," in *Selected Works, Vol. 4: Hermeneutics and the Study of History*, edited by Rudolf A. Makkreel and Frithjof Rodi, translated by Theodore Nordenhaug, 33–227. Princeton, NJ: Princeton University Press, 1996.
Leben Schleiermachers (1870). In *Gesammelte Schriften*, vols 13–14.
Einleitung in die Geisteswissenschaften: Versuch einer Grundlegung für das Studium der Gesellschaft und der Geschichte (1883). In *Gesammelte Schriften*, vol. 1. Published in English as *Selected*

Works, Vol. 1: Introduction to the Human Sciences, edited by Rudolf A. Makkreel and Frithjof Rodi, translated by Michael Neville. Princeton, NJ: Princeton University Press, 1989.

Beiträge zur Lösung der Frage vom Ursprung unseres Glaubens an die Realität der Außenwelt und seinem Recht (1890). In *Gesammelte Schriften*, vol. 5, 90–138. Published in English as "The Origin of Our Belief in the Reality of the External World and its Justification," in *Selected Works, Vol. 2: Understanding the Human World*, edited by Rudolf A. Makkreel and Frithjof Rodi, translated by Rudolf Makkreel and Jacob Owensby, 30–96. Princeton, NJ: Princeton University Press, 2010.

"Ideen über eine beschreibende und zergliedernde Psychologie" (1894). In *Gesammelte Schriften*, vol. 5, 139–240. Published in English as *Descriptive Psychology and Historical Understanding*, translated by Richard M. Zaner and Kenneth L. Heiges. The Hague: Nijhoff, 1977.

Die Entstehung der Hermeneutik (1900). In *Gesammelte Schriften*, vol. 5, 317–38. Published in English as *The Rise of Hermeneutics*, in *Selected Works, Vol. 4: Hermeneutics and the Study of History*, edited by Rudolf A. Makkreel and Frithjof Rodi, translated by Fredric R. Jameson and Rudolf Makkreel, 235–58. Princeton, NJ: Princeton University Press, 1996.

Das Erlebnis und die Dichtung: Lessing, Goethe, Novalis, Hölderlin [1905]. In *Gesammelte Schriften* vol. 26. Partly published in English as *Selected Works, Vol. 5: Poetry and Experience*, edited by Rudolf A. Makkreel and Frithjof Rodi, translated by Christopher Rodie and Joseph Ross. Princeton, NJ: Princeton University Press, 1985.

Das Wesen der Philosophie (1907). In *Gesammelte Schriften*, vol. 5, 339–416. Published in English as *The Essence of Philosophy*, translated by Stephen A. Emery and William T. Emery. Chapel Hill, NC: University of North Carolina Press, 1954.

Der Aufbau der geschichtlichen Welt in den Geisteswissenschaften (1910). In *Gesammelte Schriften*, vol. 7. Published in English as *Selected Works, Vol. 3: The Formation of the Historical World in the Human Sciences*, edited by Rudolf A. Makkreel and Frithjof Rodi. Princeton, NJ: Princeton University Press, 2002.

7

FRENCH SPIRITUALIST PHILOSOPHY

F. C. T. Moore

Félix Ravaisson and his protégé Jules Lachelier are the chief representatives of what is known as "French spiritualist philosophy," sometimes called "neo-spiritualism" or "*l'école réflexive*" in the nineteenth century. Despite their differences, they had it in common to emphasize the primacy of free action, the priority of organic wholes over their parts, and an overarching role for the divine creator. They rejected materialistic and deterministic views of reality. They influenced Henri Bergson, who succeeded Ravaisson in the Academy of Moral and Political Sciences.

Indeed, it is possible to trace some affinities and influences between Ravaisson and Lachelier and some of their predecessors, contemporaries, or successors, thereby giving a broader reach to the label "spiritualist philosophy," and providing a context for their work. A full list of authors who could be included among the spiritualists is not offered here, but some scholars would include Charles Renouvier, and may cite Maine de Biran and even Antoine-Augustin Cournot among the predecessors, and Bergson among the successors. But such a way of proceeding has to be treated with caution, because of the very considerable differences between these thinkers.

It is worth noting the contrast between them and Auguste Comte. His positivism rested on a systematic rejection of metaphysics and traditional religion, and advocacy of a form of scientism that could be applied not only to inert matter, but also to social life. Indeed, he is viewed as a founder of sociology. At first sight there could be no deeper divergence than that between spiritualism and the positivism of Comte. Yet curiously, late in his life Comte came to advocate a new religion of humanity, described in his "positivist catechism" based on love and altruism.[1]

---

1. Auguste Comte, *Catéchisme positiviste* (Paris: Éditions du Sandre, [1852] 2009).

Positive religion, he claimed, was a natural and normal feature of human life, which needed to be cleansed of previous baggage. Thus, despite the deep divergence between positivism and spiritualism, we seem in the end to observe an affinity, even if it is vanishingly remote.[2]

Here, the authors named earlier as forming a group around neospiritualism are discussed, but little attempt has been made to provide evidence of actual influences, where they can be documented. Some common themes found in the work of all the writers treated are an emphasis on the will, and rejection of hard forms of determinism or materialism. Let us turn briefly to the background.

I. THE BACKGROUND

The background to the developments in which French spiritualist philosophy has its place is to be found in a rift that arose between thinkers interested in the sciences of life. Increasingly in the eighteenth century the received paradigm of the mechanical philosophy had begun to appear inadequate in this area. There was extensive empirical inquiry and elaborate speculation. The work of Swiss naturalist Charles Bonnet[3] is emblematic. He received numerous high honors from European academies for his work on insects, in particular for his discovery of the parthenogenesis of aphids. But later in his life, having become nearly blind perhaps because of intensive use of the microscope, as he himself believed, he engaged in high speculation about the history of life in the world. He was a preformationist, holding that the development of individual organisms, and the general history of life, were determined by preexisting germs, and advocating an evolutionary theory on this basis.[4] It was only toward the end of the century that the epigenetic approach began to prevail. However, speculation of the sort engaged in by Bonnet and contrary materialistic speculation, as illustrated in the work of Julien Offray de La Mettrie[5] entitled *L'Homme-machine*

---

*2. Comte's work is discussed in the essays by Alan Sica and Dale Jacquette in this volume.

3. Charles Bonnet (1720–93) was a Swiss naturalist and philosopher. He studied insects and the structure and functions of leaves, and developed what is known as the catastrophe theory of evolution.

4. Charles Bonnet, *Considérations sur les corps organizés* (Amsterdam: M. M. Rey, 1762) and *Palingénésie Philosophique* (Amsterdam: M. M. Rey, 1769). The latter work claims that the evolution of life proceeds by catastrophic natural disasters, after which newer and higher forms of life appear from the same germs.

5. Julien Offray de La Mettrie (1709–51) was a French physician and philosopher who advocated a materialist account of life. His atheism and materialistic views forced him to leave Paris in 1745 and Holland in 1748. He was welcomed in Berlin by Frederick the Great.

(1748),[6] lacked scientific bases that might lead toward a resolution until, at the end of the century, Antoine-Laurent Lavoisier's advocacy of oxygen (as opposed to phlogiston) and Alessandro Volta's work on electricity.[7] For his part, Lavoisier was responsible not only for the discovery of oxygen and hydrogen, which he named, but for a more general reform of chemistry that made it much more apt for the study of processes in living matter. Volta's invention of the first batteries arose from his attempt to repeat and explain Luigi Galvani's[8] observation of frogs' legs twitching under dissection, and he found that an electrical current arose from the two different metals holding the leg in place. Both of these advances, chemical and electric, were rightly seen as important in the study of life.[9] Such developments ushered in a new sort of interest in the will, seen, for instance, in the work of Arthur Schopenhauer,[10] as the rift between materialistic and antimaterialistic approaches to life took an entirely new shape. But we turn now to Maine de Biran, because his interest in the will provides some of the more immediate environment for the work of the spiritualists.

II. MAINE DE BIRAN

The young Maine de Biran[11] had a strong mathematical bent, and it was suggested to him that he should apply for a Chair of Mathematics in 1803. But he did not follow this suggestion, and not much of his surviving work is marked by math-

---

6. Julien Offray de La Mettrie, "L'Homme-Machine," in *Œuvres Philosophiques Corpus de Philosophie en langue française* (Paris: Fayard, [1748] 1987); published in English as *La Mettrie: Machine Man and Other Writings*, Ann Thomson (ed. and trans.) (Cambridge: Cambridge University Press, 1996).
7. Antoine-Laurent Lavoisier (1743–94) was a French scientist who transformed chemistry; he was executed by the French Revolutionary authorities for allegedly improper use of his privileges as a tax-collector. Alessandro Volta (1745–1827) was an Italian scientist who made important early steps in the understanding of electricity, building on the work of Luigi Galvani.
8. Luigi Galvani (1737–98) was an Italian physician and physicist, and a pioneer of bioelectricity. He studied medicine at the University of Bologna, and in 1762 was appointed a lecturer in anatomy. He later became a professor of obstetrics and, in 1772 was named president of the university.
9. Electricity also provided a link to the early Romantics, as evinced in Mary Shelley's *Frankenstein: or the Modern Prometheus* (1818).
*10. For a discussion of Schopenhauer, see the essay by Bart Vandenabeele in *The History of Continental Philosophy: Volume 1*.
11. Marie François Pierre Gontier de Biran (Maine de Biran) was born on November 29, 1766, in Bergerac, France. He studied law at the University of Poitiers before entering the guard of Louis XVI at Versailles. After the French Revolution, he returned to the countryside and, after the Reign of Terror, he held public office under successive regimes. He died on July 20, 1824, in Paris.

ematical concerns, apart from a continuing interest in logic, although he tended to have a psychological rather than mathematical conception of logic.[12] Instead, Maine de Biran made it his life-work to establish foundations for psychology, and through this for the human sciences in general, although in practice his numerous and significant duties in public life under different political regimes in those turbulent times were a significant and almost continuous distraction. For about the last twelve years of his life he worked on a single book that would provide these foundations. But the projected book changed in form and content over this period and was never completed. As Henri Gouhier[13] wrote: "He was a one-book man: but he never wrote the book."[14] But the work sometimes came quite close to completion, and a scholarly edition of his writings, mostly unpublished during his lifetime, is available today in thirteen parts (twenty volumes[15]), replacing less scholarly and less complete editions produced since the 1840s.[16]

Although initially avowing a robust empiricism, Maine de Biran placed central emphasis from an early date on the consciousness of willed activity, and later in his life a more metaphysical and then mystical and religious direction also came into his work. He was steeped in the work of various predecessors, including Locke and Condillac, as well as numerous scientific and medical writers, educationalists, and other philosophers. Despite the weight he gave to empirical investigation, he did not accept strong reductivist versions of materialism, as evinced, for instance, in the work of La Mettrie or Pierre-Jean-Georges Cabanis.[17]

---

12. I did find among Maine de Biran's papers in the library of the family *chateau* near Bergerac a sketchy attempt to prove the trisection of a given angle with ruler and compass. This problem goes back to the ancient Greeks, and much ingenuity was expended on it from ancient times onward. It was only after the death of Maine de Biran that such a construction was proved to be impossible.
13. Henri Gouhier (1898–1994) was a distinguished scholar of philosophy at the Sorbonne, where he taught from 1941 to 1968. Gouhier published a number of books, mainly on the history of French philosophy, including several books on Descartes as well as books on Bergson, Comte, Maine de Biran, Malebranche, Pascal, and Rousseau. He was elected to the Académie Française in 1979.
14. Henri Gouhier, *Les Conversions de Maine de Biran* (Paris: Vrin, 1947), 6, my translation.
15. François Azouvi (ed.), *Les Œuvres de Maine de Biran, Tomes I à XIII-3* (Paris: Vrin, 1986-2001).
16. Victor Cousin's few editions, for instance, were very tardy, and crucially incomplete. He would just pick and choose bits and pieces that he thought represented the "best" aspects of the "isms" that he had crudely identified.
17. Pierre-Jean-Georges Cabanis (1757–1808) was a materialist philosopher and physiologist. He was the author of *Sur les Rapports du physique et du moral de l'homme* (1802), and was acquainted with many of the most distinguished figures of his day, including d'Alembert, Condillac, Condorcet, d'Holbach, Diderot, Benjamin Franklin, and Thomas Jefferson.

His influence on later thought was varied. In 1821, Antoine-Athanase Royer-Collard,[18] a specialist in mental disorders, requested Maine de Biran's help in preparing a course of lectures, and Maine de Biran, reworking a previous prize-winning work, sent him the *Nouvelles Considérations sur les rapports du physique et du moral de l'homme*. Royer-Collard's notes on this were published by his son in 1843 in the second issue of the *Annales Médico-psychologiques*. This journal represented a significant step in the development of empirical psychology in the nineteenth century. So Maine de Biran had a role in the early stages of this science.

It can be claimed also that he was a predecessor of phenomenology, given his insistence that "nothing is present to our consciousness except as a relation."[19] I have found no evidence that Franz Brentano knew his work, although later phenomenologists – including Maurice Merleau-Ponty and Michel Henry[20] – were acquainted with it.

Maine de Biran from an early stage distinguished between the "animal life" in humans, in which the organism followed its own ways, which were not always present to consciousness, and the "conscious life," which had at its foundation the awareness of willed effort. This notion was not abstruse; Maine de Biran often illustrated it by the simple example of a person knowingly raising an arm. But such awareness constituted what Maine de Biran called a "primitive fact" presented by "the inner sense." At the same time, the conscious life presupposed the "animal life," and Maine de Biran thought that there might one day be a "new Columbus"[21] who would explore the underlayer of our conscious life, so in a certain way anticipating Freud. To these "two lives," Maine de Biran later added a third level, the "life of the spirit." It is this last that gives some support to making Maine de Biran a predecessor of French spiritualist philosophy, although the various writings in which these ideas about the "third life" were developed by Maine de Biran were not in fact published until the twentieth century. Thus Maine de Biran cannot have been a predecessor of the spiritualists directly, through their knowledge of his published writings. Nevertheless, it is

---

18. Antoine-Athanase Royer-Collard (1768–1825) was a French doctor who worked with the "insane." In 1806 he was named chief physician at the Charenton mental asylum, where his patients included the Marquis de Sade. In 1819, he was appointed to the first Chair of *médecine mentale* in the Faculté de Médecine in Paris.
19. Henri Gouhier (ed.), *Maine de Biran: Journal, Édition intégrale* (Neuchâtel: la Baconnière, 1954–55), vol. II, 376.
*20. For a discussion of Merleau-Ponty, see the essay by Mauro Carbone in *The History of Continental Philosophy: Volume 4*; Henry in discussed in the essay by Bruce Ellis Benson in *The History of Continental Philosophy: Volume 7*.
21. Gouhier, *Maine de Biran: Journal*, vol. I, 176.

arguable that influences may tread more subtle paths, such as those outlined in the notion of the "epidemiology of ideas" recently developed by Dan Sperber.[22]

III. COURNOT

Antoine-Augustin Cournot (1801–77), by contrast, was a mathematician of note, both in mathematical theory and in applied mathematics, including economic theory. One of his most important legacies is in probability theory. Pierre-Simon Laplace,[23] perhaps the hardest of all determinists, had taken the view that the role of probabilistic mathematics was simply to make up for our insufficient knowledge as finite humans of the evolution of the universe. If we were all-knowing we could predict precisely the entire future of the universe from the current position and momentum of all elementary particles using the laws of physics. But Cournot, by contrast, considered that probabilistic techniques were founded in features of the real world, rather than being a substitute for our ignorance of it. He was greatly interested in chance, as an unavoidable aspect of our world. In this he may be considered to have anticipated from a great distance the later advent of quantum mechanics, although, of course, he was far from having any of the empirical findings or underlying theoretical work on which quantum theory would later depend.[24]

His major work in economics, *Researches into the Mathematical Principles of Wealth*,[25] was to have an important influence in the later development of economic theory, although, to his disappointment, its importance was not

---

22. Dan Sperber (ed.), "The Epidemiology of Ideas," special issue of *The Monist* 84 (2001). The analogy with epidemiology is that despite sound knowledge of the aetiology of various diseases, there is no general epidemiological law to explain their distribution since entirely different factors can affect their spread or failure to spread in different populations and areas. Analogically, and contrary to the claims of memeticists, there are no general principles to explain the spread of ideas. Cases vary considerably, and overt or provable influences through personal contacts or the written or printed word are just one of many different ways in which ideas spread.
23. Pierre-Simon Laplace (1749–1827) was a French mathematician and astronomer who advocated strong determinism. Author of the five-volume *Mécanique Céleste* (Celestial mechanics; 1799–1825), he contributed to the development of mathematical astronomy, made significant contributions to mathematics and probability theory, and aided in the development of the metric system.
24. Antoine-Augustin Cournot, *Exposition de la théorie des chances et des probabilités* (Paris: Hachette, 1843).
25. Antoine-Augustin Cournot, *Recherches sur les principes mathématiques de la théorie des richesses* (Paris: Hachette, 1838).

recognized when he published it. Some of his work prefigured the much later development of game theory, including the Nash equilibrium.[26]

In later life, he became increasingly interested in "vitalism," according to which there are laws or principles or forces governing living beings that are distinct from those governing inert matter.[27] This was a common enough preoccupation at the time, and indeed, earlier, Maine de Biran already had a considerable knowledge of and interest in eighteenth-century forms of vitalism. Later Bergson was to reject not only crude vitalism but also crude mechanism. Although current biological orthodoxy rejects vitalism in all its forms, some twentieth-century scientists, such as René Thom, D'Arcy Thompson, and C. H. Waddington, have maintained quasi-finalistic positions.[28]

But, despite these interests, Cournot is now respected primarily for his important mathematical work. The significant thing he shares with the spiritualists is his rejection of strong determinism.

---

26. Game theory is not about games as we normally understand them, but about any human interactions in which there can be different outcomes for the parties according to what they do. A Nash equilibrium occurs when "players" in a "game" know each other's strategy, and therefore know what to do. However, the existence of a Nash equilibrium does not guarantee that the players will get the best possible payoffs (which could be achieved if their strategies were different). The most well-known example of this is the "Prisoner's Dilemma," in which each of two prisoners will get the best outcome (namely, minimal or no prison sentence) if they both keep quiet under questioning, yet it seems to each of them rational to confess, since if the other keeps quiet a small sentence will result.
27. See Antoine-Augustin Cournot, *Considérations sur la marche des idées et des événements dans les temps modernes* (Paris: Hachette, 1872).
28. See, for example, René Thom, *Structural Stability and Morphogenesis: An Outline of a General Theory of Models*, D. H. Fowler (trans.) (Reading, MA: W. A. Benjamin, 1975); D'Arcy Wentworth Thompson, *On Growth and Form* (New York: Dover, [1942] 1992); and C. H. Waddington, *Principles of Embryology* (London: George Allen & Unwin, 1956). D'Arcy Thompson (1860–1948) demonstrated with beautiful diagrams the existence of common and related forms in living organisms that appeared not to be susceptible to ordinary evolutionary explanation. Thom (1923–2002) argued for a form of qualitative dynamics, based on his Fields Medal work in topology, also named by him "catastrophe theory," which would explain the occurrence of seemingly unrelated forms in nature, such as the forms of the erect penis, the mushroom *Phallus Impudicus*, and certain similarly shaped geological formations. Waddington (1905–75) introduced the idea of "chreods" (necessary paths), that is, the idea that organisms were constrained in their possible paths of development. For instance, he considered that evolutionary processes as conventionally conceived will not produce animals with, say, three, five, or seven legs. These arguments made by distinguished if unconventional scientists are not "vitalist" in the strong sense of appealing to a natural force responsible for what happens in living organisms as opposed to inert matter, as earlier eighteenth- and nineteenth-century thinkers had claimed. But they present quasi-finalist challenges to conventional biological and evolutionary wisdom.

IV. RAVAISSON

Maine de Biran and Cournot can be shown to have had major and diverse influences on subsequent thought, directly and indirectly. The same can be said of Félix Ravaisson,[29] whose own thought was influenced by, among others, Maine de Biran, Victor Cousin[30] (with whose positions he often found himself in disagreement), and F. W. Schelling (whom he travelled to Munich to meet in 1839). In addition to his interest in the fine arts,[31] drawing on Maine de Biran's psychological insights and Schelling's metaphysics, Ravaisson's writings had a profound influence on both Catholic philosophy and the development of personalism in France. In 1835, Ravaisson won a prize for a study of Aristotle's metaphysics, leading to later publication of a two-volume work.[32] Ravaisson's fresh approach to Aristotle's *Metaphysics* represented a new return to Aristotle's original thinking, and in the second volume, published nine years after the first volume appeared in 1837, he discussed Aristotle's philosophy in relation to Greek thought in general. However, Ravaisson's spiritualism is not Aristotelian in character, except in the role it gives to teleology, a theme later taken further by Lachelier.

Ravaisson's doctoral thesis about habit should be noted, since an early work of Maine de Biran (one of the very few works published in his lifetime) was about the influence of habit on our thinking, a work in which we see for the first time Maine de Biran's distinction between "two lives" in us. Maine de Biran's position depended on his advocacy of a reflective psychology. At this stage of his life, Maine de Biran entirely rejected metaphysical reasoning. Ravaisson describes habit as "the middle term between the will and nature."[33] This statement is not of itself alien to Maine de Biran's views, but Ravaisson immediately glosses it in terms of Spinoza's metaphysical distinction between *natura naturans* (namely what exists in itself and is thought through itself, or God the free cause, or

---

29. Jean-Gaspard Félix Lacher, dit Ravaisson-Mollien (October 23, 1813–May 18, 1900; born in Namur; died in Paris).
30. Victor Cousin (1792–1867) was a French eclectic philosopher who chose what he thought best of the four "-isms" – by some accounts rationalism, empiricism, spiritualism, and mysticism – among previous philosophers. Influenced by Hegel and Schelling, Cousin was a member of the Council of Public Instruction (1830), of the Académie Française (1831), and of the Académie des Sciences Morales et Politiques (1832). His influence dominated the French educational system, and in particular philosophical education, for a considerable period.
31. Henri Bergson succeeded Ravaisson at the Academy of Moral and Political Sciences, and he delivered in 1904 a *Notice sur la vie et les Œuvres de M. Félix Ravaisson-Mollien* in which he claimed that Ravaisson's philosophical work had its roots in his reflections on beauty and on works of art.
32. Félix Ravaisson, *Essai sur la Métaphysique d'Aristote*, 2 vols (Paris: Imprimerie Royale, 1837–46).
33. Félix Ravaisson, *De l'habitude*, in *Corpus des Œuvres de philosophie en langue française* (Paris: Fayard, 1984), 34, my translation.

attributes of substance that show an eternal and infinite essence), and *natura naturata* (namely all that follows from the necessary existence of God). Habit, says Ravaisson, is of the second kind, displaying the work of the first.[34] For this reason, it allows us to escape from nature, and invites an idealist view of reality. This claim is remote from the early thought of Maine de Biran, and is a crucible for the development of Ravaisson's "spiritualism."

In 1839, he became Inspector of Libraries; in 1852 he was chairman of a commission on the teaching of drawing in schools (Delacroix and Ingres were members) and had a continuing interest in the nature of beauty. In 1852, Ravaisson became Inspector General of Higher Education (a position he would occupy until 1888), producing in 1867 at the request of Victor Duruy, the Minister of Public Instruction, a report on the state of philosophy in France: *La Philosophie en France au XIXème Siècle*.[35] This report contrasted mechanical and organic modes of apprehension. It also compared the creation of works of art with God's loving creation of the universe. It rejected outright materialism as a position impossible to sustain and concluded with a theory of beauty, according to which the order and harmony of the whole is prior to and gives sense to the parts.

What is particularly interesting is Ravaisson's extended critique of the eclectic philosophy of Cousin, which continued to be dominant in the French educational system. This account displays Cousin as an unscholarly and superficial thinker, and Cousin's aesthetics is picked out for especially strong criticism, since it depicts ideal beauty in an abstract and general way. Ravaisson's own approach is illustrated in his discussion of the Venus de Milo, which concentrates in detail on the particularity of the work, to the point of arguing persuasively that a mistake had been made in its reconstruction, causing a blemish, namely a violation of Leonardo da Vinci's rule about figures posed on one foot specifying the relative heights of the shoulders and the line from the knot of the throat to the supporting foot. This is a nice illustration of Ravaisson's more general claim that philosophy must emphasize the particular (he cites Aristotle to this effect). Thus his statement that the pose of the Venus expresses love and peace, and that teleological understanding is fundamental in fine art, rests on the conviction that the beauty of an object resides in its concrete existence, contrary to the opinion of Cousin.

All this led Ravaisson to concentrate on the old distinction between analysis and synthesis. Analysis, as described and practiced by so many, from Descartes to Bertrand Russell, aimed at achieving understanding by breaking down a phenomenon or problem or object into its constituent parts. A clear

---

34. *Ibid.*, 35.
35. Félix Ravaisson, *La Philosophie en France au XIXème Siècle* (Paris: Hachette, 1867).

picture of the parts, their nature, workings, and interactions, should resolve any puzzles about the wholes. The alternative and preferred philosophical approach, according to Ravaisson, was synthesis: here we find a constructive approach, which strives toward the infinite. He wrote a "philosophical testament,"[36] of which versions have subsequently been published, although it remained incomplete at his death. Here, he praises enthusiasm, emphasizes the role of feeling in the search for truth, claims that generosity and love are the foundation of education and of social morality, and argues that belief in immortality is natural to humans. What we retain is that this "spiritualist" rested his position, at least in part, on a concern for the concrete.

V. RENOUVIER

Charles Bernard Renouvier[37] was a contemporary of Ravaisson. He is often described as a neo-Kantian, taking up in his own way Kant's concern with the *a priori* conditions of knowledge. However, he differed from Kant in many respects, claiming that relations, rather than things, are fundamental. Maine de Biran had already made a similar claim. Renouvier also gave an important role to liberty, in a way quite different from Kant's treatment of free will. Although he was a founding figure of French neo-Kantianism, these were not Renouvier's only departures from Kant: he repudiated the notion of things that are not represented ("things in themselves"), and departed from Kant in his treatment of time and space: unlike Kant, Renouvier thought that these could not be posited, by whatever reasoning, without generating the paradoxes of actual infinity.[38]

He rejected the notion of substance. Relation was the basis of representations. He also rejected the notion of actual infinity: reality is finite. Furthermore, certainty rested on liberty. In ethics, it was necessary to take into account the existence of desires and interests to which history testifies. Here, too, he diverged from Kant's notion of duty.

After his time at the École Polytechnique (1834–36), he published a work on Cartesianism,[39] in which he contended that belief in the reality of the infinite

---

36. Félix Ravaisson, *Testament Philosophique et fragments: Précédés de la notice lue en 1904 à l'Académie des Sciences morales et politiques, par Henri Bergson*, Charles Devivaise (ed.) (Paris: Boivin, 1933).
37. Charles Bernard Renouvier (January 1, 1815–September 1, 1903; born in Montpellier; died in Prades).
*38. For a detailed discussion of Renouvier and Lachelier in the context of neo-Kantianism, see the essay by Sebastian Luft and Fabien Capeillères in *The History of Continental Philosophy: Volume 3*.
39. Charles Renouvier, *Manuel de philosophie moderne* (Paris: Paulin, 1842).

gave rise to contradictions, and argued for "neo-criticism," which would combine phenomenalism, finitism, and apriorism. Renouvier continued to explore this position throughout his life, the fruits of which can be found in his most influential work, the four-volume *Essais de critique générale* (1854–64). In his later years, Renouvier was drawn to a Leibnizian metaphysical position that, conjoined with his emphasis on liberty and reflective consciousness as defining characteristics of human persons, led him to put forward an early version of personalism.[40]

VI. LACHELIER

Jules Lachelier, through his teaching at the École Normale Supérieure from 1864–75 as well as his administrative posts as Inspecteur Général (1879–1900) and president of the *jury d'agrégation de philosophie* (1900–10), was perhaps the most influential philosopher in France for almost forty years.[41] Like his teacher Ravaisson, Lachelier considered that naive acceptance of the supposed findings of "science" was dangerous. After all, science did not always deliver hard results, or more precisely, the results it did yield could lead to divergent views of the world and of our place in it. Consider the radical difference about chance between Laplace and Cournot, discussed above. It might be thought, however, that such divergences do not impugn the main merit of the scientific method, namely its objectivity. But Lachelier denied this claim to objectivity, developing a form of idealism in which there was indeed objectivity, but an objectivity that resides in thought. Mind, in this conception, is the underlying reality, and the panoply of the natural world and its order derives from thought. Thought here is not to be construed subjectively. Thus Lachelier developed a position that can be described as a form of Neoplatonism.

We can follow this line of thought by considering the arguments of his doctoral thesis on induction.[42] Induction, considered as generalization from specific facts or findings, needed a proper basis. But how is this to be provided? Lachelier devoted ten pages at the beginning of his thesis to John Stuart Mill's

---

40. Charles Renouvier, *Le Personnalisme* (Paris: Félix Alcan, 1903). [*] For a discussion of personalism later in the twentieth century, see the discussions of Emmanuel Mounier in the essays by Andreas Grossman and Felix Ó Murchadha in *The History of Continental Philosophy: Volume 4*.
41. Among those who studied with Jules Lachelier (May 27, 1832–January 26, 1918; born in Fountainbleu; died in Paris) at the École Normale were Jules Lagneau (1851–94) and Émile Boutroux (1845–1921), and his influence can be seen in the work of Léon Brunschvicg (1869–1944), Maurice Blondel (1861–1949), and Henri Bergson.
42. Jules Lachelier, *Du fondement de l'induction* (Paris: Librairie philosophique de Ladrange, 1871). This work was dedicated to Ravaisson.

account of this procedure.[43] He claimed that although Mill's methods might "work," say for very large numbers of stellar motions over very many years, they failed to account for the very possibility of passing from the particular to the general. We need to start with the One, not the many. "Pure mechanism," he wrote, "has no real existence, even phenomenally. It is just the limit of resolution of organic living entities in their material conditions."[44]

Now we must accept the existence of a law of efficient causes established in Kantian style, but this will not by itself justify or explain inductive procedures. A further and more fundamental underpinning is needed. We shall give first place to the concrete existence of teleologically organized individuals. A whole is an end when containing within itself the reason for the organization of its parts (e.g. a stable chemical compound, or a living organism). A number of consequences followed from the existence and recurrence of such wholes. First, such objects presuppose the existence of a law of final causes. Their teleological structure has the form of being willed. In this sense freedom is fundamental in the universe. Second, given that organisms vary in their degree of organization, we are led to discern a hierarchy of beings of increasing order and harmony. Third, we come once more to the underlying reality of thought.

As with other forms of idealism, the question arises: what of material existence? Given that Lachelier takes the existence of self-organizing wholes as a starting-point, are these wholes not material? A pure idealist might say that the material is an illusion: it does not really exist. Yet Lachelier oscillates between his Neoplatonizing arguments and a belief in the reality of matter. As Millet wrote: "Lachelier recognizes that his philosophical system cannot give an account of that principle which is matter, yet he holds on to the system; he is aware that such a problem is fundamental, that matter is irreducible, yet his system leads him to reduce it to non-existence."[45]

VII. BERGSON

Henri Bergson is discussed elsewhere in this collection.[46] But a brief treatment here will serve to provide a perspective on some of the various authors whose work is outlined above.

We find very varied positions among all these thinkers with regard to science. Maine de Biran, while not trained as a scientist, was well read in numerous

---

*43. For a discussion of Mill's views on induction, see the essay by Dale Jacquette in this volume.

44. Jules Lachelier, *Œuvres* (Paris: Félix Alcan, 1933), vol. I, 86, my translation.

45. Louis Millet, *Le Symbolisme dans la philosophie de Lachelier* (Paris: Presses Universitaires de France, 1959), 213, my translation. See also the conclusion to this work, 255–64.

*46. See the essay by John Mullarkey in *The History of Continental Philosophy: Volume 3*.

aspects of the physical and medical science of his day, and took it very seriously. Ravaisson, by contrast, was not similarly inclined. For instance, he used his treatment of habit mentioned above as a handle to escape from mechanism, while for Maine de Biran the topic was a first step in the development of a systematic psychology that was to give a strong place to the underground workings of the organism, and give a strong role to empirical investigation. Various scientific disciplines and social-scientific disciplines, according to Maine de Biran, would play a significant part in developing "the science of man."

Looking ahead to Bergson, we find once more a detailed treatment of topics in the biological and psychological sciences in *Time and Free Will* (1889; dedicated to Lachelier), *Matter and Memory* (1896) and *Creative Evolution* (1907), and of physical science in *Duration and Simultaneity* (1922), which is a treatment of relativity theory. Although we can see some real continuities with the thought of the spiritualists in Bergson's later work and his growing interest in religion, his respect for and detailed interest in scientific investigation also marks him off from spiritualism. One cannot imagine a spiritualist saying what Bergson said in a lecture on "Philosophical Intuition" in 1911:

> Here, if you like, is a man who, over a long period of time, has followed a certain scientific method and laboriously gained his results, who says to us: "Experience, with the help of reasoning, leads to this point; scientific knowledge begins here; it ends there; such are my conclusions"; and the philosopher would have the right to answer: "Very well, leave it to me, and I'll show you what I can do with it! The knowledge you bring me unfinished, I shall complete. What you put before me in bits I shall put together. ...." Truly a very strange pretension! How could the profession of philosopher confer upon him who exercises it the power of advancing farther than science in the same direction as science? ... Such a conception of the role of the philosopher would be unfair to science. But how much more unfair to philosophy![47]

Nineteenth-century debates had seen a rift develop between the many advocates of a positivistic and mechanistic view of reality such as Comte, and others, such as the spiritualists, who rejected this view. With Bergson, we return to a less simple position. *Creative Evolution*, perhaps his most well-known work, was not an attack from a "spiritualist" perspective on the biological science of the time,

---

47. Henri Bergson, "Philosophical Intuition," in *The Creative Mind*, Mabelle L. Andison (trans.) (New York: Citadel Press, [1946] 1992), 122–3, translation mine.

but an informed attempt to put that science in a rather different perspective.[48] And his book about relativity theory was another major and informed attempt to reconcile his own arguments about duration with the relativistic treatment of simultaneity.[49]

Thus any attempt to categorize each of these thinkers as scientistic or spiritualistic would be inadequate. Despite their spiritualist aspects, many of them were interested in or contributed to the scientific enterprise. Consider, for example, Maine de Biran's attempt to provide foundations for psychology, Cournot's treatment of chance, Renouvier's emphasis on data as essentially relational and his adoption of finitism, Lachelier's investigation of regulative principles, and Bergson's treatment of human reason as an evolutionary acquisition destined for our pragmatic needs.

Few thinkers are static. This is why the doxographic approach to the history of thought, which proceeds by "isms," is usually unsatisfactory. And it is why we have here indicated connections as well as divergences between the itineraries of the thinkers discussed in order to place the main representatives of "French spiritualist philosophy" – Ravaisson and Lachelier – in a certain intellectual landscape.

MAJOR WORKS

Antoine-Augustin Cournot

Recherches sur les principes mathématiques de la théorie des richesses. Paris: Hachette, 1838. Published in English as *Researches into the Mathematical Principles of the Theory of Wealth*, translated by N. T. Bacon. New York & London: Macmillan, 1897.

Essai sur les fondements de nos connaissances et sur les caractères de la critique philosophique. Paris: Hachette, 1851.

Traité de l'enchaînement des idées fondamentales dans les sciences et dans l'histoire. Paris: Hachette, 1861.

Considérations sur la marche des idées et des événements dans les temps modernes. Paris: Hachette, 1872.

Matérialisme, vitalisme, rationalisme. Étude sur l'emploi des données de la science en philosophie. Paris, 1875.

---

*48. For a discussion of Bergson's *Creative Evolution*, see the essay by Keith Ansell-Pearson, Paul-Antoine Miquel, and Michael Vaughan in *The History of Continental Philosophy: Volume 3*.

49. It is worth noting that Bergson did not wish this book to be republished in his lifetime, since he thought that he might not be able to sustain his position with sufficient mathematical expertise.

Jules Lachelier

Du fondement de l'induction. Paris: Librairie philosophique de Ladrange, 1871. Republished as *Du fondement de l'induction suivi de Psychologie et Métaphysique et de Notes sur le pari de Pascal*. Paris: Félix Alcan, 1924. Published in English in *The Philosophie of Jules Lachelier, Du Fondement de L'Induction, Psychologie et Métaphysique, Notes sur le Pari de Pascal*, together with *Contributions to Vocabulaire Technique et Critique de la Philosophie*, and *a Selection From His Letters*, edited and translated by Edward G. Ballard. The Hague: Martinus Nijhoff, 1960.

Œuvres. 2 vols. Paris: Félix Alcan, 1933.

Lettres (1856–1918). Paris: G. Girard, 1933.

Cours de Logique. École Normale Supérieure 1866–67. Paris: Éditions Universitaires de France, 1990.

Félix Ravaisson

Essai sur la métaphysique d'Aristote. 2 vols. Paris: Imprimerie Royale, 1837–46.

De l'habitude. Paris: Imprimerie de H. Fournier, 1838. Last ed. 1894. Published in English as *Of Habit*, translated by Clare Carlisle and Mark Sinclair. London: Continuum, 2009.

La Philosophie en France au XIXème siècle. Paris: Hachette, 1867. New ed. 1895, comprenant le *Rapport sur le prix Victor Cousin* (le scepticisme dans l'antiquité), 1884. For the later editions, see *De l'habitude/La Philosophie en France au XIXème siècle* in *Corpus des Œuvres de philosophie en langue française*. Paris: Fayard, 1984.

La Venus de Milo. Paris: Hachette, 1871.

Testament philosophique et fragments: Précédés de la notice lue en 1904 à l'Académie des Sciences morales et politiques, par Henri Bergson. Text reviewed and presented by Charles Devivaise. Paris: Boivin, 1933.

Charles Renouvier

Manuel de philosophie moderne. Paris: Paulin, 1842.

Essais de Critique Générale. Paris: Lagrange, 1854–64.

Le Personnalisme. Paris: Félix Alcan, 1903.

Critique de la Doctrine de Kant. Paris: Félix Alcan, 1906.

8

THE EMERGENCE OF SOCIOLOGY AND ITS THEORIES: FROM COMTE TO WEBER

Alan Sica

Where and when philosophy ends and so-called "classical social theory" begins is not a question readily or credibly answered in simple terms. It is easy enough to ask, for instance: which philosophical streams most forcefully stimulated the thinking of Comte, Marx, Spencer, Durkheim, Tönnies, Simmel, or Weber? Yet for many reasons a precise set of answers that pertains to each is elusive, not least because all were Victorian polymaths who read widely and thought deeply to an extent remote from today's scholarly world, besieged as it is by electronic diversions. Their minds operated within different spheres of application and comprehension than do ours. They were also egocentric enough (Comte, Marx, and Spencer in particular) to refuse to acknowledge thinkers from whom they borrowed heavily, but whose disciples they did not want to appear to be.

I. HERBERT SPENCER

Consider, for example, the remarkable case of Herbert Spencer (1820–1903), identified in the nonpareil eleventh edition of the *Britannica* (1910) as simply an "English philosopher," yet now remembered principally as a sociologist or political theorist, and for his indispensable role in the proliferation of "social Darwinism." Both his *Autobiography* and *The Life and Letters* remain indispensable in connecting the philosophical with the sociological, in showing how they were linked in this quintessential Victorian mind. The former work occupies two thick volumes published in April 1904, the year following his death at eighty-three, totaling 1258 close-set pages. He likely regarded this work, left to languish in a drawer for fifteen years, as relatively trivial when placed beside his genuinely scientific works. Yet even though it is indeed free of deep psychological insight – his one-sided relationship with Marian Evans ("George Eliot") merits little attention[1] – the magnitude of detail is in its own way uniquely informative.

We learn, for instance, that Spencer's relation with philosophical thought was antinomically creative. He dismisses Kant easily:

> I found in Mr. Wilson's house ... a copy of a translation of Kant's *Critique of Pure Reason* ... This I commenced reading, but did not go far. The doctrine that Time and Space are "nothing but" subjective forms – pertain exclusively to consciousness and have nothing beyond consciousness answering to them – I rejected at once and absolutely; and, having done so, went no further. Being then, as always, an impatient reader, even of things which in large measure interest me and meet with a general acceptance, it has always been out of the question for me to go on reading a book the fundamental principles of which I entirely dissent from.[2]

He also notes that "belief in the unqualified supremacy of reason is the superstition of philosophers,"[3] and criticizes Comte and the numerous "Comtists" who labeled Spencer a follower of the former in his ideas about sociology. Spencer vigorously denies this in detail and repeatedly,[4] while also dismissing "the schemes of Oken and Hegel, each of whom preceded Comte in the attempt to organize a system of philosophy out of the sciences arranged in serial order."[5] Despite all this, philosophy for Spencer remained indispensable in that its arguments – those few that he seemed to have studied – forced him to clarify his own in, for instance, his *Principles of Psychology*, which he realized would have "lacked its organizing principle"[6] without philosophy as its foil.

Like Darwin, his confederate in evolutionary theory, Spencer began life in the midst of an intensely religious family, and carried with him into the study of the natural and social worlds a heavy load of religio-philosophical baggage. It is no accident that "the Unknowable" figures prominently in his early work, *First Principles* (1862), since Spencer believed there were metaphysical questions neither he nor other humans could possibly answer, and should best be left to some external power beyond their ken.

---

1. See Herbert Spencer, *An Autobiography* (New York: D. Appleton, 1904), vol. 2, 428–31.
2. *Ibid.*, vol. 1, 289.
3. *Ibid.*, 290.
4. See e.g. *ibid.*, 292 n., 518.
5. *Ibid.*, 518.
6. *Ibid.*

If Spencer had died at thirty-two, he would have established himself as a minor speculative thinker, but he persisted through fifty more years of rigorous study as an autodidact, probing and amalgamating biology, education, sociology, political theory, psychology, ethics, and comparative anthropology. By inventing the phrase "survival of the fittest," he forever connected himself with the Darwinian camp of his walking partner, Thomas H. Huxley (1825–95), and others. Yet one cannot view Spencer's gigantic *Synthetic Philosophy* (sixteen volumes) without realizing that the merely empirical, measurable, and palpable operated in his system under the sign of a philosophical commitment tending toward the teleological, which surely inspired him in his tireless pursuit of data. That he was attacked late in life by "Spencer smashers" for being insufficiently ardent in his religiosity did not undermine his fundamental claim on philosophical speculation. Lester Frank Ward, first president of the American Sociological Association, defended Spencer in 1894 against a phalanx of theologians on precisely these grounds.[7]

If Spencer is now known as a champion of *laissez-faire* governmental forms (*Man Versus the State*; 1884), a believer in evolutionary progress, and a proponent of industrial versus militaristic social order, he was first of all a self-taught ontologist and epistemologist. His materialist view of the physical world, alternating between decomposition and reconstitution toward some desirable evolutionary end, all orchestrated around a unique lexicon (persistence of force, necessary rhythm, evolution versus dissolution, instability of the homogeneous, etc.), clearly revealed his hope of being accepted as a major philosopher – and as such triumphant over the German idealists he did not read carefully. His regimen of mental hygiene (not unlike Auguste Comte's some years earlier) included careful avoidance of other philosophers' ideas, so as to protect his creativity from the possible pollutants that might be loosed by conscientious reading of his competitors' works. Yet the shadow of philosophy stayed with him throughout, as revealed in his *Autobiography*, where an essential chapter in the second volume is entitled "A System of Philosophy Projected."

One wishes we had similarly detailed accounts for the other classical theorists of the kind that Spencer provided. His *Life and Letters*, assembled by an acolyte in 1908, is another 600-page "tome" (for once, the correct term), and again illustrates the astonishing dimensions of nineteenth-century thought at its highest levels. The classical theorists did not suffer imprisonment within the narrow, shallow disciplinary identities that trap most scholars today, and gloried in their ability to move freely among whatever fields of learning they found pertinent to their self-defined tasks. It is therefore unsurprising that Spencer in his prime

---

7. See Anonymous, "Spencer-smashing at Washington," *Popular Science Monthly* (February 1894): 856–7.

was often named "the nineteenth century's Aristotle," which seemed as plausible to his contemporaries as it appears preposterous now.[8]

As a further indicator of the many puzzles that arise when trying to filiate social thought with philosophy, one might posit as nascent "social theorists" or even "sociologists," the following: Mary Astell, Montesquieu, Turgot, Adam Smith, Adam Ferguson, John Millar, Kant (his *Anthropology* or *Ethics*), Condillac, Bentham, Wollstonecraft, Condorcet, Hegel (*Phenomenology of Spirit* or *Philosophy of Right*), Malthus, Sismondi, de Maistre, Saint-Simon, Carlyle, or Fourier – for a persuasive case could be made for each.[9] But if one follows convention and categorizes them instead as philosophers, economists, or historians, no one could reasonably object given current constraints on disciplinary identities. Thus the difficulty of drawing a plausible line between, on the one hand, what since the Presocratics had been "philosophy" proper, and on the other, the neologistic "social sciences" – springing up like wildflowers in the nineteenth century – has been recognized for a long time.

The learned, forgotten American sociologist Charles Ellwood had this to say about this very topic in 1902 in the opening paragraph of "Aristotle as a Sociologist," an article of continuing utility:

> Sociology is ordinarily spoken of as a "new science." In a certain sense this is true; yet social thought is as old as history, and social philosophy as an organized discipline has existed, at least, since Aristotle. Only in a very special sense, therefore, is it right to speak of sociology as a new science. If we understand by sociology merely the effort to apply to social phenomena the method of quantitative measurement, and to interpret these phenomena as merely the most complex manifestation of the forces of the physical universe, then we are justified in regarding it as a new science; for sociology in this sense is the product of modern positivism. But those who reject the mechanical theory of society, together with the idea that the scientific interpretation of society must be limited thereto, have no right to speak of sociology as a new science. *When we regard modern sociology as "the more critical, more systematized study of the social reality," we do not make it a "new" science, but rather a renovated and*

---

8. See Mark Francis, *Herbert Spencer and the Invention of Modern Life* (Stocksfield: Acumen, 2007); J. D. Y. Peel, *Herbert Spencer: The Evolution of a Sociologist* (New York: Basic Books, 1971); Steven Shapin, "Man with a Plan: Herbert Spencer's Theory of Everything," *New Yorker* (August 13, 2007); Barry Werth, *Banquet at Delmonico's: Great Minds, the Gilded Age, and the Triumph of Evolution in America* (New York: Random House, 2009).

9. See Alan Sica (ed.), *Social Thought: From the Enlightenment to the Present* (Boston, MA: Allyn & Bacon, 2005).

reorganized science. The beginnings of sociology as a science in this sense certainly lie far back of the modern scientific era.[10]

Thus the question of when sociology's classical theories began to evolve as such is impossible to answer definitively, even if we do know precisely when "sociology" got its name – a more modest discovery to be sure.

II. AUGUSTE COMTE

Standard accounts of sociology's history always begin with Auguste Comte (1798–1857), not because he single-handedly invented the field, but because he named it. He was a mathematics prodigy, admitted to France's premier engineering school aged sixteen, and tutored mathematics thereafter. But unlike most engineers being trained at the École Polytechnique, Comte was a fierce republican, rebellious at every turn, and even tried to arrange emigration to the United States in order to teach in a nation free of monarchy. His life was filled with professional and personal frustrations, especially after he began lecturing and publishing his *Course of Positive Philosophy* in 1826, which at first met with success, but later, owing partly to his repeated psychological crises, failed to win the kind of adoration that he thought was his due. Yet he could hardly be viewed as an intellectual failure. No less a figure than John Stuart Mill (1806–73) supported him financially, popularized his work in England by means of a small book (*August Comte and Positivism*; 1865), and patiently tolerated his egocentrism throughout their long friendship. And the noted British feminist, Harriet Martineau (1802–76), invested tremendous effort in freely translating his work into digestible English. There was a time when Comteanism (or "Comtism") was a respectable label recognized worldwide among those interested in political and cultural change, and his works were widely discussed by a large anglophone audience as well as in Brazil,[11] Mexico, Turkey, India, and elsewhere.

On the afternoon of Saturday, April 27, 1839, Comte in Paris "wrote and underlined the word" *sociology* in his manuscript, "embarrassed by coining

---

10. Charles Ellwood, "Aristotle as a Sociologist," *Annals of the American Academy of Political Science*, vol. 19 (1902), www.efm.bris.ac.uk/het/aristotle/ellwood.htm (accessed June 2010), emphasis added.
11. Several of the individuals involved in the coup that overthrew the Brazilian emperor and established the Brazilian republic in 1889 were followers of Comte's ideas. To this day, the flag of Brazil bears the motto *Ordem e Progresso* (Order and progress), which was inspired by Comte's positivist motto: "*l'Amour pour principe; l'Ordre pour base; et le Progrès pour but*" (Love as a principle; Order as the basis; and Progress as the goal), which appears on the title page of each of the four volumes of Comte's *Système de politique positive*.

another neologism."[12] His own development as an intellectual historian and theorist, and by self-proclamation as "the first sociologist," cannot be understood without examining a few of his many predecessors and peers, most of whom were deeply philosophical. Like most French intellectuals, ever since Pascal and Descartes, Comte learned to venerate the Gallic tradition as a schoolboy, but he managed to go far beyond it in his search for "universal" knowledge. Mary Pickering's heroically detailed spadework[13] has revealed, for example, that Hume was not only Comte's favorite historian, but also, by his own admission, his "principal philosophical predecessor" – not the usual French standard-bearers, Montesquieu, Condorcet, or Turgot, as textbooks sometimes claim.[14] Comte's strident, encompassing version of religio-positivism made it impossible for him properly to "grasp the depth of Hume's skepticism and relativism"[15] – which was typical of his peculiar mode of incorporating others' ideas into his own lumbering architectonic. More surprising yet, he claimed Condorcet, the German phrenologist and biologist Franz Joseph Gall (1758–1828), and the arch-conservative Joseph de Maistre (1753–1821), as his major influences overall.[16] By working at fevered pitch for decades, he vigorously practiced a piratical version of what Robert K. Merton dubbed "OBI": obliteration by incorporation.[17] Yet he read so broadly, even manically, that virtually any thinker of the Enlightenment figured positively or negatively in his *Cours de philosophie positive* (six volumes; 1830–42) and his *Système de politique positive* (four volumes; 1851–54), even if often only in caricature. As Pickering put it, "It is evident that Comte had absorbed the ideas of Montesquieu and Condorcet and was influenced by Constant, Staël, Say, Cabanis, and Destutt de Tracy"[18] – among many others.

Comte represents that rare social theorist who combines top-level mathematical and scientific capacities with a passionate commitment to history, intellectual and political, fired by an unconstrained desire for liberating social change. He was not the economist that Marx or Vilfredo Pareto were to become, and less well schooled in philosophical argument than were Durkheim, Simmel, or Weber. Yet, by elaborating the teaching of his sometime employer, Henri

---

12. Mary Pickering, *Auguste Comte: An Intellectual Biography, Volume 1* (Cambridge: Cambridge University Press, 1993), 615.
13. *Ibid.*, 313, 306–8, 600.
14. E.g. Jonathan Turner *et al.*, *The Emergence of Sociological Theory*, 2nd ed. (Chicago, IL: Dorsey Press, 1989), 7–13.
15. Pickering, *Auguste Comte*, 312.
16. *Ibid.*, 263.
17. Robert K. Merton, *Social Theory and Social Structure*, enl. ed. (New York: Free Press, 1968), 27–8, 35–7.
18. Pickering, *Auguste Comte*, 241.

Saint-Simon, he did lay out in great detail a form of methodological positivism that inspired generations of social scientists during the ensuing century, even when they repudiated its more grandiose aspects.

Comte believed that humankind had historically progressed from theological entrapment in myth and fetish-worship to a metaphysical stage of skilled speculation, then finally achieving maturity in the positivist era – his own, of course, as he described it in the 1830s – which would put evidence and reasoned argument to use in establishing truth. Not only did he study and analyze religious and philosophical history, but also mathematics, astronomy, physics, chemistry, and biology in his far-flung attempt to prove that sociology would become the "queen of the sciences." Comte's vision for the social sciences generally, that they would put to use quantitative methods and data along with standard inductive practices, led him to argue that once sociologists had been installed as the secular priests of the social order, calamities such as the French Revolution would become unnecessary. Yet sociology's roots for Comte always lay in philosophy, as he explained in "The Intellectual Character of Positivism":

> To effect this necessary intervention is the proper sphere of politics. But a right conception cannot be formed of it without the aid of the philosopher, whose business it is to define and amend the principles on which it is conducted. With this object in view, the philosopher endeavors to co-ordinate the various elements of man's existence, so that it may be conceived of theoretically as an integral whole.[19]

The philosophical legacy of Comte continues to live invisibly in all modern social science, since the unspoken assumption underlying today's research coincides perfectly with Comte's fondest hope: once the unvarying "laws" of social behavior are uncovered through rigorous positivistic research, behavior can be tailored to fit society's and individuals' needs like a glove, and political miseries of the kind he knew during his own lifetime in France will no longer trouble the human condition. Comte's simple notion of positivism, his theory of the three stages of human thought, and the so-called "religion of humanity" over which he and other "sociologist-priests" would preside via scientific method no longer appeal in the way they did among Mill's peers. Yet this does not detract from Comte's singular role in the early legitimation of sociology, and the necessary linkage he shaped between it and its philosophical heritage. And it is probably no accident that Comte was rediscovered, yet again, during the 1960s and 1970s, the "Age of Aquarius," given that he introduced his "religion of humanity"

---

19. In *Auguste Comte and Positivism*, Gertrude Lenzer (ed.) (New York: Harper & Row, 1975), 320.

this way: "Love, then, is our principle; order our basis; and progress our end."[20] He learned late in life, through a beloved woman who died too soon after they had met, that love is the great motivating force in social life, and "reason" alone cannot inspire humans to develop a "religion of humanity" of the sort he envisioned in a trouble-free world.

The instance of Turgot[21] is similarly interesting and illustrative in this regard, not only as it pertains to Comte's development, but also as revealing the way early social theorists often routinely turned philosophical ideas to their own purposes. Turgot set out a three-stage theory of historical change in his famous 1750 address, "A Philosophical Review of the Successive Advances of the Human Mind,"[22] which won high praise from Condorcet and others whom Comte also admired. One could therefore surmise (as did the noted chronicler Harry Elmer Barnes[23]) that Turgot's ideas directly influenced Comte when, seventy-two years later in 1822, he created his own tripartite theory of cultural "advance" (the theological–metaphysical–positivist eras). Yet, according to Pickering's careful scrutiny of the evidence, this is not likely, because Comte apparently read Turgot only in 1852 or 1853, long after his own theory had been formulated.[24] Moreover, his library contained none of Turgot's own works, but instead, a well-used copy of Condorcet's *Vie de Monsieur Turgot* (1787).

An intriguing intersection among the three thinkers occurs at the beginning of Condorcet's "Essay on the Application of Mathematics to the Theory of Decision-Making" (1785), which opens with what from our vantage point can only seem poignant hopefulness:

> A great man, Monsieur Turgot, whose teaching and example, and above all whose friendship I shall always mourn, was convinced that the truths of the moral and political sciences are susceptible of the same certainty as those forming the system of the physical sciences, even those branches like astronomy which seem to approach mathematical certainty.

---

20. *Ibid.*, 381. As noted above (note 11), this motto served as inspiration for the creation of the Brazilian flag.
21. Anne-Robert-Jacques Turgot (1727–81) was a French economist and statesman, and an early proponent of economic liberalism. In his "A Philosophical Review of the Successive Advances of the Human Mind" is found what is considered the first complete statement of the Enlightenment "Idea of Progress."
22. In *Turgot on Progress, Sociology and Economics*, Ronald L. Meek (ed.) (Cambridge: Cambridge University Press, 1973), 41–59.
23. Harry Elmer Barnes, *An Introduction to the History of Sociology* (Chicago, IL: University of Chicago Press, 1948), 72.
24. Pickering, *Auguste Comte*, 200 n.32.

This opinion was dear to him, because it led him to the consoling hope that the human race will necessarily progress toward happiness and perfection, as it has done in the knowledge of truth.[25]

Such sentiments are virtually identical with Comte's, and continue even now to inspire a significant portion of modern sociological labors, even if usually in far more modest terms, chastened as they are by postmodern reflexivity and the failure of various large-scale social programs that were based on positivistic research (e.g. the James Coleman "busing report" of 1966).

III. HENRI-CLAUDE DE SAINT-SIMON

Even a cursory glance at Comte's road to the creation of "sociology," by name if not by practice, must pay special attention to Henri-Claude de Saint-Simon (1760–1825),[26] for whom Comte served as a research associate from summer 1817 until March 1824. If the Marx/Engels relationship seems the least troubled, most productive, and "brotherly" of all such team efforts, it could be said that Saint-Simon's and Comte's – they were respectively forty-seven and nineteen when they met – represents the "dysfunctional family" model of collaboration at its worst. What began as worshipful attention of the younger for the elder ended as a paranoid tragedy in which Comte repudiated everything good about Saint-Simon's ideas and person.

The parallels between the pair's ideas have become increasingly obvious since their feuding bands of followers disappeared. Unlike Comte, who represented himself in logorrheic fashion, Saint-Simon's ideas were best presented by his disciples (e.g. Amand Bazard's *Exposition de la doctrine de St. Simon*; two volumes; 1828–30), and not in Saint-Simon's own forty-seven volumes of collected writings (1865–78). He admitted in a letter to M. de Redern "to have thought a great deal and to have read very little to produce really new ideas,"[27] which is wholly at odds with Comte's synthesizing and inclusive mode of theorizing.

The notion so close to Comte's heart, that science would guide "industrial society" toward universal prosperity and freedom, and that superstitious beliefs would be left behind, is indeed Saint-Simon's. The latter thought that industrialists could be trusted to organize and run modern society (one is reminded of

---

25. In *Condorcet: Selected Writings*, Keith Baker (ed.) (Indianapolis, IN: Bobbs-Merrill, 1976), 33.
*26. For a discussion of Saint-Simon, see the essay by Diane Morgan in *The History of Continental Philosophy: Volume 1*.
27. Claude-Henri comte de Saint-Simon, *Œuvres*, 6 vols (Paris: Anthropos, 1966) [Geneva: Slatkine Reprints, 1977], 1.1.110.

Thorstein Veblen's paean a century later to a guiding "soviet of engineers"[28]), and that a Christianized socialism would evolve from their efforts. Here a utopian condition would obtain in which the worst features of human behavior would "naturally" evaporate. Ironically, it was Saint-Simon's late injection of religiosity into his program for social change that alienated Comte, who would himself late in life make almost precisely the same move when he fashioned his "Religion of Humanity."

In *The New Christianity* (1825), Saint-Simon argued that the ultimate goal of his utopian society would be to eliminate poverty and to elevate what Marx would call "the proletariat" to a healthy and respectable condition. He envisioned the elimination of war, anarchy, and the egotistical impulses that gave rise to both when his religiously based social order was in place, one built on the conventional Catholic virtues of obedience and devotion to a larger, collective good. It must be remembered that Saint-Simon had suffered imprisonment and near-execution during the revolution, so his feelings for organized aggressiveness were not warm. Similarly, Comte grew up with the shadowy memory of the Terror, so, like many of their countrymen, including rightists such as de Maistre, he posited as the supreme societal virtue the elimination of war and anarchic brutality among its citizens. Saint-Simon's utopia would also give women the vote and would abolish inheritance, themes picked up by many revolutionary groups that followed him. His high regard for women is another theme adopted by Comte as the latter entered his concluding years of creative work, around 1852.

IV. ÉMILE DURKHEIM

A telling yet neglected work that bridges many of these ideas is Émile Durkheim's *Socialism and Saint-Simon*, a dense set of lecture notes from 1895–96, which he delivered at Bordeaux, assembled posthumously in 1928 by his nephew, Marcel Mauss.[29] Durkheim (1858–1917) planned to write a comprehensive history of socialism drawn from separate lecture courses on Saint-Simon, Proudhon, Lasalle, Marx–Engels, and others, but his manifold duties – including the single-handed founding of French sociology! – prevented him from going beyond the first course. Many of Durkheim's students and colleagues were committed leftists, and even though he sympathized with their goal of ameliorating the grim

---

28. Thorstein Veblen, *The Engineers and the Price System* (New York: Viking, 1921).
29. Émile Durkheim, *Socialism and Saint-Simon*, Alvin W. Gouldner (ed.), Charlotte Sattler (trans.) (Yellow Springs, OH: Antioch Press, 1958).

lives of the working classes, he stood back from the fray and evaluated this broad movement "scientifically," following his usual tack.

His opinion of Saint-Simon's work was quite high, and he did not hesitate to point out the relative weakness of Comte's theorizing, and its heavy reliance on the older man's more fundamental innovations: "Comte owed him much more than he acknowledged."[30] In fact, as Alvin Gouldner points out in his introduction to the English translation, "Durkheim firmly denies to Comte, and bestows on Saint-Simon, the 'honor' of having founded both positivist philosophy and sociology."[31] The argument hinges on the 1813 *Mémoire sur la science de l'homme* by Saint-Simon, published in 1859, where the lineaments of a positivist social science are clearly spelled out. Gouldner speculates that perhaps Saint-Simon's "socialism" besmirched the less politically loaded term "sociology" to which Comte laid claim, and early historians of the field so wished to distance themselves from public association with the Left that they elected to remember Comte rather than his mentor. Either way, sociology of the French variety was born within a context of serious philosophical discussion, fusing aspects of Enlightenment secularism, newly formed positivism, and latent idealism.

Durkheim shrewdly observed that Saint-Simon, as rebellious youth, received encouragement and refinement from his acquaintance with D'Alembert, fueling his desire to update the *Encyclopedia* with an eye to advances in the natural sciences.[32] Yet for all his materialism, Saint-Simon's positivism rests on an idealist base: "knowledge ... according to him is the moving power of progress ... For it is the positive source of all social life. A society is above all a community of ideas."[33] This notion, contrary to Marx's desires, was absorbed into twentieth-century sociology through ideas such as "norms," "value consensus," and "societal belief-systems." And this stream clearly began with Saint-Simon's unique transformation of Enlightenment skepticism and materialism. In fact, Saint-Simon went so far as to claim that "philosophy appears as a branch of sociology,"[34] another notion firmly taken up by Comte.

Durkheim thought that he was in genuine intellectual competition with Spencer, but prior to battling his British foil, he first needed to trounce Comte's version of the discipline in order to advance his own. He believed that Comte misunderstood, perhaps by denying Saint-Simon's insights, the true nature of industrializing Europe. For Durkheim, of course, modern life's multiplying interdependencies were cause not for alarm, but for rejoicing, since they meant that philosophic and practical differences between individuals and their

---

30. *Ibid.*, 86.
31. Alvin Gouldner, "Introduction," in *ibid.*, ix.
32. *Ibid.*, 82.
33. *Ibid.*, 91.
34. *Ibid.*, 93.

affiliated groups would "naturally" diminish over time. There was no need, so thought Durkheim, for a Comtean priesthood of propagandizing sociologists intent on controlling the unruly masses. The magical "division of labor" would resolve whatever tensions were left over from the shocking degradation of village "mechanical solidarity" into the steely social structures of modern, urban life that constituted "organic solidarity." This profound transformation of human life was most memorably analyzed by Durkheim's German competitor, Ferdinand Tönnies (1855–1936), whose *Gemeinschaft und Gesellschaft* (1887) gave sociology two of its immortal and most contested terms. Tönnies understood that small-town life (*Gemeinschaft*) was made up of "community" relations, a naturally formed face-to-face intimacy that humans had perfected over millennia as an end in itself, whereas urban existence (*Gesellschaft*) bore within it an unavoidably alienating set of forces that has typified modern life, and led to a great number of "dysfunctions" (famously portrayed by Georg Simmel in "The Metropolis and Mental Life" of 1903).[35] Problems with *anomie*, which Comte described without using the term itself, would vaporize, so Durkheim argued in opposition to Tönnies, as modern citizens assembled into professional groups that would legislate morality along "organic" rather than "mechanical" lines.

For Durkheim (whose early scholarship dealt with Kant) the major problem of industrialized social life was controlling the Byronic passions for superindividuality and egocentricity – perhaps of the very type that Comte perfected in his own sad life – that leads inevitably to social disorganization and crises. As he famously wrote in *Suicide* when defining "altruistic" self-destruction, "If, as we have seen, excessive individuation leads to suicide, insufficient individuation has the same results. When a man has become detached from society, he encounters less resistance to suicide in himself, and he does so likewise when social integration is too strong."[36] This broad-scale argument within theorizing, capsulized in the mid twentieth century as the "personality versus social structure" debate, was already "an issue" for the Scottish moralists (Adam Smith, Adam Ferguson, John Millar, Dugald Stewart) by 1750, and, with Durkheim's embrace of Saint-Simon and Comte, assumed the role of foundational timber for all sociology that followed.

---

35. Reprinted in Donald N. Levine (ed.), *George Simmel on Individuality and Social Forms*, Donald N. Levine (trans.) (Chicago, IL: University of Chicago Press, 1971), 324–39.
36. Émile Durkheim, *Suicide: A Study in Sociology*, George Simpson (ed.), John A. Spaulding (trans.) (New York: Free Press, 1951), 217; a newer translation is less rhetorically powerful, if more literally accurate: see Durkheim, *On Suicide*, Robin Buss (trans.) (London: Penguin, 2006), 234.

V. GERMAN SOCIAL THEORY

One could surely go on in pursuing the Gallic sociological tradition – from Condorcet to Saint-Simon to Sismondi to Comte, de Maistre, Fourier, Quetelet, Gobineau, LePlay, Coulanges, to Tarde and Le Bon.[37] It is an astonishing progression of thought, with deep roots in the Enlightenment consciousness of Voltaire, Montesquieu, Rousseau, and others, yet equally at home in part with the arch conservatism of the counter-Enlightenment. But it is only a third of the major story one might tell about the origins of classical social theory and its links with philosophy *per se*. Much was also going on, of course, in Germany and Britain – not to mention Italy, Russia, and Central Europe, as outlined in Barnes's uniquely informative volume,[38] as well as in Pitirim Sorokin's early masterpiece, where an international cast of hundreds flits across his stage.[39] In some ways, though, the German and British components are better known than the French, at least in the United States. This is mainly because the founding fathers of American sociology were profoundly directed by Europeans – Marx, Weber, Durkheim, Simmel, and Tönnies – yet only one member of the early pantheon was French. And Durkheim's viewpoint was so conceptually opposed to Tönnies's in particular, and, by implication, to Weber's and Marx's, that most sociologists in the US have favored either the Gallic path or the Teutonic one, but seldom both.

The manifold connections between philosophical reflection and social theory as practiced in Germany has been explored many times in the US and Britain, as exemplified most forcefully by Talcott Parsons's *The Structure of Social Action* in 1937. However, enthusiasm for Kant, Hegel, Dilthey, and Nietzsche, among others, has run high in these intellectual circles for two centuries. Even Goethe has been brought into discussions of social theory (e.g. regarding Marx, Weber, Simmel, and Georg Lukács), given the "elective affinity" these thinkers found in his Faust drama and other works. Friedrich Schiller's[40] role is similarly valued, not so much for his plays as for his *Aesthetic Letters* (1794), wherein a theory of freedom as play (*Spieltrieb*) and invention is proposed, the sociological influence of which has stretched from his time to Herbert Marcuse's *Eros and Civilization*.[41] It was unsurprising, then, in 1975 when Marx's dissertation on Democritus was first translated into English, to find that his membership in Berlin's "Doctors'

---

37. See Sica (ed.), *Social Thought*.
38. Barnes, *An Introduction to the History of Sociology*.
39. Pitirim Sorokin, *Contemporary Sociological Theories* (New York: Harper & Brothers, 1928).
*40. For a discussion of Schiller, with particular reference to his aesthetics, see the essay by Daniel Dahlstrom in *The History of Continental Philosophy: Volume 1*.
41. Herbert Marcuse, *Eros and Civilization: A Philosophical Inquiry into Freud* (Boston, MA: Beacon Press, 1955), 185ff. [*] For a discussion of Marcuse's work, see the essay by John Abromeit in *The History of Continental Philosophy: Volume 5*.

Club" – a talented group of Young Hegelians who, alienated from the right-wing University of Berlin faculty and administration, met nightly for intellectual exchange[42] – was more than mere sociality. He had been a serious philosopher long before he turned in earnest to economics and politics. In fact, it is a truism among Marxists that his early works cannot be understood without prior grounding in Hegel, Feuerbach, Fichte, Bruno Bauer, and others who made up his philosophical worldview.[43] The relationship between Dilthey,[44] a great philosophical talent of his era, and Weber, Tönnies, or Simmel is less easily specified, but is always assumed to have mattered deeply to the younger men. Dilthey was the great pedagogue of the age at Berlin, and his biography of Schleiermacher, his theory (following Mill) of how the *Geisteswissenschaften* must differ from the *Naturwissenschaften*, and his pre-Husserlian version of phenomenological apperception all fed directly into the origins of German classical social theory.[45] It is impossible to conceive, for instance, of Simmel's *Philosophy of Money* (1900) or Weber's theory of *Verstehen* without giving Dilthey his due. Simmel's monumental study of how "the cash nexus" (to use Marx's term) affected interpersonal and intrapersonal life owes a great deal to philosophical currents swirling around him in Berlin. His *Philosophy of Money* exhaustively documents how monetary exchange "rationalizes" social life, even in its most intimate settings (art or sex), and strips away the formerly unique qualities that inhered within such social realms, converting "quality into quantity." Unlike Marx, however, Simmel did not view this in always negative terms, since quantification and the transformation of values that goes with it can lead to individual freedom that is impossible to experience in a premonetized social environment.

Weber's *verstehende Soziologie* ("interpretive" or "understanding" sociology) has been analyzed repeatedly since he proposed it around 1915, and shows its debt to a number of philosophical voices, beginning with Dilthey's. Humans operate within a zone of meanings that they constitute "automatically" by the sheer operation of their consciousnesses. When trying, as they must, to understand the motivations of one another, they must leave aside positivist notions of evidence and proof that work well in the natural sciences, and instead "participate" through empathy in the meaningful orbits of others in order to comprehend

---

42. See Francis Wheen, *Karl Marx: A Life* (New York: Norton, 1999), 32–3.
43. See, among many, David McLellan, *Karl Marx: His Life and Thought* (New York: Simon & Schuster, 1973), and Robert Tucker, *Philosophy and Myth in Karl Marx* (Cambridge: Cambridge University Press, 1961). [*] See also the essays by Terrell Carver and William Clare Roberts in this volume.
*44. For a discussion of Dilthey, with particular reference to hermeneutic theory, see the essay by Eric Sean Nelson in this volume.
45. Wilhelm Dilthey, *Introduction to the Human Sciences*, Rudolf A. Makkreel and Frithjof Rodi (eds), Michael Neville (trans.) (Princeton, NJ: Princeton University Press, 1989).

the significance of various actions as lived by the actors themselves. Arguments over how exactly to carry out social science, as then understood, is what inspired the battle beginning in 1883 fought between Carl Menger (1840–1921; representing the more theoretical Austrian School) and Gustav von Schmoller (1838–1917; representing the historical school) over proper methods for economics. Menger believed that economics should become mathematized and follow the scientific methods already put to sterling use in the natural sciences, whereas Schmoller, a capable historian, thought that searching for the invariant "laws of economic action" would ruin the field, sacrificing the unique details of the past for models that failed to describe any particular economic data accurately. Menger's followers in the twentieth century "won" the battle, but it remains to be seen if "economics as natural science" will forever hold the field, or if a resurgence of Schmoller's historicist viewpoint will occur. The lineaments of this protracted argument were codified by the philosophy teacher Wilhelm Windelband in 1894, drawing attentive social theorists into its orbit for their entire professional lives.[46]

As explained by Weber in numbing detail in *Roscher and Knies*, these were no small matters to his peer group of innovators, since these decades-long squabbles among epistemologists defined what the social sciences would or should become in the twentieth century.[47] Weber's virtuoso performance of critique, published between 1903 and 1906, deals not only in excruciating detail with the methodological practices of Wilhelm Roscher and Karl Knies,[48] but also considers the views of Benedetto Croce, Simmel, Hugo Münsterberg, and Friedrich Gottl as they bore on various conundrums concerning "laws" of social behavior. In its rigor and analytic depth, it is unique in the history of classical social theory, nearly matched only by some of Simmel's work on historiographical methods[49] and by Durkheim's lectures on pragmatism[50] or the recently "discovered" lectures on philosophy proper.[51] In these essays, Weber works very hard at distinguishing the criteria for "truth" within the social sciences versus philosophy proper, and begins to lay out the ideas he would later immortalize in "Science as a Vocation"

---

46. Wilhelm Windelband, *A History of Philosophy*, James H. Tufts (trans.) (New York: Macmillan, 1893), 648–60; Sven Eliasen, *Max Weber's Methodologies: Interpretation and Critique* (Cambridge: Polity, 2002), 138.
47. Max Weber, *Roscher and Knies: The Logical Problems of Historical Economics*, Guy Oakes (trans.) (New York: Free Press, 1975).
48. Wilhelm Roscher (1817–94) and Karl Knies (1821–98) were German economists and founding figures in the historical school of political economy.
49. George Simmel, *The Problem of the Philosophy of History: An Epistemological Essay*, Guy Oakes (trans.) (New York: Free Press, 1977).
50. Émile Durkheim, *Pragmatism and Sociology*, J. C. Whitehouse (trans.) (Cambridge: Cambridge University Press, 1983).
51. Émile Durkheim, *Durkheim's Philosophy Lectures*, N. Gross and R. A. Jones (trans.) (Cambridge: Cambridge University Press, 2004).

and "Politics as a Vocation," just prior to his death in 1920.[52] In these two canonical lectures (delivered in 1917 and 1919) he explained, among many things, how scholarship differs definitively from political action, with the responsibility of scholars always to the truth as best they can define it, whereas politics calls for heartless attention to the maintenance of power and support for a stated cause. They are naturally antinomical, so he claimed, based in part on his witnessing of German and French professors prostituting themselves during the First World War as propagandists for their governments. Weber's famous "fact–value distinction" has given rise to endless debate to this day. The question he confronted, as have many before and since, is whether a "social scientist" – as opposed to an ethicist, theologian, or moralist – has any intellectually legitimate role to play in defining the ultimate values by which people carry out their lives. Weber argued rigorously that those thinkers who desire a leadership role in the realm of ethics ought not to become sociologists, since, as Tolstoy said and as Weber quoted, the only really important question in life is how we are going to live it in a way that is meaningful. And to this question, social science has no answers. For instance, when Weber accompanied the official German peace delegation to Versailles in 1919 as their constitutional law expert, the "fact" that Germany had lost the First World War was paramount, yet the "values" or "meanings" that the world took from this event varied enormously, country by country – with disastrous consequences twenty years later.

Thus we see that social theory, classically imagined and then practiced, is most properly considered a heterodox, troubled branch of philosophy from the late eighteenth century to the early twentieth century. The prolonged struggle that most now view as needlessly prolix and indecisive, between the 1880s and the First World War, which sought to distance the social "sciences" from the humanities on epistemological grounds, and involving dozens of protagonists in Europe (and the US), did not succeed as completely as Durkheim, for instance, would have wished. The links between the theoretical apparatus of the *Geisteswissenschaften*, despite its reaching for a "scientific" identity, and the philosophical tradition that must include Rousseau, Kant, Hegel, Nietzsche, Husserl, and others have, if anything, become stronger over the past few decades. After Foucault, Derrida, Habermas, Giddens, Bourdieu, and their epigoni reintroduced Enlightenment philosophy into the social sciences during the 1960s and 1970s, it became obvious to all but the most hardened and unreflective positivists that the joint journey of philosophy and social theory would continue, as indeed it should.

---

52. Max Weber, *From Max Weber: Essays in Sociology*, Hans Gerth and C. Wright Mills (ed. and trans.) (New York: Oxford University Press, 1946).

9

DEVELOPMENTS IN PHILOSOPHY OF SCIENCE AND MATHEMATICS

Dale Jacquette

I. AGE OF ROMANCE, AGE OF REVOLUTION

Nineteenth-century science and mathematics is an erratic continuation of the monumental innovations of the Enlightenment. The eighteenth century laid the groundwork for so much of what was to happen in the late modern period, and was in turn prepared for these advances by the remarkable progress in the new observational and pure and applied mathematical sciences of the seventeenth century.[1]

Philosophy of science in this early period was not thematically or methodologically distinguished from scientific commentary on the practice of science itself, and did not emerge as a distinct field of study until relatively late in the nineteenth century. It is from the 1800s onward, particularly in the writings of Bernard Bolzano, Auguste Comte, and Arthur Schopenhauer, among others, that philosophy and philosophy of science gained recognition as a subdiscipline standing on its own apart from the pursuit of knowledge in the most general sense of *scientia*. Mathematics throughout this same epoch was understood as belonging to a higher intellectual order, available to all as a tool and model of exact reasoning. It served, as it did from antiquity, for the quantitative expression of ideas and calculation of formal consequences in pure theory and in innumerable practical applications.[2]

---

1. David Oldroyd, *The Arch of Knowledge: An Introductory Study of the History of the Philosophy and Methodology of Science* (London: Methuen, 1986), esp. 48–99.
2. See, *inter alia*, W. S. Anglin, *Mathematics: A Concise History and Philosophy* (New York: Springer, 1994); David M. Burton, *The History of Mathematics: An Introduction* (Boston, MA:

The expansion of knowledge in the nineteenth century nevertheless was not merely a steady conservative building upon the precedents of early modern philosophy and Enlightenment science in a single unified direction. Rather, the century witnessed a number of important revolutions in both science and mathematics that were to have profound implications for the emergence of the philosophy of science as a separate field with an identifiable subject matter and methodology. Whereas in the eighteenth century, Robert Boyle and Isaac Newton, among other leading figures, could still think of themselves as natural philosophers – and Newton, like so many others in these centuries, could without irony or pretension refer to his work as a contribution to *philosophia naturalis*, even in the title of his great treatise on kinematics – by the time of Charles Darwin, while still intelligible, as it is to us today, such identifications were an increasingly less recognized practice that had already started to become quaint-sounding. Natural philosophy thereafter becomes natural science, and in many contexts and for all practical purposes simply science, meaning that whatever can be explained is progressively considered as theoretically reducible to a purely mechanical physical phenomenon. The philosopher William Whewell is frequently credited with having coined the word "scientist" in his 1834 review of Mary Somerville's *On the Connexion of the Sciences*, but the terminology did not find widespread acceptance until near the very end of the century.[3]

A snapshot of the transition from natural philosophy to (natural) science can be found in the history of the physics of electricity and magnetism in Scotland in the latter half of the nineteenth century. As late as the 1880s, the University of Glasgow and University of Edinburgh maintained a Chair in Natural Philosophy, occupied in 1846 in Glasgow by William Thomson (Lord Kelvin) and in 1860 in Edinburgh by Peter Guthrie Tait. Both of these researchers were practicing modern scientists making contributions to mathematics, physics, and chemistry, especially the theory of electrical phenomena, while publishing influential texts featuring the phrase "natural philosophy."[4] The same is true of Michael Faraday

---

Allyn & Bacon, 1985); Sasaki Chikara et al. (eds), *The Intersection of History and Mathematics* (Basel: Birkhäuser-Verlag, 1994); Johan L. Heiberg, *Mathematics and Physical Science in Classical Antiquity* (Oxford: Oxford University Press, 1922); Jens Hoyrup, *In Measure, Number, and Weight: Studies in Mathematics and Culture* (Albany, NY: SUNY Press, 1994); Joseph F. Scott, *A History of Mathematics from Antiquity to the Beginning of the Nineteenth Century*, 2nd ed. (London: Taylor & Francis, 1960); John W. N. Sullivan, *The History of Mathematics in Europe: From the Fall of Greek Science to the Rise of the Conception of Mathematical Rigour* (Oxford: Oxford University Press, 1925).

3. William Whewell's review appears anonymous in *Quarterly Review* 51 (1834): 54–68.
4. The most valuable recent resource is Edward Grant, *A History of Natural Philosophy: From the Ancient World to the Nineteenth Century* (Cambridge: Cambridge University Press, 2007). See also Salvo D'Agostino, *A History of the Ideas of Theoretical Physics: Essays on the Nineteenth and Twentieth Century Physics* (Boston, MA: Kluwer, 2000); P. M. Harman, *Energy, Force, and*

at Marischal College in Aberdeen. Although James Clerk Maxwell, another great Scottish scientist and electromagnetic theorist, author of the well-known Maxwell equations unifying electricity and magnetism within a single applied mathematical framework, is also described as a "natural philosopher," that exact term seldom appears in his writings, and his work falls squarely in the domain of experimental science as the concept has since come to be defined.[5]

The gradual terminological shift from natural philosophy to natural science, or, simply, science, is itself of profound significance for understanding the history of developments in twentieth-century philosophy of science and mathematics.[6] These subdivisions within philosophy arose precisely at this time, beginning in the nineteenth century with the first formulations of *positivism* as a generalized theory of meaning and explicitly scientific philosophy. The writings of Comte inspired a later generation of scientifically trained philosophers who radicalized positivism as the conceptually most far-reaching *logical positivism* in the philosophy of science, and, in the process, tried to reduce all of philosophy to a so-called logical positivist theory of the limited kinds of meanings available to thought in the sciences. Philosophy thereby became philosophy of science, and philosophy of science started to look increasingly like actual science, even as scientific explanation often appeared to be philosophical. Reflecting on the legacy of logical positivism – regardless of whether we celebrate its successes or bemoan the aftermath of its temporary stranglehold on metaphysics, philosophy of religion, and value theory – we should not lose sight of the fact that its origins derive in large part from Comte as a prominent nineteenth-century continental thinker, about whom we shall have more to say.[7] The nineteenth

---

Matter: The Conceptual Development of Nineteenth-Century Physics (Cambridge: Cambridge University Press, 1982); J. L. Heilbron, *Electricity in the Seventeenth and Eighteenth Centuries: A Study of Early Modern Physics* (Berkeley, CA: University of California Press, 1979); David M. Knight and Matthew D. Eddy, *Science and Beliefs: From Natural Philosophy to Natural Science, 1700–1900* (Aldershot: Ashgate, 2005).

5. P. M. Harman, *The Natural Philosophy of James Clerk Maxwell* (Cambridge: Cambridge University Press, 1998); John Hendry, *James Clerk Maxwell and the Theory of the Electromagnetic Field* (Bristol: Hilger, 1986); John Theodore Merz, *A History of European Thought in the Nineteenth Century*, 2 vols (New York: Dover, 1965); Robert D. Purrington, *Physics in the Nineteenth Century* (New Brunswick, NJ: Rutgers University Press, 1997).

*6. For a discussion of developments in science and their relationship to continental philosophy in the early decades of the twentieth century, see the essay by Babette Babich in *The History of Continental Philosophy: Volume 3*.

7. Peter Achinstein and Stephen F. Barker, *The Legacy of Logical Positivism: Studies in the Philosophy of Science* (Baltimore, MD: Johns Hopkins University Press, 1969); John Losee, *Philosophy of Science and Historical Enquiry* (Oxford: Clarendon Press, 1987), pt 4, "Prescriptive Philosophy of Science: A Historical Survey," 36–61; Ernan McMullin, "The Development of Philosophy of Science, 1600–1900," in *Companion to the History of Modern Science*, R. C. Olby et al. (eds) (London: Routledge, 1990), 816–37; Oldroyd, *The Arch of Knowledge*, 168–208.

century is notable also for incubating Darwin's and Alfred Russel Wallace's evolutionary theory of the natural selection of species, and for the logic, metaphysics, scientific methodology, and the rigorous development of the formal ideas of such philosophers and mathematicians as Charles Sanders Peirce, George Boole, Gottlob Frege, and Bertrand Russell. As the century progressed, increasing attention was paid to the philosophical foundations of geometry, occasioned by the logically consistent axiomatization of non-Euclidean geometries by Georg Friedrich Bernhard Riemann and Nikolai Ivanovich Lobachevsky. In addition, David Hilbert's formalistic philosophy of mathematics and program for the transparently formal metatheory of mathematical logic set a high standard for logically correct mathematical reasoning, while laying down specific goals for mathematical investigations within the principles prescribed by a well-articulated philosophy of mathematics.[8]

Revolutionary developments in nineteenth-century science, mathematics, and philosophy of science and philosophy of mathematics need also to be understood against the background of other strands of thought that characterize this era, curiously enough, as a time of *Romantic* thought. By Romance in this context is not meant anything specifically erotic, but rather the conflict of human freedom with social, political, and causal necessity and constraint. The latter category has profound implications for the Romantic quest for freedom as natural science comes increasingly to paint a picture of all natural phenomena as subject to deterministic forces and antecedent physical events.[9] The problem of understanding human choices in a world in which freedom seems to be denied by natural or political factors was certainly not new to the nineteenth century. It dates back at least to Aristotle's problem of the sea battle tomorrow in *De Interpretatione*.[10] As with other cultural trends, and owing to the convergence of a complex variety of independently interesting circumstances, the nineteenth century was ripe for an especially lively and literary as well as penetrating philosophical consideration of the struggle of human will against the forces of social conformity and political oppression in the economic and intellectual circumstances of the times. The opposition of freedom and necessity, with implications

---

8. A useful contemporary source is Michael Detlefsen, *Hilbert's Program: An Essay on Mathematical Instrumentalism* (Dordrecht: Reidel, 1986).
9. Jacques Barzun, *Romanticism and the Modern Ego* (New York: Little, Brown, 1943); Lilian R. Furst, *The Contours of European Romanticism* (Lincoln, NE: University of Nebraska Press, 1979); Isaiah Berlin, *The Roots of Romanticism* (Princeton, NJ: Princeton University Press, 1999).
10. Aristotle, *De Interpretatione* 9. In *The Complete Works of Aristotle: Revised Oxford Translation*, Jonathan Barnes (ed.) (Princeton, NJ: Princeton University Press, 1984), vol. 1. See Richard Gaskin, *The Sea Battle and the Master Argument: Aristotle and Diodorus Cronus on the Metaphysics of the Future* (Berlin: de Gruyter, 1995).

also for the rise of modern science on which its philosophical discussion was predicated, itself became a topic of close philosophical scrutiny. The Romantic struggle as a reflection of the human condition attained an extraordinary degree of self-awareness among philosophers at the time, examining the prospects of science and mathematics, not only for their explanatory successes and engineering possibilities, but as yet another threat to the Romantic sense of the freedom of will. This was a rather deep-felt philosophical concern that we may not share today, but that alongside more traditional scientific and philosophical preoccupations also characterizes the nineteenth century as an extraordinarily complex chapter of philosophy.[11]

II. HISTORICAL OVERVIEW OF NINETEENTH-CENTURY PHILOSOPHY OF SCIENCE AND MATHEMATICS

The plan of this section is to offer a historical overview of nineteenth-century philosophy of science and mathematics. The expansion of science and mathematics during this period is itself such an extensive subject that no single essay could possibly do justice to the discoveries made and the philosophical controversies that ensued. It is equally futile to try to fit into such a compact discussion all of the important movements in philosophy of science and mathematics during one hundred years of active philosophizing about the nature, meaning, and methodology of science and mathematics.

We cannot expect to offer more than a flavor of this rich and turbulent epoch, seen in retrospect and from a particular set of philosophical prejudices and predispositions. Interested readers are encouraged at every step to further explore the history of these subjects from other perspectives, and from the standpoint of an ever-expanding historical and philosophical commentary on the nineteenth-century development of the natural sciences. What is proposed instead is a sampling of characteristic moments spanning the period that helps shed light on particular chosen aspects of what makes the nineteenth century unique, and that also constitute forerunners of major topics that were later to figure prominently in philosophy of science and mathematics in the twentieth and twenty-first centuries. The organization of these separate discussions is topical rather than strictly chronological, highlighting aspects of nineteenth-century philosophy of science and mathematics that collectively sketch a portrait of philosophy of science and mathematics in the era. The episodes chosen for

---

11. A valuable collection of essays on this topic is found in Isser Woloch (ed.), *Revolution and the Meanings of Freedom in the Nineteenth Century* (Stanford, CA: Stanford University Press, 2000).

review embody in their selection, arrangement, and emphasis a particular view of the most noteworthy events in this field over the course of one hundred extraordinary active years in philosophy of science as it emerged into philosophical awareness. Accordingly, we shall consider ideas concerning the theory and practice of natural science and mathematics in featured writings of leading nineteenth-century thinkers, among numerous others equally deserving of attention: J. S. Mill and certain of his immediate predecessors, Bolzano, Comte, and Frege.

As we concentrate on these representative thinkers of nineteenth-century philosophy, we should not lose sight of the fact that philosophy of science and mathematics at this time was nourished by the new findings of such important scientists, mathematicians, and philosophers as Boole, Darwin, Augustus De Morgan, Charles Lyell, John Venn, and Wallace in Great Britain; William Rowan Hamilton in Ireland; Franz Brentano, Georg Cantor, Franz Joseph Gall, Hermann von Helmholtz, Alexander von Humboldt, and Schopenhauer in Germany; Ludwig Eduard Boltzmann, Sigmund Freud, Ernst Mach, and Gregor Mendel in Austria; Georges Cuvier, Jean-Baptiste Lamarck, Louis Pasteur, and Henri Poincaré in France; William James and Peirce in the United States. It was marked by powerful advances in physics, chemistry, biology, medicine, and technology. It was the century of the Lewis and Clark Expedition, of Darwin's voyage aboard the *Beagle* to the Galapagos Islands and elsewhere in South and Central America, of analytic geometry and non-Euclidean geometry, of Carl Friedrich Gauss and Karl Weierstrass, of Abelian group and complex function and invariant theory, of the discovery of predicate logic or functional calculus, of Hilbert, and of the ill-fated but highly instructive and influential hybrid mathematical–philosophical program of nineteenth-century logicism. All of these scientific, mathematical, and philosophical innovations had enormous repercussions and resonances that, despite rather spectacular failures in some instances, continue to reverberate into the present century.[12]

When this part of the intellectual, scientific, and philosophical milieu of the nineteenth century begins to come into focus, it needs, in turn, to be supplemented by an appreciation for the art and music of the time, of Ludwig van Beethoven, Hector Berlioz, Johannes Brahms, Frédéric Chopin, Franz Liszt, Felix Mendelssohn, and Piotr Illitch Tchaikovsky, of the French Academy and Impressionism, the fabulous world of the nineteenth-century novel and other forms of literature, and important political events, including the rise of nationalism and socialism, and accompanying decline of monarchism, Napoleon

---

12. Michael Friedman, *The Kantian Legacy in Nineteenth Century Science* (Cambridge, MA: MIT Press, 2006).

Bonaparte, the American Civil War, and countless other socially-philosophically significant occurrences.

III. BRITISH EMPIRICIST METHODOLOGY OF INDUCTIVE REASONING

The success of modern science owes much of its momentum to the articulation in the nineteenth century of explicit methods of inductive reasoning. The principal exponents of induction include such figures as John F. W. Herschel (1792–1871), William Whewell (1794–1866), John Stuart Mill (1806–73), and George Boole (1815–64).[13] The general topic of induction is not new to this period of thought, since we know from David Hume's *A Treatise of Human Nature* in the previous century that philosophers were already concerned about the logical credentials of inductive inference.[14] It is perhaps no accident that many of the most important contributions to philosophy of science in the nineteenth century occurred in Great Britain and, to a lesser extent, in the United States, in the work of such logicians and mathematical philosophers as Peirce,[15] where the experimental sciences at the time were most rigorously pursued.[16]

Prior to Mill's publication in 1843 of *A System of Logic: Raciocinative and Inductive*, his most notable predecessor was John F. W. Herschel. Herschel was the son of the famous astronomer William Herschel, and an accomplished mathematician and contributor to astronomy, optics, and other physical sciences. Herschel in 1830 wrote an important volume titled *Preliminary Discourse on Natural Philosophy*. The book is noteworthy not only for its philosophical content, but because it was the first English-language text in the philosophy of science written by a respected practicing scientist. Herschel, in keeping with a well-established tradition in expositions of scientific methodology, distinguishes

---

13. Ian Hacking provides invaluable historical background to the British tradition in inductive reasoning in *The Emergence of Probability: A Philosophical Study of Early Ideas About Probability, Induction and Statistical Inference* (Cambridge: Cambridge University Press, 1984); also his *An Introduction to Probability and Inductive Logic* (Cambridge: Cambridge University Press, 2001). The earliest source, of direct influence on nineteenth-century philosophy of science in relation to inductive methods, occurs in William Whewell, *History of the Inductive Sciences, Founded Upon Their History*, 3 vols (London: J. Parker, 1837).
14. David Hume, *A Treatise of Human Nature* [1739–40], L. A. Selby-Bigge (ed.), 2nd ed., P. H. Nidditch (rev.) (Oxford: Clarendon Press, 1978), bk I, pt III, §§1–6. See also David Hume, *An Enquiry Concerning Human Understanding*, in Hume, *Enquiries Concerning Human Understanding and Concerning the Principles of Morals*, L. A. Selby-Bigge and P. H. Nidditch (eds), 3rd ed. (Oxford: Clarendon Press, 1975), §§4.1.20–27, §§4.2.28–33.
*15. Peirce is the focus of the essay by Douglas R. Anderson in this volume.
16. See Chung-ying Cheng, *Peirce's and Lewis's Theories of Induction* (Leiden: Martinus Nijhoff, 1969).

between two phases of discovery and validation or justification. He discounts the means by which scientific hypotheses and other discoveries might be reached, focusing instead on their verification according to prescribed rules, regardless of how they are arrived at or presented to the scientific imagination. Herschel further distinguishes, also in the tradition of commentary on the interpretation of scientific findings originating with Galileo and John Locke, between primary and secondary qualities. He illustrates the distinction in one place by means of what he describes as a preliminary scientific analysis of the occurrence of sound, which he distinguishes as motion (primary quality) and sensation (secondary quality). He describes the purpose of science as the determination of causes of observed phenomena and is one of the first theorists to articulate the concept of a natural law.[17]

Herschel accordingly offers ten "general rules for guiding and facilitating our search, among a great mass of assembled facts, for their common cause."[18] Mill, in turn, in *A System of Logic*, condenses and summarizes the rules as:

(1) Method of agreement: Constant conjunction of antecedent (cause) and consequent (effect).
(2) Method of difference: Absence of consequent in the absence of antecedent.
(3) Joint method of agreement and difference: Combination of (1) and (2).
(4) Method of residues: Elimination of whatever part of a phenomenon is known by previous inductions to be the effect of particular antecedents, leaves whatever is left over as consequent of the remaining antecedents.
(5) Method of concomitant variations: Whatever phenomenon varies when another phenomenon varies in a certain way, is either an antecedent or consequent of that phenomenon, or is connected with it through some fact of causation.[19]

What is significant in Mill's inductive method is not so much the content of the principles themselves, but the fact that in presenting them he is offering both a descriptive characterization of scientific method and prescriptive advice about how scientific inquiry should be conducted. It is characteristic of nineteenth-century philosophy of science that it is conceived as an effort not only to explain

---

17. John Frederick William Herschel, *Preliminary Discourse on the Study of Natural Philosophy: The Cabinet Cyclopaedia* (London: Longman, Rees, Orme, Brown, Green and Longman, and John Taylor, 1830), vol. 1, 98–9.
18. *Ibid.*, 151–2.
19. See John Stuart Mill, *A System of Logic* (London: John W. Strand, 1843), bk III, ch. 8.

what science is and how it is done, but to legislate scientific practice by providing rules for correct empirical research. This is important in turn because it indicates a self-consciousness on the part of thinkers in addressing the methodology of science as a topic for philosophical reflection in which philosophy can contribute by standing back from the practice of science and considering the conditions for its success and failure. Mill, after Whewell, is one of the first philosophers to take this stance, and it is historically noteworthy that this happens in the nineteenth century when professional philosophy for the first time thematizes the methods of science. Mill builds on Whewell, but Whewell, unlike Mill, is a practicing scientist. It is always contentious to try to pinpoint the origin of a field of study to a particular time or particular author or publication. A case can nevertheless be made for Mill's *A System of Logic* as the first work in philosophy of science, as a subject that emerges for philosophy for the first time in English-language philosophy.[20]

Mill's study is remarkable for its combined philosophy of logic and mathematics. Having laid down the rules for determination of cause and effect relations and proper inductive reasoning, Mill presents an account of the nature of logic and mathematics as a formal theory of empirically encountered patterns of thought. His approach has frequently been criticized by such commentators later in the century as Frege, who accuses Mill of psychologism. Psychologism is the venial sin, from a Platonic realist standpoint, of confusing objective matters of abstract logical and mathematical relations, about which the mind is capable of forming opinions, with purely subjective aspects of the psychology of thinkers who reflect on and draw conclusions concerning the mind-independent truths of logic and mathematics.[21]

Mill would not have been disheartened by these criticisms. He deliberately chooses the empirical method in preference to any form of Platonism or rationalism, because he believes that experience is the only path to substantive truth. In another context, discussing the concept of nature and of laws of nature, in his essay "On Nature," published as the first of three expositions in his collected volume of 1874, *Nature, the Utility of Religion and Theism*, Mill writes:

> Adopting this course [of clarifying the meaning of a term] with the word "nature," the first question must be, what is meant by the "nature" of a particular object, as of fire, of water, or of some individual plant or animal? Evidently the ensemble or aggregate of its

---

20. Similar opinions are advanced by Oskar A. Kubitz, *The Development of John Stuart Mill's System of Logic* (Urbana, IL: University of Illinois Press, 1932) and by Geoffrey Scarre, *Logic and Reality in the Philosophy of John Stuart Mill* (Dordrecht: Kluwer, 1989).
21. Gottlob Frege, *The Foundations of Arithmetic: A Logical-Mathematical Investigation into the Concept of Number*, Dale Jacquette (trans.) (New York: Pearson/Longman, 2007), 23–6.

> powers or properties: the modes in which it acts on other things (counting among those things the senses of the observer), and the modes in which other things act upon it; to which, in the case of a sentient being, must be added its own capacities of feeling, or being conscious. The nature of the thing means all this; means its entire capacity of exhibiting phenomena. And since the phenomena which a thing exhibits, however much they vary in different circumstances, are always the same in the same circumstances, they admit of being described in general forms of words, which are called the laws of the thing's nature. Thus it is a law of the nature of water that, under the mean pressure of the atmosphere at the level of the sea, it boils at 212 degrees Fahrenheit.[22]

As a sign of his reliance on empirical observation in the sciences, Mill posits unaided direct observation as the basis for discerning natural laws in every area of scientific inquiry. It is striking to see in this connection that Mill does not recognize the extent to which idealization beyond anything immediately perceptible to sensation is standardly required in the discovery and formulation of scientific laws.

Considering the typical case of Newton's first law of motion, according to which a moving projectile unimpeded by impressed forces continues indefinitely in a straight line, most laws of nature involve the postulation of entities that not only are nowhere observed in nature, but that are definitely known not to exist in nature. There are no moving bodies unimpeded by impressed forces, according to Newton's own law of universal gravitation, since one and all are impeded by impressed forces, even if only negligibly across vast apparently empty distances of space. Mill seems oblivious to these aspects of idealization in the discovery of scientific laws of nature, which he claims in every instance are the direct result of empirical experience. It is with good reason, then, that some of Mill's oversimplified claims about the nature of science and its methodology have come under criticism by later philosophers of science as naive and uninformed about actual scientific practice.[23] Mill continues:

> Since all phenomena which have been sufficiently examined are found to take place with regularity, each having certain fixed conditions, positive and negative, on the occurrence of which it invariably

---

22. John Stuart Mill, "On Nature," in *Nature, the Utility of Religion and Theism* (London: Watts & Co. for the Rationalist Press, 1904), 7–8.
23. See Struan Jacobs, *Science and British Liberalism: Locke, Bentham, Mill and Popper* (Aldershot: Ashgate, 1991), and John C. Rees, *Mill and his Early Critics* (Leicester: University of Leicester Press, 1956).

happens, mankind have been able to ascertain, either by direct observation or by reasoning processes grounded on it, the conditions of the occurrence of many phenomena; and the progress of science mainly consists in ascertaining those conditions. When discovered they can be expressed in general propositions, which are called laws of the particular phenomenon, and also, more generally, Laws of Nature. Thus the truth, that all material objects tend towards one another with a force directly as their masses and inversely as the square of their distance, is a law of nature. The proposition, that air and food are necessary to animal life, if it be, as we have good reason to believe, true without exception, is also a law of nature, though the phenomenon of which it is the law is special, and not, like gravitation, universal.[24]

An impressive feature of Mill's characterization of natural law is the large extent to which it agrees with what philosophers of science are still inclined even today to say about the object of scientific inquiry. Many of Mill's detractors still admire his sense of what constitutes science, and confine their criticisms primarily to what they consider to be his misguided efforts to extend his notion of what constitutes good science to areas beyond its proper purview. In his own time, Mill was criticized most notably by Whewell, in his 1849 pamphlet *On Induction, with Especial Reference to Mr. J. Stuart Mill's System of Logic*. Whewell takes issue with Mill's uncompromising empiricism in the philosophy of logic and mathematics. Thus, Whewell writes:

> But the elements and materials of Science are necessary truths contemplated by the intellect. It is by consisting of such elements and such materials, that Science *is* Science. Hence a use of the term *Induction* which requires us to obliterate this distinction, must make it impossible for us to arrive at any consistent and intelligible view of the nature of Science, and of the mental process by which Science comes into being.[25]

We see played out in Whewell's nineteenth-century opposition to Mill a confrontation of rationalism with empiricism that goes back to Aristotle's no doubt turbulent apprenticeship to Plato, and in later centuries between René Descartes, G. W. Leibniz, and Baruch de Spinoza, on the one hand, and, as

---

24. Mill, "On Nature," 8.
25. William Whewell, *On Induction, with Especial Reference to Mr. J. Stuart Mill's System of Logic* (London: J. W. Parker, 1849), 13.

the Enlightenment gained traction, George Berkeley, Hume, and Thomas Reid. Later critics have objected to Mill's interpretation of the ontic and epistemic status of logical and mathematical laws as all of a piece with the laws of nature, including the lawlike principles governing the psychology of logical and mathematical reasoning.

Mill's philosophy of logic and mathematics as methods of empirical science, when compared with his moral and political philosophy, and the social policies philosophically grounded in Mill's contributions to utilitarianism, had relatively scant influence on the European continent in his own day. His concept of logic and of mathematical principles was believed to have been discredited in some circles by virtue of its psychologism, as Frege and others were afterward to charge. Empiricist thinkers such as Brentano nevertheless saw in Mill's empiricist foundations of logic and mathematics, and in his philosophy of science more generally, a powerful ally. A young Brentano in particular sought to meet with Mill, and was prevented from doing so after arriving in England only by the senior philosopher's sudden unexpected death. The impact of Mill as well as Hume is tangible in Brentano's work especially in philosophical psychology – *Deskriptive Psychologie, Phenomenologie,* and *Psychognosie* – developed by Brentano specifically as reflecting a Mill- and Hume-inspired empiricist anti-post-Kantian philosophy of science of "inner perception" (*innere Wahrnehmung*).[26]

IV. BOLZANO'S NEORATIONALIST PHILOSOPHY OF SCIENCE AND MATHEMATICS

At roughly the same time, Bernard Bolzano, writing in Czechoslovakia in German, was laying the groundwork for a very different approach to the philosophy of science, logic, and mathematics, in his highly influential 1837 *Wissenschaftslehre, Versuch einer ausführlichen und grösstetheils neuen Darstellung der Logik, mit steter Rücksicht auf deren bisherige Bearbeiter* (*Theory of Science, Attempt at a Detailed and in the Main Novel Exposition of Logic with Constant Attention to Earlier Authors*).

Bolzano's approach to the philosophy of science is in obvious ways diametrically opposed to Mill's. Where Mill offers purely empirical interpretations of the natural sciences extended to logic and mathematics in order to provide logical foundations for all the sciences, Bolzano instead offers conceptual abstractions, including part–whole or mereological relations, abstract objects and their

---

26. See Reginald Jackson, *An Examination of the Deductive Logic of John Stuart Mill* (Oxford: Oxford University Press, 1941); and Kubitz, *The Development of John Stuart Mill's System of Logic.*

attributes, formal syntax, propositions as the abstract meanings of sentences (*Sätze an sich*), sums and sets, collections, substances, adherences, subjective ideas, judgments, and sentence-occurrences, as the metaphysical basis for all of science. Bolzano proposes an *ontology* for science, conceived as an elaboration of his earlier work in the philosophy of mathematics, in which he similarly develops a distinction between the objective relationships holding between logical consequences and subjective understanding of the relations that obtain. Bolzano does not consider it sufficient to produce verification of mathematical or natural scientific truths, but regards it as the purpose of the pure and applied sciences to search for and articulate justifications for its conclusions in terms of more fundamental truths that are not always intuitively self-evident.[27]

Bolzano's commitment to a kind of Platonism in the philosophy of science, represented especially by his doctrine of propositions, is complemented by his reception of actual numerical and geometrical infinities, a concept challenged by empiricist thinkers such as Berkeley, Hume, and Mill. Bolzano's 1851 *Paradoxien des Unendlichen* (*Paradoxes of the Infinite*) does not pose but rather offers to resolve many traditional paradoxes concerning the concept of infinity that other thinkers of a more empiricist bent had previously put forward in the philosophy of mathematics.[28] As a mathematician, Bolzano made original contributions in his proof of theorems concerning the areas of similar rhombi, and what has since come to be called the Bolzano–Weierstrass theorem in real analysis (calculus). Later independently discovered by Weierstrass, but jointly redesignated when historians discovered that Bolzano had previously derived a proof, the result shows that a subset of real-numbered extension is sequentially compact if and only if it is both bounded and closed. Bolzano provided the first fully rigorous definition of a mathematical limit, in his 1817 *Rein analytischer Beweis* ("Purely Analytic Proof"), which also presents a version of the differential calculus unencumbered by the concept of infinitesimals.[29] Bolzano's practical knowledge is in constant dialectic with his philosophical explorations of the nature of mathematics. The interaction of Bolzano's mathematical and philosophical interests is exemplified by his *Theorie der reelen Zahlen* ("Pure Theory

---

27. Bernard Bolzano, *Wissenschaftslehre, Versuch einer ausführlichen und grösstetheils neuen Darstellung der Logik, mit steter Rücksicht auf deren bisherige Bearbeiter*, 4 vols (Sulzbach: J. E. von Seidel, 1837).
28. Bernard Bolzano, *Paradoxien des Unendlichen* (Leipzig: Felix Meiner, 1921); published in English as *Paradoxes of the Infinite*, in *The Mathematical Works of Bernard Bolzano*, Steve Russ (ed. and trans.) (Oxford: Oxford University Press, 2004).
29. Bernard Bolzano, *Rein analytischer Beweis: Des Lehrsatzes, dass zwischen je zwey Werthen die ein entgegengesetzes Resultat gewähren, wenigstens eine reelle Wurzel der Gleichung liege* (Leipzig: Wilhelm Engelmann, 1817); published in English as "Purely Analytic Proof," in *The Mathematical Works of Bernard Bolzano*, Russ (ed. and trans.).

of Numbers"), unpublished during his lifetime but included in his handwritten *Nachlaß*, incorporating a theory of real functions, and by his efforts predating Riemann and Lobachevsky to define a geometry independently of Euclid's fifth or parallel postulate.[30]

V. COMTE'S POSITIVISM

Comte[31] was born before Mill and died before Mill, but his legacy in philosophy of science extends beyond many of his contemporaries and far beyond the boundaries of nineteenth-century France where he worked. Comte was primarily a sociologist; indeed, he invented the term "sociology," which he first referred to as *physique sociale*, or "social physics," and later renamed *sociologie*. His contributions to philosophy of science were far-reaching, affecting not only the social sciences, but exerting a profound influence also on the conception of the physical sciences and their methodology.[32]

As a sociologist, Comte argued that all sciences were subject to what he designates the "Law of Three Phases." According to this thesis, societies progress through three distinct periods: Theological, Metaphysical, and Scientific. Human knowledge moves from phase to phase as it advances from belief in gods and God, and in the divine origin of the universe and intervention in the world of nature. Belief progresses from faith to a more philosophical attitude marked by the development of metaphysical systems that propose to explain the world and the place of human beings in natural events in terms of philosophical principles. Eventually, in the third phase, thought advances to a widespread acceptance of natural scientific explanations that take the quantitative physical sciences and the verification of hypotheses by inductive methods as their model. Comte refers to the third and final phase as "Positive," exploiting the meaning of the word by which it represents something affirmative, improved, and superior. In large measure, Comte's philosophy of science is oriented toward the natural sciences as a norm of human progress, in which knowledge naturally inclines toward and eventually attains the standards

---

30. Bernard Bolzano, *Theorie der reelen Zahlen, Betrachtungen aus der Logik in Bolzanos handschriftlichen Nachlasse*, Karel Rychlík (ed.) (Prague: Central Archives of the Czech Academy of the Sciences, 1962); published in English as "Pure Theory of Numbers," in T*he Mathematical Works of Bernard Bolzano*, Russ (ed. and trans.).

*31. Comte is also discussed in the essay by Alan Sica in this volume.

32. Auguste Comte, *Cours de philosophie positive*, 2 vols (Paris: Hermann, [1830–42] 1975). For a thorough exposition of Comte's ideas, see George Henry Lewes, *Comte's Philosophy of the Sciences: Works in the Philosophy of Science 1830–1914*, facsimile ed. (London: Thoemmes Continuum, 1999).

of scientific explanation that, from the time of the seventeenth century and beyond, the Enlightenment had proved were so successful in understanding the world and controlling natural forces through observation, experiment, and engineering applications.

In psychology, for example, in keeping with Comte's model for greater rigor in the social sciences, Brentano carried forward an effort to make the study of mind a scientific enterprise in his 1874 (and later editions) *Psychologie vom empirischen Standpunkt* (*Psychology from an Empirical Standpoint*), and posthumously published (1982) lectures on *Deskriptive Psychologie* (*Descriptive Psychology*). Brentano also conducted basic scientific experiments in empirical cognitive psychology, and some of his students founded the first European laboratories for experimental psychology. As a consequence of his lectures on descriptive psychology, which he also referred to as *Psychognosie*, Brentano established the foundations for phenomenology as it was later to take shape in the philosophy of Edmund Husserl.[33]

Comte, in keeping with his special interests, places considerable confidence especially in applications of scientific method to social problems. The practical aspects of science as a solution to society's woes puts Comte very much in the vanguard of other nineteenth-century thinkers who in some general sense of the word "science" were also hoping that science would solve social predicaments and lead to a betterment of society. Here we find a common theme in nineteenth-century philosophy of science that runs through the writings of Karl Marx, Thomas Robert Malthus, Jeremy Bentham, James and John Stuart Mill, Sigmund Freud, and others in this period. Comte's concept of a progressive scientific phase of social evolution was considered philosophically advanced and humanitarian, although eventually it came to be regarded as too closely and naively wedded to an ideal that was more appropriate to the exact physical sciences than anything realistically achievable in the social sphere. Comte's "law of three phases" is nevertheless rightly heralded as a groundbreaking attempt to formulate a theory of social evolution. In this respect, Comte led the way for later theorists, including Darwin, Herbert Spencer, Thomas H. Huxley, Oswald Spengler, and, looking ahead to the beginning of the twentieth century, Otto Weininger.

Comte also proposes an encyclopedic system for organizing and hierarchically classifying the sciences. His categories include the inorganic and organic, incorporating physics, chemistry, astronomy, and the earth sciences under the heading of inorganic sciences; and biology, psychology, and sociology as

---

33. The iconic nineteenth-century scientific social reformer is perhaps Edwin Chadwick (in the field of health and sanitation). See David Gladstone (ed.), *Setting the Agenda: Edwin Chadwick and Nineteenth-century Reform* (Pioneers in Social Welfare) (London: Routledge, 1997).

organic sciences. In a variety of recognizable guises, something like this division of sciences and their organization, first articulated in Comte's philosophy, is preserved to the present time as a scheme for arranging and categorizing the sciences. More important than the classification itself is the fact that Comte understood precisely these disciplines as "scientific," and was prepared to include them in the larger project of scientific knowledge in the third stage of human social evolution culminating in the Scientific phase. Comte's concept of a social science that was not merely philosophical was not unprecedented, but the extent to which he elevated the social sciences to a position of importance not only among the sciences but within a larger agenda of social reform, and the resolute way he advanced his project, was at once distinctive of his thought and characteristic of nineteenth-century philosophical and scientific movements. Comte, also typically of the nineteenth century, understands his own preferred sociological science as the final moment in the development of all the sciences, to which they are reducible. He believes that sociology will eventually encompass all the other sciences and integrate their discoveries into a single unified all-embracing master science.[34]

Comte's project is interesting in this respect as a harbinger of Vienna Circle logical positivism from the first decade of the twentieth century. Comte is often credited as having inspired the positivism of a later era, and, within limits and the proper qualifications, this is undoubtedly true. It is nevertheless important to remember that for Comte sociology was the apotheosis of science that would bring all the other sciences together. Nor is this a delusional concept, since, after all, physics, chemistry, biology, astronomy, and the other so-called "hard" quantitative physical sciences are the products of individual thinkers living and working in and supported educationally, culturally, financially, and in countless other ways by social communities. The fact that Comte places sociology at the top of his unity of sciences model should nevertheless give pause to the idea that the logical positivists of the Vienna Circle merely continued a project set in motion half a century earlier by Comte. Although Comte in many respects takes the physical sciences as his prime example of a science that he thought a mature sociological science should imitate, ultimately he regards sociology as standing above and subsuming the physical sciences. This form of the unity of sciences is upside down from the standpoint of the later project of logical positivism as it was to define itself in the early part of the twentieth century. The later positivists, while recognizing their debt to Comte, considered physics to

---

34. The most authoritative source on Comte's life and philosophy is Henri Gouhier, *La Jeunesse d'Auguste Comte et la formation du positivisme*, 3 vols (Paris: Vrin, 1933). A critical overview is offered by Larry Laudan, *Science and Hypothesis: Historical Essays on Scientific Methodology* (Dordrecht: Reidel, 1981), ch. 9, "Towards a Reassessment of Comte's 'Méthode Positive,'" 141–62.

be the ultimate science, incorporating whatever aspects of sociology could be made scientifically respectable by relying on public and repeatable phenomena and some form of hypothetical-deductive method for confirming and explaining natural occurrences.

It is a characteristic but by no means idiosyncratic feature of Comte's form of positivism that it should place a science other than physics at the pinnacle of the unity of sciences. Other philosophers in the twentieth century, reacting against the suffocating effect of logical positivism, were to propose similar inversions of the unity of sciences model, as R. G. Collingwood does when he suggests in his later writings that history is the ultimate science encapsulating all others.[35] Collingwood offers his reduction on grounds similar to those of Comte, reasoning that all sciences are the artifact of human reasoning dealing with the problems presented to and solved by means of reason at particular moments in the past.[36]

---

35. Collingwood puts the complex interrelation of history and philosophy into perspective when he writes: "History without philosophy is history seen from the outside, the play of mechanical and unchanging forces in a materialistically conceived world: philosophy without history is philosophy seen from the outside, the veering and backing, rising and falling, of motiveless winds of doctrine. 'Both these are monsters.' But history fertilized by philosophy is the history of the human spirit in its secular attempt to build itself a world of laws and institutions in which it can live as it wishes to live; and philosophy fertilized by history is the progressive raising and solving of the endless intellectual problems whose succession forms the inner side of this secular struggle. Thus the two studies which, apart, degenerate into strings of empty dates and lists of pedantic distinctions ... become, together, a single science of all things human" (*Essays in the Philosophy of History*, William Debbins [ed.] [Austin, TX: University of Texas Press, 1965], 4).

36. Collingwood's understanding of the relation between history and philosophy, which evolved during the course of his career, has naturally given rise to controversies about his final considered opinion, and about the exact status of his views at any point in their development. See, for example, William Debbins's "Introduction" in Collingwood's *Essays in the Philosophy of History*: "'Croce's Philosophy of History' is a critical review of Croce's *Teoria e Storia della Storiografia* (1917). Collingwood criticizes Croce for reducing philosophy to history; he argues that they are distinct disciplines even though there is an interrelation and dependence of each on the other. If it is true, as I have argued above, that philosophy *of* history was for Collingwood a critical examination of some of the problems encountered by the historian in the course of his work, then it would seem to follow that Collingwood consistently rejected the identification of philosophy and history" (Debbins, "Introduction," in Collingwood, *Essays in the Philosophy of History*, xxxii). Compare E. W. F. Tomlin: "In studying a historical process, our task is to think ourselves into the action to discern the thought of its agent ... Thus 'all history is the history of thought' ... If all history is the history of thought, so all knowledge is historical knowledge. And since historical knowledge is that which the historian absorbs into his own experience, the activity of historical thinking is simultaneously a means of self-knowledge ... History is therefore 'the self-knowledge of mind' ... The identification of philosophy and history was in effect an identification of theory and practice" (*R. G. Collingwood* [London: Longmans, Green, 1953], 30–33).

Ironically, but inevitably, perhaps, many of what Comte would have considered his most important contributions to the quantitative science of sociology have since come to be regarded as unscientific. Comte's work in science has in this respect become the unexpected victim of the unanticipated success of his own philosophy of science.

VI. FREGE'S SCIENTIFIC SEMANTICS AND PHILOSOPHY OF MATHEMATICS

Frege is best known for his discovery of a prototype of the functional calculus or predicate-quantificational logic, and for his later treatment of philosophical semantics as represented by the distinction between the conventional and indirect sense (*Sinn*) and reference (*Bedeutung*) of proper names or individually referring terms and sentences. Frege postulates an ideal language or *Begriffsschrift* (literally, concept-script or concept-writing) for the scientific expression of meaning.[37]

Frege hammers out a symbolic logic in order to formalize the foundations of arithmetic in his 1879 *Begriffsschrift: Eine der arithmetischen nachgebildete Formelsprache des reinen Denkens* (Concept-writing: a formula-language for pure thought modeled on arithmetic). A *Begriffsschrift*, in Frege's sense, in addition to satisfying other requirements of expressive adequacy, must prohibit the occurrence of multiple terms for the same entity (redundancy), the same term for distinct entities (ambiguity and equivocation), and disallow nondesignating singular terms such as those that purport to refer to fictional nonexistent objects, such as "Pegasus," "Santa Claus," or "the greatest even number" (putative reference to nonexistent objects). A *Begriffsschrift* is meant to be a purely formal symbolic language, in effect, a mathematical notation, for the expression of any proposition in any area of discourse and, in particular, of any proposition dealing with the predications of properties to objects individually and in universal or existential quantifications.[38]

Frege adopts a Platonic theory of *Gedanken* or propositions, as the abstract meanings of inscribed sentences, like Bolzano's *Sätze an sich*. Translation from one language to another is then a matter of grasping the sense of the thought as expressed in one language and rendering the same abstract thought within

---

37. Gottlob Frege, *Conceptual Notation and Related Articles*, Terrell W. Bynum (trans.) (Oxford: Oxford University Press, 1972); originally published as *Begriffsschrift: Eine der arithmetischen nachgebildete Formelsprache des reinen Denkens* (Halle: Louis Nebert, 1879).
38. See Michael Dummett, *Frege: Philosophy of Mathematics* (Cambridge, MA: Harvard University Press, 1991); Danielle Macbeth, *Frege's Logic* (Cambridge, MA: Harvard University Press, 2005); Pavel Tichý, *The Foundations of Frege's Logic* (New York: de Gruyter, 1988).

the grammar and vocabulary of another language. The analogy that suggests itself is that of the distinction in mathematics between numbers and numerals. Numbers are often thought to be abstract entities, say, the number 2 that exists on the number line in a particular position precisely between 1 and 3, while there are unlimitedly many different concrete numerals in unlimitedly many different concrete mathematical languages by means of which the same number can be expressed, including "2," "II," "two," "|√4|," "1 + 1," "9 – 7," "6/3," and so on.[39]

Frege, in his later writings after 1890, offers a theory of meaning in which the reference or *extension* of terms and sentences is determined by their sense or *intension*. The conventional sense of a term is the set of properties the designated object possesses. The sense of the name "Aristotle," for example, is the abstract set of all of Aristotle's properties, including being Macedonian, born in Stagira, a student of Plato, teacher of Alexander the Great, author of the *Nicomachean Ethics*, and all the many other things that are true of him. The reference of the name "Aristotle" is that unique existent entity that has just the set of properties belonging to the sense of the name. This is the manner in which, according to Frege's semantic theory, the sense of a term determines its reference, or intension determines extension. Where sentences are concerned, the sense of a sentence is a function of the senses of its significant terms or, broadly construed, proper names, including definite descriptions. The reference of a sentence is in turn a reified truth-value, which Frege designates as "the True," in case the sentence is true, and "the False," in case the sentence is false. Singular referring terms and sentences in colloquial language outside a *Begriffsschrift* on Frege's distinction can have sense while lacking reference. An example of each is "Pegasus" and "Pegasus is a winged stallion." The indirect reference of a name or sentence, according to Frege, is its conventional sense. If I quote a term in a context predicating a property of the term, as in "'Aristotle' contains nine letters," then the name "Aristotle" does not refer directly to Aristotle, but to the conventional sense of the name. By this distinction, Frege proposes to avoid a number of difficulties in understanding the complex uses of language in talking about itself and referring to the contents of thoughts, quoting what another person says, and similar challenges to interpreting the expression of meaning and determination of truth value.[40]

---

39. Gottlob Frege, "Thoughts," in *Collected Papers on Mathematics, Logic and Philosophy*, Max Black *et al.* (eds) (Oxford: Blackwell, 1984); originally published as "Der Gedanke," *Beiträge zur Philosophie des deutschen Idealismus* 1 (1918–19).
40. Gottlob Frege, "On Sense and Meaning," in *Collected Papers on Mathematics, Logic and Philosophy*, Max Black *et al.* (eds); originally published as "Über Sinn und Bedeutung," *Zeitschrift für Philosophie und philosophische Kritik* 100 (1892). For useful commentary, see, as recommended in a vast secondary philosophical literature, Michael Beaney, *Frege: Making*

Frege requires that the meaning of a term be understood holistically or contextually in light of its contribution to the meaning of an entire sentence. This condition is related in turn to what has come to be known as Frege's *compositionality* thesis. Frege further rejects and polemicizes vehemently against psychologism in logic and semantics, and his objections have inspired generations of extensionalistically minded logicians and meaning-theorists also to avoid psychological, phenomenological, or generally intentional factors in understanding the nature of meaning. Indeed, one of the principal targets of his attack against psychologism, as we have already noted, is Mill's *A System of Logic*. Frege wants semantic theory to be scientific, generally defined, and so he shuns any explanation that involves private psychological subjective factors that can be different in the thoughts of every different thinker and are, in that sense, at best accidental to the objective meaning of a word or sentence.[41]

Frege's researches in logic and theory of meaning provide the foundation for his groundbreaking efforts to advance the philosophical program of *logicism*. Logicism is the project to reduce all of mathematics, beginning with the basic concepts of arithmetic, to more basic principles of logic. It is this program that we find Frege trying to advance in his 1884 *Grundlagen der Arithmetik: Eine logisch-mathematische Untersuchung über den Begriff der Zahl* (*The Foundations of Arithmetic: A Logical-Mathematical Investigation into the Concept of Number*). If we think of logic as the most fundamental discipline, one that sets the standards of good reasoning for all other fields, then the idea of reducing arithmetic and eventually all of mathematics to logic can exert a very strong appeal to the philosophical imagination. If the reduction of arithmetic to logic were to succeed, then it would guarantee the starting place of that part of mathematics concerning number the absolute certainty that we expect to hold of deductively valid inferences in logic, and we would have simplified our understanding of mathematics as nothing more than a complicated outgrowth of purely logical principles. Logicism in its original form, as Frege and others in the late nineteenth and early twentieth centuries tried to develop it, ultimately failed. It did so, nonetheless, in an instructive way that continues to inform philosophical discussion, and that in refined revisionary versions has been more recently exploited again in new quasilogicist approaches to the philosophy of mathematics.[42]

Sense (London: Duckworth, 1996); Wolfgang Carl, *Frege's Theory of Sense and Reference* (Cambridge: Cambridge University Press, 1994); Dummett, *Frege: Philosophy of Language*, 2nd ed. (Cambridge, MA: Harvard University Press, 1981); Kevin C. Klement, *Frege and the Logic of Sense and Reference* (London: Routledge, 2002).

41. See note 21 above.
42. A recent assessment of the history and prospects of logicism appears in a special issue of *Notre Dame Journal of Formal Logic* 41(3–4) (2000) on "Logicism and the Paradoxes: A Reappraisal I, II."

Early in his career, Frege believed that Kant's proto-intuitionistic account of space and time as pure forms of intuition constituting the transcendental grounds respectively of geometry and arithmetic was correct with respect to geometry but not with respect to arithmetic. The failure of his efforts to provide an independent logicist foundation for arithmetic in concepts of logic eventually prompted Frege to rethink this position. Later in life, particularly after Russell in 1901 revealed a contradiction in Frege's final formulation of a predicate logic reduction of arithmetic in Frege's 1893 *Grundgesetze der Arithmetik*, Frege began to rethink his view that Kant was wrong about arithmetic having an intuitive foundation in innate preconditions for the human experience of time, and began to consider more seriously again a unified Kantian approach to the perceptual basis of both arithmetic and geometry.[43]

Frege's extraordinary accomplishments in logic, philosophy of language, philosophical semantics, and philosophy of mathematics, along with his careful, self-conscious methodological reflections in theory and practice, in many ways laid the groundwork for mainstream analytic philosophy that has flourished from Frege's time to the present day.[44]

VII. PHILOSOPHY OF SCIENCE AND MATHEMATICS ON THE THRESHOLD OF A NEW CENTURY

Whereas there is some truth and legitimacy to the oversimplifications by which the seventeenth century in philosophy is characterized as the period of rationalism, and the eighteenth century as the period of enlightenment and empiricism, the nineteenth century in dramatic contrast does not lend itself to such misleading labels as these for previous eras in the philosophy of science and mathematics, and philosophical methodology more generally. Especially on the European continent at this time, there is set loose a wide diversity of philosophical programs that defy easy summary or ideological sloganeering. In philosophy of science and mathematics, what generalization will serve to encapsulate a century over a stitched-together topography of philosophically very different European cultures that managed to produce such thinkers as Fichte and Cantor, Schelling and Darwin, Hegel and Frege, Schopenhauer and Hilbert, Marx and Dedekind, Nietzsche and Boole, to name but a few intellectual contrarieties?

The best we can do, after emphasizing all the appropriate caveats and qualifications, is to identify selected major trends that seem to be exemplified by the

---

43. See Anthony Kenny, *Frege* (Harmondsworth: Penguin, 1995).
44. See especially, among numerous sources, Alberto J. Coffa, *The Semantic Tradition from Kant to Carnap* (Cambridge: Cambridge University Press, 1991).

most influential and highly regarded philosophers of science and mathematics from this dynamic century. We can suggest how the work of some important historical figures paved the way for later developments in what was soon to be a relatively unified transition to philosophy of the exact sciences in the twentieth century. From its fractured precursor, representing one hundred years of philosophical endeavor, twentieth-century philosophy of science and mathematics, using especially the machinery of formal symbolic logic, increasingly tracks the rigor demanded of formal mathematical and empirical scientific inquiry. As the sciences themselves continued to develop within an increasingly self-conscious methodology of what is properly meant by "science," in practical terms as well as abstract theory, so the philosophy of science and mathematics has interpreted the requirements for maximizing the discovery of interesting truths to satisfy our need for information, while minimizing the risk of error in empirical judgment.

No account of nineteenth-century philosophy of science would be complete without taking notice of the idealistic movement that characterized much of the period and lent its influence to the Romantic strain of nineteenth-century thought. Unlike their intellectual forebear, the philosophers after Kant for the most part did not think of science as a continuation of the same observational and experimental hypothesis-testing tradition begun by Galileo, Descartes, Boyle, and Newton. They freely used the word "science" (*Wissenschaft*) to describe their own work in philosophy, but, with the exception of Schopenhauer, who began his university studies in medicine, most of the other German philosophers after Kant, including at least those mentioned above, were much more interested in art and literature than in the natural science of their time. Nor were any of this line of philosophers, beginning with Kant and this time including Schopenhauer, known for having made any contributions to, or demonstrated any serious command of, mathematics. Not being scientists or mathematicians does not necessarily preclude any of these thinkers in principle from doing respectable work in the philosophy of science or philosophy of mathematics, but when their actual lack of personal training and experience in the rigorous sciences is considered together with the content of their writings and what they have to say about what they call science and mathematics, it raises interesting questions as to what exactly they mean by the use of the words "science" and "scientific." The follow-up inquiry is then to ask whether what they as philosophers have to say about what they call science should be considered a chapter in the history of the philosophy of science, or whether they are not rather doing metaphysics or epistemology, or something other than philosophy of science in the sense of the kind of science practiced by Galileo, Descartes, and Newton, and by such nineteenth-century contemporaries as Darwin, Ernst Haeckel, Hilbert, Cantor, and others in the mainstream of scientific and mathematical investigations.

Although nineteenth-century science and mathematics continued to refine its methods, nineteenth-century philosophy of science and philosophy of mathematics in some philosophical subcultures did not keep pace, but persisted in *a priori* generalizations and expectations of how independently accessible truth must be projected onto the world without the benefit of good observational or experimental evidence and what in the twentieth century came to be known as the scientific evaluation and interpretation of such empirical evidence. The archetypal example of this confusion of sound scientific methods with unscientific speculative philosophical conjecture is perhaps Hegel's 1801 doctoral dissertation (*De orbitus planetarum*, University of Jena), in which he takes seriously an argument from Plato's *Timaeus* about the occurrence of arithmetical sequences in nature to suggest that there could be only seven planets in our solar system, in a bid to challenge the truth of Bode's law concerning the orbital distances of planets, which has since been vindicated by more contemporary astrophysics.

In this respect, and seen from the perspective of contemporary science and mathematics and philosophy of science and mathematics, the leading lights of nineteenth-century continental philosophy of science and philosophy of mathematics are not Hegel or Fichte or the other *a priori* transcendentalists in which the nineteenth century excelled, but figures such as Mill, Whewell, Frege, Hilbert, Cantor, Darwin (indulging in methodological asides), Boole, and others. It is this latter group, and not the nineteenth-century idealists, who self-consciously share a recognizably similar general modern scientific outlook, which might be partly described as a commitment to rigorously collected, carefully evaluated, interpreted, and reliably tested scientific truths about the properties of abstract formal structures and spatiotemporal empirical phenomena.

As science and mathematics and philosophy of science and mathematics came to define themselves in the nineteenth century, many lineages of philosophical thought were not carried into the twentieth century as fruitful approaches to explaining the nature, and understanding the methods, of mathematics and the natural sciences. As a result, what we see is the absence of a viable contemporary Hegelian, Fichtean, Schellingian, Marxist and so on philosophy of science and mathematics in the ensuing centuries. We see as well that the greatest thinkers of nineteenth-century continental philosophy – excluding Frege and Hilbert and the others we have already singled out as early exponents of a kind of rigorous scientific philosophy that emerged from the century's free experimentation with ideas under the constraint of agreement with properly accepted and interpreted abstract formal relations and empirical facts – made their greatest contributions not to philosophy of science or mathematics, but to ethics and aesthetics, philosophy of culture and politics, social thought, and the struggles of the heart.

Whether this intellectually seething century, marked as much by a Romantic idealist struggle of freedom with necessity as by the steam engine and transfinite cardinals, would have produced the breakthroughs in mathematics and natural science that in turn provided the basis for new developments in nineteenth-century continental philosophy of science and mathematics in the absence of Hegel, Fichte, and others since deemed to have been unscientific in their philosophical reflections, is difficult to affirm or to deny with any confidence. We know that philosophy is a dialectical activity, a conversation, between thinkers and themselves, and we know that philosophy only thrives within a culture and by interaction with that culture's triumphs and tragedies. We see concretely during this productive time in human thought that Frege developed his ideas partly in response to his criticisms of Mill, that Brentano labored to make philosophical psychology scientific in a sense both modern and reaching back to Aristotle's empiricism, specifically against the dominant trend in his day of post-Kantianism among the followers of Hegel, Fichte, and Schelling. If that is so, then perhaps the ideological preparation needed for the progression from nineteenth- to twentieth-century mathematical and scientific discoveries, and their traces in the transition from nineteenth- to twentieth-century philosophy of science and mathematics, would never have occurred or taken quite the historical form and content that they have in the twentieth century as a more distinctly scientific age.

10

PEIRCE: PRAGMATISM AND NATURE AFTER HEGEL

Douglas R. Anderson

I. PEIRCE AND PRAGMATISM

On the contemporary scene, pragmatism, under the influence of the work of Richard Rorty,[1] is often misleadingly regarded as an antirealist, constructivist philosophy of language. I say "misleadingly" because however much contemporary pragmatism meets this description, the work of the early pragmatists Charles Sanders Peirce,[2] William James, F. C. S. Schiller, and John Dewey is not captured by such an account.[3] Early pragmatism was a philosophy of experience, not of language. Importantly, experience was not thought to be a veil between mind and world nor a barrier to our knowing the world. Rather, experience was considered to be the site of our direct engagement with that which environs us. As Dewey put it, "if anything seems adequately grounded empirically it is the

---

*1. For a discussion of Rorty, see the essay by David R. Hiley in *The History of Continental Philosophy: Volume 6*.

2. Charles Sanders Peirce (September 10, 1839–April 19, 1914; born in Boston, MA; died in Milford, PA) was educated at Harvard College (BA 1859, MA 1862), Lowell Scientific School (BS 1863). His influences included Aristotle, Augustus De Morgan (1806–71), Hegel, Kant, Leibniz, and Scotus, and he held an appointment at Johns Hopkins University (1879–84).

3. William James (1842–1910), psychologist and philosopher at Harvard University and close friend of Peirce, gave pragmatism its name in a talk entitled "Philosophical Conceptions and Practical Beliefs" in 1898. John Dewey (1859–1952) was the third original American pragmatist. He identified himself as an instrumentalist and experimentalist, and developed educational and political theories that were influential in the twentieth century. Schiller (1864–1937) was a German-born, British-trained philosopher who developed a version of pragmatism he named "humanism." He corresponded at length with James regarding their mutual philosophical interests.

existence of a world which resists the characteristic functions of the subject of experience, which goes its way, in some respects, independently of those functions, and which frustrates our hopes and intentions."[4] In its own way early pragmatism was "realist" in the sense that our beliefs about things are directly constrained by what is sometimes called an "external world." Even James, whose notion of truth is misconstrued as antirealist, argued: "All our truths are beliefs about 'Reality'; and in any particular belief the reality acts as something independent, as a thing *found*, not manufactured."[5] To get a fuller sense of pragmatism, of its importance for the history of philosophy, and, indeed, even of its contemporary guise, it is important to revisit the work of Peirce, who found a "pragmatic" tradition in the history of Western philosophy and brought it to the American scene in the late nineteenth century.

In 1868 Peirce published "On a New List of Categories" in *Proceedings of the American Academy of Arts and Sciences*. In it Peirce took himself to be rethinking the universal categories established by Aristotle and Kant. Peirce did not use the word "pragmatism" in the essay, but he sketched the structural outline for what he would later call his "pragmaticism." Peirce's three universal categories – what he later named Firstness, Secondness, and Thirdness – are derived from his reconception of perception. These categories appear across the board in Peirce's work. In ontology they are the reality of qualitativeness, the reality of otherness, and the reality of generality or continuity. He immediately put them to work in several important ways. He offered his first published account of the triadic structure of a sign in which an interpretant understands a correlate's reference to a ground or relate. Peirce exemplified this process of representation as follows: "a word represents a thing to the conception in the mind of the hearer, a portrait represents the person for whom it is intended to the conception or recognition, a weathercock represents the direction of the wind to the conception of him who understands it."[6] Peirce proceeded to make his first triadic distinction among signs: likenesses (later called icons), indices, and symbols. Finally, he brought his categories to bear on arguments and made an initial attempt to show the differences among hypothesis (later abduction or retroduction), deduction, and

---

4. John Dewey, *On Experience, Nature, and Freedom*, Richard J. Bernstein (ed.) (Indianapolis, IN: Bobbs-Merrill, 1960), 36.
5. William James, *Pragmatism* (New York: Longmans, Green, 1907), 243–4. Ralph Barton Perry, James's student and biographer, wrote: "Some pragmatists, such as James, are avowedly, and on the whole consistently, realistic" (*Present Philosophical Tendencies* [New York: Longmans, Green, 1912], 214). The key is that while the pragmatists believed that reality constrained inquiry and belief, they did not believe that all ideas were imagistic "copies" of reality.
6. Charles Sanders Peirce, *The Essential Peirce, Volume 1: Selected Philosophical Writings (1867–1893)*, Christian Kloesel and Nathan Houser (eds) (Bloomington, IN: Indiana University Press, 1992), 5. Hereafter cited as EP I followed by the page number.

induction. This last triad came to play an important role in Peirce's rethinking scientific and philosophical inquiry; this rethinking in turn influenced James's reconsideration of the limits of science and Dewey's development of what he called "experimental method."

Peirce developed his interest in method more fully in a series of six papers published in *Popular Science Monthly* in 1877-78. He entitled the series "Illustrations in the Logic of Science," and in them he laid the groundwork for pragmatism as theory of meaning but also for the larger experiential and experimental philosophy that would become identified with the word pragmatism at the turn of the century. The first two papers of the series are among the best known of Peirce's work: "The Fixation of Belief" and "How to Make Our Ideas Clear." In "Fixation," Peirce argued for an experimental method of inquiry that is self-correcting and can therefore trump what he took to be the *a priori* process of most modern philosophers. He also laid the ground for a pragmatic notion of true belief as that which satisfies our doubts. "The most that can be maintained," he argued, "is, that we seek for a belief that we shall *think* to be true" (EP I: 115). In the second paper we find the basis for a pragmatic theory of meaning that looks to the potential effects, fruits, consequences, or implied habits of a concept rather than its origin. Peirce provided here his first rough attempt at the pragmatic maxim: "Consider what effects, which might conceivably have practical bearings, we conceive the object of our conception to have. Then, our conception of these effects is the whole of our conception of the object" (EP I: 132). With method and meaning addressed, the key concepts of pragmatism were in place. However, it is important not to overlook the other themes that appeared in these early essays; these themes help provide a much fuller picture of pragmatism and its projects.

In "How to Make Our Ideas Clear," Peirce applied his new maxim to the philosophical conception of reality. His idea, which he modified significantly over the course of his career, was to show that reality's independence of any particular perceiver or thinker could be cashed out by linking it to inquiry because the "sensible effect" of that which is real is to cause belief. Thus the real could finally be articulated by way of the beliefs of an indefinite run of inquiry; the real is that which would be agreed to by all good inquirers in the long run. It is easy to see the linkage here with James's later focus on pragmatic truth as that which is "expedient in the way of our thinking"[7] and Dewey's focus in his own logic on what he called "warranted assertability."[8] These underpinnings of later

---

7. James, *Pragmatism*, 222.
8. John Dewey, *Logic: The Theory of Inquiry*, in *John Dewey: The Later Works, vol. 12*, Jo Ann Boydston (ed.) (Carbondale, IL: Southern Illinois University Press, 1991), 15-17.

pragmatism come into sharper focus if we take into account as well the final four essays of Peirce's *Popular Science Monthly* series.

In these essays Peirce developed the relations between inquiry and reality, and foreshadowed not only his own later thought but some key ideas in the work of James and Dewey. In general he argued that deduction is inadequate as a method of philosophy. We must instead make conjectures that are initially plausible, use the pragmatic meaning of the conjectures to make deductive predictions about what "would follow" if the conjecture were true, and then inductively establish ways to test for the prediction. Peirce outlined this method in the final essay, "Deduction, Induction, and Hypothesis." This method is set against Peirce's rethinking of the "order of nature." He rejected the modern notion of a stable, solid-state universe that is shot through with order and necessity. He suggested instead that there is real chance and diversity in a universe that is constantly evolving. Moreover, this universe, Peirce argued, reveals continuity and indefiniteness in origin and future. Peirce suggested here what he later explicitly stated. Statistical inquiry is crucial to the development of science not only because of the finitude of inquirers but because it captures the "tychistic" – or chance-laden – nature of the world. In these essays, the tychism and focus on continuity that influenced James's notion of a "pluralistic universe" are apparent in incipient form. On the inquiry side, we find explicit foreshadowings of Dewey's emphasis on the communal nature of science. In "The Doctrine of Chances," Peirce argued:

> logicality inexorably requires that our interests shall *not* be limited. They must not stop at our own fate, but must embrace the whole community. This community, again, must not be limited, but must extend to all races of beings with whom we can come into immediate or mediate intellectual relation. It must reach, however vaguely, beyond this geological epoch, beyond all bounds. He who would not sacrifice his own soul to save the whole world, is, as it seems to me, illogical in all his inferences, collectively. Logic is rooted in the social principle. (EP I: 149)

The linking of logic and reality in a very down-to-earth manner became the trademark of early American pragmatism, and it reveals the importance of empiricism as an avenue of knowing. This connection, one made repeatedly by James, is well established. However, this linking of logic and ontology also discloses a close affinity between pragmatism and German idealism, where the logic of the inquirer is revelatory of an objective logic. The pragmatists, we might say, kept the objective logic but loosened the hold necessity had on that logic such that the logic of inquirers is an experimental and statistical logic and the logic of Nature is tychistic and pluralistic.

II. THE HEGELIAN SETTING IN THE UNITED STATES

As Loyd D. Easton and others have adequately shown, the philosophical thought of Hegel appeared on the American scene well before the Civil War.[9] In New England, Theodore Parker and Frederick Henry Hedge introduced German idealism to the transcendentalist movement. In 1848, Judge J. B. Stallo of Ohio published his *General Principles of the Philosophy of Nature* developing Hegelian themes. Then, in the 1850s, the St. Louis Hegelians, led by Henry Brokmeyer, William Torrey Harris, and Denton Snider, brought Hegel to the heart of the US.[10] Harris edited the *Journal of Speculative Philosophy* from 1867 to 1893, and published work by Peirce, James, and Dewey. Thus Hegel's work – and much of German idealism – was not only a living option for the early pragmatists, but was infused into the very history of thought through which their own work came to life.

William James and Hegelianism

James was well known for his ongoing combat with the American and British Hegelians of his day, rejecting what he took to be their conception of the universe as a closed or "box" system. Hegel's system, James remarked, "resembles a mouse-trap, in which if you once pass the door you may be lost forever."[11] James began reading Hegel as early as 1867 while studying in Germany. Over the course of his career he consistently exposed and argued against the "Hegelisms" in the work of his contemporaries. He was also adamantly opposed to what he took to be the mechanical progress of Hegel's dialectical method: it offered too neat a picture of history and human experience. Nevertheless, he believed some features of Hegel's outlook were redeemable, given proper reorientation. Thus, in *A Pluralistic Universe* he came to the conclusion that:

> Taken in the rough, Hegel is not only harmless but accurate. There is a dialectical movement in things, if such you please to call it, one

---

9. Loyd D. Easton, *Hegel's First American Followers* (Athens, OH: Ohio University Press, 1966).
10. Henry Brokmeyer (1818–1906) was a German immigrant who, after engaging in a variety of enterprises, settled in St. Louis and helped establish a group to study the thought of Kant and Hegel. He was the spiritual leader of the St. Louis Hegelians and made his own translation of Hegel's *Logic*. William Torrey Harris (1835–1909), a New England transplant, became superintendent of St. Louis schools, introducing kindergarten to American culture. He also created and edited the *Journal of Speculative Philosophy* and later taught at the Concord Summer School in Massachusetts. He also served as US Commissioner of Education. Denton Snider (1841–1925) was another member of the St. Louis movement who wrote extensively on philosophy and education and worked for a time with Jane Addams at Hull House in Chicago.
11. William James, *The Will to Believe* (New York: Dover, 1956), 275.

that the whole constitution of concrete life establishes; but it is one that can be described and accounted for in terms of the pluralistic vision of things far more naturally than in the monistic terms to which Hegel finally reduced it.[12]

It would be a mistake, then, to maintain that James was merely an anti-Hegelian and that no Hegelian influence found its way into his version of pragmatism. As his student and biographer Ralph Barton Perry (1876–1957) pointed out:

> Despite this early and lasting dislike of its form James continued his study of Hegelian philosophy intermittently throughout his life, with what was on the whole an increasing respect. In the 70s and 80s he was reading the translations and expositions of Hegel published in the *Journal of Speculative Philosophy* by W. T. Harris, "our most prominent American Hegelian."[13]

Two features of Hegel's work struck James as especially significant for his pragmatism. The first was what he considered to be Hegel's evolutionary conception of truth: that is, that final truth arrives at the end of a long, historical process. The difference was that James insisted on a dialectical procession that was non-necessitarian. Understood in this light, "the pragmatist view of truth lends … a cordial hand to the evolutionary side of Hegelianism."[14] The second important feature was, for James, closely tied to the first, because the intellectualist truth toward which inquiry aimed began for Hegel in immediate perception. As James put it:

> Hegel connects immediate perception with ideal truth by a ladder of intermediary concepts – at least, I suppose they are concepts. The best opinions among his interpreters seems to be that ideal truth does not abolish immediate perception but preserves it as an indispensable "moment." … In other words, Hegel does not pull the ladder up after him when he gets to the top, and may therefore be counted as a non-intellectualist, in spite of his desperately intellectualist *tone*.[15]

---

12. William James, *A Pluralistic Universe* (Lincoln, NE: University of Nebraska Press, 1996), 90.
13. Ralph Barton Perry, *The Thought and Character of William James* (Boston, MA: Little, Brown, 1935), vol. 2, 726.
14. William James, "Seminary in the Theory of Knowledge," in *Works of William James, Vol. 19: Manuscript Lectures* (Cambridge, MA: Harvard University Press, 1988), 433.
15. William James, *Some Problems of Philosophy* (New York: Longmans, Green, 1919), 92 n.2.

For James's pragmatism, being nonintellectualist was a central virtue. When James turned to Hegel's *Phenomenology*, he found in Hegel a kindred spirit who immersed himself in immediate perception. In this much, Hegel's work was among the influences on James's development of his radical empiricism, an empiricism that did not rely on atomistic, external sense impressions but dwelled in what James called the "thickness" of experience. If one kicks away the structure of the "mouse-trap," one can see the Hegel who "plants himself in the empirical flux of things and gets the impression of what happens. His mind is in very truth *impressionistic*."[16] James thus found kinship in a loose sense of dialectical development that worked through history in the direction of truth and in Hegel's impressionistic mode of inquiry. Dewey, on the other hand, whose instrumentalist pragmatism grew out of his reading of James and Peirce, was initially tempted by Hegel's absolute. Ultimately, however, his own focus on social transformation led him away from the absolute toward a Hegelian manner of conceiving the means and structures of such transformation.

John Dewey and Hegelianism

From its inception, Dewey's pragmatism was threaded with strands of Hegel's philosophical outlook. While a graduate student at Johns Hopkins University, Dewey studied Hegel with his mentor G. S. Morris (1840–89). However, as did James, Dewey resisted necessitarianism and thus conceived Hegelian dialectic as retaining some contingency. Moreover, as James Good suggests, "the American Hegelian tradition encouraged Dewey to see Hegel as a politically liberal and eminently practical philosopher, to embrace his view of the individual's relationship to society and his concept of positive freedom, and to develop a theory of learning and human growth similar to Hegel's."[17] Dewey was much less interested in the wholesale system of Hegel's *Logic* than in its import for social development, which he believed took the form of reconstruction of historical circumstances in light of new ideas. Despite the "necessary interdependence of idea and machinery, of thought and institution," Dewey argued, "there comes a time when one side conflicts with the other. At such a period reconstruction is necessary."[18] Throughout his early career, Dewey aligned social reconstruction with Hegel's descriptions of historical development. Later, he learned to pursue reconstruction in his own ways, having kicked away the Hegelian ladder.

---

16. James, *A Pluralistic Universe*, 87.
17. James Good, "John Dewey's 'Permanent Hegelian Deposit' and the Exigencies of War," *Journal of the History of Philosophy* 44(2) (2006), 295.
18. John Dewey, *Early Works, vol. 4*, Jo Ann Boydston (ed.) (Carbondale, IL: Southern Illinois University Press, 1972), 97.

> There was a period extending into my earlier years at Chicago when, in connection with a seminar in Hegel's Logic I tried reinterpreting his categories in terms of "readjustment" and "reconstruction". Gradually I came to realize that what the principles actually stood for could be better understood and stated when completely emancipated from Hegelian garb.[19]

As Dewey indicates, his movement away from Hegel and Hegelian influences was gradual and never fully completed. He claimed that he *drifted* away from Hegel's absolutism toward his own pragmatic reconception of social development, and that his later work retained traces of Hegel's influence. One of the most pervasive traces of this influence can be found in Dewey's belief that selves, institutions, and cultures are achieved outcomes and not ready-made essences. Moreover, such achievements have to take full account of their cultural and historical settings. Understanding one's situation is an initial condition of one's development, growth, or reconstruction.

The responsibility Dewey laid on human communities required adequate means for considering *how* given situations might be moved forward or ameliorated. Thus, late in his career Dewey developed the experimental logic he had begun in earlier years. It is not surprising that this logic reveals more affinities with Hegel's logic than it does with the narrowly deductivist practices that came to define logic in the twentieth century. For Dewey logic is, in its broadest sense, a theory of inquiry that provides tools for transforming the very nature of the situations in which we find ourselves.

Finally, Dewey noted early on that Hegel "elaborated the idea that the chief function of the state is educational."[20] This focus on education follows from the general belief that the primary function of all social institutions was "to further the realization of the freedom of all."[21] Dewey openly embraced the centrality of education and the empowering of individuals through social institutions. In his hands education became the key condition for any culture that tried to live democratically. However, he noted that Hegel remained "haunted by his conception of an absolute goal,"[22] and in the end failed to accomplish anything more than to "consecrate the Prussian State to enshrine bureaucratic absolutism."[23]

---

19. Jane Dewey, "The Biography of John Dewey," in *The Philosophy of John Dewey*, Paul Schilpp (ed.) (Evanston, IL: Northwestern University Press, 1939), 18.
20. John Dewey, *Middle Works, vol. 9*, Jo Ann Boydston (ed.) (Carbondale, IL: Southern Illinois University Press, 1989), 102.
21. John Dewey, *Middle Works, vol. 12*, Jo Ann Boydston (ed.) (Carbondale, IL: Southern Illinois University Press, 2008), 188.
22. Dewey, *Middle Works, vol. 9*, 64.
23. Dewey, *Middle Works, vol. 12*, 188–9.

We see, then, that James loosely borrowed the spirit of immediate perception from Hegelianism and Dewey appropriated Hegel's dialectic in the service of social reconstruction. Peirce, the most systematic of the pragmatists, was not initially enamored of Hegel's thought. But over the course of his career he came to respect Hegel's insights and to use Hegel's system as a standard by which to consider his own architectonic, and particularly his conception of Nature.

Peirce and Hegelianism

Peirce's assessment of Hegel as a thinker varied considerably over the course of his career. Early on, Peirce read the *Encyclopedia* and the *Logic*. Nevertheless, by his own strict standards of scholarship he disavowed a sufficient understanding of Hegel. Indeed, as late as 1897 he noted, regarding some lectures he was preparing: "It is not my intention at all to attempt a criticism of Hegel. I have not studied him deeply enough to do so. But certain remarks about him strike me, from time to time; and those I insert."[24] Peirce was not always this circumspect, and throughout his career worried about three aspects of Hegel's thought: (i) what he took to be Hegel's inadequate background in math and logic; (ii) what he took to be Hegel's *a priori* and thus private method; and (iii) what he construed as Hegel's ultimate abandonment of two of the three "categories" he initially introduced. Of the first, he remarked that "Hegel had the misfortune to be unusually deficient in mathematics" and that "Hegel's dialectical method is only a feeble and rudimentary application of the principles of the calculus to metaphysics."[25] Regarding his second concern, he argued that "The Absolute Knowledge of Hegel is nothing but G. W. F. Hegel's idea of himself" (CP 8.118). Peirce's final criticism was the one he most often leveled at Hegel: that he introduced the three categories only to take back two of them:[26]

> The third stage is very close indeed to Thirdness, which is substantially Hegel's *Begriff*. Hegel, of course, blunders monstrously, as we shall all be seen to do; but to my mind the one fatal disease of his philosophy is that, seeing that the *Begriff* in a sense implies

---

24. Charles Sanders Peirce, *The Charles S. Peirce Papers*, The Houghton Library (Cambridge, MA: Harvard University Library Microreproduction service, 1963–66), MS 943.
25. Charles Sanders Peirce, *The Collected Papers of Charles S. Peirce*, Charles Hartshorne and Paul Weiss (eds, vols 1–6) and Arthur W. Burks (eds, vols 7–8) (Cambridge, MA: Harvard University Press, 1931–58), vol. 1, para. 368. Hereafter cited as CP followed by volume and paragraph numbers.
26. Peirce often aligned his own categories of Firstness, Secondness, and Thirdness with Hegel's three stages of thought as well as with other triadic structures in Hegel's thought. I will describe the Peircean categories more fully below.

> Secondness and Firstness, he failed to see that nevertheless they are elements of the phenomenon not to be *aufgehoben*, but as real and able to stand their ground as the *Begriff* itself. (CP 8.268)[27]

Amid Peirce's criticisms, we find his deep respect and admiration for Hegel. As we note in the claims just cited, he repeatedly aligned his own universal categories of Firstness (qualitative immediacy), Secondness (otherness), and Thirdness (mediation) with Hegel's three stages of thought. "My three categories," he claimed, "are nothing but Hegel's three grades of thinking" (CP 8.213).[28] He also appreciated the historical and evolutionary dimension of Hegel's objective logic and argued that "Hegel's system of Nature represents tolerably the science of his day" (CP 1.524). We can see here the implicit suggestion that it will be up to Peirce, the pragmatists, and others to take the Hegelian method and bring it into alliance with the evolutionary science of the late nineteenth century. And, finally, Peirce, like James, appreciated the down-to-earthness of the *Phenomenology*. Whatever the instrumental importance of logic may be, philosophy is a science that employs "attentive scrutiny and comparison of the facts of everyday life, such as present themselves to every adult and sane person, and for the most part in every day and hour of his waking life."[29] To begin such a science, we ought to follow Hegel's lead: "We must not begin by talking of pure ideas – vagabond thoughts that tramp the public roads without any human habitation – but must begin with men and their conversation" (CP 8.112). Thus, for Peirce, Hegel was "in some respects the greatest philosopher that ever lived" (CP 1.524). This remark is worth remembering because pragmatism is so often viewed simply as an antagonist of the neo-Hegelian idealisms in Britain and the US at the turn of the twentieth century. On the contrary, pragmatism was one of the avenues by which Hegel's thought found its way into twentieth-century America. To overlook this, as many who currently fly the flag of pragmatism do, is to misunderstand pragmatism at its roots, as Peirce argued:

> The truth is that pragmatism is closely allied to the Hegelian absolute idealism, from which it is sundered by its vigorous denial that the third category ... suffices to make the world .... Had Hegel, instead of regarding the first two stages with his smile of contempt, held on

---

27. See also CP 5.79, 8.41, 8.272.
28. For more detail on the relation of Peirce's categories to Hegel's thought, see Martin Suhr, "On the Relation of Peirce's 'Universal Categories' to Hegel's 'Stages of Thought,'" *Graduate Studies Texas Tech University* 23 (1981).
29. Charles Sanders Peirce, *The Essential Peirce, Volume 2: Selected Philosophical Writings (1893–1913)*, Peirce Edition Project (ed.) (Bloomington, IN: Indiana University Press, 1998), 146. Hereafter cited as EP II followed by the page number.

> to them as independent or distinct elements of the triune Reality, pragmaticists might have looked up to him as the great vindicator of their truth. (CP 5.436)

Indeed, as early as 1893 Peirce described his relation to Hegel as follows: "The principles supported by Mr. Peirce bear a close affinity with those of Hegel; perhaps are what Hegel's might have been had he been educated in a physical laboratory instead of in a theological seminary" (CP 8, bibliography note).

My aim at this juncture is not to see to what extent Peirce got Hegel right.[30] I want simply to explore one avenue by which German idealism makes an appearance in early pragmatism. I have noted Peirce's affinities and disaffinities with Hegel's thought. It is worth adding to this that Peirce often described himself as a Schellingian. Schelling, perhaps more than Hegel, at least in Peirce's eyes, kept freedom and Firstness more alive as a category. Moreover, he brought to life Fichte's relation of the "me" and the "not-me" in his conception of Nature. Through both Hegel and Schelling, Peirce arrived at a conception of Nature that is quite at odds with the conception held by the likes of Herbert Spencer, Karl Pearson, Thomas H. Huxley and others working out the tradition of British empiricism. In exploring Peirce's idealistic conception of Nature, we can begin to see the pragmatic differences it makes in a philosophy of science – differences in the aims of science, in the uses of statistics, and in the general methods of inquiry. These differences, as many contemporary readers of Peirce have suggested, clearly separate Peirce's thought from what has come to be called pragmatism in the early twenty-first century. Using Peirce's conception of Nature as a marker for pragmatism is not, however, arbitrary. As we noted earlier, pragmatism began as a description of meaning and for Peirce, as well as for Dewey and James, evolved into a notion of inquiry that tested proposed hypotheses by checking experimental results against deduced predictions. Thus, in 1903 Peirce offered a lecture entitled "Pragmatism as the Logic of Abduction" (EP II: 226). For Peirce, the logic of abduction hinged on an affinity between the mind of the human inquirer and the world. "I infer," Peirce stated, "in the first place that man divines something of the secret principles of the universe because his mind has developed under the influence of these same secret principles" (CP 7.46, see also 1.81, 5.604). Thus an idealistic conception of Nature in which the logic of the natural inquirer was attuned to the logic of events made sense for Peirce as a way of understanding how our scientific practices are possible. In this regard, he saw Schelling and Hegel as his intellectual progenitors.

---

30. For a close exploration of Peirce's understanding of Hegel, see Robert Stern, "Peirce, Hegel, and the Category of Secondness," *Inquiry* 50(2) (April 2007).

III. PEIRCEAN NATURE

Peirce is well known for his scientific practice and his writings on the philosophy of science. He invariably described himself as "a scientific man," and he believed thinkers who had worked in laboratories made better philosophers (CP 1.618). Indeed, he argued that nineteenth-century philosophy suffered "because it had been pursued by men who have not been nurtured by dissecting rooms and other laboratories, and who consequently have not been animated by the true scientific *Eros*" (CP 1.620). His pragmaticistic method was, after all, an experimental method. Thus it seems ironic to some that he identified himself as an idealist, asserting that "the one intelligible theory of the universe is that of objective idealism that matter is effete mind" (CP 6.685). As a consequence, various commentators on Peirce's work have tried to argue that this dimension of his thought is old-fashioned or outmoded. However, Peirce understood very well what he was doing in claiming idealism as his own. As he saw it, he was looking forward not backward. For this reason it makes sense to at least try to understand what he meant.

For Peirce, the old-fashioned and outmoded version of philosophy was the nominalism that was traceable back to William of Ockham. As Peirce saw it, "all modern philosophy of every sect has been nominalistic" (CP 1.19). It was especially true, he believed, of the British empirical tradition, which was also associated with what Peirce called the "daughters of nominalism": "sensationalism, phenomenalism, individualism, and materialism" (CP 8.38). By the end of the nineteenth century, he complained, it was almost impossible to find a scientifically minded person who was not also a materialist. Peirce's objective idealism was, on the contrary, built on a strong scholastic realism that argued for real generality and continuity in the universe, and that was capable of underwriting the reality of the laws of Nature.

For Peirce, idealism and scholastic realism together provided a better account of the practices of scientists than did materialistic nominalism. Moreover, they made it easier to grasp the import of the most significant scientific theory of the late nineteenth century: biological evolution. In short, Peirce believed that the common nominalistic conception of Nature was inadequate and that it needed to be replaced with an idealistic conception of Nature. In a 1908 letter to Cassius Keyser, he remarked that a "logical, Hegelian-like evolution must be recognized as logically preceding the temporal evolution."[31]

Peirce's conception of Nature began, as did all of his metaphysical thought, with his logic. On this score, he saw himself in the tradition of Aristotle and Hegel. Logic, for Peirce, dealt not only with deduction but with the full range

---

31. Peirce, MS L233, 4.

of human reasoning. His pragmaticism and his semiotic were both featured parts of his logical theory. Logic, then, as a theory of inquiry seeks to describe and prescribe, in a general way, scientific practice. What impressed Peirce most was that many, although not all, scientists of his day believed they were coming to understand Nature, to find out truths about it. And the history of sciences, according to Peirce, confirmed this belief from a pragmatic point of view. That is, the ideas of the sciences reveal their truth in history through their effectiveness in dealing with the world. True ideas bear an experimental track record: "We call them in science established truths, that is, they are propositions into which the economy of endeavor prescribes that, for the time being, further inquiry shall cease" (CP 5.589).

If scientists are right about their mission, and Peirce believed they were, then human inquirers must be able to know Nature. Nature, that is, must be intelligible to human inquirers. As Peirce acknowledged to a group of Harvard students, he agreed with the "popular notion that modern science is so very great a thing as to be commensurate with Nature and indeed to constitute of itself some account of the universe" (CP 5.585). Or again, "The only end of science, as such, is to learn the lesson that the universe has to teach it" (CP 5.589). This requires a fittingness on both ends of the inquiry process. The human inquirer must be *able* to know Nature; and Nature must be *able* to be known. Of the first Peirce says, "I am quite sure that you must be brought to acknowledge that man's mind has a natural adaptation to imagining correct theories of some kinds" (CP 5.591). On various occasions he stated that persons have an instinct for "guessing right" – not all of the time, but more often than not. Only such a belief could underwrite Peirce's abductive/inductive theory of inquiry. Creating and selecting fitting or plausible hypotheses from an infinite realm of logically possible hypotheses requires this instinct for guessing or imagining. "It is somehow more than a mere figure of speech," he argued, "to say that nature fecundates the mind of man with ideas which, when those ideas grow up, will resemble their father, Nature" (CP 5.591). On the side of Nature, he maintained, "Nature only appears intelligible so far as it appears rational, that is, so far as its processes are seen to be like processes of thought" (CP 3.422). Nature must have an element that is idea-like, that is akin to the working of the human mind. This should *not* be surprising if the human mind is itself a feature of Nature, as Spinoza, Schelling, and Hegel suggested. Thus the process of inquiry must be a working, living analogy between inquirers and Nature: "It is certain that the only hope of retroductive reasoning ever reaching the truth is that there may be some natural tendency towards an agreement between the ideas which suggest themselves to the human mind and those which are concerned in the laws of nature" (CP 1.81). This hypothesis that Nature is in some part idea-like is the beginning of Peirce's idealistic conception of Nature. However, idealism in its extreme forms argues that Nature is *nothing but* Idea, Spirit, or Mind. As we noted earlier, Peirce often charged Hegel with precisely this reductive sort of move. "The capital error of Hegel," he wrote, "is that he almost altogether ignores the Outward Clash" of experience (CP 8.41). In the terms of Peirce's own philosophical vocabulary: Hegel regards "Category the Third as the only true one. For in the Hegelian system the other two are only introduced in order to be *aufgehoben*" (CP 5.79). This concern led Peirce, in his conception of Nature, to return to his early essay "On a New List of Categories." As we noted, in this piece he provided his own revision of the Aristotelian and Kantian categories of the Real. He argued that both logically and phenomenologically reality reveals itself as three-categoried, and he named these three, simply but awkwardly, Firstness, Secondness, and Thirdness. Unlike either the materialist or the extreme idealist, Peirce refused to excommunicate any of the categories or to reduce any one of them to the others. The reason to appropriate the term "idealism" was that it could include Thirdness without needing to get rid of Firstness and Secondness. Peirce's idealism involved a reciprocal order of dependence among the categories akin to that operative among Kant's relata of substance, cause, community. There, causality is first described as the interaction of two substantive individuals. However, for full causality, the entire situation or *communitas* in which the individuals interact is required. Thus, community cannot occur without substance and the dual relation of cause and effect, but the individuals and their interaction cannot be sustained without a community that provides the continuity of the relation. Materialism, on the contrary, had no way by which to include Thirdness. Thus Peirce revised idealism in light of his new list of categories, and this in turn led to his revised conception of the Nature into whose workings scientists inquire. Again, the argument is initiated by logic. Given an affinity between the reasoner and Nature, "It follows," Peirce said, "that if we find three distinct and irreducible forms of rhemata, the ideas of these should be the three elementary conceptions of metaphysics" (CP 3.422). Nature must, therefore, be rethought in terms of the ideas attending "the three forms of rhemata ... firstness, secondness, and thirdness; firstness, or spontaneity; secondness, or dependence; thirdness, or mediation" (CP 3.422). Elsewhere he described Firstness as variety and indeterminacy, Secondness as resistance, and Thirdness as generality and continuity.

Peirce believed that Nature revealed to inquirers traits of each of the three categories. Firstness was to be found in Nature's growing variety, in the actuality of possibility and spontaneity, and in Nature's statistical form. Secondness is disclosed most clearly in human experience where we find ourselves constrained in action and belief by Nature's "facts." Moreover, our residual belief in "things" or "individuals" is an indication of our acquaintance with Secondness in Nature. Finally, Nature's Thirdness is found in its generality, continuity, and lawfulness.

It is not difficult to see Hegel's stages of thought lurking in Peirce's categoriology. What is missing is not the historical development of Nature and culture, but a lock-step process of necessity by which this development occurs. Let me provide a sketch of each of Peirce's categories of Nature in turn.

Nature's Firstness

From early on in his career Peirce was dissatisfied with what John Stuart Mill called the "uniformity of nature." But his rejection of such uniformity was not grounded in an atomism or nominalism that outrightly rejected the reality of lawfulness or uniformity. Rather, it was his scientifically based belief in Nature's growth that resisted the picture of uniformity in a steady-state universe. What science tended to find, Peirce argued, was not perfect regularity and determinateness, but a regularity accompanied by surprises, change, and growth. Uniformity or perfect regularity in Nature may be a "natural belief" but, as Peirce consistently maintained, "Natural beliefs ... also require correction and purification from natural illusions" and so "the adaptations of nature, beautiful and marvelous as they verily are, are never found to be quite perfect; so that the argument is *against* the absolute exactitude of any natural belief, including that of the principle of causation" (CP 6.50).[32] The uniformity of Nature is a reasonable ontological hypothesis but it fails to square with experience, as does the philosophical determinism that is its intellectual companion. Peirce argued:

> Nature is not regular. No disorder would be less orderly than the existing arrangement. It is true that the special laws and regularities are innumerable; but nobody thinks of the irregularities, which are infinitely more frequent. Every fact true of any one thing in the universe is related to every fact true of every other. But the immense majority of these relations are fortuitous or irregular. (CP 5.342)

Peirce's evolutionary conception of Nature required a nonmechanistic outlook, one that admitted conditions for genuine growth.

Peirce, whose father helped create the first English translation of Laplace, rejected Laplace's suggestion that chance or probability in Nature was simply a function of human ignorance.[33] Nature rather seemed to disclose a wide range of "unlawful" or "irregular" events. In everyday experience, for example, whom we encounter and under what circumstances we encounter them are for the most

---

32. See also *ibid.*
33. Pierre-Simon Laplace (1749–1827) was a French astronomer and seminal thinker in mathematical statistics.

part unlawful events. On the intellectual front, evolutionary theory and developments in statistics led Peirce to his "tychism," the belief that there is always an element of chance or spontaneity in the universe. To his friend Chauncey Wright, a defender of both Mill and Darwin, Peirce stated, "Mill's doctrine was nothing but a metaphysical point of view to which Darwin's theory, which was nourished by positive observation, must be deadly" (CP 5.64). That is to say, Darwin's observations suggested that there are real possibilities in Nature's developments, real *may be*s as opposed to a seamless system of *must be*s and *would be*s: "The principle of sporting is the principle of irregularity, indeterminacy, chance" (EP II: 272). Tychism is supported by the simple observation of increased variety in Nature. From our limited perspective on earth, we see new species come and go and within species we find individuals that push the boundaries of the class. "The premises of Nature's own processes," Peirce argued, "are all independent uncaused elements of facts that go to make up the variety of nature which the necessitarian supposes to have been in existence from the foundation of the world, but which the Tychist supposes are continually receiving new accretions" (CP 5.119). Against Herbert Spencer's influential blend of mechanism and evolutionary theory, he held that since Nature reveals both its growth and its diversification, we must abandon mechanism since "mechanical law can never produce diversification" (CP 1.174). Thus, for Peirce, just as in our logical theory we must shift from a deductivist and necessitarian outlook to an abductive/inductive logic, so in ontology we must move from an assumption of the uniformity of Nature to a tychistic ontology and cosmology that includes the spontaneity that can account for increased diversification. Nature is *itself* probabilistic – statistics describe its being directly: "if the laws of nature are still in process of evolution from a state of things in the infinitely distant past in which there were no laws, it must be that events are not even now absolutely regulated by law." And:

> just as when we attempt to verify any law of nature our observations show irregular departures from law owing to our errors, so there are in the very facts themselves absolutely fortuitous departures from law ... which ... must manifest themselves in some indirect way on account of their continual occurrence. (CP 7.514)

Peirce willingly acknowledged that his tychistic conception of Nature was hypothetical. But he believed it better accounted both for our ordinary experiences of indeterminacy and for the late-nineteenth-century developments in science than did the uncritical adoption of the uniformity of Nature and determinism. I believe his outlook on this score remains viable in the twenty-first century, although we are still occasionally tempted by the natural belief of uniformity.

Nature's Secondness

The category of Secondness in Nature is the least problematic, I think, for contemporary science. Our human practice of scientific inquiry requires Nature's Secondness. A Nature that is pure Secondness or atomistic actuality is the Nature of the late-nineteenth-century mechanist and nominalist. Peirce's difficulty here is not so much to persuade scientists that Nature reveals Secondness, but to show that an idealistic conception of Nature can include Secondness. In other words, he must show that he is not Hegelian as he understood Hegelianism. Trading on evolutionary theory, Peirce recognized human beings as a natural result of evolution: humans are a feature of Nature. However, the human ability to inquire and to know seems to establish, as Fichte suggested, a duality in the midst of Nature. As inquirers, we become Nature knowing itself: "we are all of us natural products, naturally partaking of the characteristics that are found everywhere throughout nature" (CP 5.613). This accounts for the affinity between our ideas and Nature's laws, as suggested at the outset, but it also insists on a fundamental otherness. There must be in reality both an ego and a non-ego; the inquirer must be able to objectify the rest of Nature, including herself. There is an inner and an outer, a subject and an object, and so forth – all *within* Nature. The key is to see these as functional features of Nature – they are not extra- or super-natural, as Dewey often put it; rightly or wrongly, Peirce seemed to believe that Schelling retained this view but that Hegel lost it by neglecting Secondness.[34] For Peirce, our experience is itself the key indicator to us of the Secondness, the otherness: what he called the "outward clash" in Nature. "Experience," he believed, "means nothing but just that of a cognitive nature which the history of our lives has forced upon us" (CP 5.539); it refers "to that which is forced upon man's recognition, will-he, nill-he" (CP 5.613). Individually and communally, our beliefs are resisted by Nature's otherness; this is the truth of any empiricism. And when as inquirers we experiment, we aim to make sense of this external constraint on our thought. Borrowing from the chemist Julius Adolph Stöckhardt (1809–86), Peirce described "experiment" as "a question put to nature" (CP 5.168).[35]

Peirce thus resisted the idealistic temptation to claim that Nature is "nothing but mind": an undifferentiated categorial whole. Material reality in the normal sense of things *is* a feature of our experience. According to Peirce, "An idealist need not deny the reality of the external world, any more than Berkeley did. For the reality of the external world *means* nothing except that real experience of duality" (CP 5.539). There are individual things and events to which we, as agents and inquirers, must respond. Indeed, one of our human purposes in

---

34. For an extended discussion of Hegel and Secondness, see Stern, "Peirce, Hegel, and the category of Secondness."
35. See also CP 5.57.

discovering Nature's truths is to be able to act more effectively within an oppositional environment. Knowing a law of Nature is not enough; we must also have the ability to act in a specific situation. As Peirce put it, "a law of nature left to itself would be quite analogous to a court without a sheriff" (CP 5.48).

Peirce shares with the nominalist a belief in the actuality of things and events; Nature has its Secondness. However, understanding Nature requires more than a bare acquaintance with individuals; we seek the intelligibility of the relations of things and the regularities of their behavior. Just as the court of law requires a sheriff for action, the sheriff reciprocally requires the court of law for guidance. It is not the individual facts and events themselves that require explanation – it seems foolish to ask in any full ontological sense why one's shirt is blue. But we do require explanation for the regular behavior of things. "Law," Peirce argued, "is *par excellence* the thing that wants a reason" (CP 6.12). All inquiry, scientific or otherwise, is an investigation into Nature's Thirdness – its lawfulness, its meaning, its reasonableness.

Nature's Thirdness

As we noted earlier, Peirce's rejection of Nature's uniformity was not a rejection of its regularity. And it is precisely this regularity about which the scientist hopes to learn. Even a statistical rather than a deterministic regularity shows that individuals in Nature have habits and ways of behaving that are general, or third-like. Peirce did not argue, therefore, for the *existence* of laws as objects or individuals – this would be to reduce them to seconds and would void their ability to cover a variety of instances. Instead, Peirce argued for the *reality* of laws, a reality that is evidenced by the past regularity of the actions of things as well as by the predictability of the future. It is here in Nature's Thirdness that Peirce put his scholastic realism to work.

For the scientific world the question of Nature's Thirdness is closely bound to our conceptions of laws of Nature. The traditional British empiricist/nominalist argued that what we call "laws" are simply arbitrary descriptions attributed by persons to things in Nature. Pearson, for example, argued that a law is "essentially a product of the human mind and has no meaning apart from man."[36] Or, as Peirce argued more generally, the conceptualists "say that the laws of nature and the properties of chemical species are the results of thinking" (CP 1.27). Given the work of Rorty and a wide variety of other thinkers, such an outlook still seems very much in vogue. Indeed, those who, like Rorty, follow the logic of nominalist reasoning to its conclusion, admit that science is a modern mythologizing and that Nature itself is a human fabrication.

---

36. Karl Pearson, *The Grammar of Science* (New York: Charles Scribner's Sons, 1892), 104.

Peirce resisted this line of reasoning not only because he believed science revealed something of Nature's intelligibility but also because we find ourselves practically constrained not only by Nature's actuality, its factual resistance, but by the force of Nature's laws. We cannot indeed truly think and act as we please. In describing gravity in a lecture, Peirce maintained that we come to believe by way of experience that any stone dropped on earth will behave in a reasonably similar way and that "there was a *real reason*, that is, a real general" that governed its falling (CP 6.99). We find a natural law that enables us to tell what would be the case in the future under certain circumstances.

The description, of course, is simple and commonplace. The difficulty seems to be in seeing the necessity of Peirce's realistic, idealistic ontology for making the description effective. The pragmatic meaning of natural laws, however, should bring the force of their reality home to us. These laws have what Peirce called "a sort of *esse in futuro* .... That is to say, they will have a present reality which consists in the fact that events *will* happen according to the formulation of those laws" (EP II: 153). A law's reality, its independence from what you or I think about it, is what enables us to make predictions according to it: "it is a prognostic generalization of observations" (EP II: 68). It is our very scientific and experimental use of Nature's laws that reveals and confirms their pragmatic meaning – gravity, for example, is found in its would-be consequences. "The scientific man," Peirce said, "looks upon a law ... as a matter of fact as objective as fact can be" (EP II: 74). Only it cannot be an individual fact or a fact of Secondness; in order for prediction to be possible through its use, a law must be general and apply to an indefinite range of possible events.

Strictly speaking, Nature's laws reveal a kind of final causality in Nature. Such a claim is antithetical to nominalism and atomism, which begin and end with efficient and proximate causes, and it sounds strange to those who think of finality only in terms of conscious beings. But since a law has its "being *in futuro*," it constrains events to take some forms and to resist others. Thus, for Peirce, "To say that the future does not influence the present is untenable doctrine .... All our knowledge of the laws of nature is analogous to knowledge of the future" (CP 2.86). To say, then, that the future is in some part governed by present laws is to argue for final causality in Nature.

Finally, Peirce's claim that Nature involves Thirdness, that generality is real, also means that Nature itself reveals generality and continuity to us as inquirers. It does this through lawfulness, as we have been arguing, but it also does so through some phenomenological features of our experience. For example, we on occasion experience sympathy with other living beings, and we quite routinely experience the efficacy of the communication of meaning. But for ideas or meanings to be communicable, Peirce claimed, we must be able to enter into them; ideas are real generals that do not reside in us but that any of us may enter into. This was the feature of Hegel's *Logic* that intrigued Peirce. Moreover, in order for me to sympathize with another person or animal, there must be continuity between their experiences and mine. Thus simple everyday experiences bring home to us the real generality of Nature; that we tend to overlook or dismiss this fact is a function of the depth of our habituation to a nominalistic version of the world. In scientific work we find such continuity similarly suggested. Evolutionary theories tend to argue for a process that moves forward by "insensible degrees." Thus, in identifying species, Peirce argued, the naturalist notes that the qualities of his specimens "are not precisely alike." Therefore "the differences are such as to lead him to believe that forms could be found intermediate between any two of those he possesses" (CP 2.646). The upshot is that natural kinds are real, but the borders between them are continuous such that new species may appear, and such that some individual specimens may partake in both – they may be border creatures.

For those who conceive of Nature as a steady-state, box universe, Peirce's three-categoried Nature may seem to involve some extravagant claims. Many in the history of Western thought have been tempted by the simplicity of materialism and extreme conceptual idealism because of the clarity they can bring to explanation. However, Peirce found in the world of scientific practice enough evidence to call the simplicity of both materialism and conceptual idealism into question. To account for our natural experiences of possibility, of physical resistance, and of predictability, Nature must be diverse and spontaneous, factual and constraining, general and evolutionary. It must be, for Peirce, the same complex and living sort of Nature to be found in the thought of Hegel and Schelling.

IV. CONCLUDING THOUGHTS

In concluding, I would recall that for Peirce one's metaphysical account of Nature is never without a practical and pragmatic meaning. It can affect whether we inquire, how we inquire, and even, as we now know, how we fund inquiry. It is for this reason, as well as for his concern for finding the truth, that Peirce worried about the nominalistic disease that had permeated not only nineteenth-century science but many features of everyday life. A nominalist lives in a Nature where truth, beauty, and goodness are not real regulative hopes but are arbitrary constructions of individual beings. Indeed, the nominalist, unlike the Peircean idealist, has no intrinsic reason to care about Nature since it bears no constitutive meaning. Peirce's Nature, as did Hegel's and Schelling's, does bear meaning and may require aesthetic and moral consideration. Let me close, then, with a final sketch of Peirce's resistance to Pearson's nominalistic account of Nature. Pearson, as we noted, argued that natural laws are in a strict sense arbitrary human conventions. And prior to Rorty, Pearson maintained that the world itself is a construction of the finite mind. Therefore, for Pearson, scientific practice could not legitimately be aimed at a real general called "truth." Instead, it must be conducted for other reasons. Specifically, he argued, the sole reasons for science are to "promote the welfare of human society, to increase social happiness," and "to strengthen social stability" (EP II: 57). At first blush these may seem worthy aims. But as Peirce was quick to point out, Pearson, an original leader of British eugenics, meant by these aims the preservation of British aristocracy. Peirce, who had by that time learned that even intelligent persons could become impoverished, retorted: "to demand that man should aim at the stability of British society, or society at large, or the perpetuation of the race as an *ultimate* end, is too much" (EP II: 60). Thus a nominalist Nature too has its consequences. As Peirce well knew, there is much more at stake in his idealistic conception of Nature than conversation among philosophers or scientists. And yet, to bring the issue full circle, this is the best reason why we, as philosophers and scientists, should continue to inquire into the efficacy and truth of such a conception. For if it is not the case that the truth is merely what works, it remains the case for Peirce that the truth will in the long run work:

> The very being of law, general truth, reason, – call it what you will, – consists in its expressing itself in a cosmos and in intellects which reflect it, and in doing this progressively; and that which makes progressive creation worth doing, – so the researcher comes to feel, – is precisely the reason, the law, the general truth for the sake of which it takes place. (EP II: 58–9)

To see Peirce's Nature in this way is to see that pragmatism's roots in German idealism are deep and strong, even when they are not stated explicitly. We also see that these roots are heavily modified by the pragmatists' experimental method, by their acceptance of a tychistic dimension of Nature, and by their evolutionary outlook. Missing this connection, however, is precisely what has unfortunately led to the many contemporary misreadings of the pragmatic tradition as antirealist, as subjective and relativistic, and as thoroughly constructivist. Especially for Peirce, pragmatism was not a radically novel philosophical outlook, but a reasonable development of the history of philosophy given the states of philosophy, science, mathematics, and logic at the close of the nineteenth century.

MAJOR WORKS

The Collected Papers of Charles Sanders Peirce. Edited by Charles Hartshorne and Paul Weiss (vols 1–6) and Arthur W. Burks (vols 7–8). Cambridge, MA: Harvard University Press, 1931–58.

Semiotic and Significs: The Correspondence between Charles S. Peirce and Victoria Lady Welby. Bloomington, IN: Indiana University Press, 1977.

Writings of Charles S. Peirce: A Chronological Edition. Edited by Max H. Fisch, Christian Kloesel, and Nathan Houser. 6 vols. Bloomington, IN: Indiana University Press, 1982– .

Reasoning and the Logic of Things. Edited by Kenneth Ketner. Cambridge, MA Harvard University Press, 1992.

11
AESTHETICS AND THE PHILOSOPHY OF ART, 1840–1900
Gary Shapiro

The question can be raised whether the category or discipline of philosophical aesthetics existed before the eighteenth century. Unlike "logic," "ethics," and "physics," a traditional Stoic division of philosophy with great staying power, "aesthetics" is clearly a product of modernity. As Paul O. Kristeller demonstrated in "The Modern System of the Arts," it was in the eighteenth century that the idea of the aesthetic as a distinctive human capacity and the parallel consolidation of the notion of the fine arts crystallized in the writings of (mostly) French, German, and English philosophers and critics.[1] The modern concepts of art and aesthetics emerged together. Any history or genealogy of aesthetics will have to confront the possible tensions between an orientation to the arts and one to aesthetic subjectivity; it should take account of the canon of the fine arts that the new field of aesthetics inherited from the eighteenth century as well as its conflicts, margins, and exclusions. We should be aware, for example, that the very notion of literature (in contrast to earlier traditions of poetics and rhetoric) arose around 1800, and almost immediately generated the idea of

---

1. Paul Oskar Kristeller, "The Modern System of the Arts," in *Renaissance Thought II*, Paul Oskar Kristeller (ed.) (New York: Harper & Row, 1965); Kristeller's essay originally appeared in 1950, anticipating the analogous contextualization of Kant's aesthetics by Hans-Georg Gadamer (in *Truth and Method*) by ten years (both were students of Martin Heidegger). Cf. Larry Shiner, *The Invention of Art: A Cultural History* (Chicago, IL: University of Chicago Press, 2001), 3–16. The first modern use of the term "aesthetics" is generally credited to Alexander Baumgarten (1714–62), in suggesting that there could be a general logic of sensibility. While Baumgarten drew on Christian Wolff's (1679–1754) Leibnizian notion of sensibility as confused cognition, he gave this formulation a new direction by considering the arts as forms of perfecting and clarifying thought in sensible form.

world literature (which, as Marx observed in 1848, is a recent invention of the bourgeoisie).[2]

There is, then, only a modern aesthetics. The Greeks and Romans were concerned with the power of poetry and music and the beauty of the *kosmos*, but had no "aesthetics," and nor did the medievals, despite their hermeneutic fascination with the meaning of biblical narrative. For the development of aesthetics in the specifically modern sense two things were required: (i) *the discovery of "man"* in the meaning that Michel Foucault gives to that term, that is the being who understands that his entire construction of the world is possible only through his own finite powers, and who sets himself the infinite and, as it turns out, impossible task of clarifying the nature of these powers, including aesthetic sensibility or taste; and (ii) the critical and practical formation of a *system of the fine arts*, in which poetry, painting, sculpture, architecture, music, and others (including some later marginalized, e.g. gardening and landscape architecture) were understood as having fundamentally similar aims and roots.[3] The arts became a philosophically crucial form for the self-understanding of the finite human being at the time when it became possible to speak of art in something like the usual modern sense. This understanding was pursued in settings and institutions such as museums and concert halls where the arts had both a privileged and a newly isolated place. Aesthetics was the experience of beauty, sublimity, and art in which the human being manifests its universal capacities, coming to a knowledge of itself as reflective subject (Kant) or as participating in the work of *Geist* (Hegel).

Both Kantian and Hegelian aesthetics are centered in the concept of a universal humanity that comes to understand some of its deepest powers through aesthetic experience, including that of the arts.[4] The Kantian form revolves around the power of reflective judgment (*Urteilskraft*) by which the mind becomes aware of the free play of its other powers and claims universal validity for its judgment. This power of reflective judgment can be exercised either in regard to the beauty and sublimity of nature or with respect to the productions of fine art. This harmony of the faculties that we glimpse in the judgment of taste is one that involves a certain indeterminacy; it does not accomplish a fully articulated understanding of either the meaning of the aesthetic object or, more importantly, of the roots and unity of the three great human powers. Hegelian aesthetics envisioned the achievement of a self-conscious human universality as a historical process that could actually be completed; the

---

2. The earliest occurrence of "literature" documented by the *Oxford English Dictionary* is 1812; the word does not appear in Grimm's *Wörterbuch*.
3. Michel Foucault, *The Order of Things* (New York: Vintage, 1970).
*4. For discussions of Kant's and Hegel's aesthetics, see the essays by Thomas Nenon and Terry Pinkard, respectively, in *The History of Continental Philosophy: Volume 1*.

grand narrative of art, as developed in Hegel's lectures, is a story of spirit coming to itself historically, within the medium of sensuous material, a medium from which it eventually twists free, transforming itself into religion and philosophy. This universal historical hermeneutics concludes elegiacally by proclaiming the notorious "death of art," or to follow Hegel more precisely, the judgment that art is no longer an original source of thought, having been surpassed by and comprehended (*aufgehoben*) in religion and philosophy. Between roughly 1840 and 1900 philosophers assumed the task of elaborating and sometimes transforming the conception of the universal aesthetic human and the meaning of art that Kant and Hegel had pursued in their distinctive ways.

I. AESTHETICS AFTER HEGEL

Although a number of Hegel's critics and commentators assume that he spoke of the "death of art," what he actually claimed was more complex and not at all as naive as this phrase sounds. Hegel had said that art had completed itself in its essential movements, that it had become a subject of science (*Wissenschaft*), and could no longer play its former role as a primary source of thought, having been superseded (*aufgehoben*) by religion and philosophy. What we could now expect was not the disappearance or death of art, but its dissolution or unraveling (*Auflösung*), which would involve stylistic experimentation, play, and ironic self-consciousness. Hegel remarks that the knee no longer bends before the painted Madonna seen as an artistic image, but art continues to be the great educator of humanity and a fertile field of cultural life.[5]

The artistic world inherited by the post-Hegelian generation was one in which relatively new institutions such as the museum and the concert hall had firmly established themselves as the sites of art, corresponding both to Kant's divisions among the cognitive, practical, and aesthetic spheres and to Hegel's elaboration of a science of aesthetics. This new situation was contingent on the rise of the bourgeoisie, greater literacy, and global markets that fostered various forms of translation. The rising middle class sought credentials for its new social standing in the exercise of universal taste (to put it in Kantian terms) or in becoming knowledgeable heirs of art's universal history (to inflect this in a Hegelian way).[6] This project fit well with the European restoration of order that prevailed from Napoleon's defeat in 1815 to the revolutionary period of 1848.

---

5. G. W. F. Hegel, *Aesthetics: Lectures on Fine Art*, T. M. Knox (trans.) (New York: Oxford University Press, 1975), vol. I, 11 (art on its highest side a thing of the past), 103 (the knee does not bend); vol. II, 593–611 (dissolution of Romantic art).
6. For a Marxist account, see Terry Eagleton, *The Ideology of the Aesthetic* (Oxford: Blackwell, 1990), esp. 1–30.

While many artists and philosophers who took this new cultural context for granted found inspiration in Hegel's aesthetics and his dialectical approach, the question arose whether Hegel had claimed premature closure in his triad of symbolic, classic, and Romantic art, and in his system of the individual arts, which traced a development from the most material and earth-bound art of architecture to the purely imaginative world of poetry. Post-Hegelians such as Karl Rosenkranz and F. T. Vischer were impressed by Hegel's dialectical procedure, but argued that he had unduly restricted the scope of aesthetics by limiting its field to the beautiful.[7] They set out instead to demonstrate that the beautiful was only one of a nest of related fundamental aesthetic forms that also included (at least) the sublime, the comic, and the ugly. In Vischer's early work *On the Sublime and the Comic* (1837), and in his later massive and encyclopedic *Aesthetics* (1846–57), he implicitly claimed to out-Hegel the master, situating the beautiful as only the first or immediate moment of the aesthetic, a moment thrown into relief by its negation in the sublime, itself a negative and excessive movement, surpassing the self-contained harmony of the former. The final, reconciling moment is the comic, conceived as combining the immediate appeal of the beautiful with the disparity and conflict typical of the sublime. Vischer, after completing his monumental eight-volume *Aesthetics*, wrote an essay acknowledging that he had vastly underestimated the role of the perceiver, or the aesthetic subject, which contributed to Benedetto Croce's later verdict that Vischer's *Aesthetics* was "the tombstone of Hegelian aesthetics."[8] Rosenkranz's *Aesthetics of the Ugly* (1853) employs a similar structure, but he pushes the dialectic further to explore the extremes of horror. While we can see how the tables of contents of Vischer's and Rosenkranz's treatises could appear to be (as F. H. Bradley said of Hegel) a "ballet of bloodless categories,"[9] Rosenkranz's stress on Hegel's "power of the negative" in aesthetics was an important (if little

---

7. Johann Karl Friedrich Rosenkranz (April 23, 1805–July 14, 1879; born in Magdeburg, Germany; died in Königsberg) was educated at the Universities of Berlin, Halle, and Heidelberg. His influences included Hegel and Schleiermacher, and he held appointments at the University of Halle (1831–33) and University of Königsberg (1833–79). His major works include *Hegels Leben* (1844), *Aesthetik des Hässlichen* (1853), and *Hegel als deutscher Nationalphilosoph* (1870).

   Friedrich Theodor Vischer (June 30, 1807–September 14, 1887; born in Ludwigsburg, Germany; died in Grunden) was educated at the University of Tübingen. His influences included Hegel, and he held appointments at the University of Tübingen (1837–55, 1866–87) and University of Zürich (1855–66). His major works include *Über das Erhabene und Komische* (1837), and *Aesthetik, oder Wissenschaft des Schönen* (1846–57).
8. Benedetto Croce, quoted in Friedrich Theodor Vischer, "Critique of My Aesthetics" (1866), Jason Gaiger (trans.), in *Art in Theory: 1815–1900*, Charles Harrison and Paul Wood with Jason Gaiger (eds) (Malden, MA: Blackwell, 2001), 686.
9. F. H. Bradley, *The Principles of Logic, Volume II* (Oxford: Oxford University Press, 1928), 591.

acknowledged) step in a tradition represented by Theodor W. Adorno, who saw Rosenkranz's aesthetics of the ugly (*Hässliche*) as anticipating a more recent concern with dissonance as a fundamental aesthetic category.[10] As Rosenkranz proceeds from the formless to disfiguration, the destruction of the image, the demonic, evil, and terror, he effectively explores a dimension of subjectivity opened up in Kant's analysis of the sublime. Reading beyond the obsessively systematic tables of contents of such works, we discover a number of philosophically rich discussions of music, literature, and other arts, some of which were read by American transcendentalists and pragmatists.[11]

Søren Kierkegaard took a different direction from Hegel. Many of his writings, especially those in the first volume of *Either/Or*, could (except for their ironic tone and pseudonymous authorship) be taken as contributions to Hegelian aesthetics like those proliferating in Germany; closer attention to context will take account of Kierkegaard's agonistic relations with contemporary Danish Hegelians.[12] In "The Tragic in Ancient Drama Reflected in the Tragic in Modern Drama," a pseudonymous author argues that the modern world is comic, insofar as it presents subjectivity as pure form; whereas in Greece the social bond brought people together in common life, the modern state, in abandoning any real claim of authority, leaves the modern subject to lead an essentially isolated life.[13] Since ethical substance is lacking in modernity, the suffering of the modern hero must be completely self-inflicted. If Hegel's analysis of *Antigone* rightly discerned the tragic in the clash of two substantial powers – the universal claims of the state and those of family and ancestral piety – the modern Antigone would be one condemned to an absolutely private existence with a secret about her father, whose anxiety would be increased by her unresolvable uncertainty as to whether her father also knew and suffered from knowing it. Kierkegaard's own pseudonymous authorship, playing as it does with various forms of the secret and the incommunicable, involves a complex strategy for awakening an intense awareness of the caesura of public and private. He deploys the forms of Romantic irony against the aestheticism of the movement, as he parodies the practices of Hegelian philosophy in order to validate the concept of individuality.

---

10. Theodor W. Adorno, *Aesthetic Theory*, Gretel Adorno and Rolf Tiedemann (eds), C. Lenhardt (trans.) (New York: Routledge & Kegan Paul, 1984), 68.
11. Much post-Hegelian and post-Schellingian aesthetics was published in translation in the *Journal of Speculative Philosophy* (1867–93), a basic source of philosophical education and discussion for such North American philosophers as Peirce, James, and Dewey (Dewey's *Art as Experience* [1934] has been said to be his most Hegelian work).
*12. For a discussion of Kierkegaard that situates his work in relation to Danish Hegelians, see the essay by Alastair Hannay in this volume.
13. Søren Kierkegaard, "The Tragic in Ancient Drama Reflected in the Tragic in Modern Drama," in *Either/Or*, Howard Hong and Edna Hong (trans.) (Princeton, NJ: Princeton University Press, 1987).

Kierkegaard would no doubt have been amused by the growth of positivist aesthetics in France and Germany later in the century. He would have seen in the "experimental" aesthetics, pursued by Johann Friedrich Herbart, Gustav Fechner, Robert Zimmermann, and Carl Stumpf, a comic exhibition of how even the aesthetic could be emptied of subjectivity in the modern age.[14] These aestheticians typically model their methods on a positivist interpretation of the natural sciences, one that imagines that theory must not only be confirmed by data but that our knowledge of laws arises from a process of accumulating observations. They wedded this to a reduced conception of the aesthetic judgment; characteristically, they have little or nothing to say about the notion of the aesthetic subject, simply taking as given the datum of the judgment of taste that Kant begins to analyze in the first four moments of his "analytic of the beautiful." Fechner distinguishes an "aesthetics from above" (in the manner of Kant, Schelling, and Hegel) and an "aesthetics from below," that involves determining the laws of pleasure and displeasure; these can be determined only by observation. Zimmermann follows Kant in distinguishing mere feelings (which may vary widely from subject to subject, being pathological in Kant's terms) from aesthetic judgments. Yet, unlike Kant, he claims that the experimental methods of the exact sciences can be used to "identify the specific relations of sound or color" that produce aesthetic judgments. This approach abandons any attempt to derive the whole of aesthetics from a single principle (such as "harmony is pleasing"). Zimmermann argues that "there are just as many objective principles of taste as there are aesthetic judgments." Aesthetics should follow the model of the exact sciences, he proposes, reducing "the most complex expressions of taste, as produced by the works of nature and art, to those original factors which are incapable of further analysis." This is a project that can be completed, Zimmermann asserts, yielding "a normative standard of eternal validity."[15] In practice this means that with respect to the visual arts, for example, experimental aesthetics attempts to understand the work in terms of responses to color, form,

---

14. Johann Friedrich Herbart (1776–1841) was an influential neo-Kantian philosopher and educational theorist. Gustav Fechner (1801–87) was a German psychologist and philosopher who is generally regarded as the originator of psychophysics. Robert von Zimmermann (1824–98) was a Czech-born Austrian philosopher who published a series of studies in aesthetics. Carl Stumpf (1848–1936) was one of the earliest students of Franz Brentano; later he turned increasingly toward empirical psychological investigations. Histories of aesthetics published around 1900 devote attention to the works of all these aestheticians, demonstrating their prominence during the nineteenth century. See Bernard Bosanquet, *A History of Aesthetic* (New York: Meridian Books, [1892] 1957), 363–92; Benedetto Croce, *Aesthetic as Science of Expression and General Linguistic*, Douglas Ainslee (trans.) (New York: Noonday Press, [1902] 1955), 370–403.
15. Robert Zimmermann, "Toward the Reform of Aesthetics as an Exact Science" (1861), Nicholas Walker (trans.), in *Art in Theory: 1815–1900*, Harrison et al. (eds), 607–9.

and other measurable and observable properties. In an 1892 critical review of the history of aesthetics, Wilhelm Dilthey argued that "experimental aesthetics is unable to explain how the work of art is more than a heap of impressions."[16] Recent efforts to construct psychological theories of art and the aesthetic are in danger of analogous reductionism, which can be put in Dilthey's terms by saying that they lack a hermeneutic dimension.[17]

Dilthey argued that the experimentalists were unable to recognize holistic properties of artworks, notably style, that they had a reductive view of thought and content in art, and so necessarily produced an arid formalism as the ground of their researches. Both experimental and rational approaches (which he identifies with a tradition including Descartes, Leibniz, and Baumgarten) omit the activity of creativity and genius that gives each work "an inner delineation," or style: "Style exudes an energy which enhances the vitality of the viewer and his feeling of life ... the psyche, by its delight in the inner form of its own activity, assumes a superiority over the crude satisfaction of impulses."[18] To this "Kantian" pronouncement, Dilthey adds the "Hegelian" insistence that the artist's spirit is necessarily formed by the spirit of his age. Dilthey concludes with programs for both the arts and aesthetics: aesthetics must be enriched by the historical sense, which will involve attention to the circumstances of the present, in which naturalism is pointing to real conditions of life; and art awaits "men of genius" who will discover styles for the new age in which we are becoming aware of "the relation of the worker to the machine and the farmer to his soil, the bond of persons working together for a common end, genealogical lines of descent and heredity, the confrontation of the sexes, the relation of passion to its social and pathological basis and of the hero to masses of unnamed people who make him possible."[19] Like so many programmatic statements, Dilthey's betrays its own limits when he declares that these are tasks for the unique depth of the "Germanic character," as distinct from the Latin, Nordic, or Slavic.

Dilthey's own distinctive contribution was his *Weltanschauungslehre*, or theory of worldviews, and after distinguishing the Greek and Roman, medieval, renaissance, and early modern views, he suggests here some of the themes of the emerging worldview of the "new age." The disclosure of worldviews, and the way in which great artists or "geniuses" dealt with these, was part of his project for a renewed hermeneutics, which was provoked by his study of Schleiermacher.

---

16. Wilhelm Dilthey, "The Three Epochs of Modern Aesthetics and its Present Task," Michael Neville (trans.), in Dilthey, *Poetry and Experience*, Rudolf A. Makkreel and Frithjof Rodi (eds) (Princeton, NJ: Princeton University Press, 1985), 205.
*17. For a discussion of Dilthey's approach to hermeneutics, see the essay by Eric Sean Nelson in this volume.
18. Dilthey, "The Three Epochs of Modern Aesthetics and its Present Task," 205–6.
19. *Ibid.*, 221–2.

That project and his critical-philosophical essays on Goethe, Novalis, Hölderlin and other poets (later collected in *Das Erlebnis und die Dichtung*, 1906) had great importance for Martin Heidegger and his student Hans-Georg Gadamer, both of whom would criticize the very notion of aesthetics, replacing it with hermeneutics and ontology.

II. AESTHETICS AND REVOLUTION: MARX AND WAGNER

The 1840s were a time of political and social unrest, marked by revolutionary demands and activity aiming at greater democracy and asserting the rights of the working class. This ferment contributed to newly expanded conceptions of the universal aesthetic subject and to programs for new forms of art that could speak to the sense of future possibility aroused by radical social movements. The composer and theorist Richard Wagner absorbed his Left Hegelianism from Feuerbach;[20] it chimed with the eclectic transmission of German idealism he received from miscellaneous sources, including Thomas Carlyle. Wagner greeted the revolutionary spirit by calling for a revolution in art. He followed the Hegelians in seeing the defining characteristic of Greek art as its public role in the *polis*. While this led to a scathing criticism of the compartmentalization of art and the aesthetic in bourgeois society, Wagner refused to accept the "death of art" entailed by this culture. He called for the new revolutionary art to draw its inspiration from the complexly organized industrial activities of the modern metropolis:

> Who, then, will be the artist of the future? The poet? The performer? The musician? The plastic artist? – Let us say it in one word: the folk [*das Volk*]. That very same folk to whom we owe the only genuine art-work, still living even in our modern memory, however much distorted by our restorations; to whom alone we owe all art itself.[21]

Yet Wagner's invocation of this apparently natural base of the people, echoing Feuerbach's call for a *Philosophy of the Future* in its naturalism, concludes with a call for an ethico-aesthetic revolution under the symbolism of the divine that will join the universal humanity of Jesus with the beauty and strength of Apollo. This puzzling synthesis was left mysterious, although it may have played a role

---

*20. Feuerbach and the Left Hegelians are discussed in the essay by Lawrence S. Stepelevich in *The History of Continental Philosophy: Volume 1*, as well as in the essay by William Clare Roberts in this volume.

21. Richard Wagner, *The Art-work of the Future*, in Wagner, *Prose Works*, William Ashton (trans.) (St. Clair Shores, MI: Scholarly Press, 1972), vol. I, 204–5.

in Nietzsche's identifying the figure of Christ in Raphael's *Transfiguration* as "Apollo."[22]

Marx's early philosophical writings disclose an analogous perspective. He saw modern industrial society as necessarily leading to the alienation of workers from their deepest human possibilities, notably involving free and spontaneous human activity and from the development of the senses. Marx's analysis of alienated labor, in which humans make themselves other than they are, presupposes a conception of the human as an aesthetic subject, which, if it were in touch with its genuine nature, would be involved in creative and expressive work. Marx did not write a single systematic work in aesthetics, and this dimension of his thought was largely ignored until it proved to be a rich inspiration for later thinkers such as Georg Lukács, Walter Benjamin, Adorno, Herbert Marcuse, and others.[23] In the 1830s Marx aspired to be a poet and a drama critic; while he soon abandoned these ambitions for philosophy, his writings draw extensively on world literature (whose reality and concept he saw as a contribution of the bourgeoisie). Marx's early aesthetic utopianism owes much to Schiller[24] and Hegel. He suggests that the whole range of human sensibility is not fixed in our nature, but the product of an ongoing historical development, one in which the arts could play a role in expanding our possibilities of perception and creation: "Only through the objectively unfolded wealth of human nature is the wealth of the subjective human sensibility either cultivated or created – a musical ear, an eye for the beauty of form, in short senses capable of human satisfaction, confirming themselves as essential human capacities."[25]

The critique of post-Hegelian philosophies of subjectivity in *The German Ideology* (co-written with Friedrich Engels) rejects any valorization of a pure consciousness that would be independent of the lived, material, and social world of human beings. The early writings identify productive labor as the human essence, or "species-being," and this activity is genuinely free only when free of physical need; in this respect Marx's very model of nonalienated labor comes close to the Kantian notion of the aesthetic as independent of practical interest. If nonhuman animals are bound by the instincts of their species in their production (e.g. of nests and dwelling places), "the human knows how to produce according to the standards of any species and at all times knows how

---

22. Friedrich Nietzsche, *The Birth of Tragedy*, Ronald Speiers (trans.) (Cambridge: Cambridge University Press, 1999), §4. Hereafter cited as BT followed by the section number.
*23. Essays treating all of these figures can be found in *The History of Continental Philosophy: Volume 5*.
*24. For a discussion of Schiller's aesthetics, see the essay by Daniel Dahlstrom in *The History of Continental Philosophy: Volume 1*.
25. Karl Marx, "Economic and Philosophic Manuscripts" (1844), in Marx, *Selected Writings*, Lawrence H. Simon (ed.) (Indianapolis, IN: Hackett, 1994), 75.

to apply an intrinsic standard to the object. Thus humans create also according to the laws of beauty."[26] "The laws of beauty" are not further defined, and taken together with Marx's later remarks on the eternal charm of Greek art, which he explains as the eternal attraction of the childhood of the species, this formulation betrays a taste solidly formed in the Kantian and Hegelian traditions.[27] Yet Marx was not completely bound by the aesthetics of the beautiful. He made a close study of Vischer's *Aesthetics* in 1857–58, and it seems that Vischer's account of the sublime as intrinsically excessive, surpassing all limits, played a role in Marx's later formulations (notably in *Capital*) of how capitalist production and social relations also embody the power of the negative, giving some theoretical grounds for the famous words of the *Communist Manifesto* that declare how in capitalism "All fixed, fast-frozen relations, with their train of ancient and venerable prejudices and opinions, are swept away, all new-formed ones become antiquated before they can ossify. All that is solid melts into air …."[28] This analysis is at the root of later interrogations of the culture industry and the feverish transformation of aesthetic style in late capitalism by Benjamin and Adorno. The poetics and rhetoric of Marx's epic, prophetic, and parodic texts (e.g. *Capital*, *The Communist Manifesto*, and *Herr Vogt*) reflect his Hegelian and post-Hegelian formation; they also show his limited adoption of an artistic, conceptual persona developed in fuller form by Kierkegaard and Nietzsche.

On one level, Marx's conception of the aesthetic subject can be seen as his translation of German idealism into the history of the laboring social body. As such it stands under the sign of the beautiful, the fundamental category of Hegel's aesthetics. Yet Marx, like the post-Hegelians, also accorded special significance to the sublime and the comic. In the opening pages of *The Eighteenth Brumaire*, he implicitly criticizes the bourgeoisie's displacement of the aesthetics of the beautiful into the political realm, remarking that:

> the tradition of all the dead generations weighs like a nightmare on the brain of the living … in such periods of revolutionary crisis they anxiously conjure up the spirits of the past to their service and borrow from them names, battle-cries, and costumes in order to present the new scene of world history in this time-honored disguise and this borrowed language.

---

26. *Ibid.*, 64.
27. Karl Marx, "From 'A Contribution to the Critique of Political Economy,'" in *Marxism and Art*, Maynard Solomon (ed.) (Detroit, MI: Wayne State University Press, 1979), 61–2.
28. Marx, *Selected Writings*, 162. See Georg Lukács, "Karl Marx und Friedrich Theodor Vischer," in *Probleme der Ästhetik* (Neuwied: Luchterhand, 1969); Mikhail Lifshitz, *The Philosophy of Art of Karl Marx*, Ralph Winn (trans.) (London: Pluto, 1973), 75–7.

Through this merger of aesthetics and politics they find "the ideals and the art-forms, the self-deceptions that they needed in order to conceal from themselves the bourgeois limitations of the content of their struggles and to maintain their passion on the high plane of great historical tragedy." The alternative is not the abandonment of the poetic for a narrowly practical and mundane realism, nor an acceptance of the capitalist divorce of work and things of the spirit, itself simply a hypertrophied development of the initial division of intellectual and manual labor. Marx's concept of human activity involves an irreducibly aesthetic dimension. A new revolutionary aesthetic will free itself from the elegiac attachment to the past: "The social revolution of the nineteenth century cannot draw its poetry from the past, but only from the future .... [In earlier revolutions,] the words went beyond the content; here the content goes beyond the words." The aesthetic of the coming revolution, formulated here in traditional terms of form and content, is sublime rather than beautiful; it acknowledges the unanticipatable character of the future; rather than imagining itself in terms of a beautiful past, it accepts the absolute novelty of futurity that lies beyond all present limits.[29]

III. SCHOPENHAUER AND NIETZSCHE: FROM PURE CONTEMPLATION TO THE PHYSIOLOGY OF AESTHETICS

Following the failure of the revolutionary activity of 1848, the time was ripe for Arthur Schopenhauer's aesthetics of pure contemplation, which offered a redeeming transcendence of the will, and so of all practical and political activity.[30] If circumstances did not allow the development of the active aesthetic human, it still seemed possible to cultivate one's own aesthetic sensibility. Schopenhauer radicalized the Kantian aesthetic subject, and his valorization of music (not poetry, as in systems of the arts like Hegel's) as the art giving the deepest insight into our subjectivity, coincided with the ongoing modern formation of taste in which music effectively serves as the ultimate test in distinguishing elite from common taste.[31] While his major work, *The World as Will and Idea*, was first published in 1818, it was the expanded edition of 1844 that marked the

---

29. All quotes in this paragraph are from Karl Marx, *The Eighteenth Brumaire of Louis Bonaparte*, in *Selected Writings*, 188–90. Cf. my "From the Sublime to the Political: Some Historical Notes," *New Literary History* 16(2) (1985); Terry Eagleton, "The Marxist Sublime," in *The Ideology of the Aesthetic*.
*30. For a detailed discussion of Schopenhauer, see the essay by Bart Vandenabeele in *The History of Continental Philosophy: Volume 1*.
31. Cf. Pierre Bourdieu: "Music represents the most radical and absolute form of the negation of the world, and especially the social world, which the bourgeois ethos tends to demand of

beginning of Schopenhauer's influence.[32] For Schopenhauer, aesthetic contemplation involves a complete suspension of the will; the latter is the obscure, dark side of the world and of human life, and as long as we are in its power we are tossed restlessly on the sea of desire, unable to be content for more than a moment with any of our satisfactions. Only pure religious resignation and philosophical contemplation offer any similar relief from the suffering that is necessarily bound up with the domination of the will that rules most lives most of the time. Like Kant, Schopenhauer distinguishes aesthetic subjectivity from cognition and desire, but raises the stakes by his claim that we are desperately in need of escape from representation and desire:

> [when consciousness] considers things without interest, without [individual] subjectivity, purely objectively .... Then all at once the peace, always sought but always escaping us on that first path of willing, comes to us of its own accord and all is well with us ... that moment we are delivered from the miserable pressure of the will. We celebrate the Sabbath of the penal servitude of willing; the wheel of Ixion stands still. (WWI 1: 196)

The artist, too, must have been in a "calm, tranquil, will-free frame of mind," something that is evident in an art form such as Dutch still life and landscape painting, where it is necessary to focus an impartial attention on the most ordinary and humble objects (WWI 1: 197). Arts other than music allow the viewer or reader to see the will objectified in the world; an attentive aesthetic contemplation will reveal the various gradations of the will or its "adequate embodiments," not as particulars but as Platonic Ideas. So Schopenhauer (like the Hegelians) constructs an extensive hierarchical system of the arts, leading from architecture, which embodies elemental resistance to the force of gravity, to tragedy, in which we observe the will in conflict with itself. Even animal painting and animal sculpture (or the aesthetic contemplation of actual animals) allows us to know the "restlessness and impetuosity of the depicted will, It is that willing, which also constitutes our own inner nature, that here appears before us in forms and figures." All of Schopenhauer's aesthetics, then, rests on this tension between the pure contemplative state and the seething, indeterminate will that we are. The simplest explanation of what we discover in the aesthetic state is to be found in the Hindu watchword "That art thou" (WWI 1: 219–20).

---

all forms of art" (*Distinction: A Social Critique of the Judgment of Taste*, Richard Nice [trans.] [Cambridge, MA: Harvard University Press, 1984], 18).

32. Arthur Schopenhauer, *The World as Will and Idea*, E. F. J. Payne (trans.), 2 vols (New York: Dover, 1966). Hereafter cited as WWI followed by volume and page number.

Schopenhauer's theory of art and the aesthetic is structured by this duality between a fully luminous consciousness and the obscure and aimless will at the heart of reality. At the point where our consciousness is clearest and least obstructed, we are confronted with the chaotic will that we really are. This ultimate dualism is the last word of Schopenhauer's aesthetics; the aesthetic subject can never become a whole. The opposition finds its highest tension and deepest resolution in music, which is "by no means like the other arts, namely a copy of the Ideas, but a *copy of the will itself*" (WWI 1: 257). Music is such a copy because it embodies the entire gamut of human feelings, not this or that particular "affliction, pain, sorrow, horror, gaiety, merriment or peace of mind," but all of these emotions, or movements of the will as they are in themselves, independent, as is music, from any specific representation such as we find in plastic art or poetry (accordingly Schopenhauer dismisses program music as an inferior form [WWI 1: 261]).

In *The Birth of Tragedy*, Nietzsche offers an analysis of the aesthetic human (*ästhetische Mensch*), a concept he takes immediately from Schopenhauer and Wagner. Nietzsche had befriended the older Wagner, who by this time had adopted Schopenhauer's thought (apparently confirming Nietzsche's later judgment in *On the Genealogy of Morality* that artists are always the "valets" of religious or philosophical ideas).[33] Nietzsche defines human art in terms of two natural art impulses, named theologically after Apollo and Dionysus. Yet these are *natural* forces, so the Apollonian can be considered initially as the dreamlike and visionary dimension of life, and the Dionysian as its intoxicated, orgiastic, and ecstatic side. Nietzsche betrays a divergence from the early Wagner in replacing the latter's projected alliance of Jesus and Apollo with the productive *agon* of the two Greek figures; so in describing Raphael's *Transfiguration* in *The Birth of Tragedy* he refers to the painter's Jesus only as the radiant Apollo (BT §4). This binary of aesthetic forces is analogous to Schopenhauer's indeterminate, surging will and the principle of individuation. Nietzsche accepts Schopenhauer's teaching that life is suffering (finding it already in archaic Greek poetry) but transvalues his idea of art: great art, like Greek tragedy, is one that affirms life in all its suffering, and involves a play between beautiful Apollonian phantasy (*Schein*) and Dionysian excess and undifferentiated multiplicity. Tragedy consists in staging various versions of the ritual in which there is a clash and creative *agon* between individual figures (heroes, actors) and the music and dance of the chorus. An artistic manifesto, as well as a rewriting of Schopenhauer (as the post-Hegelians rewrote Hegel), *The Birth of Tragedy*

---

33. Friedrich Nietzsche, *On the Genealogy of Morality*, Carol Diethe (trans.) (Cambridge: Cambridge University Press, 2007), Essay III, §5. Hereafter cited as GM followed by the essay and section number.

expands Schopenhauer's idea of music with Richard Wagner's program of the *Gesamtkunstwerk* (the total work of art), and deploys it in a call for a renewed cultural nationalism that requires its own tragic myth, a myth that must be independent of morality in order to safeguard its place in the "purely aesthetic sphere" and which admits the ugly, the disharmonious, and the dissonant (BT §24).

In 1886, Nietzsche severely criticized this early statement for its Hegelian attempt to produce a grand aesthetic synthesis through opposed concepts, and its failure to find an appropriate voice for his thought, which was a confused medley of poetry and prose. He continued to affirm the necessity of a tragic worldview and *The Birth of Tragedy*'s general project of situating the question of science within that of art, and that of art within the question of life. Nietzsche's later philosophy of art involves a scathingly direct attack on the Kantian–Schopenhauerian theory of disinterested contemplation (GM III: §6) and sketches a philosophy of life as the will to power. In this later perspective, the Greeks are no longer the privileged origin of art, but simply its finest practitioners as well as its finest enemies, as in Socrates' replacing the multiplicity of perspectives staged by tragedy with the "one great Cyclops eye" of reason and science (BT §14). In another late work, Nietzsche says that what he learned from the Greeks was the eternal recurrence of life; so the questions of origin, teleology, and return that are basic to Hegelian aesthetics are folded into an antidialectical vitalism of difference.[34] Art no longer has a privileged origin or goal, but in its sheer excess and affirmation it is now seen as the will to power articulating itself for itself. Nietzsche announced the project of a "physiological aesthetics."[35] Indications are that this was to be centered on the artist, and the receptive experience was to be understood as an analogous quickening of powers. The indispensable "physiological condition" of artistic creativity is *Rausch* (intoxication, frenzy, or excess); while *Rausch* had been specifically associated with the Dionysian in *The Birth of Tragedy*, Nietzsche says in *Twilight of the Idols* that the Apollonian too is a form of *Rausch*, being a frenzy of the eye. Music as we know it is "only the remnant of a much fuller world of expression of the affects, a mere residue of the Dionysian histrionicism."[36] While Nietzsche's discussions of music and literature (to use the names of these reduced genres) are much more extensive than his writings on architecture, painting, and landscape design, he

---

34. Friedrich Nietzsche, *Twilight of the Idols*, Walter Kaufmann (trans.), in *The Portable Nietzsche*, Walter Kaufmann (ed. and trans.) (New York: Viking Penguin, 1954), "What I Owe the Ancients."
35. Nietzsche, GM III: §8; cf. Friedrich Nietzsche, *Sämtliche Werke: Kritische Studienausgabe in 15 Bänden*, Giorgio Colli and Mazzino Montinari (eds) (Berlin: dtv/de Gruyter, 1980), vol. 13, 529–30.
36. Nietzsche, *Twilight of the Idols*, "Skirmishes of an Untimely Man," §§8–11.

was already concerned in *The Birth of Tragedy* with the diagram of forces that enables the perspectivism of the Greek theater, and in *Twilight of the Idols* he exempts architecture from the Apollonian–Dionysian duality, seeing it as an eloquence of power capable of "the grand style," which is powerful enough to eschew being pleasing. There is then in Nietzsche the sketch of an aesthetics oriented as much to spatial construction as to musical composition. It is telling that when he cites Heraclitus to explain the Dionysian phenomenon, he chooses an unusual variant of one of his sayings, comparing the "world-forming power" to a primitive architectural activity, to "a playing child who sets down stones here, there, and the next place and who builds up piles of sand only to knock them down again" (BT §24).[37]

IV. THE AESTHETIC HUMAN: NEW VERSIONS, ALTERNATIVES, AND QUESTIONS

Alain Badiou takes Nietzsche to be the typical philosopher of the "age of the poets," an era whose beginning and end can be designated by the names of Hölderlin and Heidegger.[38] In this era philosophy not only takes the poem or artwork as its organon (a position already announced by Schelling) but sees philosophy itself as a form of poetry. Nietzsche confirms the designation when he says that the fundamental opposition is that between Plato and Homer (GM III: §25), or in writing what he took to be his most important work, *Thus Spoke Zarathustra*, as a poetic narrative that parodically plays with multiple genres. Nietzsche develops the idea that all language is poetic, as in the celebrated claim, in his unpublished essay "On Truth and Lies in a Non-moral Sense," that "truth is a mobile army of metaphors and metonymies" or figures of speech. On this view there is no absolutely literal level of language that can serve as contrast term to the poetic; the philosopher who is true to this insight will have to become something of a poet in order not to perpetuate the illusion of a purely cognitive language. Yet to the extent that it is language that speaks us (adopting a

---

37. Editors typically cite this as fragment 52 in the Diels-Kranz numbering; however, the phrase comes from Plutarch ("On the E at Delphi," in *Moralia* V, 393F) and is not there specifically attributed to Heraclitus. In context, a speaker in Plutarch's dialogue cites lines from Homer (*Iliad* 15.360–64) to demonstrate the folly of speaking of Apollo, who is absolutely one, as changing or entering into human affairs, after accusing Heraclitus of similar theological blasphemies. So Nietzsche has both transformed condemnation into praise and adapted a spatial and architectural metaphor to the description of music, ordinarily taken to be a temporal art.
38. Alain Badiou, *Manifesto for Philosophy*, Norman Madarasz (trans.) (Albany, NY: SUNY Press, 1999), 69–78. [*] For a discussion of Badiou's aesthetics, see the essay by Gabriel Rockhill in *The History of Continental Philosophy: Volume 8*.

Heideggerian locution that Nietzsche anticipates) we might speak of an age of poetry rather than poets, a gloss that accords with Nietzsche's treatment of the "I" or ego as a misleading metaphysical interpretation of grammar and helps to explain his importance for poststructuralist thinkers such as Foucault and Derrida.[39] By suggesting the primacy of language, Nietzsche points the way toward a nonhumanist aesthetics, one in which the primary concepts are rhetorical and textual, rather than psychological. Language or corresponding sets of conventions, styles, and diagrammatic procedures could be seen as replacing the individual creative genius; the reception of art was then described not as the quickening of the deep subject (Kant), the assumption of a purely contemplative consciousness (Schopenhauer), or the virtual model of the freely productive human (Marx), but in terms of activities such as reading and interpreting. At the same time that Nietzsche was opening up such possibilities with his philosophy of language, Charles Sanders Peirce was developing a general theory of signs (growing in part out of his own Hegelian and Schellingian criticisms of Cartesian intuitionism), which had analogous consequences in a variety of semiotic approaches to the arts in the next century.[40]

Two important texts from around 1900, Benedetto Croce's *Aesthetic* (1902)[41] and Freud's *The Interpretation of Dreams* (1899/1900), are marked by the contrast between the continuing quest to define the aesthetic human on the one hand, and the articulation of alternative, more linguistically oriented approaches to art and the aesthetic on the other.[42] Croce's full title explains that he considers aesthetics "as science of expression and general linguistics." As expression, the artwork is to be seen as the unique completion of a process of intuition; it is an ideal fact, not to be confused with a physical artifact or text. In contrast to all attempts in the Aristotelian and rhetorical traditions to formulate the rules and principles by which artworks are formed, Croce argued for an absolute distinction between the expressive-intuitive work of art, whose result can never be anticipated, and the product of craft, which presupposes a prior intention

---

*39. Nietzsche's importance for Foucault and Derrida is discussed in detail in the essay "French Nietzscheanism" by Alan D. Schrift in *The History of Continental Philosophy: Volume 6*.

40. For Peirce's semiotics see *Collected Papers of Charles Sanders Peirce*, Charles Hartshorne and Paul Weiss (eds) (Cambridge, MA: Harvard University Press, 1931–58), vol. II, paras 219–444; the editors thoughtfully entitle this selection "Speculative Grammar," calling attention to Peirce's medieval sources for thinking about language and categories; some of Heidegger's early thinking on these topics emerges from his study of Duns Scotus, one of Peirce's sources. [*] For a detailed discussion of Peirce, see Douglas Anderson's essay in this volume.

*41. For a discussion of Croce's place in Italian philosophy in the twentieth century, see the essay by Silvia Benso and Brian Schroeder in *The History of Continental Philosophy: Volume 7*.

42. Croce, *Aesthetic*; Sigmund Freud, *The Interpretation of Dreams*, in *The Standard Edition of the Complete Psychological Works of Sigmund Freud*, James Strachey (trans.) (London: Hogarth Press, [1899/1900] 1962), vols 4 and 5.

and rules of technique. The artist is not a maker but a creator; *poēsis* excludes *technē*. Linguistics is to be freed from grammar because "language is perpetual creation."[43] The upshot is a valorization of what "new critics" in the anglophone world came to call "the poem itself," a self-sufficient totality or organic unity in which form and content are ultimately indistinguishable, and these very categories may be abandoned because they are embedded in the inappropriate model of craft or *technē*.

If Croce reduces linguistics to poetics, Freud's work points in a very different direction.[44] *The Interpretation of Dreams* seems to echo Schopenhauer, portraying human life as dominated by unconscious desires (which are disclosed by artists, as in Sophocles' and Shakespeare's depiction of the Oedipus complex); it also agrees with Nietzsche in seeing the dream as a prototype of artistic production. Freud articulates a poetics for interpreting the dream that recalls the rhetorical tradition that Croce seeks to demolish. Looking at the dream on the analogy of a hieroglyphic text, Freud identifies elementary procedures of its composition: condensation, displacement, scenic representation, and secondary revision. This is, of course, an unconscious rhetoric, but one that can be reconstructed by the analyst in interpreting and decoding the dream. In Freud's later essays on literature and the visual arts, these principles are put to critical work, while he nevertheless retains more traditional concepts, confessing that psychoanalysis still cannot unravel the secret of genius, which distinguishes great art from mundane production.

V. THE QUESTION OF THE CANON: NATURAL BEAUTY AND LANDSCAPE GARDENING

In *What is Art?* Leo Tolstoy offers a version of expressionist aesthetics, but one that dispenses with the concept of genius, or reassigns it to the collective spirit of the people. Authentic expression must be sincere and communal, the expression of religious feelings of a universal humanity, the expression of common feeling that is universally intelligible. While this leads to Tolstoy's repudiation of all high art (including Shakespeare and his own famous novels), his celebration of folk art coincides in some respects with the programs of Wagner, early Nietzsche, and others who see art in terms of the need to recapture an authentic origin that has been obscured by what they see as modernity's compartmentalization of aesthetics. Like Dilthey and Croce, Tolstoy supports this position with

---
43. Croce, *Aesthetic*, 150.
*44. Freud's work and its influence on subsequent philosophy are discussed in detail in the essay by Adrian Johnston in *The History of Continental Philosophy: Volume 3*.

a critical history of aesthetics, which he sees as the rationalization of elite tastes that resolve themselves into markers of social distinction. Aesthetics turns out to be nothing but an ideological dodge for justifying class superiority. However crude Tolstoy's judgments of high art and folk art may be, his manifesto highlights an otherwise unthought presupposition of the history of aesthetics from its mid-eighteenth-century beginnings to his own time, that is, the question of the canon. He argues that there is a circular and unexamined relationship between the art valued by cultured taste and the principles of aesthetics that aim to explain and justify the production and appreciation of such art:

> [T]his science of aesthetics consists in first acknowledging a certain set of productions to be art (because they please us), and then framing such a theory of art that all those productions which please a certain circle of people should fit into it.[45]

> ... what is considered the definition of art is no definition at all but only a shuffle to justify existing art.[46]

Later writers such as Mikhail Bakhtin and Pierre Bourdieu[47] argue in similar fashion for a more explicitly social conception of taste and the artistic canon; Bourdieu in effect reformulates Tolstoy by declaring that "taste is an acquired disposition to 'differentiate' and 'appreciate' ... It functions as a sort of social orientation, a 'sense of one's place.'"[48]

The nineteenth century was marked by a number of disputes about the canon. Wagner, at first an outrageous rebel, became a touchstone for poets as well as musicians. The impressionists and postimpressionists, initially excluded from the salons, overshadowed the academicians who had ridiculed them. Nevertheless, as Tolstoy would point out, such disagreements still took place within certain implicit boundaries and were resolved within relatively cohesive social groups (indeed, it was the Emperor Louis-Napoleon who sponsored the Salon des refusés that allowed Manet to exhibit his scandalous *Le Déjeuner sur l'herbe* in 1863 when it was refused by the official Salon). More telling is the way in which some forms of art disappear from the canon or reappear unexpectedly. For example, the eighteenth-century formation of modern aesthetics coincided with a taste that accorded a high place among the arts to landscape

---

45. Leo Tolstoy, *What is Art?*, Aylmer Maude (trans.) (Indianapolis, IN: Library of Liberal Arts, 1960), 44.
46. *Ibid.,* 47.
*47. For a discussion of Bourdieu, see the essay by Derek Robbins in *The History of Continental Philosophy: Volume 6*.
48. Bourdieu, *Distinction*, 466.

design, but European taste after Hegel meant, as a recent historian of the art has noted, that "garden encyclopedias replaced treatises in aesthetics."[49] While Kant, following a number of British critics, sees landscape gardening as a major art (a form of painting), Hegel represents a drastic change in taste that was typical of the culture by 1830 when he dismisses parks and gardens as trivial accompaniments to architecture. The disappearance of gardens from the canon also coincided with a decided turn away from a concern with natural beauty (and its affines, the sublime and the picturesque). Ten years after writing his massive, systematic *Aesthetics*, Vischer issued a self-criticism in which he declared that his entire long treatment of natural beauty was a fundamental mistake, and that his "agreeable excursion through the domain of natural beauty" was fundamentally flawed because he had not begun by making the crucial point that beauty is a subjective production, a thesis that he came to only in the third moment of his original system.[50] Schopenhauer and Nietzsche are striking exceptions to the general neglect or exclusion of both the aesthetics of nature and various forms of landscape and land art. Schopenhauer compares the poet to the hydraulic engineer who creates displays of water in fountains and cascades; both present Platonic Ideas by exploring the extremes and not just the ordinary conditions of what they depict (WWI 1: 152). Nietzsche's philosophical-poetic *Thus Spoke Zarathustra* is, among other things, a landscape poem that follows its protagonist through complex geographical and climatic variations. When he wakes from confronting his most abysmal thought, Zarathustra's animals tell him what he must believe as the teacher of eternal recurrence, but the only part he accepts of what they say is that "the world awaits you like a garden." In *Beyond Good and Evil*, Nietzsche devotes a chapter to "Peoples and Fatherlands," which is in effect a geoaesthetics in which national cultures and their representative arts, specifically music, are situated with respect to human and natural geography; for example, Wagner's music and Hegel's philosophy are both said to be foggy and nebulous, echoing the German climate. North and south (and similar concepts) become aesthetic categories in this hint of a "physiological aesthetics" that could remind us of Marx's concept of the earth as "the human's inorganic body" and that looks forward to Heidegger's investigations of place in Greek and German poetry and Deleuze and Guattari's discussion of music as a way of occupying space.[51]

---

49. Elizabeth Barlow Rogers, *Landscape Design: A Cultural and Architectural History* (New York: Harry N. Abrams, 2001), 314.
50. Vischer, "Critique of My Aesthetics," 687.
51. Heidegger's geoaesthetics is developed most perspicuously in "The Origin of the Work of Art," in *Poetry, Language, Thought*, Albert Hofstadter (trans.) (New York: Harper & Row, 1971), *Hölderlin's Hymn "The Ister"*, William McNeill and Julia Davis (trans.) (Bloomington, IN: Indiana University Press, 1996); and *Elucidations of Hölderlin's Poetry*, Keith Hoeller (trans.)

VI. CONCLUSION: TENDENCIES AND DIRECTIONS

In the wake of Hegel's monumental and systematic aesthetics, later philosophers and critics were left with the task of either revising his system within the framework he established or striking out along new paths. In a revisionary mode the primacy of beauty was challenged within the Hegelian school by new analyses of the sublime, the ironic, and the comic that were still indebted to the dialectical approach and the idea of history as a meaningful development of spirit. More radical departures took the form of reversing Hegel's notion of the transformation of art into the science of art by exploiting the supposed irreducible and ironic discrepancy of the internal and the external (Kierkegaard), or rethinking art as the engine of a new cultural revolution (Wagner, Marx, the younger Nietzsche). These radicalized forms of aesthetics could be seen as the intensification of what Hegel called "moments" of the Absolute: irony and the unhappy consciousness in the case of Kierkegaard, or (impossible) reversions to an art-oriented society of the sort Hegel saw in ancient Greece, as with the cultural revolutionaries. Both tendencies continued to be effective in the twentieth century. The arts saw a variety of minimalist projects that seemed to question the fullness and harmony of the beautiful (e.g. the painters Malevich, Mondrian, and Reinhardt), while surrealism encouraged a transformation of daily life and, not coincidentally, frequently acknowledged its debt to Hegel (this tendency is represented in continental philosophy by Georges Bataille and Jacques Lacan, who linked the Freudian unconscious to the Hegelian dialectic[52]).

While even Baumgarten had already spoken of semiotics as one of the main dimensions of aesthetics, it was left to the structuralist and poststructuralist thinkers of the twentieth century to work out the implications of aesthetics's "linguistic turn." Roland Barthes, Jacques Derrida, and Julia Kristeva were inspired by Nietzsche's and Freud's meditations on language as well as by Saussure's. The contest between hermeneutics and semiotics tended to refashion the contrast between philosophies of the self-knowing aesthetic subject (as in Hegel) and notions of language as an autonomous system. The questions that thinkers such as Tolstoy had begun to raise about the social and economic presuppositions of the idealist aesthetics that dominated the nineteenth century were sharpened and intensified with different emphases by, for example, the social theorist Bourdieu and philosophers such as Derrida (e.g.

(Amherst, NY: Humanity Press, 2000). For Gilles Deleuze and Félix Guattari's discussion of music as a form of territorialization, see "The Refrain," in *A Thousand Plateaus*, Brian Massumi (trans.) (Minneapolis, MN: University of Minnesota Press, 1987).

*52. For further discussion of Bataille and Lacan, see the essays by Peter Tracy Connor and Ed Pluth in *The History of Continental Philosophy: Volume 5*.

in "Economimesis"). Such inquiries led to increased questioning of the canon of high or great art that thinkers as different as Hegel and Nietzsche had taken for granted, so that by the second half of the twentieth century writers such as Barthes, Umberto Eco, and Jean Baudrillard were deploying their analytic energies in explicating such putative artistic sites and genres as television wrestling and Disneyland rather than Sophoclean tragedy or Italian Renaissance painting.

CHRONOLOGY

	PHILOSOPHICAL EVENTS	CULTURAL EVENTS	POLITICAL EVENTS
1620	Bacon, *Novum organum*		
1633		Condemnation of Galileo	
1634		Establishment of the Académie Française	
1637	Descartes, *Discourse on Method*		
1641	Descartes, *Meditations on First Philosophy*		
1642		Rembrandt, *Nightwatch*	English Civil War begins
1651	Hobbes, *Leviathan*		
1662	*Logique du Port-Royal*		
1665		Newton discovers calculus	
1667		John Milton, *Paradise Lost*	
1670	Pascal, *Les Pensées* (posthumous) Spinoza, *Tractatus theologico-politicus*		
1675		Leibniz discovers calculus	
1677	Spinoza, *Ethics*		
1687		Newton, *Philosophiae naturalis principia mathematica*	
1689	Locke, *A Letter Concerning Toleration* (–1690) Locke, *An Essay Concerning Human Understanding* and *Two Treatises of Civil Government*		

	PHILOSOPHICAL EVENTS	CULTURAL EVENTS	POLITICAL EVENTS
1694	Birth of Voltaire		
1695		Bayle, *Dictionnaire historique et critique, vol. I*	
1712	Birth of Jean-Jacques Rousseau		
1714	Leibniz, *Monadologie*		
1724	Birth of Immanuel Kant		
1727	Birth of Anne-Robert-Jacques Turgot		
1739	Hume, *A Treatise of Human Nature*		
1742		Handel, *Messiah*	
1743	Birth of Nicholas de Condorcet		
1744	Birth of Johann Gottfried Herder		
1748	Hume, *An Enquiry Concerning Human Understanding*		
1749	Birth of Pierre-Simon Laplace		
1750	Turgot, "A Philosophical Review of the Successive Advances of the Human Mind"		
1751	Diderot and D'Alembert, *Encyclopédie, vols 1 & 2*		
1755	Rousseau, *Discours sur l'origine et les fondements de l'inégalité parmi les hommes*		
1759	Birth of Friedrich Schiller	Voltaire, *Candide*	
1760	Birth of Henri de Saint-Simon		
1762	Rousseau, *Du contrat social* and *Émile ou de l'éducation*		
1766	Birth of Maine de Biran		
1768	Birth of Friedrich Schleiermacher	Laurence Sterne, *A Sentimental Journey Through France and Italy*	
1770	Birth of G. W. F. Hegel		
1774		Goethe, *Sorrows of Young Werther*	Louis XVI becomes king of France
1775	Birth of Friedrich von Schelling		
1776	Death of Hume	Adam Smith, *Wealth of Nations*	American Declaration of Independence
1779		Lessing, *Nathan the Wise*	

262

CHRONOLOGY

	PHILOSOPHICAL EVENTS	CULTURAL EVENTS	POLITICAL EVENTS
1781	Birth of Bernard Bolzano Death of Turgot Kant, *Kritik der reinen Vernunft*		Joseph II initiates important reforms in Austria including elimination of serfdom and full civil rights for non-Catholics
1783	Kant, *Prolegomena zu einer jeden künftigen Metaphysik*		
1784	Kant, "Beantwortung der Frage: Was ist Aufklärung?"		
1785	Condorcet, "Essay on the Application of Mathematics to the Theory of Decision-Making" Kant, *Grundlegung zur Metaphysik der Sitten*		
1786	Death of Moses Mendelssohn		Death of Frederick the Great of Prussia, succeeded by Frederick William II
1787	Condorcet, *Vie de Monsieur Turgot*		US Constitution
1788	Birth of Arthur Schopenhauer Kant, *Kritik der praktischen Vernunft*	Gibbon, *The Decline and Fall of the Roman Empire*	
1789	Death of d'Holbach	Adoption of *La Déclaration des droits de l'Homme et du citoyen*	French Revolution and the establishment of the First Republic
1790	Kant, *Kritik der Urteilskraft*	Edmund Burke, *Reflections on the Revolution in France*	
1791		Mozart, *The Magic Flute* Tom Paine, *The Rights of Man*	Jewish Emancipation in France
1792	Birth of John F. W. Herschel Mary Wollstonecraft, *Vindication of the Rights of Women*		French Revolutionary Army begins occupation of parts of the Rhineland
1794	Birth of Peter Chaadaev and William Whewell Death of Condorcet Schiller, *Über die ästhetische Erziehung des Menschen, in einer Reihe von Briefen*	Creation of the École Normale Supérieure	Death of Robespierre
1795	Schiller, *Briefe über die ästhetische Erziehung des Menschen*		
1796	(–1797) Fichte, *Grundlage des Naturrechts nach Principien der Wissenschaftslehre*		Frederick William II of Prussia succeeded by Frederick William III, who introduces stricter censorship

CHRONOLOGY

	PHILOSOPHICAL EVENTS	CULTURAL EVENTS	POLITICAL EVENTS
1796	(–1799) Fichte, *Wissenschaftslehre nova methodo*		
1797	Schelling, *Ideen zu einer Philosophie der Natur als Einleitung in das Studium dieser Wissenschaft*	Hölderlin, *Hyperion Vol. One*	
1798	Birth of Auguste Comte	Thomas Malthus, *Essay on the Principle of Population*	
1799	Schleiermacher, *Über die Religion*		
1800	Fichte, *Die Bestimmung des Menschen* Schelling, *System des transcendentalen Idealismus* Schleiermacher, *Soliloquies*	Beethoven's First Symphony	Rhineland occupied by France
1801	Birth of Antoine Augustin Cournot		
1803	Death of Herder		Louisiana Purchase
1804	Birth of Ludwig Feuerbach Death of Kant		Napoleon Bonaparte proclaims the First Empire Introduction of the French civil code
1805	Birth of Karl Rosenkranz Death of Schiller	Publication of Diderot, *Le Neveu de Rameau*	
1806	Birth of John Stuart Mill and Max Stirner	Goethe, *Faust, Part One* Reinstatement of the Sorbonne by Napoleon as a secular university	Napoleon brings the Holy Roman Empire to an end
1807	Birth of Friedrich Theodor Vischer Hegel, *Die Phänomenologie des Geistes*		
1808	Birth of David Friedrich Strauss		
1809	Birth of Bruno Bauer and Pierre-Joseph Proudhon		Wilhelm von Humboldt becomes director of education in Prussia
1811	Schleiermacher, *Dialektik*	Krupp opens his first steel factory in Essen	
1812	(–1816) Hegel, *Wissenschaft der Logik*		
1813	Birth of Søren Kierkegaard and Félix Ravaisson Saint-Simon, *Mémoire sur la science de l'homme* (published 1859)		Beginning of the German wars of liberation against Napoleon

CHRONOLOGY

	PHILOSOPHICAL EVENTS	CULTURAL EVENTS	POLITICAL EVENTS
1813	Schopenhauer, *Über die vierfache Wurzel des Satzes vom zureichenden Grunde*		
1815	Birth of Charles Bernard Renouvier	Jane Austen, *Emma*	Battle of Waterloo; final defeat of Napoleon
1817	Bolzano, *Rein analytischer Beweis* Hegel, *Encyclopedia*	Ricardo, *Principles of Political Economy*	
1818	Birth of Karl Marx	Mary Shelley, *Frankenstein, or, The Modern Prometheus*	
1819	Schleiermacher, *Hermeneutik* Schopenhauer, *Die Welt als Wille und Vorstellung* Schopenhauer, *Über das Sehn und die Farben: Eine Abhandlung*	Byron, *Don Juan*	
1820	Birth of Friedrich Engels and Herbert Spencer		
1821	Hegel, *Grundlinien der Philosophie des Rechts* Schleiermacher, *Der christliche Glaube*	Birth of Fyodor Dostoevsky	Death of Napoleon
1823		Beethoven's Ninth Symphony	
1824	Death of Maine de Biran		
1825	Death of Saint-Simon Saint-Simon, *Nouveau Christianisme*		
1827	Death of Laplace		
1828	Birth of Nicolai Chernyshevsky		
1830	Herschel, *Preliminary Discourse on Natural Philosophy* (–1842) Comte, *Cours de philosophie positive* in six volumes	Stendhal, *The Red and the Black*	
1831	Death of Hegel	Victor Hugo, *The Hunchback of Notre Dame*	
1832	Birth of Jules Lachelier Death of Bentham	Death of Goethe Clausewitz, *Vom Kriege*	
1833	Birth of Wilhelm Dilthey (–1837) Feuerbach, *Geschichte der neueren Philosophie*	Pushkin, *Eugene Onegin*	Abolition of slavery in the British Empire
1834	Death of Schleiermacher		

	PHILOSOPHICAL EVENTS	CULTURAL EVENTS	POLITICAL EVENTS
1835	Strauss, *Das Leben Jesu*	The first volume of Alexis de Tocqueville's *Democracy in America* is published in French	
1836	Schopenhauer, *Über den Willen in der Natur*		
1837	Birth of Franz Brentano Bolzano, *Wissenschaftslehre, Versuch einer ausführlichen und grösstetheils neuen Darstellung der Logik, mit steter Rücksicht auf deren bisherige Bearbeiter* (–1846) Ravaisson, *Essai sur la métaphysique d'Aristote* Vischer, *Über das Erhabene und Komische* Whewell, *History of the Inductive Sciences, Founded Upon Their History*	Louis Daguerre invents the daguerreotype, the first successful photographic process	
1838	Bauer, *Kritische Darstellung der Religion des Alten Testaments* Cournot, *Researches into the Mathematical Principles of Wealth* Ravaisson, *De l'habitude*	Charles Dickens, *Oliver Twist*	
1839	Birth of Charles Sanders Peirce Feuerbach, *Zur Kritik der Hegelschen Philosophie*		
1840	Bauer, *Kritik der evangelischen Geschichte des Johannes* Proudhon, *Qu'est ce que la propriété?* Ravaisson, "Les Fragments philosophiques de Hamilton"	Birth of Claude Monet Death of Niccolò Paganini	King Frederick William IV takes the throne in Prussia
1841	Bauer, *Kritik der evangelischen Geschichte der Synoptiker* Feuerbach, *Das Wesen des Christentums* Kierkegaard, *On the Concept of Irony with Constant Reference to Socrates* Maine de Biran, *Œuvres philosophiques de Maine de Biran*	R. W. Emerson, *Essays: First Series*	
1842	Birth of William James	Death of Stendhal (Marie-Henri Beyle)	

CHRONOLOGY

	PHILOSOPHICAL EVENTS	CULTURAL EVENTS	POLITICAL EVENTS
1842	Stirner, *Das unwahre Prinzip unserer Erziehung; oder: Humanismus und Realismus* and *Kunst und Religion*	Honoré de Balzac, Preface (*Avant-propos*) to *La Comédie humaine*	
1843	Birth of Antonio Labriola Feuerbach, *Grundsätze der Philosophie der Zukunft* Kierkegaard, *Either/Or* and *Fear and Trembling* Mill, *A System of Logic*	Felix Mendelssohn founds the Leipzig Conservatory	
1844	Birth of Friedrich Wilhelm Nietzsche Engels and Marx, *The Holy Family* and *The Condition of the Working Class in England in 1844* Marx writes *Economic-Philosophic Manuscripts*	Alexandre Dumas, *The Count of Monte Cristo*	
1845	Stirner, *Der Einzige und sein Eigentum*	Alexander von Humboldt, *Kosmos*, Volume One	Fergus O'Connor founds the National Land Company as the Chartist Cooperative Land Company
1846	Kierkegaard, *Concluding Unscientific Postscript* (–1857) Vischer, *Aesthetik, oder Wissenschaft des Schönen*		
1847	Boole, *The Mathematical Analysis of Logic*	Helmholtz, *On the Conservation of Force*	Factory Act (aka Ten Hours Act) in Great Britain
1848	Birth of Gottlob Frege Death of Bolzano	Publication of the *Communist Manifesto*	Beginning of the French Second Republic
1849	Comte, "Positivist Calendar"	Death of Frédéric Chopin Robert Schumann completes the music for Byron's *Manfred*	
1850	Birth of Eduard Bernstein	Death of Balzac Nathaniel Hawthorne, *The Scarlet Letter*	
1851	Bolzano, *Paradoxien des Unendlichen* (–1854) Comte, *Système de politique positive* Feuerbach, *Vorlesungen über das Wesen der Religion* Ravaisson, *Rapport sur le stoïcisme*	Herman Melville, *Moby Dick* Herbert Spencer, *Social Statics* Giuseppe Verdi, *Rigoletto* The Great Exhibition is staged in the Crystal Palace, London	
1852		Death of Louis Braille	Napoleon III declares the Second Empire

CHRONOLOGY

	PHILOSOPHICAL EVENTS	CULTURAL EVENTS	POLITICAL EVENTS
1853	Rosenkranz, *Aesthetik des Hässlichen*	Johannes Brahms meets Robert and Clara Schumann in Düsseldorf	(–1856) Crimean War
1854	(–1864) Renouvier, *Essais de critique générale*	H. D. Thoreau, *Walden*	
1855	Chernyshevsky, *Aesthetic Relations to Art of Reality*	Walt Whitman, *Leaves of Grass*	
1856	Birth of Sigmund Freud and Georgi Plekhanov Death of Chaadev and Stirner		
1857	Birth of Ferdinand de Saussure Death of Comte	Charles Baudelaire, *The Flowers of Evil* Gustav Flaubert, *Madame Bovary*	
1858	Birth of Émile Durkheim and Georg Simmel	Expedition led by Richard Burton and John Hanning Speke reaches Lake Tanganyika and Lake Victoria in Central Africa	
1859	Birth of Henri Bergson, John Dewey, and Edmund Husserl Saint-Simon, *Mémoire sur la science de l'homme*	Death of Alexander von Humboldt Charles Darwin, *Origin of Species*	Treaty of Zurich, signed by the Austrian Empire, the French Empire, and the Kingdom of Sardinia
1860	Death of Schopenhauer Dilthey, "Das hermeneutische System Schleiermachers in der Auseinandersetuzung mit der älteren protestantischen Hermeneutik"		
1861	Mill, *Utilitarianism*	Johann Jakob Bachofen, *Das Mutterrecht* Fyodor Dostoevsky, *The House of the Dead*	Death of Frederick William IV of Prussia, and accession of his brother as William I (William the Great) Tsar Alexander II abolishes serfdom in Russia
1862		Victor Hugo, *Les Misérables*	
1863	Chernyshevsky, *What is to be Done?*	Fyodor Dostoevsky, *Notes from the Underground*	Death of King Frederick VII of Denmark Abraham Lincoln issues the *Emancipation Proclamation*
1864	Birth of Max Weber	Charles Babbage, *Passages from the Life of a Philosopher*	
1865	Death of Proudhon	(–1869) Leo Tolstoy, *War and Peace* Premiere of Richard Wagner's *Tristan und Isolde*	Surrender of General Robert E. Lee signals conclusion of American Civil War
1866	Birth of Benedetto Croce Death of Whewell	Fyodor Dostoevsky, *Crime and Punishment*	The Peace of Prague ends the Austro-Prussian War

	PHILOSOPHICAL EVENTS	CULTURAL EVENTS	POLITICAL EVENTS
1867	Marx, *Das Kapital, Vol. I*	Birth of Maria Skłodowska (Marie Curie) in Warsaw	
1868	Birth of Émile Chartier ("Alain") Peirce, "On a New List of Categories" Ravaisson, *La Philosophie en France au XIXe siècle*	Birth of W. E. B. Du Bois Premiere of Wagner's *Die Meistersinger von Nürnberg* Creation of the École Pratique des Hautes Études (EPHE)	
1869	Mill, *The Subjection of Women* Renouvier, *Science de la morale*	Birth of Henri Matisse (–1870) Jules Verne, *Twenty Thousand Leagues Under the Sea*	Completion of the Suez Canal
1870			Birth of Vladimir Lenin (–1871) Franco-Prussian War Establishment of the Third Republic
1871	Death of Herschel Lachelier, *Du fondement de l'induction*	Darwin, *The Descent of Man* Eliot, *Middlemarch* Premiere of Giuseppi Verdi's *Aida*	Paris Commune Unification of Germany: Prussian King William I becomes Emperor (*Kaiser*) of Germany and Otto von Bismarck becomes chancellor
1872	Nietzsche, *Die Geburt der Tragödie*		
1873	Death of Mill Mill, *Autobiography*	(–1877) Tolstoy, *Anna Karenina*	End of German Occupation following France's defeat in the Franco-Prussian War
1874	Birth of Nikolai Berdiaev and Max Scheler Death of David Strauss Émile Boutroux, *La Contingence des lois de la nature* Brentano, *Psychologie vom empirischen Standpunkt* Mill, *Nature, the Utility of Religion and Theism*	Premiere of *Danse Macabre*, by Camille Saint-Saëns First Impressionist Exhibition staged by the Société anonyme des peintres, sculpteurs et graveurs (Pissarro, Monet, Sisley, Degas, Renoir, Cézanne, Guillaumin and Berthe Morisot)	
1875		Premiere of Georges Bizet's *Carmen*	
1876		Death of George Sand (Amantine Aurore Luciles Dupin) Premiere in Oslo of Ibsen's *Peer Gynt*, with incidental music composed by Edvard Grieg	
1877	Death of Cournot (–1878) Peirce, "Illustrations in the Logic of Science"	Henry Morton Stanley completes his navigation of the Congo River	

CHRONOLOGY

	PHILOSOPHICAL EVENTS	CULTURAL EVENTS	POLITICAL EVENTS
1878	Engels, *Anti-Dühring*		Birth of Joseph Stalin King Leopold II of Belgium engages explorer Henry Morton Stanley to establish a colony in the Congo
1879	Death of Rosenkranz Frege, *Begriffsschrift*	Fyodor Dostoevsky, *The Brothers Karamazov* Henrik Ibsen, *A Doll's House* Georg Cantor (1845–1918) becomes Professor of Mathematics at Halle Thomas Edison exhibits his incandescent light bulb	Germany and Austria-Hungary form the Dual Alliance
1880	Engels, *Socialism: Utopian and Scientific*		
1881	Death of Dostoevsky		Assassination of Czar Alexander II
1882	Death of Bauer	Premiere of Wagner's *Parsifal* in Bayreuth Robert Koch announces his discovery of the bacterium that causes tuberculosis	Formation of the Triple Alliance as Italy joins Germany and Austria-Hungary
1883	Birth of Karl Jaspers and José Ortega y Gasset Death of Marx Dilthey, *Einleitung in die Geisteswissenschaften* (–1885) Nietzsche, *Also Sprach Zarathustra*	Death of Wagner Cantor, "Foundations of a General Theory of Aggregates"	
1884	Birth of Gaston Bachelard Engels, *The Origin of the Family, Private Property and the State* Frege, *Die Grundlagen der Arithmetik*	Mark Twain, *Adventures of Huckleberry Finn*	(–1885) Berlin Conference (aka Africa or Congo Conference)
1885	Birth of Ernst Bloch and György Lukács Chernyshevsky, *The Nature of Human Knowledge*	Émile Zola, *Germinal*	
1886	Nietzsche, *Jenseits von Gut und Böse*	Death of Franz Liszt	
1887	Death of Vischer Nietzsche, *Zur Genealogie der Moral*	Vincent van Gogh, *Self-Portrait with a Straw Hat* Foundation of the Pasteur Institute in Paris	
1888	Birth of Jean Wahl	Johan August Strindberg, *Miss Julie*	William II becomes German emperor and king of Prussia

CHRONOLOGY

	PHILOSOPHICAL EVENTS	CULTURAL EVENTS	POLITICAL EVENTS
1889	Birth of Martin Heidegger, Gabriel Marcel, and Ludwig Wittgenstein Death of Chernyshevsky Bergson, *Essai sur les données immédiates de la conscience*	Paris World's Fair, featuring the Eiffel Tower	
1890	William James, *Principles of Psychology*	Death of van Gogh	William II dismisses Chancellor Otto von Bismarck and repeals the Anti-Socialist Law of 1878
1891	Birth of Antonio Gramsci	Monet, *Haystacks*	
1892	Frege, "Über Sinn und Bedeutung"	Paul Cézanne, *The Card Players*	Franco-Russian Alliance Military Convention
1893	Xavier Léon and Élie Halévy cofound the *Revue de métaphysique et de morale*		Birth of Mao Zedong
1894			Captain Alfred Dreyfus (1859–1935), a Jewish-French army officer, is arrested and charged with spying for Germany
1895	Birth of Max Horkheimer	The Lumière brothers hold the first public screening of projected motion pictures Wilhelm Conrad Röntgen discovers X-rays	
1896	Bergson, *Matière et mémoire* Dewey, "The Reflex Arc Concept in Psychology" Labriola, *Essays on the Materialistic Conception of History*	Athens hosts the first Olympic Games of the modern era	
1897	Birth of Georges Bataille Durkheim, *Le Suicide* James, *The Will to Believe and Other Essays in Popular Philosophy* Labriola, *Socialism and Philosophy*		
1898	Birth of Herbert Marcuse James, *Human Immortality*	Zola, article "J'accuse" in defense of Dreyfus Premiere of Giacomo Puccini's *La Bohème*	
1899	Bernstein, *Evolutionary Socialism* Dewey, *The School and Society*		Start of the Second Boer War
1900	Birth of Hans-Georg Gadamer	Freud, *Interpretation of Dreams*	

CHRONOLOGY

	PHILOSOPHICAL EVENTS	CULTURAL EVENTS	POLITICAL EVENTS
1900	Death of Nietzsche and Ravaisson Dilthey, *Die Entstehung der Hermeneutik* (–1901) Husserl, *Logische Untersuchungen* Simmel, *Philosophie des Geldes*	Planck formulates quantum theory	
1901	Birth of Jacques Lacan		
1902	Croce, *Aesthetic as Science of Expression and General Linguistic* James, *The Varieties of Religious Experience*		
1903	Birth of Theodor W. Adorno and Jean Cavaillès Death of Renouvier and Spencer	Du Bois, *The Souls of Black Folk*	
1904	Death of Labriola Spencer, *Autobiography, or The Life and Letters* (–1905) Weber, *Die protestantische Ethik und der Geist des Kapitalismus*		
1905	Birth of Jean-Paul Sartre and Raymond Aron	Einstein formulates the special theory of relativity	Law of Separation of Church and State in France
1906	Birth of Hannah Arendt and Emmanuel Levinas	Birth of Léopold Sédar Senghor	The Dreyfus Affair ends when the French Court of Appeals exonerates Dreyfus of all charges
1907	Birth of Jean Hyppolite Bergson, *L'Evolution créatrice* Dilthey, *Das Wesen der Philosophie*	Pablo Picasso completes *Les Demoiselles d'Avignon*	
1908	Birth of Simone de Beauvoir, Claude Lévi-Strauss, Maurice Merleau-Ponty, and W. V. O. Quine Plekhanov, *Fundamental Problems of Marxism*		
1909	Birth of Isaiah Berlin Lenin, *Materialism and Emperio-Criticism: Critical Comments on a Reactionary Philosophy*		
1910	Death of William James Dilthey, *Der Aufbau der geschichlichen Welt in den Geisteswissenschaften*		

CHRONOLOGY

	PHILOSOPHICAL EVENTS	CULTURAL EVENTS	POLITICAL EVENTS
1911	Death of Dilthey Victor Delbos publishes the first French journal article on Husserl: "Husserl: Sa critique du psychologisme et sa conception d'une Logique pure" in *Revue de métaphysique et de morale*	The Blaue Reiter (Blue Rider) group of avant-garde artists is founded in Munich	
1913	Birth of Albert Camus, Aimé Césaire, and Paul Ricoeur Husserl, *Ideen*	Marcel Proust (1871–1922), *Swann's Way*, the first volume of *Remembrance of Things Past* Stravinsky's *Rite of Spring* first performed	
1914	Death of Peirce		Germany invades France
1915	Birth of Roland Barthes	Franz Kafka, *Metamorphosis*	
1916	Berdiaev, *The Meaning of the Creative Act* Dewey, *Democracy and Education* Publication of Saussure's *Cours de linguistique générale*	James Joyce, *A Portrait of the Artist as a Young Man*	
1917	Death of Durkheim and Brentano		Russian Revolution
1918	Birth of Louis Althusser Death of Georg Cantor, Lachelier, Plekhanov, Renouvier, and Simmel Bloch, *Principle of Hope*		First World War ends Proclamation of the Weimar Republic
1919		German architect Walter Gropius (1883–1969) founds the Bauhaus School	
1920	Death of Max Weber		Ratification of the 19th amendment to the US Constitution extends suffrage to women
1922	Birth of Karl-Otto Apel Bergson, *Duration and Simultaneity* Dewey, *Human Nature and Conduct* Wittgenstein, *Tractatus Logico-Philosophicus* Bataille begins his twenty-year career at the Bibliothèque Nationale	T. S. Eliot, *The Waste Land* Herman Hesse, *Siddhartha* James Joyce, *Ulysses*	
1923	Berdiaev, *The Meaning of History* and *Dostoevsky's Worldview*	Kahil Gibran, *The Prophet*	

273

PHILOSOPHICAL EVENTS	CULTURAL EVENTS	POLITICAL EVENTS
1923 Lukács, *Geschichte und Klassenbewusstsein* Institut für Sozialforschung (Frankfurt School) is founded		
1924 Birth of Jean-François Lyotard Lachelier, *Du fondement de l'induction suivi de Psychologie et Métaphysique et de Notes sur le pari de Pascal* Sartre, Raymond Aron, Georges Canguilhem, Daniel Lagache, and Paul Nizan enter the École Normale Supérieure	André Breton, *Le Manifeste du surréalisme* Thomas Mann, *The Magic Mountain*	Death of Vladimir Lenin
1925 Birth of Zygmunt Bauman, Gilles Deleuze, and Frantz Fanon Death of Frege Dewey, *Experience and Nature*	Franz Kafka, *The Trial* First Surrealist Exhibition at the Galerie Pierre, Paris	
1926 Birth of Michel Foucault Jean Hering publishes the first French text to address Husserl's phenomenology: *Phénoménologie et philosophie religieuse*	The film *Metropolis* by German director Fritz Lang (1890–1976) premieres in Berlin The Bauhaus School building, designed by Walter Gropius (1883–1969), is completed in Dessau, Germany	
1927 Heidegger, *Sein und Zeit* Marcel, *Journal métaphysique*	Virginia Woolf, *To the Lighthouse*	
1928 Birth of Noam Chomsky The first work of German phenomenology appears in French translation: Scheler's *Nature et formes de la sympathie: Contribution à l'étude des lois de la vie émotionnelle*	Bertolt Brecht (1898–1956) writes *The Threepenny Opera* with composer Kurt Weill (1900–1950) The first television station begins broadcasting in Schenectady, New York	
1929 Birth of Jürgen Habermas Heidegger, *Kant und das Problem der Metaphysik* and *Was ist Metaphysik?* Husserl, *Formale und transzendentale Logik* and "Phenomenology" in *Encylopedia Britannica* Wahl, *Le malheur de la conscience dans la philosophie de Hegel* Husserl lectures at the Sorbonne	Ernest Hemingway, *A Farewell to Arms* Erich Maria Remarque, *All Quiet on the Western Front*	

	PHILOSOPHICAL EVENTS	CULTURAL EVENTS	POLITICAL EVENTS
1930	Birth of Pierre Bourdieu, Jacques Derrida, Félix Guattari, Luce Irigaray, and Michel Serres Levinas, *La Théorie de l'intuition dans la phénoménologie de Husserl*	(–1942) Robert Musil, *The Man Without Qualities*	
1931	Heidegger's first works appear in French translation: "Was ist Metaphysik?" in *Bifur*, and "Vom Wesen des Grundes" in *Recherches philosophiques* Husserl's *Ideas* is translated into English Levinas and Gabrielle Peiffer publish a French translation of Husserl's *Cartesian Meditations*	Pearl Buck, *The Good Earth* Gödel publishes his two incompleteness theorems	
1932	Birth of Stuart Hall Death of Eduard Bernstein Bergson, *Les Deux sources de la morale et de la religion*	Aldous Huxley, *Brave New World* BBC starts a regular public television broadcasting service in the UK	
1933	University in Exile is founded as a graduate division of the New School for Social Research (–1939) Alexandre Kojève lectures on Hegel at École Pratique des Hautes Études		Hitler becomes Chancellor of Germany
1935		Penguin publishes its first paperback	
1936	Husserl, *Krisis der europäischen Wissenschaften und die transzendentale Phänomenologie* Sartre, "La Transcendance de l'égo" in *Recherches philosophiques*	Benjamin, "The Work of Art in the Age of Mechanical Reproduction" First issue of *Life Magazine*	(–1939) Spanish Civil War
1937	Birth of Alain Badiou and Hélène Cixous Death of Gramsci Berdiaev, *The Origin of Russian Communism* Zedong, *On Contradiction*	Picasso, *Guernica*	
1938	Death of Husserl Berlin, *Karl Marx: His Life and Environment*	Sartre, *La Nausée*	

CHRONOLOGY

	PHILOSOPHICAL EVENTS	CULTURAL EVENTS	POLITICAL EVENTS
1938	Stalin, *Dialectical and Historical Materialism*		
1939	Berdiaev, *Slavery and Freedom* (–1941) Hyppolite publishes his translation into French of Hegel's *Phenomenology of Spirit* Establishment of Husserl Archives in Louvain, Belgium Founding of *Philosophy and Phenomenological Research*	Joyce, *Finnegans Wake* John Steinbeck, *The Grapes of Wrath*	Nazi Germany invades Poland (September 1) and France and Britain declare war on Germany (September 3)
1940	Death of Benjamin	Richard Wright, *Native Son*	
1941	Death of Bergson Marcuse, *Reason and Revolution*	Arthur Koestler, *Darkness at Noon*	Japan attacks Pearl Harbor, and US enters the Second World War Germany invades the Soviet Union
1942	Birth of Étienne Balibar Camus, *L'Étranger* and *Le Mythe de Sisyphe: Essai sur l'absurde* Merleau-Ponty, *La Structure du comportement* Lévi-Strauss meets Roman Jakobson at the École Libre des Hautes Études in New York		
1943	Death of Simone Weil Farber, *The Foundation of Phenomenology* Sartre, *L'Être et le néant*	Herman Hesse, *The Glass Bead Game* Ayn Rand, *The Fountainhead*	
1944		Jorge Luis Borges, *Ficciones*	Bretton Woods Conference and establishment of the International Monetary Fund (IMF) Paris is liberated by Allied forces (August 25)
1945	Merleau-Ponty, *Phénoménologie de la perception*	George Orwell, *Animal Farm* Sartre, Beauvoir, and Merleau-Ponty begin as founding editors of *Les Temps modernes*	End of the Second World War in Germany (May); Atom bombs dropped on Hiroshima and Nagasaki; end of War in Japan (September) Establishment of the United Nations
1946	Hyppolite, *Genèse et structure de la "Phénoménologie de l'esprit" de Hegel*	Bataille founds the journal *Critique*	Beginning of the French Indochina War Establishment of the Fourth Republic

CHRONOLOGY

	PHILOSOPHICAL EVENTS	CULTURAL EVENTS	POLITICAL EVENTS
1946	Sartre, *L'Existentialisme est un humanisme*		
1947	Adorno and Horkheimer, *Dialektik der Aufklärung* Beauvoir, *Pour une morale de l'ambiguïté* Heidegger, "Brief über den Humanismus"	Camus, *The Plague* Anne Frank, *The Diary of Anne Frank* Thomas Mann, *Doctor Faustus*	Creation of General Agreement on Tariffs and Trade (GATT) (–1951) Marshall Plan
1948	Death of Berdiaev Althusser appointed *agrégé-répétiteur* ("caïman") at the École Normale Supérieure, a position he holds until 1980 (–1951) Gramsci, *Prison Notebooks*	Debut of *The Ed Sullivan Show*	The United Nations adopts the Universal Declaration of Human Rights
1949	Beauvoir, *Le Deuxième sexe* Heidegger's *Existence and Being* is translated Lévi-Strauss, *Les Structures élémentaires de la parenté*	Orwell, *1984* Cornelius Castoriadis and Claude Lefort found the revolutionary group and journal *Socialisme ou Barbarie*	Foundation of NATO
1950	Ricoeur publishes his translation into French of Husserl's *Ideas I*		Beginning of the Korean War
1951	Death of Alain and Wittgenstein Arendt, *The Origins of Totalitarianism* Quine, "Two Dogmas of Empiricism"	Marguerite Yourcenar, *Memoirs of Hadrian*	
1952	Death of Croce, Dewey, and Santayana Merleau-Ponty is elected to the Chair in Philosophy at the Collège de France	Samuel Beckett, *Waiting for Godot* Ralph Ellison, *Invisible Man*	
1953	Wittgenstein, *Philosophical Investigations* (posthumous) Lacan begins his public seminars	Crick and Watson construct the first model of DNA Lacan, together with Daniel Lagache and Françoise Dolto, founds the Société française de psychanalyse	Death of Joseph Stalin Ceasefire agreement (July 27) ends the Korean War
1954	Lyotard, *La Phénoménologie* Scheler, *The Nature of Sympathy* appears in English translation		Following the fall of Dien Bien Phu (May 7), France pledges to withdraw from Indochina (July 20) Beginning of the Algerian revolt against French rule
1955	Marcuse, *Eros and Civilization*	Vladimir Nabokov, *Lolita*	

CHRONOLOGY

	PHILOSOPHICAL EVENTS	CULTURAL EVENTS	POLITICAL EVENTS
1955	Cerisy Colloquium *Qu'est-ce que la philosophie? Autour de Martin Heidegger*, organized by Jean Beaufret		
1956	Sartre's *Being and Nothingness* appears in English translation		Hungarian Revolution and Soviet invasion The French colonies of Morocco and Tunisia gain independence
1957	Chomsky, *Syntactic Structures* Founding of *Philosophy Today*	Jack Kerouac, *On the Road* Camus receives the Nobel Prize for Literature	Rome Treaty signed by France, Germany, Belgium, Italy, the Netherlands, and Luxembourg establishes the European Economic Community The Soviet Union launches *Sputnik 1*, the first man-made object to orbit the Earth
1958	Lévi-Strauss, *Anthropologie structurale*	Chinua Achebe, *Things Fall Apart* William S. Burroughs, *Naked Lunch* (–1960) The first feature films by directors associated with the French "New Wave" cinema, including, in 1959, *Les Quatre Cent Coups* (*The 400 Blows*) by François Truffaut (1932–1984) and, in 1960, *A bout de souffle* (*Breathless*) by Jean-Luc Godard (1930–) The Sorbonne's "Faculté des Lettres" is officially renamed the "Faculté des Lettres et Sciences Humaines"	Charles de Gaulle is elected president after a new constitution establishes the Fifth Republic
1959	Lévi-Strauss is elected to the Chair in Social Anthropology at the Collège de France	Günter Grass, *The Tin Drum* Gillo Pentecorvo, *The Battle of Algiers*	
1960	Death of Camus Gadamer, *Wahrheit und Methode* Sartre, *Critique de la raison dialectique* Spiegelberg, *The Phenomenological Movement*	First issue of the journal *Tel Quel* is published The birth control pill is made available to married women	
1961	Death of Fanon and Merleau-Ponty Fanon, *Les Damnés de la terre*, with a preface by Sartre	Joseph Heller, *Catch 22*	Erection of the Berlin Wall Bay of Pigs failed invasion of Cuba

CHRONOLOGY

	PHILOSOPHICAL EVENTS	CULTURAL EVENTS	POLITICAL EVENTS
1961	Foucault, *Histoire de la folie à l'âge classique* Heidegger, *Nietzsche* Levinas, *Totalité et infini: Essai sur l'extériorite*		
1962	Death of Bachelard Deleuze, *Nietzsche et la philosophie* Thomas Kuhn, *The Structure of Scientific Revolutions* Lévi-Strauss, *La Pensée sauvage* Heidegger, *Being and Time* appears in English translation Merleau-Ponty, *Phenomenology of Perception* appears in English translation First meeting of SPEP at Northwestern University, Evanston, Illinois	Rachel Carson, *Silent Spring* Ken Kesey, *One Flew Over the Cuckoo's Nest*	France grants independence to Algeria Cuban Missile Crisis
1963	Arendt, *Eichmann in Jerusalem*	Betty Friedan, *The Feminine Mystique* The first artificial heart is implanted	Assassination of John F. Kennedy Imprisonment of Nelson Mandela
1964	Barthes, *Eléments de sémiologie* Marcuse, *One-Dimensional Man* Merleau-Ponty, *Le Visible et l'invisible* (posthumous)	Lacan founds L'École Freudienne de Paris The Beatles appear on *The Ed Sullivan Show*	Gulf of Tonkin Incident US Civil Rights Act outlaws discrimination on the basis of race, color, religion, sex, or national origin
1965	Death of Buber Althusser, *Pour Marx* and, with Balibar, *Lire "Le Capital"*	Truman Capote, *In Cold Blood*	Assassination of Malcolm X
1966	Adorno, *Negative Dialektik* Deleuze, *Le Bergsonisme* Foucault, *Les Mots et les choses: Une archéologie des sciences humaines* Lacan, *Écrits*	Alain Resnais, *Hiroshima Mon Amour* Jacques-Alain Miller founds *Les Cahiers pour l'Analyse* *Star Trek* premieres on US television Johns Hopkins Symposium "The Languages of Criticism and the Sciences of Man" introduces French theory to the American academic community	(–1976) Chinese Cultural Revolution Foundation of the Black Panther Party for Self-Defense by Huey P. Newton and Bobby Seale
1967	Derrida, *De la grammatologie*, *La Voix et le phénomène*, and *L'Écriture et la différence*	Gabriel Garcia Marquez, *One Hundred Years of Solitude*	

CHRONOLOGY

	PHILOSOPHICAL EVENTS	CULTURAL EVENTS	POLITICAL EVENTS
1967			Confirmation of Thurgood Marshall, first African-American Justice, to the US Supreme Court
1968	Deleuze, *Différence et répétition* and *Spinoza et le problème de l'expression* Habermas, *Erkenntnis und Interesse*	Beatles release the White Album Carlos Casteneda, *The Teachings of Don Juan: A Yaqui Way of Knowledge* Stanley Kubrick, *2001: A Space Odyssey*	Events of May '68, including closure of the University of Nanterre (May 2), police invasion of the Sorbonne (May 3), student demonstrations and strikes, and workers' occupation of factories and general strike Prague Spring Assassination of Martin Luther King Tet Offensive
1969	Death of Adorno and Jaspers Deleuze, *Logique du sens* Foucault, *L'Archéologie du savoir* Paulo Freire, *Pedagogy of the Oppressed*	Woodstock Music and Art Fair Neil Armstrong is the first person to set foot on the moon	Stonewall riots launch the Gay Liberation Movement
1970	Death of Carnap Adorno, *Ästhetische Theorie* Foucault, *The Order of Things* appears in English translation Husserl, *The Crisis of European Philosophy* appears in English translation Founding of the *Journal of the British Society for Phenomenology* Foucault elected to the Chair of the History of Systems of Thought at the Collège de France Ricoeur begins teaching at the University of Chicago	Millett, *Sexual Politics* First Earth Day Founding of *Diacritics*	Shootings at Kent State University Salvador Allende becomes the first Marxist head of state to be freely elected in a Western nation
1971	Death of Lukács and Marcuse Lyotard, *Discours, figure* Founding of *Research in Phenomenology*	Reorganization of the University of Paris	End of the gold standard for US dollar
1972	Death of John Wild Bourdieu, *Esquisse d'une théorie de la pratique* Deleuze and Guattari, *Capitalisme et schizophrénie. 1. L'Anti-Oedipe*		Watergate break-in President Richard Nixon visits China, beginning the normalization of relations between the US and PRC

CHRONOLOGY

	PHILOSOPHICAL EVENTS	CULTURAL EVENTS	POLITICAL EVENTS
1972	Derrida, *La Dissémination, Marges de la philosophie,* and *Positions* *Radical Philosophy* begins publication Colloquium on Nietzsche at Cerisy		
1973	Death of Horkheimer Derrida, *Speech and Phenomena* appears in English translation Lacan publishes the first volume of his *Séminaire*	Thomas Pynchon, *Gravity's Rainbow* (–1978) Aleksandr Solzhenitsyn, *The Gulag Archipelago* Roe *v.* Wade legalizes abortion	Chilean military coup ousts and kills President Salvador Allende
1974	Irigaray, *Speculum: De l'autre femme* Kristeva, *La Révolution du langage poétique*	Founding of *Critical Inquiry* Creation of the first doctoral program in women's studies in Europe, the Centre de Recherches en Études Féminines, at the University of Paris VIII–Vincennes, directed by Hélène Cixous	Resignation of Nixon
1975	Death of Arendt Foucault, *Surveiller et punir: Naissance de la prison* Irigaray, *Ce sexe qui n'en est pas un* Derrida begins teaching in the English Department at Yale Foucault begins teaching at UC-Berkeley Foundation of GREPH, the Groupe de Recherches sur l'Enseignement Philosophique	Cixous and Clément, *La Jeune née* *Signs* begins publication The Sixth Section of the EPHE is renamed the École des Hautes Études en Sciences Sociales	Death of Francisco Franco Andrei Sakharov wins Nobel Peace Prize Fall of Saigon, ending the Vietnam War First US–USSR joint space mission
1976	Death of Heidegger and Bultmann Foucault, *Histoire de la sexualité. 1. La Volonté de savoir* Derrida, *Of Grammatology* appears in English translation Barthes is elected to the Chair of Literary Semiology at the Collège de France	Foundation of the International Association for Philosophy and Literature	Death of Mao Zedong Uprising in Soweto
1977	Death of Ernst Bloch Deleuze and Guattari, *Anti-Oedipus* appears in English translation	The Centre Georges Pompidou, designed by architects Renzo Piano (1937–) and Richard Rogers (1933–), opens in Paris	Egyptian president Anwar al-Sadat becomes the first Arab head of state to visit Israel

CHRONOLOGY

	PHILOSOPHICAL EVENTS	CULTURAL EVENTS	POLITICAL EVENTS
1977	Lacan, *Ecrits: A Selection* appears in English translation	240 Czech intellectuals sign Charter 77	
1978	Death of Kurt Gödel Arendt, *Life of the Mind* Derrida, *La Vérité en peinture*	George Perec, *Life: A User's Manual* Edward Said, *Orientalism* Birmingham School: Centre for Contemporary Culture releases *Policing the Crisis* Louise Brown becomes the first test-tube baby	Camp David Accords
1979	Death of Marcuse Bourdieu, *La Distinction: Critique sociale du jugement* Lyotard, *La Condition postmoderne: Rapport sur le savoir* Prigogine and Stengers, *La Nouvelle alliance* Rorty, *Philosophy and the Mirror of Nature*	Francis Ford Coppola, *Apocalypse Now* Edgar Morin, *La Vie de La Vie* Jerry Falwell founds Moral Majority The first cognitive sciences department is established at MIT	Iranian Revolution Iran Hostage Crisis begins Margaret Thatcher becomes British Prime Minister (first woman to be a European head of state) Nicaraguan Revolution
1980	Death of Sartre and Barthes Deleuze and Guattari, *Capitalisme et schizophrénie. 2. Mille plateaux* Derrida, *La Carte postale* Foucault, *The History of Sexuality*, Vol. One appears in English translation	Murder of John Lennon Umberto Eco, *The Name of the Rose* Lacan officially dissolves the École Freudienne de Paris Cable News Network (CNN) becomes the first television station to provide twenty-four-hour news coverage	Election of Ronald Reagan Solidarity movement begins in Poland Death of Yugoslav president Josip Broz Tito
1981	Death of Lacan Habermas, *Theorie des kommunikativen Handelns* Bourdieu is elected to the Chair in Sociology at the Collège de France	The first cases of AIDS are discovered among gay men in the US Debut of MTV	Release of American hostages in Iran François Mitterrand is elected as the first socialist president of France's Fifth Republic Confirmation of Sandra Day O'Connor, first woman Justice, to the US Supreme Court
1982	Foundation of the Collège International de Philosophie by François Châtelet, Jacques Derrida, Jean-Pierre Faye, and Dominique Lecourt	Debut of the Weather Channel	Falklands War
1983	Death of Aron Lyotard, *Le Différend* Sloterdijk, *Kritik der zynischen Vernunft*	Alice Walker, *The Color Purple* Founding of *Hypatia*	
1984	Death of Foucault Lloyd, *The Man of Reason*	Marguerite Duras, *The Lover*	Assassination of Indira Gandhi

	PHILOSOPHICAL EVENTS	CULTURAL EVENTS	POLITICAL EVENTS
1985	Habermas, *Der philosophische Diskurs der Moderne* First complete translation into French of Heidegger's *Sein und Zeit*	Don Delillo, *White Noise* Donna Haraway, *Cyborg Manifesto*	Mikhail Gorbachev is named General Secretary of the Communist Party of the Soviet Union
1986	Death of Beauvoir Establishment of the Archives Husserl de Paris at the École Normale Supérieure		Chernobyl nuclear accident in USSR Election of Corazon Aquino ends Marcos regime in Philippines
1987	Derrida begins his appointment as Visiting Professor of French and Comparative Literature at UC-Irvine	Toni Morrison, *Beloved* Salman Rushdie, *The Satanic Verses* Discovery of Paul de Man's wartime journalism damages the popularity of deconstruction in America	In June Gorbachev inaugurates the *perestroika* (restructuring) that led to the end of the USSR The First Intifada begins in the Gaza Strip and West Bank
1988	Badiou, *L'Être et l'événement*		Benazir Bhutto becomes the first woman to head an Islamic nation Pan Am Flight 103, en route from London to New York, is destroyed by a bomb over Lockerbie, Scotland
1989	Heidegger, *Beiträge zur Philosophie (Vom Ereignis)* Žižek, *The Sublime Object of Ideology*	*Exxon Valdez* oil spill in Alaska Tim Berners-Lee submits a proposal for an information management system, later called the World Wide Web	Fall of the Berlin Wall Students protest in Tiananmen Square, Beijing
1990	Death of Althusser Butler, *Gender Trouble*	The World Health Organization removes homosexuality from its list of diseases Beginning of the Human Genome Project, headed by James D. Watson	Nelson Mandela is released from prison Reunification of Germany Break-up of the former Yugoslavia and beginning of the Yugoslav Wars Lech Walesa is elected president of Poland
1991	Deleuze and Guattari, *Qu'est-ce que la philosophie?*	Fredric Jameson, *Postmodernism, or, The Cultural Logic of Late Capitalism* The World Wide Web becomes the first publicly available service on the internet	First Gulf War
1992	Death of Guattari Guattari, *Chaosmose*		Maastricht Treaty is signed, creating the European Union

CHRONOLOGY

	PHILOSOPHICAL EVENTS	CULTURAL EVENTS	POLITICAL EVENTS
1992			Dissolution of the Soviet Union
1993	Gilroy, *Black Atlantic*		Dissolution of Czechoslovakia; Vaclav Havel is named the first president of the Czech Republic
1994	Grosz, *Volatile Bodies* Publication of Foucault's *Dits et écrits*	The Channel Tunnel opens, connecting England and France	Genocide in Rwanda End of apartheid in South Africa; Nelson Mandela is sworn in as president North American Free Trade Agreement (NAFTA), signed in 1992, goes into effect
1995	Death of Deleuze, Levinas		End of Bosnian War World Trade Organization (WTO) comes into being, replacing GATT
1996		Cloning of Dolly the Sheep (died 2003)	Death of Mitterrand
1997	Death of Isaiah Berlin		
1998	Death of Lyotard		
1999	Badiou leaves Vincennes to become Professor and Head of the Philosophy Department at the École Normale Supérieure		Introduction of the Euro Antiglobalization forces disrupt the WTO meeting in Seattle
2000	Death of Quine Negri and Hardt, *Empire*		The Second Intifada
2001	Balibar, *Nous, citoyens d'Europe? Les Frontières, l'État, le peuple*		Terrorist attack destroys the World Trade Center
2002	Death of Gadamer and Bourdieu		
2003	Death of Davidson and Blanchot	Completion of the Human Genome Project	Beginning of Second Gulf War Beginning of conflict in Darfur
2004	Death of Derrida	Asian tsunami	Madrid train bombings
2005	Death of Ricoeur	Hurricane Katrina	Bombings of the London public transport system
2006	Badiou, *Logiques des mondes. L'Être et l'événement, 2.*		Bombings of the Mumbai train system
2007	Death of Rorty and Jean Baudrillard		
2008		Death of Robbe-Grillet	
2009	Death of Lévi-Strauss		

BIBLIOGRAPHY

Major works of individual philosophers are collected at the end of the relevant essay in the text.

Achinstein, Peter, and Stephen F. Barker. *The Legacy of Logical Positivism: Studies in the Philosophy of Science*. Baltimore, MD: Johns Hopkins University Press, 1969.
Adorno, Theodor W. *Aesthetic Theory*. Edited by Gretel Adorno and Rolf Tiedemann. Translated by C. Lenhardt. New York: Routledge & Kegan Paul, 1984.
Allison, Henry E. "Christianity and Nonsense." *Review of Metaphysics* 20(3) (1967): 432–60. Reprinted in *Kierkegaard: Critical Assessments of Leading Philosophers*, edited by Daniel W. Conway, vol. 3, 7–29. London: Routledge, 2002.
Althusser, Louis. "On Feuerbach." In *The Humanist Controversy and Other Writings (1966–67)*, edited by François Matheron, translated by G. M. Goshgarian, 85–154. London: Verso, 2003.
Anglin, W. S. *Mathematics: A Concise History and Philosophy*. New York: Springer, 1994.
Anonymous. "Spencer-smashing at Washington." *Popular Science Monthly* (February 1894): 856–7.
Ansell-Pearson, Keith. *Viroid Life: Perspectives on Nietzsche and the Transhuman Condition*. London: Routledge, 1997.
Aristotle. *The Complete Works of Aristotle: Revised Oxford Translation*. Edited by Jonathan Barnes. 2 vols. Princeton, NJ: Princeton University Press, 1984.
Arthur, C. J. *Dialectics of Labour: Marx and his Relation to Hegel*. Oxford: Blackwell, 1986.
Aschheim, Stephen E. *The Nietzsche Legacy in Germany 1890–1990*. Berkeley, CA: University of California Press, 1992.
Azouvi, François, ed. *Les Œuvres de Maine de Biran, Tomes I à XIII-3*. Paris: Vrin, 1986–2001.
Bacon, Francis. *The New Organon and Related Writings*. Edited by Fulton H. Anderson. Translated by James Spedding, Robert Leslie Ellis, and Douglas Denon Heath. Indianapolis, IN: Bobbs-Merrill, 1960. Originally published as *Novum Organon* (1620).
Badiou, Alain. *Manifesto for Philosophy*. Translated by Norman Madarasz. Albany, NY: SUNY Press, 1999.
Baker, Keith, ed. *Condorcet: Selected Writings*. Indianapolis, IN: Bobbs-Merrill, 1976.
Barnes, Harry Elmer. *An Introduction to the History of Sociology*. Chicago, IL: University of Chicago Press, 1948.

BIBLIOGRAPHY

Barrett, William. *Irrational Man: A Study in Existential Philosophy*. New York: Doubleday Anchor, 1962.

Barzun, Jacques. *Romanticism and the Modern Ego*. New York: Little, Brown, 1943.

Bauer, Bruno. *Christ and the Caesars: The Origin of Christianity from Romanized Greek Culture*. Translated by Frank E. Schacht. Charleston, SC: A. Davidonis, 1998. Originally published as *Christus und die Cäsaren: Der Ursprung des Christenthums aus dem römischen Griechenthum*. Berlin: Grosser, 1879.

Bauer, Bruno. *Christianity Exposed: A Recollection of the 18th Century and a Contribution to the Crisis of the 19th*. Edited by Paul Trejo. Lewiston, NY: Edwin Mellen Press, 2002. Originally published as *Das Entdeckte Christentum: Eine Erinnerung an das 18. Jahrhundert und ein Beitrag zur Krisis des 19*. Zürich & Winterthur, 1843.

Bauer, Bruno. *Die Judenfrage*. Braunschweig: Friedrich Otto, 1843. In part published in English as *The Jewish Problem*, translated by Helen Lederer, in *The Young Hegelians*, edited by Stepelevich, 187–97.

Bauer, Bruno. *Kritik der evangelischen Geschichte der Synoptiker und des Johannes, Dritter und letzter Band*, 3 vols. Braunschweig: Friedrich Otto, 1840–42.

Bauer, Bruno (anonymously). *The Trumpet of the Last Judgment against Hegel the Atheist and Antichrist: An Ultimatum*. Translated by Lawrence S. Stepelevich. In *The Young Hegelians*, edited by Stepelevich, 177–86.

Beaney, Michael. *Frege: Making Sense*. London: Duckworth, 1996.

Beiser, Frederick C. "Schleiermacher's Ethics." In *Cambridge Companion to Friedrich Schleiermacher*, edited by Mariña, 53–71.

Benson, Bruce Ellis. *Pious Nietzsche: Decadence and Dionysian Faith*. Bloomington, IN: Indiana University Press, 2008.

Bergson, Henri. *Creative Evolution*. Translated by Arthur Mitchell. New York: Dover, [1911] 1998. Published in French as *L'Évolution créatrice*. Paris: Presses Universitaires de France, [1907] 1986.

Bergson, Henri. *The Creative Mind*. Translated by Mabelle L. Andison. New York: Citadel Press, [1946] 1992.

Bergson, Henri. *Duration et Simultanéité*. Paris: Presses Universitaires de France, [1922] 1985. 237–71. Paris: Presses Universitaires de France, [1904] 1987.

Bergson, Henri. *L'Intuition philosophique*. In *La Pensée et le mouvant*. Paris: Presses Universitaires de France, [1911] 1987.

Bergson, Henri. *Matter and Memory*. Translated by N. M. Paul and W. S. Palmer. New York: Zone Books, 1994. Originally published as *Matière et Mémoire: Essai sur la relation du corps à l'esprit*. Paris: Presses Universitaires de France, [1896] 1985.

Bergson, Henri. *Time and Free Will: An Essay on the Immediate Data of Consciousness*. Translated by F. L. Pogson. Whitefish, MT: Kessinger Publishing Company, 1910. Originally published as *Essai sur les données immédiates de la conscience*. Paris: Presses Universitaires de France, [1889] 1988.

Bergson, Henri. "La Vie et les Œuvres de Ravaisson." In *La Pensée et le mouvant: essais et conférence*, Berkowitz, Peter. *Nietzsche: The Ethics of an Immoralist*. Cambridge, MA: Harvard University Press, 1995.

Berlin, Isaiah. *Four Essays on Liberty*. New York: Oxford University Press, 1970.

Berlin, Isaiah. *The Roots of Romanticism*. Princeton, NJ: Princeton University Press, 1999.

Bolzano, Bernard. *Paradoxes of the Infinite*. In *The Mathematical Works of Bernard Bolzano*, edited and translated by Steve Russ, 591–678. Oxford: Oxford University Press, 2004. Originally published as *Paradoxien des Unendlichen*. Leipzig: Felix Meiner, 1921.

Bolzano, Bernard. "Pure Theory of Numbers." In *The Mathematical Works of Bernard Bolzano*, edited and translated by Steve Russ, 355–428. Oxford: Oxford University Press, 2004. Originally published as *Theorie der reelen Zahlen, Betrachtungen aus der Logik in Bolzanos handschriftlichen*

Nachlasse. Edited by Karel Rychlík. Prague: Central Archives of the Czech Academy of the Sciences, 1962.
Bolzano, Bernard. "Purely Analytic Proof." In *The Mathematical Works of Bernard Bolzano*, edited and translated by Steve Russ, 251–77. Oxford: Oxford University Press, 2004. Originally published as *Rein analytischer Beweis: Des Lehrsatzes, dass zwischen je zwey Werthen die ein entgegengesetzes Resultat gewähren, wenigstens eine reelle Wurzel der Gleichung liege*. Leipzig: Wilhelm Engelmann, 1817.
Bolzano, Bernard. *Wissenschaftslehre, Versuch einer ausführlichen und grösstetheils neuen Darstellung der Logik, mit steter Rücksicht auf deren bisherige Bearbeiter*. 4 vols. Sulzbach: J. E. von Seidel, 1837.
Bonnet, Charles. *Considérations sur les corps organizés*. Amsterdam: M. M. Rey, 1762.
Bonnet, Charles. *Palingénésie Philosophique*. Amsterdam: M. M. Rey, 1769.
Bontekoe, Ronald. *Dimensions of the Hermeneutic Circle*. Atlantic Highlands, NJ: Humanities Press, 1996.
Bosanquet, Bernard. *A History of Aesthetic*. New York: Meridian Books, [1892] 1957.
Bourdieu, Pierre. *Distinction: A Social Critique of the Judgment of Taste*. Translated by Richard Nice. Cambridge, MA: Harvard University Press, 1984.
Bowie, Andrew. *Aesthetics and Subjectivity: From Kant to Nietzsche*. 2nd ed. Manchester: Manchester University Press, 2003.
Bowie, Andrew. "The Philosophical Significance of Schleiermacher's Hermeneutics." In *Cambridge Companion to Friedrich Schleiermacher*, edited by Mariña, 73–90.
Bradley, F. H. *The Principles of Logic, Volume II*. Oxford: Oxford University Press, 1928.
Brandes, George (Georg). *Friedrich Nietzsche*. Translated by A. G. Chater. London: William Heinemann, 1914.
Breckman, Warren. *Marx, the Young Hegelians, and the Origins of Radical Social Theory: Dethroning the Self*. Cambridge: Cambridge University Press, 1999.
Bulhof, Ilse Nina. *Wilhelm Dilthey: A Hermeneutic Approach to the Study of History and Culture*. The Hague: Martinus Nijhoff, 1980.
Burton, David M. *The History of Mathematics: An Introduction*. Boston, MA: Allyn & Bacon, 1985.
Butler, Judith. *Giving an Account of Oneself*. New York: Fordham University Press, 2005.
Cabanis, Pierre-Jean-Georges. *Rapports du physique et du moral de l'homme*. Paris: Crapart, Caille & Ravier, 1802.
Callinicos, Alex. *Marxism and Philosophy*. Oxford: Oxford University Press, 1983.
Caputo, John D. *More Radical Hermeneutics: On Knowing Who We Are*. Bloomington, IN: Indiana University Press, 2000.
Carl, Wolfgang. *Frege's Theory of Sense and Reference*. Cambridge: Cambridge University Press, 1994.
Carver, Terrell. "Communism for Critical Critics? A New Look at *The German Ideology*." *History of Political Thought* 9(1) (1988): 129–36.
Carver, Terrell. "*The German Ideology* Never Took Place." *History of Political Thought* 31(1) (2010): 107–27.
Carver, Terrell. *The Postmodern Marx*. Manchester: Manchester University Press/New York: St. Martin's Press, 1998.
Chamberlain, Lesley. *Lenin's Private War: The Voyage of the Philosophy Steamer and the Exile of the Intelligentsia*. New York: St. Martin's Press, 2007.
Cheng, Chung-ying. *Peirce's and Lewis's Theories of Induction*. Leiden: Martinus Nijhoff, 1969.
Chikara, Sasaki, Sugiura Mitsuo, and J. W. Dauben, eds. *The Intersection of History and Mathematics*. Basel: Birkhäuser-Verlag, 1994.
Clark, Maudemarie. *Nietzsche on Truth and Philosophy*. Cambridge: Cambridge University Press, 1990.

BIBLIOGRAPHY

Clowes, Edith. *Fiction's Overcoat.* Ithaca, NY: Cornell University Press, 2004.
Coffa, Alberto J. *The Semantic Tradition from Kant to Carnap.* Cambridge: Cambridge University Press, 1991.
Cohen, Gerald A. *Karl Marx's Theory of History: A Defence.* Oxford: Clarendon Press, 1978.
Cohen, Gerald A. *Self-Ownership, Freedom and Equality.* Cambridge: Cambridge University Press, 1996.
Collingwood, R. G. *Essays in the Philosophy of History.* Edited by William Debbins. Austin, TX: University of Texas Press, 1965.
Comte, Auguste. *The Catechism of Positive Religion.* Translated by Richard Congreve. 3rd rev. ed. London: Kegan Paul, Trench, Trübner, 1891; Reprinted New York: Augustus Kelley, 1973. Published in French as *Catéchisme positiviste.* Paris: Éditions du Sandre, [1852] 2009.
Comte, Auguste. *Cours de philosophie positive.* 2 vols. Paris: Hermann, [1830–42] 1975.
Comte, Auguste. *The Positivist Library.* Translated by Frederic Harrison. London: Reeves & Turner, 1886. Reprinted New York: Burt Franklin, 1971.
Conant, James. "Kierkegaard, Wittgenstein and Nonsense." In *Pursuits of Reason,* edited by Ted Cohen, Paul Guyer, and Hilary Putnam, 195–224. Lubbock, TX: Texas Technical University Press, 1993.
Conway, Daniel. *Reader's Guide to Nietzsche's* On the Genealogy of Morals. London: Continuum, 2008.
Conway, Daniel. "Revisiting the Death of God: On the Madness of Nietzsche's Madman." *Acta Kierkegaardiana* 4 (2009): 105–32.
Cournot, Augustin. *Considérations sur la marche des idées et des événements dans les temps modernes.* Paris: Hachette, 1872.
Cournot, Augustin. *Exposition de la théorie des chances et des probabilités.* Paris: Hachette, 1843.
Croce, Benedetto. *Aesthetic as Science of Expression and General Linguistic.* Translated by Douglas Ainslee. New York: Noonday Press, 1955. Published in Italian as *Estetica: Come scienza dell' espressione e linguistica generale.* Milan: Adelphi, [1902] 2005.
D'Agostino, Salvo. *A History of the Ideas of Theoretical Physics: Essays on the Nineteenth and Twentieth Century Physics.* Boston, MA: Kluwer, 2000.
Davison, Ray. *Camus: The Challenge of Dostoevsky.* Exeter: University of Exeter Press, 1997.
Deleuze, Gilles, and Félix Guattari. *Anti-Oedipus: Capitalism and Schizophrenia.* Translated by Robert Hurley, Mark Seem, and Helen R. Lane. Minneapolis, MN: University of Minnesota Press, 1983.
Deleuze, Gilles, and Félix Guattari. "The Refrain." In *A Thousand Plateaus,* translated by Brian Massumi, 311–50. Minneapolis, MN: University of Minnesota Press, 1987.
Detlefsen, Michael. *Hilbert's Program: An Essay on Mathematical Instrumentalism.* Dordrecht: Reidel, 1986.
Dewey, Jane. "The Biography of John Dewey." In *The Philosophy of John Dewey,* edited by Paul Schilpp, 3–45. Evanston, IL: Northwestern University Press, 1939.
Dewey, John. *Early Works, vol. 4.* Edited by Jo Ann Boydston. Carbondale, IL: Southern Illinois University Press, 1972.
Dewey, John. *Logic: The Theory of Inquiry.* In *John Dewey: The Later Works, vol. 12.* Edited by Jo Ann Boydston. Carbondale, IL: Southern Illinois University Press, 1991.
Dewey, John. *Middle Works, vol. 9.* Edited by Jo Ann Boydston. Carbondale, IL: Southern Illinois University Press, 1989.
Dewey, John. *Middle Works, vol. 12.* Edited by Jo Ann Boydston. Carbondale, IL: Southern Illinois University Press, 2008.
Dewey, John. *On Experience, Nature, and Freedom.* Edited by Richard J. Bernstein. Indianapolis, IN: Bobbs-Merrill, 1960.
Dilthey, Wilhelm. "The Three Epochs of Modern Aesthetics and its Present Task." Translated by Michael Neville. In *Poetry and Experience,* edited by Rudolf A. Makkreel and Frithjof Rodi,

BIBLIOGRAPHY

175–222. Princeton, NJ: Princeton University Press, 1985. Originally published as "Die drei Epochen der modernen Ästhetik und ihre heutige Aufgabe," *Die Deutsche Rundschau* 18 (1892): 267–303.

Dostoevsky, Fyodor. *The Brothers Karamazov*. Translated and annotated by Richard Pevear and Larissa Volokhonsky. New York: Farrar, Straus & Giroux, 1990.

Dostoevsky, Fyodor. *Notes from Underground*. Translated by Richard Pevear and Larissa Volokhonsky. New York: Vintage, 1993.

Dostoevsky, Fyodor. *A Writer's Diary, vol. 2, 1877–1881*. Translated by K. A. Lantz. Evanston, IL: Northwestern University Press, 1994.

Dummett, Michael. *Frege: Philosophy of Language*. 2nd ed. Cambridge, MA: Harvard University Press, 1981.

Dummett, Michael. *Frege: Philosophy of Mathematics*. Cambridge, MA: Harvard University Press, 1991.

Duncan, David. *The Life and Letters of Herbert Spencer*. London: Methuen, 1908.

Durkheim, Émile. *Durkheim's Philosophy Lectures*. Translated by N. Gross and R. A. Jones. Cambridge: Cambridge University Press, 2004.

Durkheim, Émile. *On Suicide*. Translated by Robin Buss. London: Penguin, 2006.

Durkheim, Émile. *Pragmatism and Sociology*. Translated by J. C. Whitehouse. Cambridge: Cambridge University Press, 1983.

Durkheim, Émile. *Socialism and Saint-Simon*. Edited by Alvin W. Gouldner. Translated by Charlotte Sattler. Yellow Springs, OH: Antioch Press, 1958.

Durkheim, Émile. *Suicide: A Study in Sociology*. Edited by George Simpson. Translated by John A. Spaulding. New York: Free Press, 1951.

Eagleton, Terry. *The Ideology of the Aesthetic*. Oxford: Blackwell, 1990.

Eagleton, Terry. "The Marxist Sublime." In *The Ideology of the Aesthetic*, 193–233. Oxford: Blackwell, 1990.

Easton, Loyd D. *Hegel's First American Followers*. Athens, OH: Ohio University Press, 1966.

Eliasen, Sven. *Max Weber's Methodologies: Interpretation and Critique*. Cambridge: Polity, 2002.

Ellson, Julie. *Delicate Subjects: Romanticism, Gender, and the Ethics of Understanding*. Ithaca, NY: Cornell University Press, 1990.

Ellwood, Charles. "Aristotle as a Sociologist." In *Annals of the American Academy of Political Science* 19 (1902). www.efm.bris.ac.uk/het/aristotle/ellwood.htm (accessed June 2010).

Engels, Frederick. *The Condition of the Working-Class in England: From Personal Observation and Authentic Sources*. In Marx and Engels, *Collected Works*, vol. 4, 295–596. London: Lawrence & Wishart, 1975–2004.

Engels, Frederick. "Karl Marx, A Contribution to the Critique of Political Economy." In Marx and Engels, *Collected Works*, vol. 16, 465–77. London: Lawrence & Wishart, 1975–2004.

Engels, Frederick. *Ludwig Feuerbach and the End of Classical German Philosophy*. In Marx and Engels, *Collected Works*, vol. 26, 353–98. London: Lawrence & Wishart, 1975–2004.

Engels, Frederick. "Outlines of a Critique of Political Economy." In Marx and Engels, *Collected Works*, vol. 3, 418–43. London: Lawrence & Wishart, 1975–2004.

Engels, Frederick. "Preface." In Marx and Engels, *Collected Works*, vol. 26, 519–20. London: Lawrence & Wishart, 1975–2004.

Ermarth, Michael. *Wilhelm Dilthey: The Critique of Historical Reason*. Chicago, IL: University of Chicago Press, 1978.

Feuerbach, Ludwig. "Towards a Critique of Hegel's Philosophy." Translated by Zawar Hanfi. In *The Young Hegelians*, edited by Stepelevich, 95–128.

Földényi, László. "Dostoevsky Reads Hegel in Siberia and Bursts into Tears." *Common Knowledge* 10(1) (2004): 93–104.

Foucault, Michel. *The Order of Things*. New York: Vintage, 1970.
Francis, Mark, *Herbert Spencer and the Invention of Modern Life*. Stocksfield: Acumen, 2007.
Frank, Joseph. *Dostoevsky: The Stir of Liberation, 1860–1865*. Princeton, NJ: Princeton University Press, 1986.
Frege, Gottlob. *Collected Papers on Mathematics, Logic and Philosophy*. Edited by Max Black, V. Dudman, P. T. Geach, H. Kaal, E.-H. W. Kluge, B. McGuinness, and R. H. Stoothoff. Oxford: Blackwell, 1984.
Frege, Gottlob. *Conceptual Notation and Related Articles*. Translated by Terrell W. Bynum. Oxford: Oxford University Press, 1972. Originally published as *Begriffschrift: Eine der arithmetischen nachgebildete Formelsprache des reinen Denkens*. Halle: Louis Nebert, 1879.
Frege, Gottlob. *The Foundations of Arithmetic: A Logical-Mathematical Investigation into the Concept of Number*. Translated by Dale Jacquette. New York: Pearson/Longman, 2007.
Frege, Gottlob. "On Sense and Meaning." In *Collected Papers on Mathematics, Logic and Philosophy*, edited by Black et al., 157–77. Originally published as "Über Sinn und Bedeutung." *Zeitschrift für Philosophie und philosophische Kritik* 100 (1892): 25–50.
Frege, Gottlob. "Thoughts." In *Collected Papers on Mathematics, Logic and Philosophy*, edited by Black et al., 351–72. Originally published as "Der Gedanke." *Beiträge zur Philosophie des deutschen Idealismus* 1 (1918–1919): 58–77.
Freud, Sigmund. *Civilization and Its Discontents*. Translated by James Strachey. New York: Norton, 1961.
Freud, Sigmund. *The Interpretation of Dreams*. In *The Standard Edition of the Complete Psychological Works of Sigmund Freud*, translated by James Strachey, vols 4 and 5. London: Hogarth Press, 1962. Originally published as *Die Traumdeutung*. Leipzig & Vienna: Franz Deuticke, 1900.
Friedman, Michael. *The Kantian Legacy in Nineteenth Century Science*. Cambridge, MA: MIT Press, 2006.
Furst, Lilian R. *The Contours of European Romanticism*. Lincoln, NE: University of Nebraska Press, 1979.
Gabriel, Gottfried. "Introduction: Carnap Brought Home." In *Carnap Brought Home: The View from Jena*, edited by S. Awodey and C. Klein, 3–20. Chicago, IL: Open Court, 2004.
Gadamer, Hans-Georg. *Hermeneutik in Rückblick*. Tübingen: Mohr Siebeck, 1995.
Gadamer, Hans-Georg. *Truth and Method*. Translated by Joel Weinsheimer and Donald Marshall. 2nd ed. New York: Continuum, 1989.
Gadamer, Hans-Georg. "Wilhelm Dilthey nach 150 Jahren: Zwischen Romantik und Positivismus." In *Dilthey und Philosophie der Gegenwart*, edited by E. W. Orth, 157–82. Freiburg: Karl Alber, 1985.
Garff, Joakim. *Søren Kierkegaard: A Biography*. Translated by Bruce H. Kirmmse. Princeton, NJ: Princeton University Press, 2005.
Gaskin, Richard. *The Sea Battle and the Master Argument: Aristotle and Diodorus Cronus on the Metaphysics of the Future*. Berlin: de Gruyter, 1995.
Gladstone, David, ed. *Setting the Agenda: Edwin Chadwick and Nineteenth-Century Reform*. London: Routledge, 1997.
Good, James. "John Dewey's 'Permanent Hegelian Deposit' and the Exigencies of War." *Journal of the History of Philosophy* 44(2) (2006): 293–313.
Gooding-Williams, Robert. *Zarathustra's Dionysian Modernism*. Stanford, CA: Stanford University Press, 2001.
Gouhier, Henri. *Les Conversions de Maine de Biran*. Paris: Vrin, 1947.
Gouhier, Henri. *La Jeunesse d'Auguste Comte et la formation du positivisme*. 3 vols. Paris: Vrin, 1933.
Gouhier, Henri, ed. *Maine de Biran: Journal*. Neuchatel: la Baconnière, 1954–55.

BIBLIOGRAPHY

Grant, Edward. *A History of Natural Philosophy: From the Ancient World to the Nineteenth Century.* Cambridge: Cambridge University Press, 2007.

Grondin, Jean. *Introduction to Philosophical Hermeneutics.* New Haven, CT: Yale University Press, 1994.

Habermas, Jürgen. *The Philosophical Discourse of Modernity: Twelve Lectures.* Translated by Frederick G. Lawrence. Cambridge, MA: MIT Press, 1987.

Habermas, Jürgen. "Religion in the Public Sphere." *European Journal of Philosophy* 14(1) (2006): 1–25.

Hacking, Ian. *The Emergence of Probability: A Philosophical Study of Early Ideas about Probability, Induction and Statistical Inference.* Cambridge: Cambridge University Press, 1984.

Hacking, Ian. *An Introduction to Probability and Inductive Logic.* Cambridge: Cambridge University Press, 2001.

Hamacher, Werner. "Hermeneutic Ellipses: Writing the Hermeneutic Circle in Schleiermacher." Translated by Timothy Bahti. In *Transforming the Hermeneutical Context: From Nietzsche to Nancy*, edited by Gayle L. Ormiston and Alan D. Schrift, 177–210. Albany, NY: SUNY Press, 1990.

Hannay, Alastair. *Kierkegaard: A Biography.* Cambridge: Cambridge University Press, 2001.

Harman, Peter M. *Energy, Force, and Matter: The Conceptual Development of Nineteenth-Century Physics.* Cambridge: Cambridge University Press, 1982.

Harman, Peter M. *The Natural Philosophy of James Clerk Maxwell.* Cambridge: Cambridge University Press, 1998.

Hartshorne, Charles, and Paul Weiss, eds. *Collected Papers of Charles Sanders Peirce, vol. 2.* Cambridge, MA: Harvard University Press, 1931–58.

Hatab, Lawrence J. *A Nietzschean Defense of Democracy.* Chicago, IL: Open Court, 1997.

Hatab, Lawrence J. *Nietzsche's On the Genealogy of Morality: An Introduction.* Cambridge: Cambridge University Press, 2008.

Hayman, Ronald. *Nietzsche: A Critical Life.* New York: Penguin, 1982.

Hegel, G. W. F. *Aesthetics: Lectures on Fine Art.* Translated by T. M. Knox. 2 vols. New York: Oxford University Press, 1975.

Hegel, G. W. F. *Early Theological Writings.* Translated by T. M. Knox. Philadelphia, PA: University of Pennsylvania Press, 1948.

Hegel, G. W. F. *Lectures on the Philosophy of World History.* Translated by H. B. Nisbet. Cambridge: Cambridge University Press, 1975.

Hegel, G. W. F. *Phenomenology of Spirit.* Translated by A.V. Miller. Oxford: Oxford University Press, 1977.

Hegel, G. W. F. *The Philosophy of Right.* Translated by Alan White. Newburyport, MA: Focus Publishing/R. Pullins Company, 2002.

Heiberg, Johan L. *Mathematics and Physical Science in Classical Antiquity.* Oxford: Oxford University Press, 1922.

Heidegger, Martin. *Einleitung in die Philosophie (Gesamtausgabe 27)*, 2nd ed. Frankfurt: Klostermann, 2001.

Heidegger, Martin. *Elucidations of Hölderlin's Poetry.* Translated by Keith Hoeller. Amherst, NY: Humanity Press, 2000.

Heidegger, Martin. *Hölderlin's Hymn "The Ister".* Translated by William McNeill and Julia Davis. Bloomington, IN: Indiana University Press, 1996.

Heidegger, Martin. *Nietzsche, Volume IV: Nihilism.* Edited by David Farrell Krell. Translated by Frank Capuzzi. San Francisco: Harper & Row, 1982.

Heidegger, Martin. "The Origin of the Work of Art." In *Poetry, Language, Thought*, translated by Albert Hofstadter, 15–87. New York: Harper & Row, 1971.

Heidegger, Martin. "The Word of Nietzsche: God is Dead." In *The Question Concerning Technology*, translated by William Lovitt, 53–112. New York: Harper & Row, 1977.

BIBLIOGRAPHY

Heilbron, John L. *Electricity in the Seventeenth and Eighteenth Centuries: A Study of Early Modern Physics*. Berkeley, CA: University of California Press, 1979.

Hendry, John. *James Clerk Maxwell and the Theory of the Electromagnetic Field*. Bristol: Hilger, 1986.

Herschel, John Fredrick William. *Preliminary Discourse on the Study of Natural Philosophy: The Cabinet Cyclopaedia*. London: Longman, Rees, Orme, Brown, Green and Longman, and John Taylor, 1830.

Higgins, Kathleen. *Comic Relief: Nietzsche's Gay Science*. Oxford: Oxford University Press, 2000.

Higgins, Kathleen. *Nietzsche's Zarathustra*. Philadelphia, PA: Temple University Press, 1987.

Hoyrup, Jens. *In Measure, Number, and Weight: Studies in Mathematics and Culture*. Albany, NY: SUNY Press, 1994.

Hume, David. *An Enquiry Concerning Human Understanding*. In *Hume, Enquiries Concerning Human Understanding and Concerning the Principles of Morals*. Edited by L. A. Selby-Bigge and P. H. Nidditch. 3rd ed. Oxford: Clarendon Press, 1975.

Hume, David. *A Treatise of Human Nature*. Edited by L. A. Selby-Bigge. 2nd ed. Revised by P. H. Nidditch. Oxford: Clarendon Press, 1968.

Jackson, Reginald. *An Examination of the Deductive Logic of John Stuart Mill*. Oxford: Oxford University Press, 1941.

Jackson, Robert Louis. "Dostoevsky Today and for All Times." *Dostoevsky Studies* n.s. 6 (2002): 11–27.

Jacobs, Struan. *Science and British Liberalism: Locke, Bentham, Mill and Popper*. Aldershot: Ashgate, 1991.

Jacquette, Dale. "Schopenhauer's Philosophy of Logic and Mathematics." In *Companion to Schopenhauer*, edited by Bart Vandenabeele. Oxford: Blackwell, forthcoming.

James, William. *A Pluralistic Universe*. Lincoln, NE: University of Nebraska Press, [1912] 1996.

James, William. *Pragmatism*. New York: Longmans, Green, 1907.

James, William. "Seminary in the Theory of Knowledge." In *Works of William James, Vol. 19: Manuscript Lectures*, 429–41. Cambridge, MA: Harvard University Press, 1988.

James, William. *Some Problems of Philosophy*. New York: Longmans, Green, 1919.

James, William. *The Will to Believe*. New York: Dover, 1956.

Janaway, Christopher. *Beyond Selflessness*. Oxford: Oxford University Press, 2006.

Janicaud, Dominique. *Une généalogie du spiritualisme français; Aux sources du bergsonisme: Ravaisson et la métaphysique*. The Hague: Martinus Nijhoff, 1969.

Jung, Matthias. *Hermeneutik zur Einführung*. Hamburg: Junias, 2001.

Kain, Philip J. *Marx and Ethics*. Oxford: Clarendon Press, 1988.

Kant, Immanuel. *Critique of Pure Reason*. Translated by Norman Kemp Smith. New York: St. Martin's Press, 1965.

Kant, Immanuel. "Idea for a Universal History with a Cosmopolitan Intent." In *Perpetual Peace and Other Essays on Politics, History, and Morals*, translated by Ted Humphrey, 29–40. Indianapolis, IN: Hackett, 1983.

Kaufmann, Walter. *Nietzsche: Philosopher, Psychologist, Antichrist*. 4th ed. Princeton, NJ: Princeton University Press, 1974.

Kearney, Richard. "Introduction." In *Modern Movements in European Philosophy*, 1–9. 2nd ed. Manchester: Manchester University Press, 1994.

Kenny, Anthony. *Frege*. Harmondsworth: Penguin, 1995.

Kierkegaard, Søren. *Papers and Journals: A Selection*. Translated by Alastair Hannay. Harmondsworth: Penguin, 1996.

Kierkegaard, Søren. *Synspunktet for min Forfatter-Virksomhed. En ligefrem Meddelelse, Rapport til Historien* [The point of view of my work as an author: a direct communication, report to history] [1859]. In *Søren Kierkegaard Samlede Værker*, edited by A. B. Drachmann, J. L. Heiberg, and H. O. Lange. Copenhagen: Gyldendal, 1962.

Kierkegaard, Søren. "The Tragic in Ancient Drama Reflected in the Tragic in Modern Drama." In *Either/Or*, translated by Howard Hong and Edna Hong, pt 1, 137–64. Princeton, NJ: Princeton University Press, 1987.

Kirmmse, Bruce H., ed. *Encounters with Kierkegaard: A Life as Seen by His Contemporaries*. Translated by Bruce H. Kirmmse and Virginia R. Laursen. Princeton, NJ: Princeton University Press, 1996.

Kirmmse, Bruce H. *Kierkegaard in Golden Age Denmark*. Bloomington, IN: Indiana University Press, 2001.

Kitching, Gavin, and Nigel Pleasants, eds. *Marx and Wittgenstein: Knowledge, Morality and Politics*. London: Routledge, 2002.

Klement, Kevin C. *Frege and the Logic of Sense and Reference*. London: Routledge, 2002.

Knight, David M. and Matthew D. Eddy. *Science and Beliefs: From Natural Philosophy to Natural Science, 1700–1900*. Aldershot: Ashgate, 2005.

Kofman, Sarah. *Nietzsche and Metaphor*. Translated by Duncan Large. Stanford, CA: Stanford University Press, 1994.

Kristeller, Paul Oskar. "The Modern System of the Arts." In *Renaissance Thought II*, edited by Paul Oskar Kristeller, 163–227. New York: Harper & Row, 1965.

Kroeker, Travis P., and Bruce K. Ward. *Remembering the End: Dostoevsky as Prophet to Modernity*. Boulder, CO: Westview Press, 2001.

Kubitz, Oskar A. *The Development of John Stuart Mill's System of Logic*. Urbana, IL: University of Illinois Press, 1932.

Laclau, Ernesto, and Chantal Mouffe. *Hegemony and Socialist Strategy: Towards a Radical Democratic Politics*. London: Verso, 1985.

La Mettrie, Julien Offray de. "Machine Man." In *La Mettrie: Machine Man and Other Writings*, edited and translated by Ann Thomson, 1–40. Cambridge: Cambridge University Press, 1996. Originally published as "L'Homme-Machine," in *Œuvres Philosophiques*. Paris: Fayard, [1748] 1987.

Lamm, Julia A. "The Art of Interpreting Plato." In *Cambridge Companion to Friedrich Schleiermacher*, edited by Mariña, 91–108.

Lampert, Laurence. *Nietzsche's Teaching: An Interpretation of* Thus Spoke Zarathustra. New Haven, CT: Yale University Press, 1986.

Laudan, Larry. *Science and Hypothesis: Historical Essays on Scientific Methodology*. Dordrecht: Reidel, 1981.

Leiter, Brian. *Nietzsche on Morality*. London: Routledge, 2001.

Lenzer, Gertrude, ed. *Auguste Comte and Positivism*. New York: Harper & Row, 1975.

Leopold, David. *The Young Marx: German Philosophy, Modern Politics, and Human Flourishing*. Cambridge: Cambridge University Press, 2007.

Levine, Donald N., ed. *George Simmel on Individuality and Social Forms*. Translated by Donald N. Levine et al. Chicago, IL: University of Chicago Press, 1971.

Levine, Norman. *Dialogue within the Dialectic*. London: George Allen & Unwin, 1984.

Lewes, George Henry. *Comte's Philosophy of the Sciences: Works in the Philosophy of Science 1830–1914*. Facsimile ed. London: Thoemmes Continuum, 1999.

Lifshitz, Mikhail. *The Philosophy of Art of Karl Marx*. Translated by Ralph Winn. London: Pluto, 1973.

Loeb, Paul. *The Death of Nietzsche's Zarathustra*. Cambridge: Cambridge University Press, 2010.

Losee, John. *Philosophy of Science and Historical Enquiry*. Oxford: Clarendon Press, 1987.

Lubasz, Heinz. "Marx's Initial Problematic: The Problem of Poverty." *Political Studies* 24(1) (1976): 24–42.

Lukács, Georg. "Karl Marx und Friedrich Theodor Vischer." In *Probleme der Ästhetik*, 233–306. Neuwied: Luchterhand, 1969.

BIBLIOGRAPHY

Luxembourg, Lilo K. *Francis Bacon and Denis Diderot: Philosophers of Science*. Copenhagen: Munksgaard, 1967.

Macbeth, Danielle. *Frege's Logic*. Cambridge, MA: Harvard University Press, 2005.

MacIntyre, Ben. *Forgotten Fatherland: The Search for Elisabeth Nietzsche*. New York: Farrar, Straus, Giroux, 1992.

Magnus, Bernd. *Nietzsche's Existential Imperative*. Bloomington, IN: Indiana University Press, 1978.

Maine de Biran, Marie François Pierre Gonthier. *Essai sur les fondements de la psychologie*, In *Œuvres complètes*, vol. 7, edited by F. C. T. Moore. Paris: Vrin, 2001.

Makkreel, Rudolf A. *Dilthey: Philosopher of the Human Studies*, 2nd ed. Princeton, NJ: Princeton University Press, 1992.

Makkreel, Rudolf A. "The Feeling of Life: Some Kantian Sources of Life-Philosophy." *Dilthey-Jahrbuch für Philosophie und Geschichte der Geisteswissenschaften* III (1985): 83–104.

Makkreel, Rudolf A. *Imagination and Interpretation in Kant*. Chicago, IL: University of Chicago Press, 1990.

Marcuse, Herbert. *Eros and Civilization: A Philosophical Inquiry into Freud*. Boston, MA: Beacon Press, 1955.

Mariña, Jacqueline, ed. *Cambridge Companion to Friedrich Schleiermacher*. Cambridge: Cambridge University Press, 2005.

Martensen, Hans Lassen. *Af Min Levnet: Meddeleser* [From my life: communications]. 3 vols. Copenhagen: Gyldendal, 1882–83.

Martin, Julian. *Francis Bacon: The State and the Reform of Natural Philosophy*. Cambridge: Cambridge University Press, 1992.

Marx, Karl. "Economic and Philosophic Manuscripts." 1844. In *Selected Writings*, edited by Lawrence H. Simon, 54–97. Indianapolis, IN: Hackett, 1994.

Marx, Karl. "From 'A Contribution to the Critique of Political Economy.'" In *Marxism and Art*, edited by Maynard Solomon, 61–2. Detroit, MI: Wayne State University Press, 1979.

Marx, Karl. *Selected Writings*. Edited by Lawrence H. Simon. Indianapolis, IN: Hackett, 1994.

Marx, Karl, and Friedrich Engels. *The German Ideology: Part 1 and Selections from Parts 2 and 3*. Edited by Christopher J. Arthur. New York: International Publishers, 1970.

Marx, Karl, and Friedrich Engels. *The Marx/Engels Collected Works*, vol. 1. New York: International Publishers, 1975.

Marx, Karl, Friedrich Engels, and Joseph Weydemeyer. *Die Deutsche Ideologie: Artikel, Druckvorlagen, Entwürfe, Reinschriftenfragmente und Notizen zu I. Feuerbach und II. Sankt Bruno*, 2 vols, *Marx-Engels-Jahrbuch 2003* (issued by the Internationale Marx-Engels-Stiftung, Amsterdam). Edited by Inge Taubert and Hans Pelger. Berlin: Akademie, 2004.

May, Simon. *Nietzsche's Ethics and his War on "Morality."* Oxford: Oxford University Press, 1999.

McBride, William L. *The Philosophy of Marx*. London: Hutchinson, 1977.

McLellan, David. *Karl Marx: His Life and Thought*. New York: Simon & Schuster/London: Macmillan, 1973.

McLellan, David. *Marx Before Marxism*. London: Macmillan, 1970.

McMullin, Ernan. "The Development of Philosophy of Science, 1600–1900." In *Companion to the History of Modern Science*, edited by R. C. Olby, G. N. Cantor, J. R. R. Christie, and M. J. S. Hodge, 816–37. London: Routledge, 1990.

Meek, Ronald L., ed. *Turgot on Progress, Sociology and Economics*. Cambridge: Cambridge University Press, 1973.

Meikle, Scott. *Essentialism in the Thought of Karl Marx*. London: Duckworth, 1983.

Merton, Robert K. *Social Theory and Social Structure*. Enl. ed. New York: Free Press, 1968.

Merz, John Theodore. *A History of European Thought in the Nineteenth Century*. 2 vols. New York: Dover, 1965.

Mészáros, István. *Marx's Theory of Alienation*. London: Merlin, 1970. 4th ed. 175.
Mill, John Stuart. "On Nature." In *Nature, the Utility of Religion and Theism*, 1–65. London: Watts & Co. for the Rationalist Press, 1904.
Mill, John Stuart. *A System of Logic*. 2 vols. London: John W. Strand, 1843.
Miller, C. A. "Nietzsche's 'Discovery' of Dostoevsky." *Nietzsche-Studien* 2 (1973): 202–57.
Miller, Richard W. *Analyzing Marx: Morality, Power and History*. Princeton, NJ: Princeton University Press, 1987.
Millet, Louis. *Le Symbolisme dans la philosophie de Lachelier*. Paris: Presses Universitaires de France, 1959.
Moore, Gregory. "Nietzsche, Medicine, and Meteorology." In *Nietzsche and Science*, edited by Gregory Moore and Thomas H. Brobjer, 71–90. Aldershot: Ashgate, 2004.
Morson, Gary Saul. "Paradoxical Dostoevsky." In *Slavic and East European Journal* 43 (1999): 471–94.
Mul, Jos de. *The Tragedy of Finitude: Dilthey's Hermeneutics of Life*. New Haven, CT: Yale University Press, 2004.
Nancy, Jean-Luc. *Hegel: The Restlessness of the Negative*. Translated by Jason Smith and Steven Miller. Minneapolis, MN: University of Minnesota Press, 2002.
Nelson, Eric Sean. "Disturbing Truth: Art, Finitude, and the Human Sciences in Dilthey." *theory@buffalo* 11 (2006): 121–42.
Nelson, Eric Sean. "Empiricism, Facticity, and the Immanence of Life in Dilthey." *Pli: Warwick Journal of Philosophy* 18 (Spring 2007): 108–28.
Nelson, Eric Sean. "Impure Phenomenology: Dilthey, Epistemology, and Interpretive Psychology." *Studia Phaenomenologica* 10 (2010).
Nelson, Eric Sean. "Interpreting Practice: Epistemology, Hermeneutics, and Historical Life in Dilthey." *Idealistic Studies* 38(1–2) (2008): 105–22.
Nelson, Eric Sean. "Moral and Political Prudence in Kant." *International Philosophical Quarterly* 44(3) (September 2004): 305–19.
Nelson, Eric Sean. "Schleiermacher on Language, Religious Feeling, and the Ineffable." *Epoché* 8(2) (Spring 2004): 297–312.
Nelson, Eric Sean. "Self-Reflection, Interpretation, and Historical Life in Dilthey." *Dilthey International Yearbook for Philosophy and the Human Sciences* 1 (2010).
Neurath, Otto, Hans Hahn, Rudolf Carnap et al. "The Scientific Conception of the World: The Vienna Circle." In *The Emergence of Logical Empiricism: From 1900 to the Vienna Circle*, edited by Sahotra Sarkar, 321–40. New York: Garland Publishing, 1996. Originally published as *Wissenschaftliche Weltauffassung: Der Wiener Kreis*. Vienna, 1929.
Nordau, Max. *Degeneration*. Lincoln, NE: University of Nebraska Press, 1993.
Olby, Robert Cecil, Geoffrey N. Cantor, John R. R. Christie, and M. Jonathan S. Hodge, eds. *Companion to the History of Modern Science*. London: Routledge, 1990.
Oldroyd, David. *The Arch of Knowledge: An Introductory Study of the History of the Philosophy and Methodology of Science*. London: Methuen, 1986.
Ollman, Bertell. *Alienation: Marx's Conception of Man*. Cambridge: Cambridge University Press, 1971. 2nd ed. 1976.
Ollman, Bertell. *Dance of the Dialectic: Steps in Marx's Method*. Urbana, IL: University of Illinois Press, 2003.
Ollman, Bertell. *Dialectical Investigations*. London: Routledge, 1993.
Owen, David. *Nietzsche's Genealogy of Morality*. Stocksfield: Acumen, 2007.
Parkes, Graham. *Composing the Soul: Reaches of Nietzsche's Psychology*. Chicago, IL: University of Chicago Press, 1994.
Parsons, Talcott. *The Structure of Social Action*. New York: McGraw-Hill, 1937.
Pearson, Karl. *The Grammar of Science*. New York: Charles Scribner's Sons, 1892.

BIBLIOGRAPHY

Peel, J. D. Y. *Herbert Spencer: The Evolution of a Sociologist*. New York: Basic Books, 1971.
Peffer, Rodney G. *Marxism, Morality and Social Justice*. Princeton, NJ: Princeton University Press, 1990.
Peirce, Charles Sanders. *The Charles S. Peirce Papers*, The Houghton Library. Cambridge, MA: Harvard University Library Microreproduction service, 1963–66.
Peirce, Charles Sanders. *The Essential Peirce, Volume 1: Selected Philosophical Writings (1867–1893)*. Edited by C. Kloesel and N. Houser. Bloomington, IN: Indiana University Press, 1992.
Peirce, Charles Sanders. *The Essential Peirce, Volume 2: Selected Philosophical Writings (1893–1913)*. Edited by Peirce Edition Project. Bloomington, IN: Indiana University Press, 1998.
Perry, Ralph Barton. *Present Philosophical Tendencies*. New York: Longmans, Green, 1912.
Perry, Ralph Barton. *The Thought and Character of William James*. 2 vols. Boston, MA: Little, Brown, 1935.
Pickering, Mary. *Auguste Comte: An Intellectual Biography, Volume 1*. Cambridge: Cambridge University Press, 1993.
Pippin, Robert. *Nietzsche, Psychology, and First Philosophy*. Chicago, IL: University of Chicago Press, 2010.
Plamenatz, John. *Man and Society: A Critical Examination of Some Important Social and Political Theories from Machiavelli to Marx*. 2 vols. Oxford: Oxford University Press, 1963.
Power, Nina. "Which Equality? Badiou and Rancière in Light of Ludwig Feuerbach." *Parallax* 5(3) (2009): 63–80.
Protevi, John, ed. *The Edinburgh Dictionary of Continental Philosophy*. Edinburgh: Edinburgh University Press, 2005.
Purrington, Robert D. *Physics in the Nineteenth Century*. New Brunswick, NJ: Rutgers University Press, 1997.
Raffoul, François, and Eric Sean Nelson, eds. *Rethinking Facticity*. Albany, NY: SUNY Press, 2008.
Ravaisson, Félix. *Essai sur la Métaphysique d'Aristote*. 2 vols. Paris: Imprimerie Royale, 1837–46.
Rees, John C. *Mill and his Early Critics*. Leicester: University of Leicester Press, 1956.
Richardson, John. *Nietzsche's New Darwinism*. Oxford: Oxford University Press, 2004.
Ricoeur, Paul. *Freud and Philosophy: An Essay on Interpretation*. Translated by Denis Savage. New Haven, CT: Yale University Press, 1970.
Ridley, Aaron. *Nietzsche's Conscience: Six Character Studies from the "Genealogy."* Ithaca, NY: Cornell University Press, 1998.
Rodi, Frithjof. *Erkenntnis des Erkannten: zur Hermeneutik des 19. und 20. Jahrhunderts*. Frankfurt: Suhrkamp, 1990.
Roemer, John E. *A General Theory of Exploitation and Class*. Cambridge, MA: Harvard University Press, 1982.
Rogers, Elizabeth Barlow. *Landscape Design: A Cultural and Architectural History*. New York: Harry N. Abrams, 2001.
Rosen, Stanley. *The Mask of Enlightenment: Nietzsche's Zarathustra*. Cambridge: Cambridge University Press, 1995.
Royer-Collard, Hippolyte. "Examen de la Doctrine de Maine de Biran sur les rapports du physique et du moral de l'homme, par Antoine-Athanase Royer-Collard." In *Annales Médico-Psychologiques: Journal de l'anatomie, de la physiologie et de la pathologie du système nerveux* 2, 1–45. Paris, 1843.
Ruben, David-Hillel. *Marxism and Materialism: A Study in the Marxist Theory of Knowledge*. Hassocks: Harvester Press/Atlantic Highlands, NJ: Humanities Press, 1977. 2nd ed. 1979.
Safranski, Rüdiger. *Nietzsche: A Philosophical Biography*. Translated by Shelley Frisch. New York: Norton, 2002.
Saint-Simon, Claude-Henri, Comte de. *Œuvres*. 6 vols. Paris: Anthropos, 1966. Reprinted Geneva: Slatkine Reprints, 1977.

Scanlan, James. *Dostoevsky the Thinker*. Ithaca, NY: Cornell University Press, 2002.
Scarre, Geoffrey. *Logic and Reality in the Philosophy of John Stuart Mill*. Dordrecht: Kluwer, 1989.
Schoenwald, Richard L. *Nineteenth Century Thought: The Discovery of Change*. Englewood Cliffs, NJ: Prentice-Hall, 1965.
Scholtz, Gunter. *Ethik und Hermeneutik*. Frankfurt: Suhrkamp, 1995.
Schopenhauer, Arthur. *On the Fourfold Root of the Principle of Sufficient Reason*. Translated by E. F. J. Payne. La Salle, IL: Open Court, 1974.
Schopenhauer, Arthur. *On Vision and Colors*. Edited by David E. Cartwright. Translated by E. F. J. Payne. Oxford: Berg, 1994.
Schopenhauer, Arthur. *On the Will in Nature*. Edited by David E. Cartwright. Translated by E. F. J. Payne. Oxford: Berg, 1992.
Schopenhauer, Arthur. *The World as Will and Representation*. Translated by E. F. J. Payne. 2 vols. New York: Dover, 1966.
Schrift, Alan D. *Nietzsche's French Legacy: A Genealogy of Poststructuralism*. New York: Routledge, 1995.
Schrift, Alan D. "Nietzsche's Nachlass." In *A Companion to Friedrich Nietzsche*, edited by Paul Bishop. London: Camden House, forthcoming.
Scott, Joseph F. *A History of Mathematics from Antiquity to the Beginning of the Nineteenth Century*. 2nd ed. London: Taylor & Francis, 1960.
Seung, T. K. *Nietzsche's Epic of the Soul*. Lanham, MD: Lexington Books, 2005.
Shapin, Steven. "Man with a Plan: Herbert Spencer's Theory of Everything." *New Yorker* (August 13, 2007): 75–9.
Shapiro, Gary. "From the Sublime to the Political: Some Historical Notes." *New Literary History* 16(2) (1985): 213–35.
Shiner, Larry. *The Invention of Art: A Cultural History*. Chicago, IL: University of Chicago Press, 2001.
Sica, Alan, ed. *Social Thought: From the Enlightenment to the Present*. Boston, MA: Allyn & Bacon, 2005.
Simmel, George. *The Problem of the Philosophy of History: An Epistemological Essay*. Translated by Guy Oakes. New York: Free Press, 1977.
Sorokin, Pitirim. *Contemporary Sociological Theories*. New York: Harper & Brothers, 1928.
Spencer, Herbert. *An Autobiography*. 2 vols. New York: D. Appleton, 1904.
Spencer, Herbert. *Principles of Sociology*. 3 vols. London: Williams & Norgate, 1882–89.
Sperber, Dan, gen. ed. "The Epidemiology of Ideas." Special Issue of *The Monist* 84 (2001).
Stepelevich, Lawrence S., ed. *The Young Hegelians: An Anthology*. Amherst, NY: Humanity Books, 1999.
Stern, Robert. "Peirce, Hegel, and the Category of Secondness." *Inquiry* 50(2) (April 2007): 123–55.
Stewart, Jon. *Idealism and Existentialism: Hegel and Nineteenth- and Twentieth-Century European Philosophy*. London: Continuum, 2010.
Stirner, Max. *The Ego and Its Own*. Edited by David Leopold. Cambridge: Cambridge University Press, 1995. Originally published as *Der Einzige und sein Eigentum*. Leipzig: Wigand, 1844.
Strauss, David Friedrich. *The Life of Jesus Critically Examined*. Edited and introduced by Peter C. Hodgson. Translated by George Eliot. Ramsey, NJ: Sigler Press, 1994. Revised and edited selection by Marilyn Chapin Massey, in *The Young Hegelians*, edited by Lawrence S. Stepelevich, 21–51. Originally published as *Das Leben Jesu, Kritisch bearbeitet*, 2 vols. Tübingen, 1835; 2nd ed. 1837; 3rd ed. 1839; 4th ed. 1842.
Strem, George. "The Theme of Rebellion in the Works of Camus and Dostoevsky." *Revue de littérature comparée* 1 (1966): 240–57.
Suhr, Martin. "On the Relation of Peirce's 'Universal Categories' to Hegel's 'Stages of Thought.'" *Graduate Studies Texas Tech University* 23 (1981): 275–9.

Sullivan, John W.N. *The History of Mathematics in Europe: From the Fall of Greek Science to the Rise of the Conception of Mathematical Rigour.* Oxford: Oxford University Press, 1925.
Thom, René. *Structural Stability and Morphogenesis: An Outline of a General Theory of Models.* Translated by D. H. Fowler. Reading, MA: W. A. Benjamin, 1975. Originally published as *Stabilité structurelle et morphogenèse.* Paris: Interéditions, 1972, 1977.
Thompson, Curtis I. and David J. Kangas. *Between Hegel and Kierkegaard: Hans L. Martensen's Philosophy of Religion.* Atlanta, GA: Scholars Press, 1997.
Thompson, D'Arcy Wentworth. *On Growth and Form.* 2nd ed. New York: Dover, [1942] 1992.
Tichý, Pavel. *The Foundations of Frege's Logic.* New York: de Gruyter, 1988.
Tolstoy, Leo. *What is Art?* Translated by Aylmer Maude. Indianapolis, IN: Library of Liberal Arts, 1960.
Tomlin, Eric W. F. *R. G. Collingwood.* London: Longmans, Green, 1953.
Trân Duc Thao. *Phenomenology and Dialectical Materialism* [1951]. Edited by Robert S. Cohen. Translated by Daniel J. Herman and Donald V. Morano. Dordrecht: Kluwer, 1986.
Tucker, Robert. *Philosophy and Myth in Karl Marx.* Cambridge: Cambridge University Press, 1961.
Turgot, Anne-Robert-Jacques. *Turgot on Progress, Sociology and Economics: A Philosophical Review of the Successive Advances of the Human Mind on Universal History [and] Reflections on the Formation and the Distribution of Wealth.* Edited and translated by Ronald L. Meek. Cambridge: Cambridge University Press, 1973.
Turner, Jonathan, Leonard Beeghley, and Charles Power. *The Emergence of Sociological Theory.* 2nd ed. Chicago, IL: Dorsey Press, 1989.
Veblen, Thorstein. *The Engineers and the Price System.* New York: Viking, 1921.
Vischer, Friedrich Theodor. "Critique of My Aesthetics" (1866). Translated by Jason Gaiger. In *Art in Theory: 1815–1900*, edited by Charles Harrison and Paul Wood with Jason Gaiger, 686–90. Malden, MA: Blackwell, 2001.
Waddington, C. H. *Principles of Embryology.* London: George Allen & Unwin, 1956.
Wagner, Richard. *The Art-work of the Future.* In *Prose Works,* vol. 1. Translated by William Ashton Ellis. St. Clair Shores, MI: Scholarly Press, 1972.
Wahl, Jean. *Études Kierkegaardiennes.* Paris: Fernand Aubier, 1938.
Wartofsky, Marx. *Feuerbach.* Cambridge: Cambridge University Press, 1977.
Weber, Max. *From Max Weber: Essays in Sociology.* Edited and translated by Hans Gerth and C. Wright Mills. New York: Oxford University Press, 1946.
Weber, Max. *Roscher and Knies: The Logical Problems of Historical Economics.* Translated by Guy Oakes. New York: Free Press, 1975.
Werth, Barry. *Banquet at Delmonico's: Great Minds, the Gilded Age, and the Triumph of Evolution in America.* New York: Random House, 2009.
Wheen, Francis. *Karl Marx: A Life.* New York: Norton, 1999.
Whewell, William. *History of the Inductive Sciences, Founded Upon Their History.* 3 vols. London: J. Parker, 1837.
Whewell, William. *On Induction, with Especial Reference to Mr. J. Stuart Mill's System of Logic.* London: J. W. Parker, 1849.
Whewell, William (published anonymously). Review of Mary Somerville, *On the Connexion of the Sciences. Quarterly Review* 51 (1834): 54–68.
White, Richard. *Nietzsche and the Problem of Sovereignty.* Champaign, IL: University of Illinois Press, 1997.
Whitlock, Greg. *Returning to Sils Maria.* New York: Peter Lang, 1990.
Wicks, Robert. *Nietzsche.* Oxford: Oneworld, 2002.
Windelband, Wilhelm. *A History of Philosophy.* Translated by James H. Tufts. New York: Macmillan, 1893.

Wittgenstein, Ludwig. *Philosophical Investigations*. Translated by G. E. M. Anscombe. Oxford: Blackwell, 1958.
Woloch, Isser, ed. *Revolution and the Meanings of Freedom in the Nineteenth Century*. Stanford, CA: Stanford University Press, 2000.
Wood, Allen W. *Karl Marx*. London and Boston, MA: Routledge & Kegan Paul. 2nd ed. New York: Routledge, 2004.
Young, Julian. *A Philosophical Biography of Friedrich Nietzsche*. Cambridge: Cambridge University Press, 2010.
Yovel, Yirmayahu. *Dark Riddle: Hegel, Nietzsche, and the Jews*. University Park, PA: Penn State University Press, 1998.
Zimmermann, Robert. "Toward the Reform of Aesthetics as an Exact Science" (1861). Translated by Nicholas Walker. In *Art in Theory: 1815–1900*, edited by Charles Harrison and Paul Wood with Jason Gaiger, 607–10. Malden, MA: Blackwell, 2001.

INDEX

a priori 219–21, 225–6
  conditions of knowledge 170
  transcendentalists 215
abductive reasoning 218, 227, 229
Abraham 80
absolute, the 20, 24–7, 74, 91, 223, 225–6, 258
abstract, the 27, 31, 57
absurd, the 74, 96, 98
Acton, H. B. 55
  Illusion of the Epoch: Marxism-Leninism as a Philosophical Creed 55
Adler, Alfred 133
Adorno, Theodor W. ix, 49, 243, 248
  Negative Dialectics 49
aesthetics viii, 13, 68, 77, 169, 239–59
  aesthetes 73
  experimental 244–5
  expressionist 255
  folk art 255
  Greek 164n, 187, 189
  history of 256
  idealist 258
  judgments 240–41, 244, 251, 256
  landscape design 256–7
  post-Hegelian 243n
  post-Schellingian 243n
  positivist 244
  sublime, the 240, 242–3, 248–9, 258
  ugly 242–3
affectivity 143

afterlife 110
aggression 111, 116
Alder, Adolph Peter 72
alienation 53, 115, 188, 247
Althusser, Louis x, 28n, 29, 54
altruism 161, 188
amor fati (love of fate) 119
analysis 169
analytic philosophy ix, 213
anarchism 94
Andersen, Hans Christian 65, 71
Anderson, Douglas R. 12
anger 38
angst 92
anomie 188
anthropology 22, 29, 88, 111, 179
  transcendent 22
  of the spirit 24–9
Anti-Climacus (Kierkegaard's pseudonym) 80
Antigone (Sophocles) 243
anti-Hegelianism 21, 23, 68, 75
anti-hero 87–8, 97n, 97–100
antiphilosophy (Marx) 62
anti-realism 218, 237
Apollo 4, 132, 246–7, 251–3, 253n
aporia 151
apprehension 29
"approaching gloom" 129
arbitrariness (power of) 89

301

INDEX

Arendt, Hannah x
"argonauts of the ideal" 130
Aristophanes 77
Aristotle 168–9, 180, 196, 203, 216, 218, 228, 230, 254
art viii–xii, 1, 5–6, 100, 142–3, 156
  history of 13
  Greek 248, 252, 258
Ast, Friedrich 156
atheism 13, 36, 105, 124, 127, 162n
atomism 231, 233, 236
attitudes 94
authenticity 32, 134
authorship 71, 81, 145, 154, 157
authoritarianism 39
authority 2, 19, 243
  theological 104–5, 114, 121
Ayer, A. J. 28

bad, the (the common) 110
Bakhtin, Mikhail 98, 256
  Problems of Dostoevsky's Poetics 98
Barrett, William 86
Barth, Karl 79, 145, 158
Bataille, Georges x
Bauer, Bruno viii, 23, 23n, 32, 40
beauty 9, 111, 113, 168, 240, 242, 244, 248–9, 257–8
being 24–5, 30, 72, 202, 220, 235–6, 240
belief (Christian, in God) 75, 127
Benjamin, Walter x, 248
Bentham Jeremy 28
Berdiaev, Nikolai 94–5, 94n, 95n
  Origin of Russian Communism 95
  Russian Idea 95
Bergson, Henri ix, 11, 161, 167, 168n, 172–4, 174n
  Creative Evolution 173
  Duration and Simultaneity 173
  Time and Free Will 173
Berlin, Isaiah 2n, 51
  Karl Marx: His Life and Environment 51
Bernstein, Eduard 49
  Evolutionary Socialism 49
Bible 38, 145–6, 158
bigotry 37
Bildung 81
Biran, Maine de 161, 163n, 164n, 163–8, 170, 173–4

black existentialism x
Blanchot, Maurice 134
Bloch, Ernst 49
  Principle of Hope 49
Bloom, Allen 135
body 116, 152
Bogbinder, Hilarius (Kierkegaard's pseudonym) 80
Bolzano, Bernard 12, 193, 198, 204–6
  Paradoxes of the Infinite 205
  Pure Theory of Numbers 205–6
  Purely Analytic Proof 205
  Theory of Science, Attempt at a Detailed and in the Main Novel Exposition of Logic with Constant Attention to Earlier Authors 204
Bonaparte, Napoleon 3, 19, 36, 198, 241
Bonnet, Charles 162, 162n
bookishness 96
Bourdieu, Pierre x, 249n, 250n, 256, 258
bourgeoisie 44, 240–1, 246–9
Bowie, Andrew 157
Brandes, Georg 132, 135
Breckman, Warren 18, 20n
Brenner, Robert 54
Brentano, Franz 204, 207, 216
  Deskriptive, Psychologie, Phenomenologie, and Psychognosie 204
Brokmeyer, Henry 221, 221n
Brown, Norman 133
Brussels 40
Buber, Martin 134
Butler, Judith 20

Cabanis, Pierre-Jean-Georges 164n
Camus, Albert 85, 95–8, 134
  Myth of Sisyphus, The 98
Cantor, Georg 215
capitalism 49–50, 55–6, 59, 248–9
care 94
Carlyle, Thomas 246
Carnap, Rudolf vii, 151, 151n
Cartesian *cogito* 140
Cartesianism 170
Carver, Terrell 7
Casey, Edward xi
categorization 14
cause 150
certainty 62, 135, 140, 170

302

INDEX

mathematic 184, 212
ontological 54
scientific 48
sensuous 26, 31
change 40, 43–5, 48, 58
cheerfulness 129, 132
Cherkasova, Evgenia V. 8–9
Chernyshevsky, Nicolai 88, 88n
  What is to be Done? 89
Christ 19, 24, 38, 66, 75, 92–3, 99, 247
  historical Jesus 112
Christianity 7, 8, 19, 23, 26–7, 36–8, 73–8, 104–5, 116, 126
  Christian (becoming a) 69–70, 73, 77
  Christian faith 8, 36, 38, 69
  confessional Christianity 38–9, 82
church 36–9, 67, 74, 104–5, 115
citizenship xii
civil society (*bürgerliche Gesellschaft*) 42
class 3, 42–5, 50, 56–7, 60
  dominant 45
  property owning 58
  worker and peasant 51
  class dominance 55
  class interest 56
  class structure 60
  class struggle 44, 48, 57
classical social theory 177
Climacus, Johannes (Kierkegaard's pseudonym) 69–74, 78–82
Clowes, Edith 86n
  Fictions Overcoat 86n
cognition 152
Cohen, G. A. 54–5
Collingwood, R. G. 209, 209n
Cologne 41
comic, the 242, 248, 258
Communication 25–6, 59, 145, 154, 235
  existential 73
  indirect 73, 81–2, 155, 157
communism 33, 34, 41, 43n, 44, 56
Communist Party (in France and Soviet Union) 50
comparative literature xi
Comte, Auguste 3, 11–14, 28, 88, 161, 173, 178–88, 181n, 193, 195, 198, 206–10
  Course of Positive Philosophy 181–2
  Law of Three Phases 163n, 166n, 231
  positivism 206–10

Système de Politique Positive 182
Comtism 181
concealment 147
concreteness 31, 153
Condillac, Etienne 164
Condorcet, Marquis de 182, 184
confession 32–3, 37
Congress of Vienna 36
conscience 95, 111
  bad conscience 111
  guilty conscience 111
consciousness 20, 29, 32, 50, 59, 62, 94, 145, 148, 151, 178, 189–90, 247, 250–1, 258
  communist 51
  eternal 73
  human 31
  hyper 96
  individual 32
  of meaning 98
  political 59
  reflective 171
  self- 20, 28–9, 33, 110, 201, 241
  self-deceiving 96–7
  sensuous 25–6
  social 45
  tempted 99
  unique 33
  of willed activity 164–5
conservatism 23–4
constitution 20
constructivism 237
consumption 42, 46, 60
content 37, 145, 151, 156–8
context 145, 151, 156–8
  relational (*Zusammenhang*) 146, 153
  life-context (*Lebenszumsammenhang*) 148–9, 155
continental philosophy vii, viii, ix, 1, 13–15, 36, 54, 57, 59, 61–2, 85, 95–6, 100, 195, 215–16, 258
contingency 59
continuity 52
contradiction 55, 98
Copenhagen 65–7
  Nietzsche in 132
correctness 143, 147
cosmopolitanism 112
cosmos 116–17
  amoral, post-theistic 118, 124, 131–2

303

courage 38
Cournot, Antoine-Augustin 161, 166–8, 171, 174
  Researches into the Mathematical Principles of Wealth 166
Cousin, Victor 164n, 168n, 168–9
cowardice 94
craftwork 53
crisis 6–7, 9, 100, 105
  of modernity x
  of the will 112, 114
critical philosophy (of Kant) vii, viii
critical theory x
  third generation xi
critique 28
critique of historical reason (Dilthey) 148, 153
Croce, Benedetto 209n, 254–5
  Aesthetic 254
cruelty 111
culture viii, 39, 110, 112, 114, 118, 128–9, 135, 215–16, 224, 231, 246, 257
  American 221
  European 3, 9, 37, 105, 114–15, 126–9, 133, 213
  German 112, 257
  Greek 133
curse 116, 118

Dadaism 77
Darwin, Charles 118, 178–9, 194, 215, 232
Darwinism 118
  English 118
  social Darwinism 11, 118, 177
De Interpretatione (Aristotle) 196
death of art 241, 246
decadence 112, 122
deception 94
deconstruction 1, 15
deductive reasoning 142, 212, 218, 220, 228
Deleuze, Gilles x, 134–5, 257
democracy 103, 112, 246
  radical xii
Democritus 189
Denmark 68
  Christianity in 74
  Golden age in 77, 81
Derrida, Jacques x, xi, 254, 258
Descartes, Rene 164n, 169, 182

Cartesian *cogito* 140
Cartesianism 170
despair 66, 75, 122
destiny 119
destruction 90
determinism 10, 40, 50, 52, 161–2, 166, 166n, 196, 201, 231–4
  scientific 49–50
deterministic Marxism 50
Dewey, John 13, 217, 217n, 219–21, 223–5, 233
  Art as Experience 243n
  growth 223–4, 258
  reconstruction 222–5
  warranted assertability 196
dialectic 2, 26, 42, 46–7, 51, 58, 74, 76, 91, 141, 154, 154n
  Hegelian (master-slave) 50, 110
  materialist 48
  Stalinist 51
Dialectic of Enlightenment (Horkheimer and Adorno) 49
diamat (dialectical materialism) 49, 51, 53–4
Dilthey, Wilhelm 3, 9–10, 13, 139n, 139–60, 245
  Beiträge zur Losung der Frage vom Ursprung unseres Glaubens an die Realität der Aubenwelt und Seinem Recht 150
  criticisms of 158
  critique of historical reason 148, 153
  "the empirical without empiricism" 147
  empiricism (nonreductive) 140, 147–8
  Formation of the Historical World in the Human Sciences 151–2
  on the human sciences 140, 140n, 147–53, 156
  Introduction to the Human Sciences 141, 147
  Life of Schleiermacher 148
  Schleiermacher's Hermeneutical System in Relation to Earlier Protestant Hermeneutics of 1860 144
  on science 140, 142–3, 148–9, 153, 157n
  "Studies toward the Foundation of the Human Sciences" 151
  "Understanding of Other Persons and Their Manifestations" 151
  whole, the 141n, 145–7, 151, 156–7
Dionysus 113, 132, 251, 253

304

disclosure 150
  of nondisclosedness 147
discourse 60
  radical 95
distribution 42, 44, 46
divination 144n
divine 21, 141
  divine assent 73
  divine law 104
Dostoevsky, Fyodor viii, 5, 8, 13–15, 85, 85n, 91–100
  Brothers Karamazov, The 86, 91, 93, 96
  Demons 91, 96
  Diary of a Writer 92n
  Notes from the House of the Dead 87
  Notes from the Underground 85–8, 91, 96n, 98
  youth 87
Duration and Simultaneity (Bergson) 173
Durkheim, Emile ix, 11–12, 182, 186–8, 191–2
  Geisteswissenschaften 156, 163n, 190, 192
  Socialism and Saint Simon 186
  Suicide: A Study in Sociology 188

Earle, William xi
earth 116, 128
École Polytechnique 170, 181
economics 1, 42n, 55, 166, 190–1
economy 37, 44
The Ego and Its Own (Stirner) 33
egoism 33
  rational 89
Ellwood, Charles 180
Elster, Jon 54
emigration (of European Jewish intellectuals) x
empiricism 147–8, 164, 203–5, 216, 223, 233
  British xii, 54, 199, 227–8
  epistemological 42
  empiricist method 12
  investigation 173
  nonreductive 140
  research 201
Engels, Friedrich viii, 8, 35, 41, 43, 46–53, 58, 61
  Anti-Dühring: Herr Eugen Duhring's Revolution in Science 48

Condition of the Working-Class in England 43
Dialectics of Nature 48
German Ideology, The 43n, 46, 46n, 49, 52, 56, 61, 247
Manifesto of the Communist Party 44, 56, 61
Enlightenment 19, 23, 133, 158, 182, 184n, 187, 189, 192–4, 204, 207, 213
  counter- 78
  non-European 3
enslavement 94
enthusiasm 11, 78, 145
epidemiology 166, 166n
epistemology 147–8, 150, 152, 158, 214
  moral 109
Eremita, Victor (Kierkegaard's pseudonym) 80
estrangement 53, 97
eternal, the 70–71, 74, 79
eternal recurrence 118–20, 252, 257
eternity 109
ethics ix, 57, 68, 70, 154, 154n, 170, 192, 211
  ethicist, the 73
  post-Holocaust 13
  utilitarian 95
ethical turn xii
ethnicity xii
Europe vii viii, 1, 9, 37, 40, 52, 85, 95, 105, 112, 115, 125, 136
  continent, the xi
  fin de siècle 132
  "good Europeans" 132
  history of 114
evil 90, 93, 110, 130, 243
  beyond good and evil 110, 130
evolution 11, 174, 226, 228, 236–7
evolutionary theory 162, 174, 179, 196, 226, 231–3, 236
  social evolution 179, 207–8
exchange 42
existence 38, 54, 72–3, 91, 155, 158
  post-theistic 131
  stages of 81
existentialism ix, 66, 86, 93, 97, 134
  non-reductive interpretive 159
  religious 95, 136
explanation 111
exploitation 55–6

theory of (Marx) 55
expression 25, 98, 151, 153, 157

fact 11, 32, 37
faith 4, 36, 39, 74, 77–8, 100, 127–8
  radical 79
family 4
fantasy 31
fatalism 19
Fechner, Gustav 244, 244n
feeling 11, 31–2, 143, 147
  of life 148, 151–2, 151n, 156
feminine, the (in association with others and their individuality) 144n
feminism x, xii, 112
Ferguson, Adam 42
Feuerbach, Ludwig viii, 2, 5, 7, 13–15, 17–18, 17n, 22, 24–9, 27n, 31–4, 38, 46, 58, 75, 86, 88, 105, 190, 246
  anthropology of the spirit 24–9
  as cryptophilosopher 26
  as materialist, proto phenomenologist, proto-positivist 28
  demonstration 24, 26
  dream, the 27–8
  Feuerbach's new philosophy 27, 30
Fichte, J. G. viii, 190, 213, 215–16, 227, 233
finite, the 22–3, 32, 73, 76, 146–7, 155
finitude 155, 157
Firstness 12, 218, 225–7, 230–1
flourishing (human) 109, 119, 121
  transhuman 109, 121
  western idea of 115
force 152
  productive forces [*Krafte*] 152
form 78–9, 146
Foucault, Michel x–xi, 135–6, 240, 254
Fourier, Jean Baptiste Joseph viii
Franco-Prussian War 5, 106
Frank, Joseph 97n
Frankfurt School, the ix, 49
free heart 93
free-market 103
"free spirits" 128
free thinking 36–8, 86
free trade 41
free will 90, 170, 198
freedom 3–4, 9, 11, 14, 20, 81, 85, 90–7, 104, 172, 190, 196, 215, 224, 227

  paradoxes of 87
  political 110
  radical 93, 97
  spiritual 93
  of choice 93
  of conscience 95
  of expression 37, 67
  of action 161–2
Frege, Gottlob vii, 12, 198, 204, 210–13, 215
  Begriffsschrift 210–11
  Concept Writing: a Formula-language for Pure Thought Modeled on Arithmetic 210
  Foundations of Arithmetic: A Logical-Mathematical Investigation into the Concept of Number 212
  Grundgesetze der Arithmetik 213
  semantic theory 211–12
  Thoughts on Death and Morality 18
French Revolution 36, 39–40, 78, 163n, 183
French Spiritualists ix, 10–11, 14, 161–75
Freud, Sigmund ix, 6, 9, 13, 15, 85, 98, 133–5, 165, 254–5, 258
  Interpretation of Dreams 254–5
Fukuyama, Francis 135
fulfillment 66, 75–6
fundamentalism 37–8

Gadamer, Hans-Georg xi, 13, 139n, 146, 154, 158, 246
Galileo, Galilei 200, 214
Galvani, Luigi 163, 163n
game theory 55, 167, 167n
Geist (spirit) 4, 7, 20, 39, 52, 240
gender xii, 10
genealogy 111, 136
general, the 10, 143, 151, 153
genius (for thinking) 25
Geras, Norman 53
  Marx and Human Nature: Refutation of a Legend 53
Gide, André 135
globalization xii
God 4, 9–10, 19–24, 29–33, 93, 103–6, 111, 123–7, 157, 168–9, 206
  authority of 114, 121
  belief in 127–8
  death of 9, 13, 104n, 104–6, 121–32, 136
  feeling of 140

as free cause 168–9
God-relationship 72
ineffability of 155
murderers of 122–3
God-Man, the 73
  transcendent 141, 141n, 145, 155
Goethe, Johann Wolfgang von 189
Gonthier, Charles 10–11
good(ness) 90, 93, 110–11
  beyond good and evil 110, 130
goods and services 42–4, 53
Gospels, the 38
Gouhier, Henri 164, 164n
Gouldner, Alvin 187
government 36, 40
grace 82
Gramsci, Antonio 50–51, 59
  Prison Notebooks 50
Grand Inquisitor, the 85–6, 91–5, 99
Grundtvig, N. F. S. 76
guilt 111, 115, 124
Gurwitsch, Aron x–xi
gymnasium education 36, 106

Habermas, Jürgen x–xi, 82, 154, 158
habit 168–9, 173, 234
Haller, Carl Ludwig von 19
Hamacher, Werner 147n
Hamann, J. G. 78
Hannay, Alastair 8
happiness 91–3, 117
  eternal 73–4
Harris, William Torrey 221, 221n
Haufniensis, Vigilius (Kierkegaard's pseudonym) 80
Hegel, G. W. F. viii, ix, 1–7, 2n, 11–13, 17–20, 23–7, 32–3, 39, 42–3, 47, 49, 52, 57, 66–80, 88, 90–91, 91n, 110, 151–2, 178, 215–16, 221–8, 230–33, 236, 240–43, 247, 259
  absolute 20, 24–7, 74, 91, 223, 225–6, 258
  aesthetics 245, 248, 252
  death of art 241, 246
  De orbitus planetarum 215
  dialectic 50, 110, 223, 225, 252
  Enzyklopädie der philosophischen Wissenschaften 69
  father of existentialism 75
  Geist 4, 7, 20, 39, 52, 240

  on history 222, 226, 241, 258
  Lectures on the Philosophy of Religion 19
  Logic 25, 223–4
  Phenomenology of Spirit 20, 25–6, 50, 223, 226
  Philosophy of Right 19, 23
  "Spirit of Christianity and its Fate" 19
  Theological Writings 75
Hegelianism viii, 1, 21, 23, 27, 72, 108
  Christian 21, 24
  Left Hegelianism 7, 14, 17–18, 21, 23, 28, 32, 91, 246
  Neo-Hegelianism 108, 226
  philosophy of history 91n
  Right Hegelianism 7, 14, 17–18, 21, 23, 57–8, 66
  St. Louis Hegelians 221, 221n
  Young Hegelians viii, 18, 39, 57, 190
Heiberg, Johan Ludvig 66–8, 72
  "Grundlinien zum System der Ästhetik als speculativer Wissenschaft" 68
Heidegger Circle, the xi
Heidegger, Martin vii, ix, 13, 79, 85, 134, 145n, 150, 151n, 152n, 154, 157n, 158, 246, 253–4, 254n
  Einleitung in die Philosophie (Gesamtausgabe 27) 157n
  on Nietzsche 113–14, 114n, 128
Hell 93
Henry, Michel 165
Heraclitus 253, 253n
Herbart, Johann Friedrich 244n
hermeneutics ix, 1, 5, 9, 10, 13, 139–58, 154n, 240, 245–6, 258
  as the art of understanding 145, 154
  of facticity 145n
  hermeneutic circle 10, 151, 156
  hermeneutic method 10
  Protestant and Enlightenment trends in 142
  Romantic 143, 146
Herschel, John F. W. 199–200
  Preliminary Discourse on Natural Philosophy 199
Hesse, Hermann 135
highest good, the 141, 141n
Hilbert, David 196, 215
Hitler, Adolf 107–8
historical efficacy 152

Hölderlin, Friedrich 253
holism 157n
  first-person 156
  organic 141n, 146, 161, 233
  strong 149
  weak 149
Homer 253, 253n
homo faber (man the worker) 58
homogeneity 2
Horkheimer, Max ix, 49
human sciences 140, 140n, 147–53, 156
humanism 7, 54, 96, 105, 217
  absolute 22, 28
  phenomenological 28
  spiritual 22
humanity 22, 28n, 38, 58, 93–4, 100, 116
  higher humanity 121–2
  natural capacities of (Kant) 23
Hume, David 28, 182, 199, 204
humor 70, 78
  humorist 70
Husserl Circle xi
Husserl, Edmund vii, ix, 28, 158, 207
Huxley, Thomas H. 118, 179

"I"/"Thou" 29–30
idealism 10, 42–3, 48, 58, 90, 171–2, 187, 214–15, 228
  German viii, 13, 17, 19, 58, 86, 132, 141, 149, 179, 220–21, 227, 237, 246, 248
  Peircian 229–30, 233, 336–7
  subjective 62
ideality 79
imagery (abstract and concrete) 26
imagination 31, 143, 147
immanence 128, 141, 151
impressionism 256
incarnation 24
income 42–3
incommunicable, the 144, 146
indecisiveness 94
independence 20, 89, 94, 104
indeterminacy 40, 59, 145, 151, 157
indifference 94
individual(s) 22, 24, 28, 21, 33, 44, 54, 68, 70–82, 97, 100, 140, 145–6, 149–57, 243
  exceptional 73
  existing 73
individuality 19, 97
  single 73–4, 81
  transcendent personality of 20
individualism 54, 149, 228
industry 43–4
ineffable, the 146, 157
inequality 43–4
infinity 10, 22, 32, 73, 76, 141, 146–7, 155, 170, 205
  felt intuition of 140
  metaphysics of 82
inner (perspective of life) 148
innovation 45, 52
inquiry 149, 154
  scientific 158, 203
instrumentalism 223
integration 4
integrity 99
intention 96
interest (material) 43
International Dostoevsky Symposium 100
interpretation 4, 9, 140, 140n, 143–5, 151–7
  grammatical 145
  psychological 145
  self 157
intersubjectivity 30, 51, 59, 151
intuition 10, 31, 140–42, 155–6, 213, 254
inspiration 145
institutions (natural) 13
Irigaray, Luce x
irony 25, 258
irrationality 98
Isaac (sacrifice of) 80

Jackson, Robert Louis 100
Jacobi, F. H. viii, 19
Jacquette, Dale 12
Jakobson, Roman x
James, William 13, 217, 219–23, 225
  pluralistic universe 220
  radical empiricism 223
Jaspers, Karl ix, 79
Journal of Speculative Philosophy 221n, 221–2, 243n
judgment 22, 39, 51, 143, 205, 214
  aesthetic 240–41, 244, 251, 256
  determinant 143
  reflective 143
Jung, Carl 13, 157n
justice 55–6, 77, 91, 95

INDEX

Kafka, Franz 96, 135
Kant, Immanuel vii–xii, 22, 42 72–4, 88, 170, 172, 188, 213–14, 218, 230, 240–41, 244
   on aesthetics 240, 243–50, 254
   categorical imperative 119
   Critique of Judgment 143
   Critique of Pure Reason 178
   neo-Kantianism 149, 158, 170, 244, 244n
   post-Kantianism 204, 216
   space and time 170, 178, 213, 215
Kapp, Christian 26
Karamazov, Alyosha 92, 99
Karamazov, Ivan 92, 93, 99
Kazantzakis, Nikos 135
Kierkegaard, Michael Pedersen 81
Kierkegaard, Søren viii, 2, 5, 8, 13, 15, 65, 65n, 66–82, 96–9, 127, 243–4, 248, 258
   as dialectical thinker 73–4, 77
   as father of existentialism 66, 79
   as humorist 71
   as philosopher 82
   as postmodernist 74, 80
   Concept of Anxiety 66
   "Concluding Simple-Minded Postscript" 69
   Concluding Unscientific Postscript to the Philosophical Crumbs 66, 68–74, 76–9, 81
   "On the Church" 76
   De Omnibus Dubitandum Est 73
   Either/Or: A Fragment of Life 66, 73, 80–81, 243
   Fear and Trembling 66, 80, 127
   From the Papers of One Still Living 65, 71
   Literary Review 78–9
   Nachlass 82
   On the Concept of Irony with Continual Reference to Socrates 65
   Philosophical Crumbs 66, 73
   Practice in Christianity 66
   pseudonymous work 66, 243
   Repetition 66
   Sickness unto Death 66, 75
   Stages on Life's Way 66, 73, 80–81
knowledge 25, 39, 44, 47, 50, 59, 136, 151–4, 159
   empirical 62
   self- 25, 91, 157

theory of knowledge (*Theorie des Wissens*) 152
Kojève, Alexandre 50
Kołakowski, Leszek 53
   Main Currents of Marxism: Its Rise, Growth and Dissolution 53
Köselitz, Heinrich (aka Peter Gast) 107, 113
Kristeller, Paul O. 239, 239n
   "Modern System of the Arts" 239
Kroeker, Travis 98

laborers 56
Labriola, Antonio 49
   Essays on the Materialistic Conception of History 49
   Socialism and Philosophy 49
Lacan, Jacques 13
Lachelier, Jules 11, 161, 168, 171–4
Laclau, Ernesto 59
laissez-faire 179
language 10, 24–6, 37, 52, 60, 144–7, 154
   acquisition of 143
   artist of 146
   identity of 146
   interpretation of 144
   ordinary discourse 144
   Platonic theory of propositions 210
   power of 156
   semantic theory 211–12
   symbolic 210
   propositional 26
Laplace, Pierre-Simon 166, 166n, 171, 231
Lavoisier, Antoine-Laurent 162, 163n
law 1, 37
law of negation of the negation 48
Law of Three Phases 11
law of transformation 48
law of unity 48
Lawrence, D. H. 135
laws of nature 12, 90, 97, 201–4, 228–9, 231, 234–6
Lefebvre, Henri 50
Leibniz, Gottfried 171
Lenin, V. I. 48, 89, 95n
   Materialism and Empirio-Criticism: Critical Comments on a Reactionary Philosophy 48
Lessing, G. E. 74
Levi-Strauss, Claude x

INDEX

Levine, Norman 52
liberal rationalism 90
liberal reform (Kierkegaard's opposition to) 78
liberalism (political) 40, 112
liberty 59, 124, 170–71
libertarianism 96
life 145n, 150, 154
  categories of 150
  historical 151
  immanence of 151
  ordinary 158
  practical 159
  social 149
life-concern 153
life-philosophy (*Lebensphilosophie*) 147
linguistic turn x, 55
linguistics 255
literary philosophizing 98
literary theory x, 147n
literature viii, 97, 100
"living life" 96–7, 96n
Locke, John 164, 200
logic 37
  epistemic 141
  experimental 224
  predicate-quantificational 210, 213
  symbolic 214
logicism 212
love 32–3, 38, 94
  Christian 66
  free love of man 93
Lukács, Georg 49, 79
  History and Class Consciousness 49
Lyotard, Jean-François x–xi
Lysenko affair 51

Mach, Ernst 28
MacIntyre, Ben 135
Madman, the 122–6, 128–30
Maimon, Salomon viii
Makkreel, Rudolf A. 140n
Malraux, Andre 134
Man, Paul de 134
Mann, Thomas 135
Marcuse, Herbert x, 49–50, 133
  Eros and Civilization 50
  One Dimensional Man 50
Marheineke, Philipp Konrad 21

marketplace, the 126
Martensen, Hans Lassen 66–8, 72, 76, 79
Martineau, Harriet 181
"Marx and justice" controversy 55–6
Marx, Karl viii, ix, 2–9, 13–18, 35n, 33–62, 74–5, 86, 89, 103, 105, 134, 182, 186–7, 189–90, 240, 247–8, 254, 257–8
  Assorted Opinions and Maxims 109n
  Capital: A Critique of Political Economy, Volume 1, Book 1: The Process of Production of Capital 55, 61, 248
  capitalism 49–50, 55–6, 59, 248–9
  "cash nexus" 190
  Contribution to the Critique of Political Economy, A 41
  "Difference Between the Democritean and Epicurean Philosophy of Nature" 40
  Economic and Philosophic Manuscripts of 1844 46, 49–53, 61
  Eighteenth Brumaire of Louis Bonaparte 61, 248
  German Ideology, The 43n, 46, 46n, 49, 52, 56, 61, 247
  Herr Vogt 248
  liberal journalist 40–41
  humanist 53
  Manifesto of the Communist Party 44–6, 56, 61
    "Preface" 44–6
  new Marx 51, 53, 55
  philosopher 36, 41–2, 47, 51, 54, 57–8
  political activist 35, 41
  postmodernist 59–60
  socialist 40
  "Thesis on Feuerbach" 46
  youth 24
Marxism x, 7, 18, 35, 48–52, 62n, 95
Marxist dialectics 49
Marxist materialism 49
Marxist philosophy 47–9, 51
Marxology 52
masculine, the (in association with the universal) 144n
masters of suspicion 9, 15, 98, 134
materialism ix, 10–11, 43, 49–52, 58, 62, 90, 161–4, 162n, 169, 187, 209n, 228, 230, 236
  Marxist 42
  ontological 42

310

mathematics viii, ix, 5, 12, 193–4, 196, 198, 210, 212
maturation 9
May, Rollo 133
meditation 72, 145, 146
melancholy 75
Mendès, Catulle 113
  Isoline 113
Mendelssohn, Moses 19
Menger, George 191
merit 74
Merleau-Ponty, Maurice ix, 28, 50, 165
metaphysics 11, 114, 140, 164, 168, 171, 183, 205, 236
  Platonic 141, 147
  western 128
method 143
  historical method 47
  scientific method 6, 11, 201, 171, 183, 191, 198, 202, 206
  universal method 47–8
Mettrie, Julien de La 162–3
  L'Homme-machine 162–3
Mill, John Stuart xii, 12, 88, 171–2, 181, 183, 198–204, 206, 212, 215–16, 231
  Logic: Raciocinative and Inductive 199–201, 212
  Nature, the Utility of Religion and Theism 201
mimicry 71
mind 62, 96, 258
minimalism 258
mirror, the 31–3
misanthropy 96
misunderstanding 142
modern man 95, 97n
modern nation-state 3–4
modernity 1, 9, 82, 87, 97–8, 112, 134–5, 141
  critique of 1, 13, 115–16
  decadent epoch 112
  European 2, 6–9, 14, 105, 118, 122
Moller, Poul Martin 67
monastic movement 79
monism 2n
morality 37, 55–7, 104–18, 122, 128–9, 134–5, 170, 188, 252
  Christian 9, 104–16, 128–9, 132
  decadent 112–13, 115
  European 105, 112

history of 135
  noble 110
  slave 110
More, Thomas 40
  Utopia 40
Mouffe, Chantal 59
movement 52
multitude, the 125–6, 129
music 156
Mussolini, Benito 107
mysticism 95, 164

Nancy, Jean-Luc 20
Napoleon 3, 19
Nash Equilibrium 167, 167n
nationalism 198
natural law 200–201, 236
natural selection 196
natural state of man 90
naturalism (scientific) 111
Naumburg 106–7
necessity 95
negation 58
Neo-Hegelianism 108, 226
neo-Kantianism 149, 158, 170, 244, 244n
neoplatonism 171–2
Newton, Isaac 194, 202
Nietzsche, Elisabeth Forster 107–8, 107n, 113
Nietzsche, Friedrich viii, ix, 2–9, 13–15, 85, 96–8, 103–36, 247–9, 251–3, 253n, 256–9
  Antichrist(ian) 112–13, 112n, 116
  Beyond Good and Evil 109, 257
  Birth of Tragedy from the Spirit of Music 108, 132–3, 251–3
  "An Attempt at Self-Criticism" (Preface) 108
  Case of Wagner, The 112
  Daybreak 109
  death 107
  death of God 9, 13, 104n, 104–6, 121–32, 136
  Dithyrambs of Dionysus 113
  Ecce Homo 108–9, 112–13, 113n
  Gay Science, The 103, 109, 118, 122, 125, 129, 132
  health 106–7, 107n
  Human, All too-Human 109, 109n

INDEX

immoralist 113
insanity 107
Nietzsche contra Wagner 113
On the Genealogy of Morality 110, 111n, 251
ressentiment (resentment) 105, 110–11
Richard Wagner in Bayreuth 109
Schopenhauer as Educator 108
slave revolt 115
Twilight of the Idols 112, 243
Untimely Meditations 108
Uses and Disadvantages of History for Life 108
Wanderer and His Shadow, The 109n
"We Fearless Ones" 122
youth 106
Nietzsche Society xi
nihilism 19, 38, 91, 94–5, 112, 114–15, 131–2
nobility 111, 113
nominalism 28, 33, 228, 231–7
novelist, the 96, 98
novice, the 74

object(s) 20, 29–31, 72
 humanized 31
objectivity 29, 48, 150, 153, 171
Oken, Lorenz 178
Ollman, Bertell 52
Olsen, Regine 65
oneness 53
ontology 42, 54–5, 141, 155, 205, 218, 220, 231–2, 234–6
opposition(s) 74–5
 Aristotelian 72
 eternity and time 74
optimism 132
orthodoxy 38
otherness 14, 110, 145, 147, 155, 157
overman (*Übermensch*) 109, 120–22, 135
outer (perspective of life) 148

pantheism 19, 38
Pantheismusstreit (pantheism controversy) 19
paradox 96
parody 71–2
partiality 48
particular 10, 33, 143, 151, 156
Pascal, Blaise 182

passion 79
passivity 29–30
paternalism 94
peace 23
Pearson, Karl 234, 236–7
Peirce, Charles S. 2–5, 12–14, 199, 217–37, 254
 "Deduction, Induction, and Hypothesis" (Peirce) 220
 Firstness 12, 218, 225–7, 230–31
 "Fixation of Belief" 219
 "How to Make Our Ideas Clear" 219
 "Illustrations in the Logic of Science" 219
 "On a New List of Categories" 218
 pragmaticism 218, 223, 228–9
 Secondness 12, 218, 225–6, 230, 233–4, 236
 Thirdness 12, 218, 225–6, 230, 234, 236
personalism 19–20, 95, 168, 171
 Christian 19
 German 18
personality 18, 20, 20n, 96
 abstract 21
 factual 80
 of God 18
 individual 141n, 154
 of the king 18
 of soul 18
 sovereign 21
 transcendent 19
perspective 152
pessimism 108, 129, 132
Petrashevsky circle, the 87
phenomenalism 150
phenomenology vii, ix, 1, 62, 62n, 165, 190, 207, 212, 228, 230, 236
 existential xi
 German 50
philosopher, the 96
philosophy 18, 24–7, 43, 53, 49, 67, 97, 100, 109, 155, 158
 Greek 37, 164n, 168, 240
 mechanistic 162, 167, 172–3, 188
 natural 36, 60, 194–5
 of creativity 95
 of experience 217–18, 233
 of history 91
 of language vii, 217, 253–4
 of logic 204

of mathematics   12, 196, 205, 210–16
of mind   69
of science   54, 193–216
Roman   37
Russian   85–6, 100
philosophy steamers   95n
Pickering, Andrew   184
Plato   40, 74, 203, 215, 253
  Meno   74
  Platonic ideas   250, 257
  Timaeus   215
Platonism   205
Plekhanov, G. V.   48, 89
  Fundamental Problems of Marxism   48
pluralism   2n, 140, 149, 220
poetry   239, 248, 253–5, 257
  Greek   251, 257
political economy   3, 42n, 42–4, 47, 60, 191n
political theory   ix, 179
  post-democratic   1
politics   viii, xii, 1, 6, 8, 37, 39, 40, 45, 56
  class   51, 44
  European   viii
  transformative   48
possession (self)   111
positivism   12, 28, 54, 88, 95, 148, 161–2, 173, 183, 185, 187, 190, 192, 195, 206–10
  logical   208–9
  modern   180
postcolonial theory   xii, 1
postimpressionism   256
postmodernism   xi, 1, 15, 74, 80, 185
poststructuralism   1, 15, 254, 258
postwar reconstruction   51
poverty   44, 53, 57
power   37, 57–61, 117, 136
  "feeling of power"   117–18, 133
  institutional   38
  language forming   145–6
practical, the   70
pragmaticism   218, 223, 228–9
pragmatism   ix, 12–13, 127, 174, 191, 217–19, 226–7, 236–7, 243
praxis   32, 51
preformationism   162
presentation   25–6
  linguistic   26
  systematic   26
Presocratics   180

primary qualities   200
'Prisoner's Dilemma'   167n
"private"   44, 46
production   42–5, 55, 60
productivity   44–6
progress   9, 13, 23, 57, 112, 134, 181n, 184, 203, 206, 209, 221
  economic and technological   90
  evolutionary   179, 207
  human   90, 183, 185, 206
progressivism (historical)   91
proletariat   33, 44, 58, 186
property   44
protective tariffs   41
Proudhon, Pierre-Joseph   viii, 43
  Poverty of Philosophy   43
  "Speech and the Question of Free Trade"   43
pseudonymity   71, 73, 76, 79–81
  pseudonymous authorship   65, 81
psychoanalysis   ix, x, 1, 13, 49, 133–4, 255
psychologism   201, 204, 212
psychology   8, 10, 131, 133, 149–50, 173–4, 204, 207, 216
  animal   133
  cognitive   207
  experimental   207
  folk   131
  human   133
  interpretive   150
  moral   109
  reflective   168
  of religion   8
psycho-physiology (human)   111
"public"   44
purpose   91, 95, 152

race   xii
radicalism   39
rank (natural order of)   113
rationalism   19, 49, 99, 201, 203
rationality   39, 85, 88, 91, 97, 100
Ravaisson, Felix   11, 161, 168–71, 173
  La Philosophie en France au XIXème Siècle   169
real, the   26, 30, 33, 39
realism   88, 201, 218, 236, 249
  Chernyshevsky's   88
  Platonic   201
  scholastic   228

INDEX

reality 74, 150, 152
reason(ing) 3, 6, 24–5, 36, 67, 88, 95, 98, 100, 156, 174, 178, 184, 193
  abductive 218, 227, 229
  deductive 142, 212, 218, 220, 228
  inductive 12, 171–2, 183, 199–201, 203, 206, 219–20, 229
  hypocrisy of 76
rebellion 96, 104
redemption 73
reductionism 164
reflection 27, 100, 144, 153
  self-reflection (*Selbstbesinnung*) 148, 153
  social-historical 156
reflective awareness 153
reform 40, 43
Reich 13, 108
Reign of Terror 163n
Reinhold, Karl Leonhard viii
relations 45, 53, 60, 136, 160
relativism 182
religion ix, xii, 1, 6, 8, 14, 27–8, 27n, 38, 57, 72, 81, 104–5, 116
  antireligion 27
  appearance of 28
  Enlightenment critics of 28n
  essence of 27
  representation of 27
  western 128
religiousness 70
  religiousness A (of immanence) 70, 74
  religiousness B (paradoxical religiousness) 70, 74
Renouvier, Charles 11, 161, 170–71, 174
  Essais de critique générale 171
repentance 82
representation 25–7
  imaginistic 27
  self 27
repulsion 73
resistance 150
resolution 53, 74
responsibility 123, 224
  existential 94
  reversal of 123, 130–31
ressentiment (resentment) 105, 110–11
"revaluation of all values" 115–16
revelation 76, 78
  self- 80

revocation 70–71
Rheinische Zeitung (Rhenish Gazette) 41
rhetoric xi, 239, 248, 254–5
Ricoeur, Paul x–xi, 13, 154
Ritschl, Friedrich 106
Roemer, John 54–5
Röcken, Prussian Saxony (Nietzsche) 106
Romanticism 10, 77, 90, 90n, 141, 196–7, 214–15, 243
Royer-Callard, Antoine-Athanase 164–5
Rorty, Richard x, 217, 234, 237
Rosenkranz, Karl 21, 242–3, 242n
  Aesthetics of the Ugly 242
Rousseau, Jean-Jacques 88, 90
Royer-Collard, Antoine-Athanase 165n
rule(s) 143–4
Russell, Bertrand vii, 169, 196, 213
Russia 85–6, 94–5
  Bolshevik 95
  nihilist-socialist movement in 88
  Russian language 86n

Sacred Court, the 92
Saint-Simon, Henri de viii, 11, 182–3, 187–8
  Memoire sur la science de l'homme 187
  New Christianity, The 186
Sartre, Jean-Paul ix, 50, 79, 85, 93, 96, 134
  Critique of Dialectical Reason 50
Saussure, Ferdinand de x
Scharff, Robert xi
Scheler, Max ix
Schelling, Friedrich von 39, 168, 216, 227, 233, 236, 253
Schiller, Friedrich viii, 189, 217, 247
  Aesthetic Letters 189
Schlegel, Friedrich viii
Schleiermacher, Friedrich 9–10, 13, 67–8, 139–60
  Christian Faith, The 142
  criticisms of 158
  Dialectic 140
  dialectics 141, 154n
  On Religion: Speeches to its Cultured Despisers 142
  youth 142
Schmitt, Carl x
Schmoller, Gustav 191
Schopenhauer, Arthur viii, 103n, 108, 163, 193, 214, 249–52, 257

aesthetics 249–54
World as Will and Idea, The 249
Schrader, George xi
Schrag, Calvin xi
Schutz, Alfred x
scientism 95, 161, 174
secondary qualities 200
Secondness 12, 218, 225–6, 230, 233–4, 236
secularism 112
security 2, 93
  material 94
self 110–11, 150–51, 157
self-deprivation 115
self-preservation 117–18
semantics (scientific) 12
semiotics 254n, 258
sensation 28–9
sensationalism 28, 228
sense(s) 29, 70, 146, 153–4
sensuous, the 31
Serres, Michel x
Shapiro, Gary 13
Shaw, George Bernard 135
Shestov, Lev 98
Sibbern, Frederick Christian 68
Siberia
  Hegel on 91n
  Dostoevsky's exile in 85, 87, 91n
sign(s) 27–8, 218, 254
Silentio, Johannes *de* (Kierkegaard's pseudonym) 80, 127
Simmel, Georg 182, 191
sin 27, 66, 75, 104
singularity 10, 18, 146, 151, 155
skepticism 72, 140, 182
slavery 110
slave, the 110–11
  revolt 115
Snider, Denton 221
social change 37, 57, 62
social Darwinism 11, 118, 177
social question, the 43, 53, 60
social theory 180, 192
socialism 41, 44, 186–7, 198
  Christian 186
  French 41
society ix, 40, 42, 44–8, 52, 55–6, 103–5, 149, 152
  ancient 45

Asiatic 45
capitalist 49, 50
civil 104–5
feudal 45
modern bourgeois 45
Society for Phenomenology and Existential Philosophy (SPEP) xi
sociology ix, 3, 5, 12, 161, 178, 180–83, 185–8, 206, 208, 210
  American 189
  positivist 28
Socrates 68, 70, 74
soul (personal) 18
sovereignty 20n, 36
  popular 40
Spanish Inquisition 92
species 24, 33
  human 22–3, 26, 30, 32, 110
  infinite 24
species-being (*Gattungswesen*) 24, 28–9, 31–2, 53, 247
species-identical 30
speech 26–8
Spencer, Herbert 11, 118, 177–81, 187, 232
  Autobiography 177, 179
  First Principles 178
  Life and Letters 177, 179
  Synthetic Philosophy 179
Spengler, Oswald 135
Spinoza, Baruch 19, 168–9
spirit 4, 11, 14, 20–28, 32–3, 33, 39, 47, 149
  Absolute 91
  finite 22
  infinite 22, 31–2
  life of 11
  objective (Hegel) 51–2
  revolution of 8
  self-conscious 28
  see also Geist
Stalin, Josef 48
  Dialectical and Historical Materialism 48
state, the 19, 21, 36, 39, 57
Stirner, Max 32–3, 32n
Strauss, David Friedrich viii, 21–4, 21n, 32–3, 38, 108
  David Strauss, the Confessor and Writer 108
  Life of Jesus Critically Examined 21, 38
Strauss, Leo 135

315

structural conditions   ix
structuralism   x, 258
  French   54
structure(s)   2, 54
struggle   57
  of opposites   48; *see also* oppositions
Stumpf, Carl   244n
subject, the   18, 20, 29, 32, 54, 72, 150
  political   21
  universal human   58
subjectivity   29–30, 78, 99, 133
sublime, the   240, 242–3, 248–9, 258
substance   19–20, 48, 72, 150, 169–70, 205, 230
suffering   92, 100, 111, 115
suffrage (in Copenhagen)   67
surrealism   258
suspicion   98
  hermeneutics of   99, 134
  school of   98
synthesis   58, 145, 169–70, 252
system(s)   39, 44, 47, 77, 90, 146
  Hegelian   68
  productive   152
systemization   4

Tait, Peter Guthrie   194
technē   255
technology   xii, 45, 149, 198
teleology   71, 168, 172, 179, 236, 252
temporality   152
text, the   81, 154, 157
Theater of the Absurd   77
theology   viii, 27–8, 69, 79, 105–6, 140
  critique of   18
  negative   1, 13, 136
  speculative   76
theoretical   70
theory of relativity   173–4
thesis-writers   98
Thirdness   12, 218, 225–6, 230, 234, 236
Thompson, D'Arcy   167n
Thomson, William   194
three laws of dialectics   48
three temptations, the   92
Tillich, Paul   134
Tolstoy, Leo   87, 192, 255–6, 258
  What is Art?   255–6
Tönnies, Ferdinand   188

Gemeinschaft und Gesellschaft   188
totalitarianism   94
totality   2, 22–3, 32
traces and seeds (*Spuren und Keime*)   147, 147n
tragedy   133
  Attic   132–3
  Greek   108
transcendence   53
  religious   141
transformation   53, 55, 62
  economic   40
  linguistic   146
  social and political   40
transgression   90
translation   26, 32, 34
  of religion   27
Turgot, Anne-Robert-Jacques   184n
  "Essay on the Application of Mathematics to the Theory of Decision-Making"   184
  "Philosophical Review of the Successive Advances of the Human Mind"   184
tychism   232, 237
tyranny   96

unconsciousness   145, 255, 258
underground man, the   88–91, 96–7, 97n, 99
underground, the   98–9
understanding   10, 25–6, 70, 142–4, 150–56, 169, 205
  individual   74
  ordinary   152
  self-   27n, 131, 157, 240
universal end   91
universality   48, 95, 156–7
unthought, the   145
utilitarianism   88, 204
utopianism   viii, 3, 11, 40, 86–7, 186, 247

validity   153
values   115, 152
  Western   115–16
verstehende Soziologie (Weber)   190
Vienna Circle   28, 54, 208
violence   36, 44, 90
Vischer, F. T.   13, 242, 242n
  Aesthetics   242, 248, 257
  On the Sublime and the Comic   242

INDEX

vitalism 11, 141, 141n 167
volia 89, 90
Volta, Allesandro 162, 163n
"voyage of discovery" 130

Wagner, Richard 13, 103n, 108, 246, 251–2, 256–8
Wahl, Jean 75
Wallace, Russel 196
wanting 89
Ward, Bruce 98
Wartofsky, Marx 27n, 30
weakness 94
wealth 42–4, 57
Weber, Max 11–12, 14, 182, 190, 192
  Roscher and Knies 191
  verstehende Soziologie 190
Whewell, William 194, 201, 203, 215
Wild, John x–xi
will 10–11, 14, 20n, 114, 162–3, 196, 251
  self- 90
  to nothingness 114, 116
  will to power 117, 251
Wissenschaft 3, 18, 42, 69, 214, 241
Wittgenstein, Ludwig ix, 61, 70
  Tractatus Logico-Philosophicus 70
word(s) 33, 157
written word, the 96
workers 40–41, 53, 58, 246
world ix, 30, 96, 141n, 150, 152, 154
Wright, Chauncey 232
Wright, Erik Olin 54
Wright, George von vii

Young Germany movement (*Junges Deutschland*) 39, 77–8, 81

Zarathustra 109, 120–22, 125
Zedong, Mao 48
  On Contradiction 48
Zimmermann, Robert 13, 244, 244n
Zoroaster 109